D1193842

José Batlle y Ordoñez of Uruguay

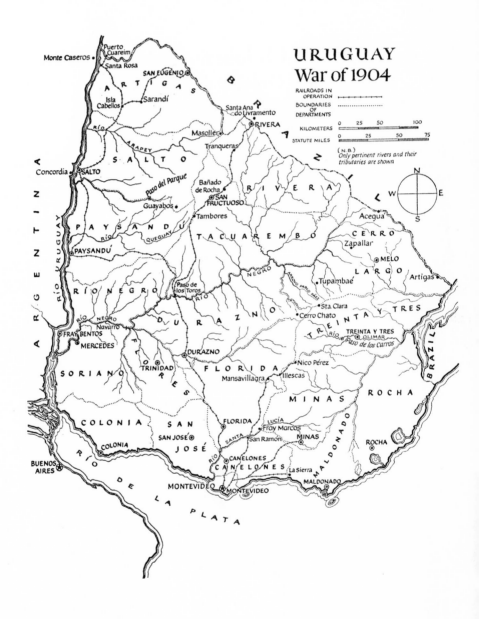

URUGUAY
War of 1904

RAILROADS IN
OPERATION
BOUNDARIES
OF
DEPARTMENTS

KILOMETERS 0   25   50   100
STATUTE MILES 0   25   50   75

(N.B.)
Only pertinent rivers and their
tributaries are shown

59588

José Batlle y Ordóñez of Uruguay

THE CREATOR OF HIS TIMES

1902 – 1907

MILTON I. VANGER

989.506
J253

HARVARD UNIVERSITY PRESS

Cambridge, Massachusetts

1 9 6 3

Alverno College

© Copyright 1963 by the President and Fellows of Harvard College

All rights reserved

Distributed in Great Britain by Oxford University Press, London

Publication of this book has been aided by a grant from the Ford Foundation

Library of Congress Catalog Card Number 62-19225

Printed in the United States of America

To

Elsa, Rachel, Rose, John,

Mark, *and* Max Vanger

PREFACE

José Batlle y Ordoñez * has fascinated those concerned with
twentieth-century Latin America, for during the years he led
Uruguay—from 1903 to his death in 1929—the country changed
from one notorious for its revolutions to Latin America's most
stable democracy. Batlle was able as well to sponsor Latin America's earliest labor legislation, government-owned business enterprises, and what in Uruguay is called moral legislation, such as laws
for divorce, protection of illegitimate children, and the end of the
death penalty. Some leaders for a few years overwhelm their national scene and then are thrown from power and their accomplishments reversed, but Batlle saved what he built and left a powerful
political party for the future.

There have been several biographies of Batlle written by Uruguayan admirers, all in one or another way campaign biographies
which make him larger than life. Since these books provide the
only information available, writers on Latin America have incorporated the exaggerations of the biographies into their own work.
The more I read the sources—including Batlle's private papers—
the more I became dissatisfied with the existing interpretations of
Batlle and the more I became convinced that what was needed was
a careful study of his career which would document exactly what
Batlle did accomplish and why, how, and with whose support he
did it. Such a study, requiring two or three volumes, would be the
best and most convincing way to evaluate Batlle's influence in
Uruguay, and would, in its way, contribute to the general historical understanding of leadership.

The present volume tells the story of Batlle's rise from just
another politician in the Colorado Party to the undisputed leader
of his party, to the man who changed Uruguay's political history
and put his country on the path to reform. The book describes the
events which transformed Batlle to BATLLE: his narrow election

---

* In Uruguay Batlle is pronounced Bah-jay, with the "j" sounded like the first
letter of the French name Jean.

as President in 1903, the uneasy year with the opposition Nationalists ending in the War of 1904, Batlle's war victory and subsequent
victory in the 1905 general elections, the next two years of admin-
istrative-legislative accomplishment, and finally, Batlle's triumphant
departure for Europe at the end of his term. The next volume will
treat Batlle's second presidency (1911–1915), which greatly extended the reforms begun and foreshadowed in 1903–1907.

This first volume tries to explain how a major Latin American
reform leader gained and consolidated power. It finds the explanation in political events, events frequently dismissed as mere surface
manifestations of deeper causes by social analysts who explain the
rise of leaders like Batlle as a response to the emergence of new
social classes. This book concludes that Batlle's success lay in his
use of the Colorado political organization and tradition, not in his
response to class needs and demands.

I am deeply grateful to César and Rafael Batlle Pacheco for per-
mitting me to go through their father's papers and for many other
services. My friend P. Fernández Prando shared the task of classi-
fying the Batlle Archive. Professor Juan E. Pivel Devoto arranged
for me to use the National Party papers, helped secure interviews,
shared his wide insight into Uruguayan history, and kept encouraging me. I will be ever fortunate to have found such scholarly co-
operativeness and personal friendship. The Director, Dionisio Trillo
Pays, the Sub-Director, Nicolás Fusco Sansone, and the staff of the
Biblioteca Nacional put up with extraordinary impositions on my
part. My twenty-month stay in Uruguay, from 1950 to 1952, was
financed by a fellowship from the Doherty Foundation.

Professor C. H. Haring first interested me in writing about Batlle
and guided my doctoral dissertation, of which this book is a several
times revised version. The staff of Widener Library assisted me in
many ways for many years. Paula Budlong Cronin handled the
rough job of typing the original manuscript aided, in my absence,
by Joseph T. Criscenti, who generously took on a number of my
burdens. Special thanks are due these two good friends. Mrs. Carol
Larsen has ably typed this version.

I want to thank the administration of Sacramento State College
for granting me a leave of absence to complete this book.

Milton I. Vanger

Sacramento, California
May 1961

CONTENTS

ILLUSTRATIONS

MAPS
(drawn by Samuel Bryant)

José Batlle y Ordoñez of Uruguay

I

Uruguay—1902

With cautious optimism, *El Siglo*, the most responsible newspaper in Montevideo, made its prognosis for 1902: a prosperous year, if there were no revolution.[1] The next President of the Republic was to be elected on March 1, 1903, and the campaign would soon begin. Responsible people were concerned that the election could destroy the present armed equilibrium between the traditional rivals, the Colorados still in the government, and the Blancos still out but much closer to power than they had been in many years. Businessmen looked with envy across the Río de la Plata to Argentina, where politics was now subordinated to progress, where progress was everywhere evident. Uruguay's progress was painful. Optimists pointed to Montevideo, a respectable city with a population close to 300,000,[2] to the proud statistic that though Uruguay was the smallest country in South America it had the highest population density. Those whose optimism had cooled remembered that Uruguay was twice the size of Portugal but had only a million inhabitants, one-third of whom lived in the capital. If more people and fewer cattle lived in the interior, maybe there would be fewer gaucho revolutions.

Foreign travelers traditionally arrived by way of the port of Montevideo, one of the best natural harbors in the South Atlantic. Ocean liners had too deep a draft to dock; passengers were landed by lighters. This would soon be remedied. A French construction company was dredging the port and constructing the most modern docks. Here was proof of progress, impressive proof, because the new port construction, the government's proudest achievement, was being financed by additional customs duties, not by a foreign loan.[3]

Once landed, the casual foreign visitor saw little to detain him in Montevideo, in preference to Rio de Janeiro or Buenos Aires, the next ports of call, north and south. The best a Spanish visitor would say was that Montevideo reminded him of a maritime city in Spain, still uncorrupted by too much cosmopolitanism. A more energetic American commercial agent wasted no time moving on to Buenos Aires.[4] But the citizens of Montevideo compared the city of today with the Montevideo they once knew, not with places elsewhere. All around were evidences of achievement: new neighborhoods, electric lights, telephones, gas, even the horsecars were on the way to being replaced by electric trolleys.

The city itself moved out from the port. The *Ciudad Vieja* (Old City), colonial Montevideo, close by the docks, was still the business heart. First came the warehouses, then in the old buildings on the winding streets were the lawyers' offices, the export and import houses, and the banks. Farther up was the old Spanish plaza, renamed Plaza Constitución, dominated by the Cathedral. The colonial Cabildo, where the Uruguayan legislature still met, faced the Cathedral across the square. Two streets farther was the bigger Plaza Independencia, whose principal edifice was Government House, a post-Independence building, small in comparison with the colonial structures. The big plaza and small building were quiet reminders of the differences between aspirations and achievements since Independence. Plaza Independencia was by now a popular promenade and opened on its far end into Montevideo's principal avenue, the 18 de Julio, again named for a patriotic date of Independence. On the 18 de Julio were the city's best shops, cafes, and *confiterías* (pastry shops). The city, made up mostly of one-story buildings, each built around a patio, continued on and ended in an outer rim of country houses.

Montevideo was Uruguay's economic center as well as its capital. All the country's railroads terminated here, bringing in cattle, sheep, wool, and hides from the interior. In Montevideo, these products were sorted, processed, and shipped abroad. Foreign houses did a good part of this business, and most banks were foreign-owned. British capital was especially prominent—all the public utilities except for the electric light system were English. The British investment in Uruguay of some £35.8 million substantially exceeded all other foreign capital. Anglo-Uruguayans even believed that England was more important in the economy of Uruguay than it was in Argentina,[5] where the English colony was so famous and so influential.

In Uruguay, a network of business interests, social activities, and marriages united foreign merchants and executives with their Uruguayan counterparts and attorneys. These men were the "conservative classes," a name they carried in honor. The conservative classes believed in business and progress, and in no-nonsense politics. They were *El Siglo* readers and shared the newspaper's laments at the aberrations of Uruguay's passionately traditional political parties. The conservative classes were the most influential organized social group in Uruguay, and President Juan Lindolfo Cuestas, that odd, squat, ugly old man who had come into office when an obscure youth assassinated his predecessor, leaned heavily on their support.

The only really large-scale industrial enterprises in Montevideo were the slaughterhouses and the old-fashioned jerked beef *saladeros* (meat-salting plants). Refrigerated packing plants were expected shortly, but beyond this the prospects for big industry were limited for there were no natural resources available. The Uruguayan market was small and local capital was timid. High tariffs, avowedly protectionist since 1888,[6] enabled a number of small firms to manufacture for internal needs. Small business predominated; 11,867 establishments, mostly retail stores, paid the business license tax.[7]

Labor unions were weak, their leadership was anarchist or Marxist, and their existence was ephemeral. Though working conditions were bad—30 pesos a month was held up as a good wage—labor organization was difficult. Not only were employers more powerful than unions but government regularly broke strikes and arrested strike leaders. As President Cuestas' newspaper put it:

Anyone who knows the peaceful and orderly spirit of our working class, can easily recognize that these movements are not spontaneous, but are the result of artificial agitation, promoted and instigated by certain individuals who come from abroad with the express purpose of agitating our people with the seductive mirage of better conditions to make them revolt.[8]

One of the sights of Montevideo was an ornate Victorian building, the railroad station. Nearly 2,000 kilometers of railroad stemmed out from the capital in three lines: the northwest line up the littoral, the central route, and the eastern line nearer the Atlantic coast. The littoral and central routes reached the Brazilian border; the eastern route stopped at Nico Pérez, a hamlet 230 kilometers from Montevideo, where stagecoaches and oxcarts took over. The whole system was supposed ultimately to connect the port of Montevideo with all southern South America.[9] The railroads, British owned and operated, had been built by British capital under Uruguayan government profit guarantees per kilometer. Recurring government financial difficulties forced renegotiation, but the government still paid the companies somewhere around one million pesos a year.

However heavy the burden on the government, regions still without railroads begged for new lines. Railroads meant higher land values, direct shipment of products to the capital, and increased prosperity. This was particularly true because roads, nicely drawn in red on the maps, were in fact nothing but wide trails, impassable mud bogs in the wet part of the year and the rest of the time dusty rutted oxcart routes, good only for horsemen or livestock on the hoof.

Railroads had been instrumental in producing the dramatic changes of the Uruguayan interior in the last thirty years. Not that great cities had grown up. On the contrary, the railroads by making Montevideo the single terminus for all the country's exports had assured the capital's urban predominance. The next largest cities, the upriver ports of Salto and Paysandú—less than 20,000 inhabitants each—were literally pygmies compared to Montevideo. The dramatic transformation was on the ranches.

Once, Uruguay had been a huge unfenced pasture where tough gauchos periodically rounded up semi-wild cattle, skinned them for hides, and let most of the meat rot. Then came the wire fence, which enabled ranchers to control breeding and produce a heavier animal. Pedigreed bulls and rams were imported, ranches were clearly marked and fenced. Fencing began in the 1870's, railroads in the '80's, significant imports of breeding stock in the '90's.[10]

Land and livestock were now valuable. Wire fences cut down the need for hands; ranchers could no longer let hordes of gaucho hangers-on, useful in roundups and war, live off the herds. Excess hands were asked, or forced, to leave. They were dragooned into the army or drifted into rural slums which grew up at crossroads or on land whose ownership was in doubt. The denizens of these *pueblos de ratas* (rat towns), though they were habituated to all the sins humanity could suffer, excited little attention or compassion. They just existed.

In 1902, the Chamber of Deputies was debating tax concessions to refrigerated packing plants. Uruguay already had the highest relation of livestock to population in the world. *Frigoríficos* (refrigerated meat-packing plants), universally welcomed, would provide a new market and by offering higher prices for heavier cattle would speed the process of livestock improvement. No one knew the exact number of livestock in Uruguay. Officially, there were 17,927,071 sheep and 7,029,078 cattle, but these numbers came from ranchers' voluntary declarations, deflated out of fear of tax collectors, and the best estimates put the real population at between 8 and 9 million cattle, with some 22 to 28 million sheep.[11]

While ranching had made dramatic progress and could be expected to upgrade rapidly once frigoríficos began operation, agriculture remained stationary. The 1900 rural census showed 14,515,104 hectares (one hectare equals 2.47 acres) of land devoted to pasture, with less than 500,000 hectares under cultivation.[12] What farming there was, mostly of wheat and corn for the local market, was marginal farming. Argentina, across the river, had become one of the world's great cereal producers, but Uruguay grew only sheep and cattle.

Profits per hectare on a successful farm were much higher than on a ranch. Agriculture would populate the interior and provide a solution for the pueblos de ratas. Ranches now entirely based on natural pasture would be vastly improved by raising alfalfa and other forage crops. One of the reasons the government had aided the railroads was the hope, forlorn so far, that railroads would bring farming.

Some blamed the lack of agriculture on poor soil; others insisted the cause was that a few ranchers owned most of the country and refused to subdivide it. There were only 22,674 ranches,[13] big and small, in all Uruguay and it was well known that some individuals controlled whole regions. Actually, there were few absolutely clear land titles since public lands had been occupied subject to later payment. Ranchers still had not paid for these *tierras fiscales* (fiscal lands), and thus were not particularly anxious for passage of the enabling legislation which would permit the government to collect in exchange for title.[14]

The Asociación Rural, founded in 1871 to propagandize in favor of the new fenced-in ranches, was holding its first Rural Congress in Montevideo. When discussion reached the "social question," the Congress revealed real concern, not for the denizens of the pueblos de ratas, but that these individuals stole cattle to feed themselves. The Congress proposed a solution: the government ought to send more police to the interior and establish prison colonies there.[15]

Everyone agreed on the desirability of public education. Uruguay had its equivalent of Argentina's Sarmiento in José Pedro Varela, who visited the United States, identified American success with its public education system, and vowed to duplicate the process in Uruguay. To accomplish this he was even willing to serve under the military dictator Colonel Latorre, whose government sponsored the centralized, free, and ostensibly compulsory public education system which began classes in 1877. The system's merits were apparent and soon won over those who originally opposed Varela, less because they opposed public education than because they opposed working with dictators. In recent years educational advance had stagnated for the usual reason, government shortage of funds. The 1900 census showed an illiteracy rate of 46.46 percent in Uruguay. Close to the Brazilian border two out of every three persons could not read, and even in Montevideo, where illiteracy was lowest, one out of three was illiterate.[16] This stagnation satisfied no one; the dream was still untarnished: education would convert lazy *criollos* (creoles) into hardworking Yankees.[17]

Everyone also favored immigration. At one time Uruguay had been flooded by newcomers, but in recent years few had come and the immigrants, Brazilian in the North and Italian in Montevideo, were increasingly assimilated. In 1860, 33.53 percent of the population were foreign-born; by 1900 the percentage had dropped to 21.64. In 1902, only 7,960 immigrants came to Uruguay.[18] Argentina's superior attractions, coupled with Uruguay's political turmoil, explained the immigration decline. Uruguayans wanted Europeans—hardworking Scandinavians would be ideal but even Italians would be welcome—to come and make the empty country produce.

Uruguayans were relatively healthy; their birth rate was high. There was no racial problem; the local Indians long since had been absorbed or killed off and Negro slavery had never been important. Illegitimacy, though, brought on by the pueblos de ratas, by ranchers' insistence that their peons stay unmarried, and by the slum life of Montevideo, was very high—one of four births was out of wedlock.[19]

This was another way of saying that the lower classes were un-churched. So were the intellectuals who, following the French example they so admired, were religious liberals. The Constitution said that Roman Catholicism was the state religion, but the liberals had eroded the tie. Convents were now limited by law, civil marriage was compulsory. There were only 122 parish priests in all the country, and in Montevideo 40 percent of the marrying couples went through just the civil ceremony and dispensed with the sacred, religious marriage.[20]

On the whole, church-state relations now were quiet. When a religious liberal presented a divorce project to the Chamber of Deputies the bill was buried in committee. President Cuestas' newspaper commended the Chamber, explaining, "we are convinced that the country is neither prepared for this radical reform nor anxious to carry it out." [21]

In spite of *El Siglo*'s prediction, 1902 was not a particularly good economic year; the collapse of several great French wool houses hurt business. Still, it was nothing like the terrible crisis year of 1890, a date businessmen still shuddered to remember.

In the late 1880's, Argentine speculation flowed over into Uruguay and contaminated local businessmen. A fabulous promoter, Emilio Reus,[22] was at the center of the boom. He was full of schemes—for new business (500 new companies were incorporated), for real-estate developments (in 1902 the unfinished streets still stood in the outskirts of Montevideo), for a new private bank under government sponsorship, the Banco Nacional. When the Banco Nacional failed, the government almost failed too since it had to settle with the creditors. Government debt shot up, its income dropped precipitately; government workers took 15 percent pay cuts. The government was left with the Montevideo electric power system on its hands, something salvaged from the crash. The total cost to government and businessmen of the economic disaster was at least 200 million gold pesos, almost equal to the entire declared property value of the country.[23] Later, the government set up a new Bank of the Republic to act as its agent and to engage in general banking. The Bank of the Republic was intended as a joint state-private bank, but though the new bank was conservatively managed private capital refused to invest.

Businessmen ceased gambling after 1890. Business gradually improved; by 1899 total foreign trade, the best single indicator of national prosperity, was back up at the 1889 level of 62 million pesos, the last boom year. Since '99, it had oscillated between 50 and 60 million.[24] These days businessmen were depositing their profits in safe banks; the uncertain political situation was reason enough for caution.

Uruguay's foreign trade was world-wide, but most of it was concentrated in dealings with its neighbors, with Western Europe, and with the United States. Ninety percent of Uruguayan exports came from its ranches—wool, hides, and meat products to Europe, hides to the United States. Import categories were revealing: in 1902, 57.20 percent of the total imports were foodstuffs, beverages, and textiles, indicative of still limited Uruguayan industrialization.[25]

Foreign trade was as crucial to the government as to the economy, for government revenues rose and fell with the level of imports. Tax specialists acknowledged that such dependence on import customs duties was dangerous and regressive, but the tariff was the traditional tax and the easiest to collect. Property taxes, though important, brought only limited revenues for it was politically impossible to tax real property at its true value. Government income for fiscal 1901–1902 bore this out: total income was around 18 million pesos, of which some 10.5 million came from customs receipts and 2 million from property taxes. Collections from no other single tax reached one million pesos.[26]

The national budget for 1901–1902 was 16.1 million pesos. Some 19,000 government employees, still suffering pay cuts from 1890, were in the budget. So was an item for 9,036,420 pesos to service the public debt—a graphic heritage of Uruguay's tragic financial history. The army required 1.7 million, the police a little more; the sums left for schools, roads, or public works were just not enough.[27]

President Cuestas was proud of his record as an administrator. He worked out the plan for financing the Montevideo port construction through additional import duties; he was ruthless with corrupt government employees. Government bonds, mostly held abroad, were rising. They were now quoted at 42.25 percent of par, low but very satisfactory considering their past levels. Cuestas had squeezed the budget and asserted at the end of his administration, to the delight of businessmen, that it was balanced. He was so proud of this accomplishment that the words NO BUDGET DEFICIT were printed with capital letters in the official message.[28]

Uruguay's political history did not permit unmixed pride. Politics had been the enemy of progress. Eduardo Acevedo felt obliged to begin his economic history of Uruguay, published in 1903, with a table, not of the economic cycles through which the country had passed, but one titled Presidencies and Dictatorships.[29] Revolutions, of all sorts, added up to nearly fifty.

Several factors could be offered in explanation. It was a truism that the Latin American republics had not been ready for nationhood when they became independent, and nowhere was this more true than in Uruguay. The principal colonial importance of the province of *La Banda Oriental del Uruguay* (the east bank of the Uruguay River) had been strategic—to keep Portugal's Brazil from bordering on the Río de la Plata. In 1810, Buenos Aires began the movement for independence from Spain; the Banda Oriental, actually the garrison town of Montevideo and its semi-populated pasture hinterland, was immediately involved. Though the *Orientales*, led by their hero Artigas, gradually developed a consciousness of being separate from the rest of the Plata region, most of them probably would have been satisfied to have their province an autonomous part of an Argentine confederation. Instead, because neither Argentina nor Brazil could win the province away from

the other by war, and because England believed a buffer state
would best preserve the balance of power in the Plata, with England
mediating, Argentina and Brazil created an independent Uruguay.
The Uruguayans welcomed independence and worked up a constitution in 1830, based on the best available models. Since Uruguay
had only one real city, federalism made little sense, so the Constitution called for a centralized government.

Artigas' two ex-lieutenants, the rival *caudillos*, Rivera and Oribe,
soon split, and the buffer became a battleground. Argentina was
going through its own difficult process of national organization;
Argentine politics spilled across the river. Imperial Brazil, better
organized, was alert for opportunities. The result was that internal
Uruguayan politics could not be separated from foreign relations.
Contending Uruguayan parties sought and received armed support
from Argentina and Brazil. Not until the middle 1870's, when
Brazilian and Argentine spoils from the Paraguayan War settled
the Plata balance of power question, and when Argentina finally
resolved its own organizational problems, was Uruguayan politics
left to the Uruguayans.

Political inexperience and the incursions of powerful neighbors
were two factors explaining Acevedo's table. A third factor was
the intensity of party feeling which developed in the post-Independence years of political turmoil. From 1843 to 1851, Oribe's
followers, wearing White Blanco ribbons, besieged the followers
of Rivera, wearing Red Colorado ribbons, inside Montevideo. The
Blancos of Oribe came aided by armies of the terrible Rosas, dictator
of Argentina. The Colorados of Rivera had French and English
naval support. Ultimately, Brazil and the upriver Argentine prov-
inces turned against Rosas, relieved the siege of Montevideo, then
swept Rosas from power into exile. During the Great Siege of
Montevideo an Uruguayan was a Colorado or a Blanco, and neither
he nor his children ever forgot it. There was little tolerance for
the other side. Party feelings transcended the purely political and
reached the religious, fellow party members called each other "coreligionaries."

Intellectuals and businessmen were appalled at this party spirit.
So much blood had been shed over those white and red rags. The
new University of Montevideo was teaching doctrinaire liberalism;
the "doctores" believed in evolution and wanted Uruguay to follow

"evolving" Argentina, to substitute parties of principle for parties of tradition, governments of law for governments of men. They preached political liberty and proportional representation, but behind this preaching was the doctores' belief that the educated elite—themselves—ought to run the country instead of letting it be misgoverned by illiterate caudillos followed by untrustworthy rabble.[30]

The elite had their chance in the early 1870's, when both parties agreed to a truce. The legislative chambers then echoed to able defenses of liberty, but in the face of a monetary crisis doctrinaire liberalism did not know what to do. This opened the way to the professional army officers who proposed to establish order and entirely ignore politics. The somber apparatus of military dictatorship was brought to bear: assassination, coercion, exile. The caudillos of the interior were broken, property rights were assured, the dispossessing of the gauchos was countenanced, and the power of the central government was established.

But the base on which the military dictators operated constantly narrowed. The doctores were horrified at dictatorial terror; younger generations within the traditional parties tried to revolt. Army leaders betrayed each other to enjoy the pleasures of power. Latorre, the first of the militarists, was exiled by his successor, General Santos. A bullet from an assassin's pistol wounded Santos, and General Máximo Tajes replaced him. Tajes recognized that the only way to stay in power was to widen the base of his political support. He therefore emphasized his Colorado background. His young chief minister, Julio Herrera y Obes, the most able of the doctores, also realized that instead of trying to do away with the traditional parties it was wiser to lead them. Tajes was able to finish out his term, and Herrera y Obes, now civilian leader of the Colorado Party, succeeded him as President in 1890, bringing back civilian government.

Both parties had survived during the militarist era. The Colorados, ostensibly in power since 1865 when Flores had defeated the Blancos with the aid of Brazil (although the militarists did not at first govern as party figures) had more public employees among their members than did the Blancos. Otherwise, there were few structural differences between the parties. Both had developed party programs during the eighties and, on paper at least, thoroughgoing organizations. Under these new influences the Blancos preferred to call themselves Nationalists. Both parties were national not sectional; whether there were more Nationalist than Colorado ranchers was not a matter of statistical investigation, but many Colorados lived in the interior, and Nationalists in Colorado Montevideo.[31]

By the last decade of the nineteenth century Uruguayan political history had its encouraging aspects. First, Argentina and Brazil now stayed out of Uruguayan politics. Second, the government's authority was national and the standard government services, such as courts and police, were reasonably well established. Third, the political parties were political organizations, not just crude working groups of leaders and followers. Fourth, Uruguayans cared greatly about politics, about their parties, and about their political traditions. As far as the conservative classes were concerned, this fourth point was scarcely an encouraging consideration.

The returned years of civilian government, from 1890 to 1902, superficially resembled the past. Revolution, assassination of the President, dictatorship, counterrevolution, and avoidance of elections all were present. Still, some of the long-sought "progress" had taken place.

Herrera y Obes governed as a partisan Colorado, and alienated the Nationalists. He was too much of an elitist to take his promises of free elections seriously—after all, the rabble were not ready—and alienated the popular faction of the Colorado Party. His government also had to confront the 1890 economic crisis. Yet Herrera y Obes dominated the situation. The army stood by to obey, not command, even through the chaotic twenty-one days after the end of his term when Herrera y Obes, whose direct re-election was prohibited by the Constitution, tried to manipulate the legislature which was electing his successor.

A subaltern member of Herrera's group, Juan Idiarte Borda, emerged as President. Borda continued Herrera's policies but lacked Herrera's prestige; his government was also openly corrupt. The popular Colorados resisted him and in 1897 the Nationalists, under Aparicio Saravia, revolted.[32]

During the militarist era there had been frequent conspiracies and barracks uprisings, as well as abortive revolutions based in

Argentina, but there had been no full-scale civil war since the Blanco revolution of 1872. Many believed that ranchers had too much at stake in their new fenced ranches to risk joining a revolution and that the era of revolutions in the interior was over. Saravia, who had learned to fight serving under his brother in the gaucho wars across the northern border in Brazil's state of Rio Grande do Sul, showed that the party spirit still lived and that full-scale revolution was indeed possible. The government, unable to defeat the revolution, agreed to an armistice in August, but the Nationalist peace terms were too high for President Borda. On Independence Day, August 25, 1897, an obscure youth, inflamed by the violent campaign of the opposition press, fired a pistol at Borda, just leaving the Cathedral after a *Te Deum*. The shot was at point-blank range and killed the victim almost immediately.[33]

The President of the Senate, Juan Lindolfo Cuestas, that old man who hobbled with the aid of a cane, took over as interim President. Cuestas showed unexpected energy and resourcefulness. He realized that the closed group around Borda was doomed, called in the negotiators, and made peace with the revolution. The 1872 Revolution had been settled by giving the Nationalists the administration of four departments—the map of Uruguay, following the French pattern, was divided into nineteen departments. Cuestas' major concession in the peace pact of '97 was his commitment to appoint Nationalist *jefes políticos* (political heads) to administer six of these departments. The pact, incidentally, was the first major Uruguayan peace settlement made without foreign mediation.

Electoral reform and administrative honesty had been the revolution's banner. Cuestas hastened to sponsor an electoral law providing for minority representation and to correct administrative abuses. A rapid political realignment took place. The Nationalists supported Cuestas; the popular Colorados who had opposed Borda now supported Cuestas, while the former pro-government Colorados, under Borda, opposed Cuestas' government. The central question was whether the legislature, elected under Borda, would vote Cuestas as President of the Republic for the regular term beginning March 1, 1898. The legislators were warned that they had two choices: Cuestas as President or Cuestas as Dictator. "Cuestas, cueste lo que cueste" (Cuestas, cost whatever he costs) was the popular slogan, and behind the slogan were the business classes, the Nationalists, and the pro-Cuestas Colorados.

The legislature refused to elect Cuestas. Thereupon Cuestas, with the army standing aside, overthrew the legislature, substituted a Council of State composed of his Colorado and Nationalist supporters, and proclaimed himself dictator. On July 4, 1898, an abortive army counterrevolt was put down. The promised electoral law was approved, but the government parties, Colorado and Nationalist, felt the situation was too delicate to risk an electoral contest under the new law. Instead they made an *acuerdo* (accord), an agreement dividing the legislative seats between them. The new legislature, elected under the acuerdo, met and on March 1, 1899, chose Juan L. Cuestas constitutional President of the Republic.

Since the Fourth of July counterrevolution Cuestas no longer trusted the army. His fears of a barracks uprising inspired by the opposition Colorados reached the point of a psychological obsession. To prevent any such movement from succeeding, Cuestas needed the support of Saravia's army, and he propitiated the Nationalist caudillo while he alienated many Colorados by his continual acts of vexation against possible dissident Colorado leaders.[34]

Saravia, who only with difficulty had assembled an army of a few thousand in '97, could now doubtless raise one double that size. Nationalist morale was high; contributions for the party treasury and Saravia's army flowed in. Saravia himself stayed on his ranch, many leagues from the nearest railroad, and refused to come to Montevideo. He sensed that in Montevideo he would appear rustic, but on his ranch Montevideo public figures would look like tenderfeet. When matters of great moment arose, the President of the Republic, and the Directorio, the Directorate of the National Party, sent emissaries to the gaucho.

Proof that Cuestas had split the Colorado Party while Saravia had united the Nationalists came in 1900, when the Nationalists won the Senate seats in five of the six departments up for election. Saravia would have liked to contest the general legislative elections of 1901 but this idea horrified Cuestas, the Nationalist Directorio, and the conservative classes, all of whom feared that a contested election could only end in civil war. Instead, the legislative seats were again divided by an acuerdo, with the Nationalists maintaining their strong minority position and the anti-Cuestas Colorados largely frozen out. To mollify Saravia, Cuestas secretly agreed not to intercept certain arms shipments the Nationalists were buying abroad and sending to Saravia's army.[35]

In agreeing to the acuerdo, the Nationalists had agreed to accept more than continuation of their minority status in the legislature. Since the Constitution provided that the President of the Republic be elected by majority vote of the legislature, not by popular election, the Nationalists had, in effect, agreed that the President to be elected on March 1, 1903, would not be a member of their party. The Nationalists did assume that since there would be several Colorado candidates no candidate could get the constitutional absolute majority of legislative voters without their votes. Therefore, Nationalist influence on the next President would continue, even increase over the party's already substantial influence on Cuestas.

Since '97, both sides had been calling for free elections and had even passed enabling legislation. Saravia was building up his army to make sure that his party's rights would be assured when the time came for free elections. The Colorados were divided among themselves, yet determined not to lose power. Under these circumstances, an appeal to armed strength somewhere along the line was quite likely. The next President would have a difficult government. One of the signs that there really had been "progress" since '97 was that none of the presidential candidates could be sure he would win.

II

Y<<<<<<<<<<<<<

Campaigners

On March 1, 1903, if nothing untoward had happened, all the Senators and Deputies would gather in the grand salon of the cabildo to elect the next President of the Republic. Each legislator would get up, announce his vote, and the candidate who won 45 votes would be the next President. The Nationalists, under the 1901 acuerdo, had 37 legislative seats, 8 short of the needed majority. Since the Colorado legislators were divided into warm followers of Cuestas, lukewarm followers of Cuestas, and even some outright opponents of Cuestas, the likelihood was that the Nationalist votes would decide among competing Colorado candidates. Given the delicate political situation, the campaign was likely to be in the back rooms, for to bring the public in might produce pressures which would end in war.

One man, Aparicio Saravia, could, if he would, deliver the Nationalist vote. Saravia had restored the National Party to a dominant position in Uruguay; he would lead it to power—by election if possible, by revolution if necessary.[1] He commanded an army with a cadre on active service (the *compañías urbanas*) made up of militarized companies of prison guards in the six Nationalist departments won in '97. His army reserve was organized down to a printed table of organization listing unit commanders and officers.[2] Saravia's arms were cached and his army waited for his word. The Nationalist legislators who were going to vote for president would

16

also hear his word. It would be enough for Saravia to suggest a name; he did not have to issue a command.

But General Saravia did not like to mix into political operations. He did not want to weaken his prestige by involving it in day to day politics; he did not trust the Montevideo politicians, still obliged to make the tiring trip to his ranch when they wanted to consult him.

Saravia's suspicions of politicians had been confirmed by the recent acuerdo. He had advised the Nationalist negotiators to hold out for better terms, but they disappointed him. He accepted the acuerdo out of party loyalty, then resigned as Honorary President of the Nationalist Directorio. The resignation was enough to topple the Directorio, and a new one headed by one of Saravia's old supporters was elected. Saravia was not mollified; late in the 1902 presidential campaign he wrote an adviser:

> Passing to the presidential question, you tell me that my influence will be decisive in the solution of that problem: permit me to remind you that I was told the same thing when the acuerdo matter was being arranged; in spite of which, and to my deep regret, my opinions were completely disregarded.[3]

Besides his unwillingness to risk his prestige by sponsoring a presidential candidate who might not be elected, Saravia was not enthusiastic about any of the Colorado candidates offered the Nationalists. So far as he could see, one of these Colorados was about the same as another; the important question was whether the candidate was prepared to respect, or increase the number of, the Nationalist departments, the Nationalist positions of strength. Saravia believed that, if the Nationalists waited before choosing a Colorado candidate, the contending candidates would make increasingly higher offers on the departments.

Old Cuestas naturally would take a hand in the campaign, especially to convince Saravia to commit himself. Cuestas believed Uruguay needed another administration like his: one dedicated to financial responsibility and based upon cooperation with the Nationalists. He also had personal reasons for wanting a friend in power, since his goal was to turn the government over in peace and go off to Europe for a rest.[4] Cuestas feared that if he stayed in Uruguay as a private citizen, one of the many men he had thrown out of office, into prison, or into exile would assassinate him. The

Constitution required an ex-president to remain in the country for a year after leaving office, but the legislature could waive the requirement and permit him to leave. For the permission and departure to go smoothly, Cuestas' successor must want to oblige his predecessor.

There were at least three avowed candidates for the succession. José Batlle y Ordoñez, Senator from Montevideo and Colorado political leader, onetime President of the Senate now somewhat distant from Cuestas, was openly in the race for President of the Republic. Juan Carlos Blanco, President of the Senate, quite distant from Cuestas and friendly with the Nationalists, hoped he would get the 37 Nationalist votes, add the remaining 8 Colorado votes, and win. Cuestas was sponsoring his old political chum and present Minister of Government, Eduardo MacEachen, and Cuestas' influence was a tremendous asset.

In addition to the avowed candidates, there were others eager to be the next President should events go their way. José Pedro Ramírez, dean of the conservative classes, the peacemaker of '97, neither a Colorado nor a Nationalist, was the one man about whom Saravia really could become enthusiastic.[5] If the Colorados so fell out among each other during the campaign that no one candidate could get a majority and a man above the strife was needed, Ramírez was available for a draft. Ex-President General Máximo Tajes also was available. His chance would come if the Nationalists tried to force events; then the Colorados might jettison Cuestas, turn to a military solution, and elect Tajes. There were other unavowed candidates, less Colorado than Tajes, less neutral than Ramírez, whose special qualities might still make one of them President.

Of the active candidates, the chances of José Batlle y Ordoñez [6] seemed the poorest. His lineage was distinguished: his father, the late General Lorenzo Batlle, one of the *prohombres* (distinguished men) of the Colorado Party, had been a Minister of War during the Great Siege of Montevideo and President of the Republic from 1868 to 1872; his grandfather, José Batlle y Carreó, had been a substantial citizen of colonial Montevideo. Batlle y Carreó, a native of Sitjes near Barcelona in Catalonia, brought his bride to Montevideo in his own ship in 1800. He built a large flour mill outside the city's fortified walls, owned—outright or in partnership—a fleet of grain ships, and in 1806 was awarded the contract to provision the Royal Spanish Navy in Montevideo. Batlle y Carreó was an enthusiast of the Spanish Crown, first against the 1806–1807 English invasions of the Plata, then against the forces of independence led by Artigas. The English confiscated his loaded ships; the patriots confiscated his merchandise; the Crown did not pay for the provisions he supplied. All told, his loyalty cost him several hundred thousand gold pesos. In 1814, he got permission from the victorious patriots to leave for Spain and collect the debt owed him by the Crown, though he was obliged to leave his wife and his four Montevideo-born children behind as a pledge of good faith; the family later reunited in Barcelona in 1818. Batlle y Carreó's long efforts to obtain payment from the Crown were fruitless; his wife died in the old family home of Sitjes in 1823; finally, in 1833, he decided to return to Uruguay and reopen the flour mill, the only real property he still had left. Batlle y Carreó lived until 1854, long enough to see his son Lorenzo Batlle an important man in Uruguay.[7]

Lorenzo Batlle had received an exceptional education in Europe, at a school in France, then at the exclusive *Colegio de Nobles y Militares* in Madrid, from which he graduated. His father sent him back to Montevideo in 1830, when Lorenzo was twenty, to start up in business and prepare for the family's return. Lorenzo Batlle's education made him stand out in rudimentary, just independent Uruguay, where he was welcomed into political life and joined the Colorados from the very beginning. When Oribe began the Great Siege of Montevideo in 1843, Lorenzo Batlle became a battalion commander of the city's Colorado defenders. He was named Minister of War in 1847, at a moment when the Defense seemed about to succumb. Rivera himself, the Colorado caudillo, defeated in the field and fearful that Montevideo's European allies were betraying her, proposed peace to Oribe. The Government of Montevideo decided to exile its caudillo and sent its Minister of War, Lorenzo Batlle, on the delicate mission of personally escorting Rivera aboard the ship that took him to Rio de Janeiro. Lorenzo Batlle was always remembered for this mission.

After Oribe was defeated and the Siege of Montevideo lifted in 1852, Lorenzo Batlle returned to the management of the now prosperous family flour mill, the *Molino Uruguayo*. During the Great War he had married Amalia Ordoñez, daughter of a tough Colorado guerrilla leader. Lorenzo Batlle continued in Colorado politics, generally in the anti-caudillo factions of the party. When Flores, Rivera's successor as Colorado caudillo, brought the party back to power in 1865, he promoted Lorenzo Batlle to General and named him Minister of War, to conciliate the moderate Colorados. In the turmoil following Flores' assassination in 1868, Lorenzo Batlle, a compromise candidate, was elected President of the Republic. His presidency was disastrous. He inherited a monetary crisis, and antagonized the doctrinaire liberalism of the doctores (already unhappy at his caution in dealing with the lesser Colorado caudillos remaining after Flores' death) by his attempts to control the private banks' emission of paper money. He proposed to govern with all factions of the Colorado Party; the lesser caudillos revolted at this. He excluded the Blancos from his government, and Timoteo Aparicio led a major civil war against him, from 1870 until several months after his administration ended in 1872. A barracks uprising in the last days of his term presaged the era of military dictatorship. Lorenzo Batlle's preoccupations were so great that he neglected the Molino Uruguayo, and it failed during his presidency. For the rest of his life to his death in 1887, he was a poor man living on his army pension, respected as a historic figure, admired in his poverty for not turning high office to personal profit, and vindicated by the doctores who came to admit that their opposition to Lorenzo Batlle had helped bring worse days for the Republic.

José Batlle y Ordoñez, born in 1856, had been 12 years old when his father's presidency began; he was now 45, still a little young to be aspiring to be the second President Batlle. Batlle was a huge man, well over six feet tall, an athlete gone to fat. He had a ponderous walk, spoke slowly with a gruff voice which fitted his physique, and his heavy features were partially covered with a beard. "Robust" was the best single word to describe his appearance.

People preferred another and less favorable word, "bohemian," to describe Don Pepe—Batlle's nickname. Stories even circulated that he drank; the irreverent called him "Don Pepe Botella (Bottle)." Actually, Batlle was a sober citizen, a model husband and proud father of four; his wife was the daughter of another hero

18 de Julio Avenue

The harbor

The Presidential House

Aparicio Saravia

Juan L. Cuestas

of the Defense of Montevideo, Manuel Pacheco y Obes. Still, the origins of their marriage were complicated. Matilde had been left by her husband, Ruperto Michaelson, perhaps abandoned, with five children and no money. The husband was Pepe's cousin, and Batlle set up household with his cousin's wife. It was an admirable act, but the embarrassing fact was that it was not until several years afterward that they could marry and have all Matilde's children with her. Batlle lived decorously, yet instead of devoting himself to building a fortune for his substantial family of children and stepchildren he spent all his time in politics and in his political newspaper *El Día*. It was well known that Batlle was honest and physically brave, but was he up to the business of government?

If Don Pepe's life had been bohemian, it had not been carefree. He and his younger brother Luis lost their mother when they were still young. Their father's years were hard, especially after his presidency. Nevertheless, Pepe's education had been the finest available. He had gone to an English school in Montevideo and in due time to the University.

The University, though, stagnated during the militarist era, and the young generation of the '70's organized the Ateneo, where they avidly discussed religion and philosophy to get around the ban on political criticism.[8] Idealists who insisted that Man's attributes are innate debated Positivists who maintained that Man's attributes are determined by the society in which he lives. In spite of furious debate, more united the two schools than divided them; both sides agreed what the desirable human virtues were, the Positivists insisting these virtues had evolved while the Idealists were convinced Man had always possessed them.[9] What the debaters were really seeking was the answer to a perplexing Uruguayan question: How could moral men avoid the corruption around them and lead their country out of despotism?

Batlle was a leading member of the Idealist side captained by Prudencio Vázquez y Vega, who gave his followers a personal answer to their central question. They must live the needed virtues; for them, austerity, morality, and friendship, and no compromises with the dictators and their economic lures.[10] Vázquez y Vega also taught from a book by Ahrens, a Belgian follower of the post-Kantian German Idealist philosopher Krause. Ahrens' *Course On*

Natural Law exalted the human personality and made proposals for the reform of society based on the innate dignity of man.[11] In later life Batlle acknowledged a great debt to Vázquez y Vega, and in 1913 on the title page of a gift copy of Ahrens he wrote, "in this great work I formed my criterion on the law and it has served me as a guide in my public life." [12]

The preoccupations of the young philosophers could easily rouse the wrath of the authorities. It was only because he feared for his son that Lorenzo Batlle consented to Pepe's proposal for a year of study in Paris, the fountainhead of philosophy. Lorenzo explained to his other son that he would not have let Pepe go "if it were not for the risk to which I saw him exposed here, because of his exaggerated political ideas." [13]

The year in Paris, 1880, was a delight, even though the father had little money to send. Pepe spent his time wandering around Paris, going to a gym, taking a course in English, and sitting in on the contending philosophical schools. In one of his infrequent letters home, the twenty-four-year-old Batlle reported:

Caro, Laffitte and Paul Zané [Janet?] are the professors I prefer to hear. But they don't take much time because Laffitte only gives classes on Sundays, and Caro and Zané only give them twice a week. Besides, the same thing happens to me here as in Montevideo: I cannot subject myself to the discipline of classes. I try to teach myself by reading the works which appear to be most useful to me.[14]

Money ran out and Pepe had to return to Montevideo, where the trip had heightened his prestige as a student of philosophy. Vázquez y Vega was dying of tuberculosis. Pepe, who went off to Minas to nurse him, had the sad responsibility of bringing the corpse to Montevideo, and then helped arrange the funeral. Batlle hoped to continue Vázquez y Vega's work and prepared himself to take over the philosophy chair of the Ateneo.[15] He was now preoccupied, he confided to a diary he kept in January 1883, with the development of his own position, not the defense of a particular philosophical school:

I have often thought of the necessity of introducing a little order into the intellectual anarchy which reigns in my brain. I want to link causes with consequences, to tie them together among themselves, to reject those that are contradictory, and through rational deduction fill the innumerable blank spots which I note in almost all the doctrines which I have accepted without any critical spirit. My thought and my life will be more original and more logical, my memory more systematic and consequently more powerful, and my imagination more regular and more brilliant—for such are some of the immediate results of meditation.

He also confided to his diary his essential timidity and sensitiveness, a side of his character which he hid in later years behind the gruff voice and his beard:

Indifferent, sensitive, languid, without even the beginning of a vigorous personality in my spirit, it seems as though I lose myself in the daily current of the stupid details of life. I want to react against this fatality, and I cannot, and it conquers me. If I could isolate myself, if I could live alone, completely alone, I would triumph.[16]

The days of keeping a diary, of preparing to be a professor or even a lawyer (he was only four courses short of completing his law degree), did not last much longer. Instead, politics became Batlle's whole life interest. The call his whole generation felt, the adventure of opposing militarism, the implications of his philosophical position, political life's freedom from fixed schedules, the Batlle family background, all made Pepe's move very natural, very easy.

The move itself was imperceptible. Batlle had already been writing for opposition newspapers and enjoying the risks. In 1886, the best young men of all parties in Montevideo organized a revolt against the government of General Santos. Batlle and his brother took part; General Lorenzo Batlle was to be one of the leaders. At Quebracho, the young idealists were routed by the regular army, but Tajes, commanding the army, disobeyed Santos' orders and spared the war prisoners' lives. Batlle returned to Montevideo and opened his own opposition newspaper, *El Día*. He suffered the physical dangers common to the trade, yet was luckier than some. Santos is supposed to have said of Don Pepe, "Does that lunatic really think I would have a son of General Batlle's assassinated?" [17]

Quebracho had great moral force. It demonstrated to Santos and to everyone how alone and despised his government was. Later that year Santos retired to Europe to recover from a would-be assassin's bullet and left Tajes in charge. Tajes saw the meaning of Quebracho, tried to broaden his base of support, and gave the young Colorados, led by Julio Herrera y Obes, a place in his government. Batlle, one of Herrera y Obes' followers, in 1887 was named jefe político of the department of Minas. A few weeks before Pepe left for Minas, Lorenzo Batlle died. *El Día*, the ex-opposition newspaper, stopped publishing shortly after Pepe's departure.

Batlle was jefe político for only six months, then resigned to go on the Colorado ticket as candidate for Deputy. He lost his place on the ticket, apparently because he protested publicly Tajes' announcement that his successor as jefe político of Minas would protect the interests of all, an announcement Don Pepe took as a slur on his honor. Don Pepe devoted the next two years to working in the Colorado clubs of Montevideo on behalf of Julio Herrera y Obes, and in 1889, with financial help from Herrera y Obes, Batlle reopened *El Día* to support Herrera y Obes' campaign for the presidency. The new *El Día* sold on the streets at two cents a copy, the first street sale of newspapers in Uruguay, the first newspaper whose aim was mass readership.[18] Herrera y Obes was elected President, and Pepe Batlle, his supporter, went to the Chamber as a Deputy.

Herrera y Obes' presidency disappointed Batlle. Batlle had been working to reorganize the Colorado Party so that it could win real elections and name presidents. Herrera y Obes saw the party's role differently: it should be the instrument of the President, not his superior; the power of the government, not the broad base of the party, would win the elections. When Herrera y Obes proceeded to name the Colorado candidates for the legislature, Batlle broke with the President. And when Idiarte Borda continued Herrera y Obes' political tactics and combined them with overt corruption, Batlle erupted in Colorado party meetings and in the press. The young grocery clerk who assassinated Borda in '97, during Saravia's revolution, had been inspired, he said, by the bitter articles against the President in opposition newspapers, but evil tongues insisted that Batlle's connection with the assassination was more direct than merely writing blistering press editorials.[19]

Batlle supported Cuestas from the very beginning, and Cuestas seized upon this support. In making peace with Saravia, Cuestas perforce had to turn against the government Saravia had been fighting. This alienated Herrera y Obes and a considerable number of Colorado supporters of that government. If Cuestas was to stay in power he desperately needed a new source of Colorado support, a source Batlle's previously insurgent Colorado group provided. Saravia's revolutionary banner, free elections and administrative honesty, coincided with part of Batlle's program. Batlle saw in Cuestas an opportunity to have free elections and to remake the Colorado Party along the lines Don Pepe had long preached.

Batlle's own star rose rapidly. He became President of the National Executive Committee of the Colorado Party, or at least the pro-Cuestas faction of the party; he was named Senator from Montevideo and then elected President of the Senate. As Senate President, he exercised the Executive Power in the crucial two weeks between Cuestas' retirement as Dictator and election as constitutional President. There was even a Nationalist move to elect Batlle as constitutional President, but Batlle declined to betray Cuestas. Cuestas appreciated Don Pepe's signal service, and by 1900 Batlle, President of the Senate, friend of Cuestas and ally of the Nationalists, considered himself likely to be elected next President of the Republic.[20]

The Senate elections that year jolted Batlle's presidential ambitions. The Nationalists recognized the Colorado disunity, refused an acuerdo, and ran candidates in all six departments up for election. It was Batlle's first chance at campaign managing; he threw all his friends, his brother, his own influence into the election. The Nationalists won five of the six seats, even winning in two departments administered by Colorado jefes políticos. Batlle explained away the dismaying results and claimed that the Colorados, expecting an acuerdo, had been taken unawares, but the fact was that many Colorados, dissatisfied with Cuestas' conciliatory attitude toward the Nationalists and persecution of the pre-'97 Colorado leadership, refused to vote.

For Batlle the defeat meant a change in strategy; he now expected that the Nationalists, having tasted victory in the Senate elections, would refuse an acuerdo for the 1901 general legislative elections. If the Nationalists won in 1901, they would be in position to elect their own candidate to succeed Cuestas as President. Batlle, if he were going to be the next President, must get the Colorado vote out for the general elections and win that vote for himself. Batlle created his opportunity. In one department, Río Negro, the Nationalist Senate election victory was disputed. Batlle advised the Nationalists he would oppose the seating of their victorious Río Negro candidate. In effect, Batlle was telling the Nationalists his alliance with them was over; their response was to refuse to vote his re-election as President of the Senate, the officer who would succeed Cuestas should he die or be assassinated, either of which was quite likely. The new President of the Senate was elected in February 1901, by one vote when three dissident Colorados joined the Nationalists to give Juan Carlos Blanco eight votes to Batlle's seven.[21]

The Senate galleries, packed with noisy Colorado supporters of Batlle, had to be cleared before voting could begin. After the session, a crowd of admirers escorted Batlle to the doors of *El Día*, where he spoke before entering. The time had come, Batlle announced, to stop treating the Nationalists with deference, the time had come to end acuerdos. His peroration was ominous: the goal of the next election should be one-party government and

. . . the reconquest of the departments, the cessation of this abnormal state, which had been aggravated from day to day, in spite of all the complacencies of the Colorado Party, and which divided the Republic into two parts, almost into two separate countries, one Colorado, the other Blanco.[22]

Many thought Batlle had lost his temper at not being elected and spoken in anger, but the speech was a calculated move. During the 1900 Senate election campaign Batlle warned a recalcitrant Colorado departmental politician that if the Nationalists won, the era of concord would end and extremist Colorados take over. "Whoever would then want to influence events, even though it would no longer be possible to direct them, at least to avoid the worst possible consequences, would have to let himself be carried along by the current of exaggeration and intransigence." [23] The reconquest-of-the-departments speech was the opening of Batlle's campaign as partisan Colorado candidate for President of the Republic.[24]

All through 1901, Batlle continued on the partisan path. He unsuccessfully defended the rights of the Colorado candidate to the Río Negro Senate seat; he harped on the differences between Colorados and Nationalists; he proposed reapportionment of the Chamber of Deputies in ways which would favor Colorado chances in the November elections. But Batlle miscalculated. The pre-'97 Colorados refused to join him. The conservative classes, Cuestas, and elements in the Directorio united in their perennial fear that an election under heightened party passions could end only in civil war, and got Saravia to agree to another acuerdo. There was nothing Batlle and his Colorado organization could do except go along.

Though there were no contests, the Colorado organization had to go through the formality of running candidates for the Chamber seats assigned to it. At this juncture, Cuestas dealt Batlle another blow; because he did not like some of the candidates on the Montevideo Colorado ticket, Cuestas used the police to get a slightly different ticket elected. As head of the Colorado organization Batlle could not avoid leading the Colorado committee which called on Cuestas to protest. Old Cuestas did not like people who protested and stopped asking Pepe Batlle in for visits.

Batlle's chances were therefore poor in 1902, when the presidential campaign really got under way. Instead of the partisan campaign Don Pepe had anticipated, victory now seemingly depended on getting the support of the Nationalists and of Cuestas. Batlle had absolutely alienated the Nationalist leadership and lost Cuestas' sponsorship.

Batlle did have some strength. The friends of his youth respected him, for in many ways he had been more faithful to their mutual ideals than they. In younger days they usually elected Pepe as officer of their clubs and organizations; now some of these friends, of both parties, were in the legislature and might once more be willing to vote for him. Also, in the nearly twenty years Batlle had devoted full time to politics, he had developed contacts throughout the country, contacts which in a sense became official when he took over as head of the Colorado organization. His political friends in the departments could influence their Colorado legislators to vote Batlle for President.

Don Pepe had a popular following, especially among young Colorados. Timid as he was, he was not a backslapping politician; his manners were formal, old-fashioned. The idea of huge Batlle bending over to kiss a baby would have provoked hilarious comments. Batlle didn't particularly enjoy speaking in public, and when he did he spoke in a straightforward, almost professorial way instead of using the grandiloquent techniques usually expected. Don Pepe preferred long conversations where he could convince his listeners by using logical tactics to destroy their positions. Perhaps the young Colorados looked up to Batlle, perhaps they liked what

they heard when he conversed with them and what they read in
El Día.

Batlle was preaching a new political era based on free elections,
a Colorado unity party organized from the bottom to the top instead of the other way around, and one-party government. The
Nationalists, plus most intellectuals, considered one-party government a primitive solution and preferred coparticipation, or the
sharing of the Executive by the parties, which could mean anything
from shared patronage to a coalition cabinet to the anomalous
division of the departmental administrations which Batlle had been
attacking. One-party government had been Lorenzo Batlle's motto.
Don Pepe brought it up to date by insisting that a doctrinal gulf,
whose specific policy differences he avoided enumerating, so separated Colorados from Nationalists as to make it impossible for
them to work together in the Executive.

Batlle always concentrated his preaching on political questions,
not on social reform. He had earlier been a Deputy and was now
a Senator, but he had never introduced any startling projects to
reform Uruguayan life, projects which would have been pigeon-
holed had he attempted them; his legislative reputation was as a
specialist in the political intricacies of electoral legislation. To be
sure, Don Pepe had spoken out against the death penalty and against
bullfights, issues which went back to his Ateneo days, and he was
one of the many Uruguayan religious liberals, although *El Día's*
anti-Catholicism had been muted in recent years. On economic
matters Batlle was known to be pro-protective tariff, but beyond
that he made no public pronouncements. Indeed, José Serrato, the
bright young Colorado economist Batlle had already marked for
a cabinet post should he be elected, doubted that Batlle had any
ideas at all on economics.[25] *El Día* criticized Borda for his use of
police as strikebreakers, but whether this represented anything
more than criticism by a systematic opponent of the government
was not clear. Lorenzo Batlle had been an economic conservative,
though he lost his personal fortune. Whether the father's views
passed to the son, here as in other areas, or whether the family's
fall from wealth made Don Pepe sympathize with the downtrodden
were not matters of public knowledge.

Few people remembered the philosophical preoccupations of
Batlle's youth. Nevertheless, he had continued his ruminations

through his years as a Colorado politician. When Don Pepe was still on good terms with Julio Herrera y Obes, he once confided some of these ruminations to the older man. Herrera y Obes was astounded, "Why, man, you're a Socialist!" [26]

Cuestas, who did not entirely trust Batlle, summed him up this way:

> This citizen is a young man of 45, well educated, the son of the late President Batlle, a newspaperman by profession, a revolutionary political agitator, a very tall man with the muscles of a Roman gladiator. He is popular with the politically active elements of the younger generation. He is not accepted by conservative opinion.[27]

Cuestas did not veto Batlle's presidential candidacy because his government still needed the Colorado political support Batlle contributed, but he had no intention of allowing Batlle to succeed him. Cuestas wanted a successor more to his liking, one who would continue his cardinal principles, strict economy and conciliation of the Nationalists; he had a candidate at hand, his own Minister of Government, Eduardo MacEachen. Cuestas and MacEachen had been cronies in the days of Santos, and in '97 Cuestas brought MacEachen into the government. MacEachen, an old bachelor around Cuestas' age, boasted a long beard and a considerable fortune—inherited from his Scotch parents. He was a substantial landowner and prominent member of the conservative classes. Politically, he was a cipher; Cuestas' support was his only capital. Nor would MacEachen engage in a campaign, *Ni un paso ni un peso* (not a step, not a peso) was the phrase commentators put into his mouth. If Juan Lindolfo Cuestas could get him elected, MacEachen would serve; if not, he would go home.

The cautious group around the Nationalist Directorio liked MacEachen. Implicit in the 1901 acuerdo was the assumption that Cuestas' successor would continue Cuestas' policies, and MacEachen was another Cuestas, although much more phlegmatic. Cuestas would influence some Colorado votes; if Saravia could be prevailed upon to accept MacEachen, MacEachen would be the next President. But the Nationalists had problems in committing themselves to MacEachen, as Saravia was well aware. How long would the ordinary Nationalist, the man who had to fight in Saravia's army or vote if it came to an election, tolerate seeing his party so submissive to the government in power? Had men died in '97 so that the Nationalists could support the candidate of the Colorado President of the Republic in '03?

Eduardo Acevedo Díaz,[28] that many-faceted literary man, Uruguay's first great historical novelist, Nationalist to the core, was asking just those questions. He had been brought back from exile by the Nationalist youth in 1895 to found the newspaper, *El Nacional*, whose passionate attacks on Borda helped stir the Nationalists to revolt. Acevedo Díaz had shared the '97 revolution with Saravia, and had expected to share the party leadership after the war. Instead, he was given decorative positions, and his relations with Saravia cooled, although superficially the two remained friendly.

Acevedo Díaz, a postwar Senator and leader of a small group of Nationalist legislators, attacked Cuestas from the beginning, had opposed the 1901 acuerdo, and was hostile to MacEachen. His views on the end of acuerdos and the need for elections paralleled Batlle's. The two had been close friends since the days they had fought together against Santos at Quebracho. Somehow, Acevedo Díaz had convinced himself that Batlle's election would be an affront to Cuestas and therefore a victory for the Nationalists. If Batlle, Acevedo Díaz' man, were elected, Acevedo Díaz' prestige in the National Party relative to Saravia's would rise.

To avoid accusations of truckling to Cuestas, the Nationalist leadership looked favorably, not on Batlle, whose talk about reconquest of Nationalist departments made him entirely unacceptable, but on his rival, Juan Carlos Blanco. Blanco, a famous orator, brilliant lawyer and professor, onetime Minister of Foreign Affairs and President of the Ateneo, was easily the most distinguished of the three avowed candidates. He too had fought as a soldier at Quebracho and been a frequent exile.[29] Blanco left the Constitutionalist Party—the last attempt of the doctores to supersede the traditional parties—to rejoin the Colorados fighting Borda. He had contributed with his oratory and presence to the first period of Cuestas' government, but it was hard for a man of principle to keep his footing during this rapidly changing situation and Blanco came to be the rallying point for those disaffected with Cuestas but opposed to the pre-'97 situation.

Juan Carlos Blanco's election as President of the Senate in 1901, mainly with Nationalist support, made him an obvious candidate for

President of the Republic. Blanco was a very attractive possibility for the Nationalists, since he could be expected to run an honest election, to abide by its results, and—his Colorado fervor being less than red-hot—not resist allowing a non-Colorado to succeed him. Blanco's major weakness was his lack of Colorado support; the pre-'97 Colorados, around Tajes and Herrera y Obes, largely unrepresented in the legislature but with considerable strength among the rank and file, classed Blanco as one of those who had contributed to their fall and would do nothing for him; the great majority of the Colorado legislators were still loyal, in greater or lesser degree, to the Cuestas regime. This left only a scattered few Colorado legislators, neither with the pre-'97 group nor with Cuestas, to support Blanco. There were some very well known men in Blanco's company but as a Colorado political force they were minimal.

The Nationalists had not proved by election that they represented the majority of Uruguayans. It was greatly feared that, should Blanco be elected by 37 Nationalist votes and only 8 or so Colorado votes, the Colorados would go to war before giving up the government. Many of Blanco's ostensible supporters, especially among the Nationalists, expected to jettison him when the danger of war loomed and, in the interests of peace, support MacEachen, just as they had justified the 1901 acuerdo. The Nationalists would then go along with Cuestas and continue the satisfactory political arrangement in existence since '97. In short, Juan Carlos Blanco looked like the classic political front runner who would fade in the home stretch.

III

⟩⟨⟨⟨⟨⟨⟨⟨⟨⟨⟨⟨⟨⟨

The Presidential Campaign Begins

Bᴀᴛʟʟᴇ normally made the *El Día* offices his headquarters, but during the campaign he expected to move around quite a bit. He decided to leave the getting out of the daily edition to his two editors—his protégé, Pedro Manini Ríos, still in his twenties, one of the brightest of the young Colorados, and Domingo Arena, an older man, Batlle's confidant and greatest admirer. Arena, born in Italy, had been taken to the interior Uruguayan town of Tacuarembó when just a child by his immigrant cobbler father. He had come to Montevideo, worked his way through the University to a degree in pharmacy and in law, and done some writing; then Batlle brought him into *El Día*. Arena was everyone's friend, although his favorite circle was with nonconformist intellectuals.

Though Arena and Manini worked well together and were devoted to advancing Batlle's interests, Don Pepe did not give them a free hand in running the paper. He decided that instead of running daily editorials throughout the campaign—editorials which would require *El Día* to take too many stands at a time which called for prudence—the newspaper should limit itself to publishing a digest of the rest of the Montevideo press.[1] Batlle also wanted to set the tone of his campaign personally, so he took the slightly unusual step of publishing two editorials over his own signature in *El Día* in January 1902.

"No more acuerdos" was Batlle's campaign theme. In "New Directions" he explained:

There can be no more just acuerdo than the one which gives each party as much influence in the State as corresponds to it under law. And the laws themselves establish the conditions of that acuerdo. Let the parties go freely to the ballot box, let them measure their forces there, and let each one of the parties have as much influence in the Republic as it earns by ballot. It will be impossible to ask the Colorado Party to give up the government to its adversary through a series of acuerdos which gradually dispossess it from power; nor can the Nationalist Party be asked, again through a series of acuerdos, to submit indefinitely to Colorado supremacy.[2]

In "Party Struggles," Batlle defended both parties from the by now standard accusation that they were responsible for Uruguay's political difficulties:

I believe that one of the benefits we owe the past is our inheritance of the traditional, or better said, historic parties. I believe that, through them, we can have a relatively superior political organization. It is better, really, to be moved by the fervor of memories whose evocation produces a more or less defined program of ideas or sentiments than to serve the private interests of a man or group of men; and our parties, even as they now are, still in formation, without clear action programs or exact goals, are better than the complete anarchy of interests and opinions which would take their place could they be successfully suppressed . . . Really, the parties, more inclined the one to authority and order, the other more inclined to liberty and progress, can constitute the two poles of all our national politics.[3]

There was nothing here about reconquest of departments or one-party government. Batlle was trying to convince the Nationalists that they could trust him to run an honest election and to turn the government over to them should they win that election. This really was Batlle's principal campaign promise. He also promised something to the Colorados, his party of liberty and progress: if they reorganized, they—the Colorados—would do the winning in that election. He let the Colorado legislators see a bit of the 1901 Batlle when he concluded:

The year we are beginning will be full of intensive and useful political labor. The issue of the Presidency of the Republic and the attempts which will be made to snatch the government from the hands of the Colorado Party will make this year profoundly interesting.[4]

The Nationalist leadership had no interest in exploring Batlle's promises. No Batlle promise now would make them recommend that the Nationalist legislators give him their votes for President.

The Nationalist leadership did prepare for the campaign. They proceeded to discipline Acevedo Díaz and smooth relations between the Directorio and Saravia. First, the Directorio inaugurated a new newspaper, *La Prensa,* to expound the party line—Acevedo Díaz' *El Nacional* still was published, but it no longer was orthodox. Next, in spite of Acevedo Díaz' objections, the leadership got Juan Carlos Blanco re-elected President of the Senate. Then a new Directorio was elected and Escolástico Imas, a political mediocrity, friend of Cuestas, brother of one of Saravia's officers killed in '97, was chosen its President. Acevedo Díaz, boxed in and furious, took a several-month vacation from the press.[5] Imas followed protocol, went to Saravia's ranch, met with Saravia—without anyone else present—and returned to assure his fellows that Saravia had agreed to forget frictions with past Directorios. Saravia, Imas announced, was delighted with the composition of the present Directorio.[6]

Cuestas was also preparing for the presidential election. In the 1901 acuerdo the Nationalists agreed not to contest the six Senate seats which would be up for election in 1902, but the dissident Colorados had made no such promise. Unless the loyal Colorado organization was able to defeat the dissidents, Cuestas feared that, when it came time to elect Juan Carlos Blanco's successor—Blanco's Senate term was expiring and Senators could not be immediately re-elected—as President of the Senate, the new dissident Senators would combine with the Nationalists and elect one of Cuestas' outright enemies. Cuestas did not want a really hostile Colorado in the chair as *de facto* Vice President at the end of his term in February 1903, when he would be at his most vulnerable.

Cuestas moved to forestall the possibility. He invited the President of the loyal Colorado organization, Don Pepe Batlle, in for a visit, the first such invitation in months. Cuestas explained to Batlle the need to get the organization moving. He assured Batlle that he wanted nothing for himself, only to turn over the government to his successor in peace; the successor would be elected in legal fashion and he, Cuestas, would not want any personal influence on the next President. Batlle, in turn, assured Cuestas that "not for a single moment" had he been anything but a member of the situation—local parlance for the group around the government—and advised the President that he would do his part to get loyal Colorados elected to the Senate.[7]

El Día described the visit as "a long and pleasant conversation." Batlle's big features were beaming as he left Cuestas' house,[8] for Cuestas had baited his request for Batlle's assistance in the Senate election with the transparent promise that no force would be used against Batlle's presidential candidacy. Batlle knew that while this promise did not mean he would win the presidency, it did mean that he could try. Who had trapped whom would be discovered on March 1, 1903.

Having secured his Colorado flank, Cuestas made a quick thrust at the Nationalists. He wasted no time with the Directorio. Instead he sent Pedro Etchegaray, his perennial emissary to Saravia, off to the caudillo's ranch. Etchegaray, a Colorado Senator and rancher, was now also the principal factotum of the MacEachen campaign; his mission was to convince Saravia to come out in favor of Mac-Eachen immediately. Saravia as usual was noncommittal, but the Montevideo Nationalists, angered at Cuestas' going over their heads, warned him in the new Directorio newspaper that he was treading on dangerous ground.[9]

Cuestas reacted to the rebuff in characteristic fashion. He would knock a few heads together so that the Nationalists could see what treatment they might expect if the next President were a Colorado enemy instead of a Colorado friend. Cuestas had given several recent exhibitions of his famous perverseness. He had two army officers arrested for not saluting him when they passed his house; the fact that they could not see him because he was hiding behind a curtained window did not alter the case. At Eastertime he ordered government employees not to leave Montevideo; good administration required that they spend their vacations in the capital not the country.

Now Cuestas turned his attention to elected officials and named two Senators and one Deputy to the board of directors of the Bank of the Republic. The Senate refused to approve the nominations on the ground that it was illegal to appoint legislators to executive positions; Cuestas countered by sending to the Senate a bill which would legalize such appointments. It was a political test of strength between Cuestas and the Nationalists. Batlle

stretched his conscience and voted for Cuestas' project.[10] The vote
was tied. Juan Carlos Blanco, President of the Senate, broke the tie
by voting against Cuestas and with the Nationalists. The police,
under Cuestas' orders, had filled the galleries with paid demonstrators who jeered Blanco and cheered Batlle.

Cuestas wasn't done with the Senate yet. The senatorship for
the department of Colonia was vacant and there was a legal ob-
scurity over whether the previously elected electoral college could
name the new Senator or whether a popular election of a new
electoral college must be held. Cuestas wanted a new election.
Batlle, now arguing a position he believed in, supported Cuestas
and got Acevedo Díaz' vote as well. Again the Senate vote was
a tie; again Juan Carlos Blanco broke the tie, defeated the project
for a new election, and gave the Nationalists another victory over
Cuestas.[11]

In June, the police uncovered a plot to assassinate Cuestas and
implicated Osvaldo Cervetti, a shady customs official with vague
ties to Tajes, who had been suspended from his position in the
Customhouse for corruption. Cuestas professed to believe that two
Colorado Senators were involved. The two, once his supporters
but now distanced from him, had voted with the Nationalists and
provided the margin which beat Cuestas. Cuestas had them arrested
and deported to Buenos Aires, in spite of their Senatorial im-
munities. There was violent excitement; the Senate insisted they
be returned. Telegrams went off to the unruffled Saravia. Finally,
after hearing the society ladies of Montevideo plead for the Senators' return, Cuestas relented. Batlle, though he joined in the
Senate's stand, also visited Cuestas regularly during the crisis.[12]

Cuestas' tantrums had hardened the lines between Colorados
and Nationalists, had given Batlle numerous opportunities to show
his loyalty to Cuestas, and given Juan Carlos Blanco the same opportunities to strengthen his ties with the Nationalists. Blanco's
candidacy apparently gained strength, for Aureliano Rodríguez
Larreta, one of the shrewdest insiders among the Nationalist leaders,
announced in the Directorio's newspaper that the next President
must be "outside and above the parties." [13] Since Blanco was not a
Nationalist, yet also did not follow the Colorado line, only he of
the avowed candidates fitted the prescription. This was underlined
when José Pedro Ramírez—the man who most comfortably fitted

Rodríguez Larreta's formula—authorized his brother to tell friends among the Nationalists that he too was supporting Blanco and was not himself an active candidate.[14]

The recent crisis also made it difficult for Acevedo Díaz to justify his rebelliousness within the National Party, for the leadership had resisted Cuestas and was leaning toward Blanco, the active candidate furthest from Cuestas. The leadership, with Saravia's full concurrence, wanted all the Nationalist legislators to agree on and vote for the same candidate in the presidential election. Of the 37 Nationalist legislators, 30 had agreed to vote together;[15] Acevedo Díaz and 6 followers were resisting. Rodríguez Larreta's "outside and above the parties" did not appeal to Acevedo Díaz and in *El Nacional* he offered a counterformula: the candidate must assure the Nationalists coparticipation and free elections; he should have enough Colorado strength to make his promises effective; and he must not be "imposed" from above. If the party could not find such a Colorado, it should give up trying to influence the election and vote for a Nationalist.[16] Acevedo Díaz' formula eliminated Blanco, who had insufficient Colorado strength; eliminated MacEachen, who, as far as Acevedo Díaz was concerned, was "imposed" from above by Cuestas; and left Batlle, who was prepared to promise coparticipation and free elections, as Acevedo Díaz well knew. Even if Acevedo Díaz succeeded only in preventing the Nationalists from voting for Blanco or MacEachen and convinced them to throw their votes away on a Nationalist, he would be helping Batlle by making it impossible for Blanco, and exceedingly difficult for MacEachen, to form the needed constitutional majority of 45.

Cuestas had his own formula for the ideal candidate. At a reception for Colorado legislators he proposed that the man be a Colorado, but not a violent Colorado, should continue Cuestas' administrative policies, and above all, that the Nationalists must not make the mistake of refusing to vote for him. Senator José Espalter, a MacEachen man, coined a new slogan—the candidate should be acceptable to the majority of both parties, not be above and outside the parties.[17] MacEachen, the personification of these virtues, had been stunned by the death of his brother and was even more distant from the presidential campaign than usual. To give him a rest and to keep him out of the way of political attack, Cuestas had Mac-

Eachen resign as Minister of Government and named him President
of the Bank of the Republic.

Cuestas wanted the Colorado legislators to come together, vote
on a candidate for President, agree that the victorious candidate
would get all their votes, and then present the candidate—he was
confident it would be MacEachen—to the Nationalists. Batlle went
along with this plan. He could not cross Cuestas and keep his
candidacy viable, for Cuestas had the force of the government
at his command. Besides, Batlle's basic hope was that when the
Colorado legislators came together he, not MacEachen, would
have the majority. If, in the interim, he had given Cuestas no cause
for overturning this result, he might be the next President of the
Republic. Batlle did get Cuestas to agree that the Colorado legislators should not come together until after the Senate elections,
so that all the potential Colorado voters would get a chance to
join. It was to Batlle's advantage to postpone the vote on the presidential candidate as long as possible, since Cuestas' influence on the
legislators would decrease as his term came close to expiration.
Don Pepe was displaying political finesse, something not at all in
keeping with his reputation for simplicity and directness.

Batlle made it a policy to continue his regular visits with Cuestas.
At one such visit, sickly old Cuestas wanted his other callers, who
were waiting in the anteroom, to think he had humbled Pepe
Batlle, the man with a Roman gladiator's physique. Cuestas sud-
denly described to Batlle how he had bawled out some individual
and demonstrated by shouting and beating his cane on the ground.
Don Pepe was worried that the listeners in the anteroom would
think Cuestas was abusing him, rather than the other unfortunate;
to set listeners straight, he forgot his pride and gave out with deep
guffaws whenever Cuestas stopped in his story.[18]

Batlle was also assiduously seeking the company of his fellow
Colorado legislators and future presidential electors. He was seen
enjoying the sun on a warm October afternoon, seated on a bench
in the Plaza Independence, exchanging pleasantries with presumed
legislative supporters of MacEachen, more sure of himself and
less careless of appearances than was his custom. He began asking
his fellow legislators to lunch, one at a time, concentrating particularly on those rumored to favor MacEachen. Batlle would

order the most elegant dishes on the menu and allow his guest to enjoy the experience without political disturbance. After dessert he would assure the satisfied legislator that nothing fundamental divided him from MacEachen, that whoever got the majority of the Colorado votes should get them all. His fellow host, the entertaining Arena, was under strict instruction to follow Batlle's example and never to ask for vote pledges.[19] What Batlle wanted of the MacEachenites was willingness to let the winner win, nothing more.

Batlle's great difficulty was that Cuestas and the Nationalists determined the major campaign developments. The best Don Pepe could do was to adapt his campaign to situations brought about by others unfavorable to his candidacy. This became apparent in November when, in the first formal development of the campaign, the Nationalist legislators announced their agreement to vote together and determine the presidential candidate of their choice.

Acevedo Díaz had given way. There was little else he could do now that the Nationalist leadership was showing itself hostile to Cuestas. Had he refused to agree, Acevedo Díaz could be accused of risking the party's chances to pick the next President merely out of personal petulance. He had, though, driven a bargain which he thought would protect Batlle's interests.

Though the Nationalist legislators issued a public manifesto, the important part of their agreement, the voting procedure, was kept secret. Originally, the manifesto was to contain new policy proposals, but then it was decided only to repeat the traditional Nationalist platform: legislative supremacy, tax reduction, constitutional reform. The candidates would not be obliged to accept these policy planks, but they would have to promise to leave the Nationalists in control of their departments as a guarantee of honest general elections in 1904—a revealing indication of post-'97 politics. The National Party did announce in the manifesto, and here Acevedo Díaz apparently had yielded, that its legislators would not vote for a Nationalist presidential candidate.[20]

The secret agreement on voting procedures had sixteen separate clauses. It outlined a series of run-off ballots to determine which candidate would get all the 37 Nationalist votes. Prior to the vote, individual Nationalist legislators would bring in written statements from the candidate of their choice listing his promises to the party;

these statements would be discussed immediately before the first ballot. Each candidate was required to prove that he had at least 8 Colorado votes, so the 37 Nationalist votes could give him the constitutional majority of 45.

Acevedo Díaz had put in several of the clauses. He got the signatories to agree that the Nationalist legislators would not be coerced into voting for a candidate. He took this to mean that they would not vote for MacEachen, but his co-signers did not agree that to vote for MacEachen was necessarily to bow to Cuestas' coercion. Acevedo Díaz had also written in the requirement that each candidate present a statement of promises, because he knew Batlle was prepared to make attractive offers to the party and thought such a formal pledge might make Batlle acceptable. Acevedo Díaz was not the sort who would accept interpretations of the cumbersome agreement he did not like, yet he agreed to abide by a majority vote of the signatories should disagreements on interpretation arise.[21]

Juan Carlos Blanco, who had the seeming support of the Directorio, most obviously benefited from the Nationalist agreement. If he could get but eight Colorado votes, the Nationalists would almost be morally bound to vote for him. Acevedo Díaz tried to deflate Blanco's hopes and restrain premature dismissals of Batlle's chances. "Up to now, no specific candidate has been considered, or excluded, in the meetings of our party's legislators," *El Nacional* reported.[22]

Acevedo Díaz wanted to widen the split between the Nationalists and Cuestas. *El Nacional* disclosed that a soldier had been beaten in barracks by order of an officer—an old evil now supposedly outlawed. Nationalist legislators called for an interpellation of the Minister of War. Cuestas refused to permit the Minister to appear in the Chamber. The air of crisis, so welcome to Acevedo Díaz, returned; but the Nationalist leadership, now that they had Acevedo Díaz' signature on the agreement, saw only danger of loss of influence in continuing an open split with Cuestas, and President Imas of the Directorio accepted MacEachen's and Etchegaray's good offices in arranging an interview with Cuestas.

The meeting was held on the evening of November 9, 1902, at Cuestas' house. The beating incident was easily settled, then talk moved to more important matters. Cuestas complained that

989.506
V253

59588

the Nationalists were not playing fair on the upcoming Senate elections. He had heard that, though no Nationalist candidates were entered, local Nationalist politicians were secretly advising their followers to vote for dissident Colorados. This violated the spirit of the 1901 acuerdo. Cuestas believed the Directorio ought publicly to ask all Nationalists to refrain from voting. Imas replied that personally he agreed with Cuestas' understanding but that others interpreted the acuerdo more loosely. They talked of the presidential election. Cuestas assured Imas he would not impose MacEachen's candidacy; it would be up to the legislators "spontaneously" to choose their candidate. Very probably Imas told Cuestas that he himself was really pro-MacEachen. The meeting ended and with it the strained relations between the National Party and the President of the Republic.[23]

The Directorio was pleased. All the Nationalist legislators had signed the agreement; good relations with Cuestas were restored. It could now quickly settle the presidential issue before Acevedo Díaz discovered a way out of the agreement. Originally, the Directorio had planned to wait until after the Senate elections before sending the delegation to Saravia which, with the caudillo, would determine the Nationalist presidential strategy. Now the Directorio met and decided to have the delegation leave before the elections. The few members of the Directorio who really were enthusiastic about Juan Carlos Blanco's candidacy wanted a large delegation so that no behind-doors briefing of Saravia could occur, but they were voted down and a three-man delegation was elected, made up of President Imas, already suspect of MacEachenism. Rodríguez Larreta, and war leader Carlos Berro.[24]

The news that the delegation already was elected, soon would be instructed, and shortly thereafter would leave galvanized Cuestas. He wanted the delegation to go to Saravia with information that the Colorado legislators would vote for MacEachen, and he got Batlle to agree to have the Colorado legislators move up their own organizational session to November 21, before the Senate elections and before the delegation's departure. As always, Batlle was cooperative.

On the morning of November 21, *La Nación*, the newspaper which existed on funds supplied by the President's office, came

Alverno College

out with a banner headline proclaiming: THE CITIZEN DON
EDUARDO MAC-EACHEN POPULAR CANDIDATE FOR
CONSTITUTIONAL PRESIDENT OF THE REPUBLIC.
According to the newspaper, unnamed Colorado Senators and
Deputies were the sponsors of the "popular candidate," [25] but there
was no doubt that Cuestas wanted the Colorado legislators meeting
that afternoon to know that he expected them to vote for Mac-
Eachen.

At 5:00 P.M., twenty-one Colorado legislators gathered in Etchegaray's home, even though Etchegaray was MacEachen's campaign
manager. Apparently a message from Imas was read urging a quick
decision before the Nationalist agreement broke apart.[26] However,
the attendance did not even comprise a majority of the Colorado
legislators, to say nothing of the full Colorado membership. Therefore a second meeting was scheduled for November 24 when, it
was hoped, more future voters would attend.[27]

The second meeting was better attended; twenty-seven Colorado
legislators appeared and nine more indicated they would join
the group later. MacEachen's supporters called for an immediate
vote; the Batllistas, led by Batlle, who was his own campaign
manager, resisted. They claimed that several members of their
group were absent and that it would be better to wait before
voting until after the Senate elections, when the "loyal" Colorado
group would be larger and might even reach the constitutional
majority of forty-five. The Batllistas did agree that the future
Colorado candidate be acceptable to the Nationalists. The Mac-
Eachen people, unsure of their own strength, decided not to press
for an immediate vote. It was agreed that future meetings be held
somewhere else than Etchegaray's home, though Batlle's suggestion that the meeting be open to the public was turned down.[28]

One fact stood out: Cuestas had not entrapped Batlle. Batlle had
more support among the Colorado legislators than previously believed, shown by his supporters' successful resistance to an immediate vote. The Directorio delegation could not now go to
Saravia with the news that MacEachen was already the candidate
of the Colorado majority.

On November 26, two days after the second Colorado meeting,
the Directorio met to instruct its delegation which would leave
the next day. A mail popularity poll conducted by the Directorio's

newspaper had resulted in 12,843 votes for Juan Carlos Blanco, 7,015 for MacEachen, and only 869 for Batlle.[29] The Directorio went through the motions of instructing its delegation and unanimously agreed that the delegation should tell Saravia that Juan Carlos Blanco was the Directorio's choice for President of the Republic.[30] But it did not instruct the delegation to say that it wanted to vote for Blanco come what may, and the fact that only one of the three members of the delegation was actively in favor of Blanco meant that Blanco was really the Directorio's conditional choice.

While the delegation was away, Senate elections were held in six departments. There had been fears that Cuestas would use force, but Batlle ran the campaigns without untoward incident. The usual limited number of voters, several hundred in each department, voted. The results must have eased Cuestas' mind and disappointed Juan Carlos Blanco, for the dissident Colorados had felt it worth while to put up candidates in but three departments, won in only two, and these two with the aid of Nationalist votes.[31] Four new "loyal" Senators would be available to vote for MacEachen or Batlle to two new dissidents who might vote for Blanco.

On December 1, the three-man delegation to Saravia returned. On December 2, the Directorio met in secret session to hear their report. They announced Saravia's message:

If you can get a majority for Dr. José Pedro Ramírez vote him without making any demands on him; if this is not possible vote Dr. Blanco and if that candidacy fails I would like MacEachen. As for Tajes and Batlle, in no case should they be voted.[32]

This was scarcely the definitive advice the Directorio had been expecting. Saravia had advanced no real strategy—Ramírez had no Colorado votes—made no clear personal choice. One could surmise that he thought the longer the party waited before deciding, the greater the demands it could make on the candidates in exchange for the Nationalist votes. At bottom, he had avoided committing himself and put the burden of decision on the Directorio.

What Saravia did not want to recognize was that without his explicit backing the Directorio lacked the authority to convince the Nationalist legislators to follow any single course. The Directorio President, Imas, had absolutely no political prestige; he was President only because he was Saravia's friend. Some of the members of the Directorio—Rodríguez Larreta, for example—were shrewd, but unless they could show that they had Saravia behind their specific recommendations, many Nationalist legislators would refuse to accept their leadership. Already, Vidal y Fuentes, Blanco's supporter in the Directorio, was publicly casting doubt on whether the version brought back by the delegation was an accurate reflection of Saravia's views.

The editor of the Directorio's newspaper wanted guidance and wrote a pleading letter to Luis Ponce de León, Saravia's private secretary:

I want to know something, anything, about the future presidency so that I can orient myself . . . You know that your opinion is good enough for me and that I respect General Saravia's with all my heart. It would be painful to proceed without knowing it because what the delegation brought is equivalent to nothing, except for the two candidates justly excluded.[33]

Something had to be given out to the public. The official explanation was that Saravia wanted Nationalist unity and did not desire to dictate to the Nationalist legislators; the Directorio announced that it had decided to wait until the Colorado situation was clearer. Saravia, said the Directorio's newspaper, "doesn't have a presidential candidate; the party's candidate will be his candidate." [34]

Nationalist unwillingness to come out clearly for Juan Carlos Blanco hurt his chances. He needed to pledge at least eight Colorado votes, and Colorado waverers did not want to pledge themselves to Blanco because they knew the Nationalists were already considering how to act when and if Blanco's candidacy failed. Nationalist confirmation of Batlle's unacceptability did not strengthen his candidacy either. MacEachen had gained, but had not gained a clear Nationalist endorsement.

The Nationalists left the next moves to the Colorados. On December 5, the Colorado legislators assembled for their third meeting in the antechambers of the Senate, a more neutral locale than Etchegaray's house. The Batllistas had exerted themselves to get Blanco's Colorado supporters to join the meeting as a stop-MacEachen device, but the Blanco group knew that there were no votes for Blanco among the "loyal" Colorados. If they attended, the Blanco men would be outvoted by the other Colorados and the result would be their disappearance as a factor in the campaign; so they refused.

Exactly twenty-nine Colorado legislators attended and six more excused their absences. This left about seven presently seated Colorado legislators—one less than the eight Blanco needed—either not yet committed or committed to Blanco. Angel Floro Costa, a colorful but discredited deputy who supported Batlle although not one of Don Pepe's inner circle, proposed that the Colorados unite around Batlle and present his candidacy to the Nationalists. This gave Antonio María Rodríguez, one of the professional politicians for MacEachen, a brilliant opening; he proposed that the names of both Batlle and MacEachen be presented to the Nationalists. The second motion would have been even more disastrous to Batlle than the first. Then, the most influential of the Batllistas, Senator Juan Pedro Castro, moved that nothing further be now done and a fourth meeting scheduled two weeks later. This motion, the continuation of Batlle's strategy of delay, carried.[35] Once more, the Batllistas had demonstrated strength among the Colorado legislators; once more, after the meeting, Batlle paid his customary social call on Cuestas.

In the interim between the third and fourth Colorado meetings, the Nationalist leadership tried to discover Blanco's real Colorado strength. On December 10, Rodríguez Larreta, in the company of Nationalist Senator Manuel Alonso, visited Blanco in his home.[36] Acevedo Díaz immediately objected, insisting that prior solicitation violated the Nationalist legislators' agreement; from somewhere a leak developed, and the previously secret Nationalist agreement was published. Cuestas did not like these Nationalist tactics either. His newspaper protested that the Nationalists were playing a devious game by giving each candidate hope that he would get the Nationalist votes.[37]

The fourth Colorado meeting, on December 19, had an attendance of thirty, only one more than previously, and six more were absent but agreeable. This meant that Nationalist votes were still decisive because, even if all six new Colorado Senators—four was more likely—later appeared, the total would still be at least three short of the constitutional majority of forty-five votes needed to elect the next President. The meeting was "harmonious and cordial." A committee was named; it met during a recess and afterwards proposed that the legislators sign a document pledging themselves not to vote for any candidate for President of the Republic who did not have at least twenty Colorado votes. The Batllistas had proposed the measure, which was designed to close off the officialist Colorado voters (the group which was now meeting) from Blanco. The motion passed because the MacEachenites were also interested in preventing defections to Blanco. *El Siglo*, which was supporting Blanco, insisted there was a loophole: the document would not be binding unless it secured forty-three Colorado signatures.[38]

The next evening MacEachen's Colorado supporters met in private session at Etchegaray's house. A document was passed around pledging each signer to vote for MacEachen as President; rumor had it that from twenty to twenty-three Colorados were already signed. Etchegaray supposedly had shown the document to the delighted Cuestas, and *La Nación*, Cuestas' newspaper, announced that when a predetermined number of signatures was reached the pledge would be published. "When this publication appears then nobody will have any doubts about the final outcome of the Presidential problem." [39]

The fifth Colorado meeting was set for the afternoon of December 27. That morning Batlle again spoke with Cuestas who, it was reported, urged him to withdraw from the campaign in favor of MacEachen. At the afternoon session, thirty-two legislators appeared and discussed the details of the agreement they would soon sign. The agreement, analogous to the Nationalist agreement, required all the loyal Colorados to vote together in run-off ballots until one candidate got a majority; this candidate would then receive all the loyal Colorado votes for President.[40]

Batlle's patient efforts had succeeded in getting the pledge he wanted—the pledge from MacEachen's supporters that they would vote for him if he won more Colorado votes than MacEachen. But Batlle seemingly had waited too long, for the word was that Mac-Eachen was three or four Colorado votes ahead of Batlle.

Juan Carlos Blanco now made his move. He had received assurances that he could count on all the thirty-seven Nationalist votes, *if* he had sufficient Colorado support. At best, Blanco had six

Colorado votes—two short—and not all of these six had promised to stay to the end. Blanco personally visited Cuestas, but Cuestas was confident of MacEachen's ultimate victory. Blanco's supporters visited Tajes, but Tajes still hoped for his own election and would do nothing for Blanco.[41] Juan Carlos Blanco could not announce that he had the precious eight Colorado votes.

When Acevedo Díaz was told that Rodríguez Larreta had offered the Nationalist votes, his own included, to Blanco, he grew violent. According to the Nationalist legislators' agreement a number of steps must be taken before the Nationalist vote was pledged to anyone. Acevedo Díaz would not be assuaged by statements that the offer was "private" not "official," and on December 31 he announced he was deciding whether or not he was still bound to vote with the Nationalist legislators.[42]

Blanco's candidacy was fading. If Acevedo Díaz and his group deserted the Nationalists, Blanco would need ten to fifteen Colorado votes, instead of eight, to combine with the Nationalist vote if he was to reach forty-five; he had no prospect of getting that many Colorado votes. Blanco was also being betrayed: President Imas of the Directorio was able to write Saravia that José Pedro Ramírez, whom Saravia so admired and who supposedly was seeking votes for Blanco, had told him, "The candidacy of Sr. Blanco is only an illusion, the Colorados will not vote for him." [43]

Now was the time for Saravia to speak out and give direction to the Nationalists. Blanco was fading; Acevedo Díaz was splitting away and doubtless would go to Batlle. The very worst might happen: Blanco's supporters, both Nationalist and Colorado, could become so disgruntled at Nationalist refusal to stand up for Blanco that they would join Acevedo Díaz and vote for Batlle. These votes might be enough to make Batlle President.

If Saravia spoke for Blanco, only a few Nationalists would follow Acevedo Díaz to Batlle, and Blanco's Colorado supporters would take heart. If Saravia thought the time had come to drop Blanco and move to MacEachen, he could announce his support for MacEachen. Surely more than thirty Nationalist legislators, protected by Saravia's prestige, would vote for MacEachen, and MacEachen had the necessary balance of Colorado votes already pledged.

Correspondents warned Saravia that his silence was hurting the party's chances to influence the outcome of the presidential election, but he would not be moved. His private secretary was going to Montevideo for the New Year holiday. On getting off the train, young Ponce de León was interviewed. He admitted he had asked Saravia what to say before leaving for Montevideo and had received this answer:

Simply the truth; that I don't have a specific candidate; that I want them to proceed with the greatest wisdom and most elevated point of view, and bring to the presidency the citizen who best meets the national interest.[44]

Cuestas closed the year 1902 in typical style. He brought the Colorado legislators together and announced that he was tired of waiting for the Senate to make up its mind on whether or not to call a new election for the vacant Senate seat from the department of Colonia. He would call a new election himself.

IV

Election

Acevedo Díaz opened the New Year of 1903 with the announcement that because of the "violation" of the Nationalist legislators' agreement he considered the agreement void.[1] It did not take long to discover who had told Acevedo Díaz of the Nationalist vote offer to Juan Carlos Blanco. Domingo Mendilaharsu, editor of *El Tiempo* and a Tajes supporter, spoke out. In mid-December he had been invited to a meeting of the seven Colorado legislators who were going to vote for Blanco; at the meeting he was told that all thirty-seven Nationalist votes were pledged to Blanco and was asked to put *El Tiempo* behind Blanco. Mendilaharsu checked the story, found that the Nationalist votes were not really pledged, and passed on to Acevedo Díaz the news that Nationalist emissaries were promising votes to Blanco.[2]

What Mendilaharsu, an eminent Colorado, did not announce was his reason for talking to Acevedo Díaz. Actually, he was in a rage at being duped by the Nationalists in his own presidential ambitions. He had come to his old friend Pepe Batlle and asked, "Between MacEachen's candidacy and mine, which would you choose?" Batlle, even though about to seal his long-sought agreement with MacEachen's supporters, answered, "Yours, without hesitation." "Well, you can make me President . . . if you give me your votes." Batlle was sure of at least fifteen votes but he gave Mendilaharsu a more cautious answer. He replied that although he had no formal pledges, he could influence eight or nine of his supporters to vote for Mendilaharsu, *if* these votes would be enough to elect him.

Mendilaharsu assured Batlle that Nationalist leader Rodríguez Larreta had promised him eighteen Nationalist votes, that he was confident he would then get the votes of the Colorados supporting Blanco, and that if he had Batlle's eight or nine votes he could pick up the balance from individual legislators. Don Pepe, who knew that no Nationalist leader could yet pledge Nationalist votes, agreed to speak to his own supporters *after* Mendilaharsu got the other assurances *in writing*. Mendilaharsu tried, discovered he could get no written assurances, and became convinced that the Nationalists had been toying with him. He went to Acevedo Díaz, not with the story that he had been offered Nationalist votes, but with the equally true story that they had been offered to Blanco.[3]

Once more, Don Pepe had operated with unexpected subtlety, and used his superior knowledge of the situation to make Mendilaharsu work for his candidacy without realizing it. Now Acevedo Díaz had an excuse for his unilateral breaking of the Nationalist agreement. Mendilaharsu, with whatever influence he possessed, felt Batlle was the only fully honest operative in the whole transaction. Batlle had also protected himself in case Mendilaharsu's doubtful dreams might be true, since by delivering the decisive votes he would have earned an important place in Mendilaharsu's government.

Saravia's unwillingness to give explicit instructions to the Directorio delegation had disoriented the Nationalist leaders, who had felt obliged to discover the candidates' strength. In order to get specific answers from the candidates, the leadership—Rodríguez Larreta had been one of the three-man delegation—made tentative vote promises to some candidates. These promises gave Acevedo Díaz the excuse he needed to free himself to vote for Batlle. Would Saravia now come out for a candidate? The Directorio hoped so; after Acevedo Díaz' announcement, it sent a telegram to Saravia asking for "his views on the presidential question," [4] and it postponed the Nationalist legislators' meeting, originally scheduled for January 16, to January 30, in the expectation that Saravia's declarations would arrive in the interim.

Etchegaray, MacEachen's campaign manager, was once more

on Saravia's ranch with a message from Cuestas urging Saravia to come out for MacEachen. Etchegaray had supposedly also delivered an eight-point memorandum from Cuestas. Abelardo Márquez, Nationalist jefe político of Rivera, one of Saravia's most trusted lieutenants, went with Etchegaray to join in urging the caudillo to support MacEachen.

On January 16, the day originally scheduled for the Nationalist legislators' meeting, Etchegaray, all smiles, returned to Montevideo. After an earlier trip, Etchegaray had reported this conversation with Saravia: "Which of the candidates do you like best, friend General? Look here, friend Don Pedro, I'd like to run it with the Englishman!" Etchegaray now announced, "I don't bring anything formal, but I do bring something in substance." [5]

News spread that Saravia had asked how the candidates stood. Etchegaray replied that MacEachen had over twenty Colorado votes, Batlle fourteen or fifteen, and Blanco six to eight conditional votes. Etchegaray then told Saravia that if he announced for MacEachen more than the needed twenty-five Nationalist legislators would follow his lead, and MacEachen would be the next President. After much urging, Saravia had agreed to find out how the Nationalist legislators felt. One version was that Saravia said if a majority of the Nationalist legislators did in fact favor MacEachen he would go along; another version had Saravia promising to support MacEachen over Batlle if Blanco's candidacy failed.[6] Either way, Saravia said nothing to Etchegaray he had not already said to the original Directorio delegation.

Etchegaray though was confident; he got thirteen hard-core Colorado MacEachen supporters together and told them that Saravia had promised him the votes of the majority of the Nationalist legislators. He next arranged the final details of the voting agreement with the Batllistas. In November, Cuestas had wanted a quick Colorado vote to enable the Directorio delegation to present Saravia with the news that MacEachen was the Colorado candidate. Now the Cuestas strategy was to postpone the Colorado vote, and so give the Nationalists time to dispose of Blanco decorously before coming out for MacEachen. Batlle had shown considerable strength among the Colorados; Cuestas now wanted the Colorados not to vote until they could vote influenced by the knowledge that the Nationalists were already pledged to MacEachen.

On January 20, twenty-seven Colorado legislators met and signed an agreement to vote together in the presidential election. They circulated the agreement, gathered a total of thirty-seven signatures—eight short of the constitutional majority—and released the document on January 23. The signatories would come together on February 16 and vote by signed and sealed ballot. After the first ballot, all candidates not obtaining a minimum of twenty Colorado votes would be dropped. After the second ballot, "all the signatories to this agreement . . . solemnly promise to proclaim as candidate for the presidency of the republic, the citizen who obtains the majority of votes." If, before February 6 (ten days before the February 16 vote), a candidate with twenty-six Colorado votes had enough other pledged votes—that is, nineteen Nationalist votes—to achieve the constitutional majority of forty-five, a special meeting would be called and all those who had signed the agreement would then vote for that candidate. Once a candidate was chosen, on February 16 or before, a committee of three would be named to negotiate for the votes of other political groups—that is, the Nationalists and the pro-Blanco Colorados.[7]

After the January 20 meeting Batlle, six of his supporters, and seven supporters of MacEachen went to Senator Canfield's house where they toasted the agreement with champagne. Of greater potential importance was a secret clause the fourteen legislators then signed: if one of the candidates had twenty Colorado votes and also received the Nationalist votes but—because the Nationalists split—did not yet have forty-five votes, then six voters for the other candidate—that is, Batllistas—would give their votes to him, to give him the constitutional majority.[8]

Batlle had accepted the MacEachen demands on every point: he agreed to delay the vote for more than three weeks; he publicly agreed to suspend the vote if MacEachen got twenty-six Colorado votes and but nineteen of a potential thirty-seven Nationalist votes; he secretly agreed to suspend the vote if MacEachen got only twenty Colorado votes plus nineteen Nationalist votes. Batlle's supporters feared he had given up too much, but Don Pepe was sure that no agreement would restrain the MacEachenites if they had enough votes to elect their man before the February 16 Colorado balloting. If MacEachen were to be the next President, Batlle did not want to be proscribed; he wanted to contribute to the

José Batlle y Ordoñez, 1903

Government House

The Cabildo

victory and continue politically with MacEachen as he had with Cuestas. At bottom, Batlle had gotten in weakened form the substance of what he always had wanted: agreement by the MacEachenites to vote for Batlle, if Batlle had more Colorado votes in the showdown than MacEachen did.

On January 21, the day after the Colorado agreement was signed, Acevedo Díaz made his formal break with the Nationalists: "for us the 'agreement' no longer exists. . . we will act with complete independence, as citizen and as party-man, as writer and member of parliament." The Directorio newspaper responded with an editorial, "Impossible Candidates," which rejected General Tajes, an anachronism, and Batlle, the one candidate who would bring war.[9] The Directorio itself moved up the Nationalist legislators' meeting to January 26 from January 30, to ascertain how many Nationalist legislators were following Acevedo Díaz.

The Directorio, naturally, wanted Saravia's support—he had not yet answered its request for his opinion on the presidential question. President Imas of the Directorio immediately advised Saravia of Acevedo Díaz' treason. So did Etchegaray. In a letter written as to a comember of the MacEachen group, Etchegaray told Saravia that Acevedo Díaz was offering ten to twelve Nationalist votes to Batlle, and that the Nationalist majority was supporting Blanco. He urged Saravia to call on Acevedo Díaz to abstain, and to request that a delegation of legislators visit his ranch. Etchegaray, who doubtless had inflated Acevedo Díaz' vote total to impress Saravia with the danger, closed with the phrase which ever made Saravia cautious: "your influence will be decisive." [10]

Saravia still could not bring himself to endorse MacEachen, the incumbent Colorado President's candidate. He did go part of the way with Etchegaray, enough almost to eliminate Blanco's chances, and wrote Imas intimating both that he would like a delegation to visit him and that it was not to "the party's interests" for the Nationalist legislators to proclaim a candidate for President immediately.[11] Saravia was accepting the MacEachen strategy of holding off the Nationalist endorsement of Juan Carlos Blanco until it was too late for Blanco to get the additional Colorado votes. Then the press would be on the Nationalist legislators to overcome their scruples and vote for Cuestas' candidate MacEachen, lest

Batlle, the Nationalist Party's enemy, combine the Colorado votes with Acevedo Díaz', and win.

Now that the Colorado agreement had been signed and another Nationalist delegation to Saravia was being readied, Batlle judged it time to present his platform as candidate for President. He could explain his position to potential Colorado voters and could once again try to convince the Nationalists that he was not their inveterate enemy. Also, the atmosphere of back-room politics which had so dominated the campaign ran against Batlle's preaching of open politics; by making declarations, Don Pepe further distinguished himself from Blanco, who would say nothing lest he topple his already shaky support, and MacEachen who evidently had nothing to say. Batlle allowed himself to be interviewed at length by Mendilaharsu's *El Tiempo* and then had *El Día* reprint the interview.

Batlle began by talking of the need for concord between the parties. "I believe that the remedy for all our ills is liberty, electoral liberty. Here is the true acuerdo, the obligatory acuerdo, to which we are all duty bound to submit." The great "task of the present" was to transfer party struggles from the battlefield to the ballot box. "As for me, I can say that this has been the ideal of my entire political life."

When asked what political role he assigned to the President of the Republic, Batlle responded with Nationalist leader Rodríguez Larreta's very phrase: "the President of the Republic should place *himself outside the parties and above them!*" As head of government the President must be impartial when he ran elections.

But the citizen who occupies the presidency of the republic, and who, in most cases, will be one of the most important members of his political organization, can not be denied the right to have his own opinions about popular movements, or the right to communicate these opinions to his friends, thus exercising a moral influence.

He went on to explain his past political attitudes, especially his reconquest-of-the-departments speech. Earlier in the interview he had stated, "The first result of electoral liberty will be one-party government." He now went on to give a soft definition of one-party government:

A truly constitutional government can not be exclusivist; it necessarily is everyone's, although principally the triumphant party's; it is a government of coparticipation . . . The minority party will always have strong representation in the National Legislature, which will permit it to achieve important positions in the public administration, in addition to those rightfully belonging to it through the obligation of every government to choose the most apt individuals for public employment, even though this would not prevent the government, when the aspirants were equal, from looking with equitable preference on men from the triumphant party.

Batlle specifically promised to continue the present policies of coparticipation in the coming government:

The new government will be the final result of the acuerdo of 1901 and, in general, of the policy of acuerdos. The new government can not be considered the work of full electoral liberty, a state into which the Republic has not yet entered. I believe, therefore, that an indispensable condition of a just policy will be to keep the present positions of the nationalist party throughout the period of the next government, positions which should still be considered as a guarantee to that party that the institutional work we are all engaged in will be completely accomplished. This is not to say that a patriotic spirit of concord should not be accentuated when it comes to the distribution of administrative posts.

Batlle's final statement was a flat pledge to keep all the promises he had just made even if he were elected entirely with Colorado votes.[12]

The platform was reminiscent of the two signed editorials with which Don Pepe had opened his presidential campaign, but the whole tone was much more conciliatory to the Nationalists. Batlle was trying hard to satisfy the Nationalists: he had just promised to let them keep their departments throughout his administration, not only until after the 1904 elections; he had even intimated that he was prepared to let the Nationalists have additional departments; his definition of one-party government had been extremely mild. The promises might convince other Nationalists to join Acevedo Díaz, and if Batlle were elected in spite of the Nationalist leadership, the promises might restrain any Nationalist revolt.

Several of Batlle's more general pledges, though, were very carefully phrased. He had promised the non-Cuestas Colorados he would exercise only "a moral influence" in party affairs; however, he had not described how he would exercise this influence. He had assured the Nationalists that when a Nationalist applicant for a government job was superior to the Colorado applicant the Nationalist applicant would get the job; only if there were no qualitative differences would the Colorado be slightly favored. Still, the Colorado government itself would presumably determine whether the Nationalist was superior, equal, or inferior to the Colorado. Batlle had given himself some room for maneuver, but his specific promises would decidedly restrict his freedom of action, should he be elected.

Batlle's declarations did not change the Nationalist hostility; to the Directorio he still was the candidate "in conflict with the highest national interests." [13] The Directorio named its second three-man delegation, and before sending it off telegraphed to Saravia a pleading announcement of the delegation's departure "to interview you, exchange ideas on the presidential question, and receive your opinion." [14] Simultaneously, Etchegaray and Saravia's lieutenant, Abelardo Márquez, went on what they hoped would be their last trip to Saravia—the one when they would convince him to come out openly for MacEachen.

The Directorio delegation left on January 28. Until it returned, little could be accomplished. The Nationalist legislators met on the 26th and again on the 30th, discussed candidates, and decided nothing. They were encouraged to see that only Lauro V. Rodríguez had joined Acevedo Díaz in staying away, and agreed therefore that the Nationalist legislators' agreement still stood.[15]

Etchegaray and Márquez were the first of Saravia's visitors to return, arriving on February 1. Márquez had gone armed with a special message from Cuestas for Saravia, in which Cuestas, to make Saravia commit himself, warned that if Batlle were elected the best thing the Nationalists could do would be to go to war.[16] Etchegaray, on returning, exuded his usual confidence: "Everything is arranged. There is nothing more to do." [17]

But everything was not arranged. Saravia had refused to come out for MacEachen. This became evident the next day, when Cuestas asked his Nationalist Minister of Foreign Relations to resign, because "the attitude of the Nationalists in parliament disgusted him, since it appeared to obey a plan of hostility to his policies." [18]

Cuestas may have heard of the order Saravia had given to Márquez on his ranch: upon returning to Montevideo, Márquez was to go with Dr. Baena, one of the few Nationalist politicians Saravia trusted, interview General Tajes, and discover whether Tajes' presidential candidacy stood any chance of victory—Tajes had been making attractive offers to the Nationalists. This may have seemed like shrewd political strategy on Saravia's ranch since the exploration of Tajes would confuse the Colorado candidates, who would then raise their offers to the Nationalists. But the Montevideo Nationalist leadership had agreed earlier with Saravia that Tajes was unacceptable, and the Directorio's newspaper had said publicly it would be anachronistic for the Nationalists to join with the old Colorado military led by Tajes. Saravia, who refused to commit himself on candidates, by ordering such an exploration could only further weaken the Directorio's attempts to be decisive in the presidential election. And for Cuestas, such a move must confirm his worst obsession—his very life might be taken by the vengeful followers of Tajes he had so long persecuted.

Baena and Márquez discovered that Tajes was bluffing. He talked of having eighteen Colorado votes, but Baena was sure it was just talk. Abelardo Márquez wrote bluntly, warning his caudillo, Saravia, to come out openly for MacEachen, otherwise Batlle would win "and your prestige and power in the Party will be supplanted by the prestige and personality of Acevedo Díaz." Saravia must have thought that Abelardo had lost his senses in the bright lights of the big city. He wrote back: "I lament that a man of your ability has let himself be influenced to the point of talking like a goose, as the common saying has it." [19]

Cuestas' informants had apprised him of a Nationalist plan, a plan which could be part of a fundamental shift in Nationalist strategy—like a move to Tajes. The Nationalist Senators would delay seating the six new Colorado Senators until after the February 14th election of President of the Senate. The Nationalists would then have a majority and would elect Vázquez Acevedo, their Senate leader, President of the Senate. If the Colorados still had not agreed on a candidate for President of the Republic by March 1, and no one candidate had the necessary forty-five votes, the Nationalists either would not appear on March 1 or would vote

for a Nationalist, with the result that no candidate could be elected
and the Nationalist President of the Senate would be the *de facto*
President of the Republic.[20] This might be the prelude to violence,
it might be merely a tactic to further the candidacy of Juan Carlos
Blanco, Vázquez Acevedo's relative, or the whole story might have
been concocted by Cuestas' informants.

Cuestas decided that a bold stroke would bring the Nationalists
around. On February 4 he called MacEachen's Colorado supporters
to his home. Word circulated that the MacEachenites told Cuestas
that MacEachen had only sixteen Colorado votes and would get no
more, that the group had asked to be released to vote for Batlle, and
Cuestas had readily assented. A variation had Cuestas supposedly
advising the group:

> Gentlemen: The National Candidate, who undoubtedly was advisable
> for the country, is Sr. Eduardo MacEachen, but I am convinced that
> the candidate of the Colorado Party, the one who best interprets its
> aspirations and responds to its desires, is Sr. José Batlle y Ordoñez.
> Therefore I ask all my friends here present to give their most decided
> support to Sr. Batlle y Ordoñez to bring him to the presidency of the
> nation.[21]

The most likely verson was that Cuestas told three MacEachen
leaders "that the Nationalists won't vote for Sr. MacEachen, that
they had deceived Sr. Etchegaray, and that in virtue of the turn
taken by events he believed it necessary to precipitate the March
solution" [22] by having the Colorado legislators come together and
vote on their candidate before February 16, the date previously
stipulated in their agreement.

Cuestas had his reasons for now wanting the Colorado vote to
come before the Senate President's election. The Nationalists would
see the Colorados were united, they would recognize the fact that
they could not prevent the election of a Colorado on March 1,
and would cease their dilatory tactics on seating the new Senators.
More important, by letting the Nationalists think that he was supporting Batlle, Cuestas was putting tremendous pressure on the
Nationalists finally to accept MacEachen, for if Cuestas went
through with his threat the Colorados would unite around Batlle.
Batlle, who already had Acevedo Díaz' votes, would win; and Batlle
was the one candidate the Nationalists absolutely refused to trust.

Batlle could have insisted that the Colorado agreement called for a February 16 vote, but Don Pepe did not protest. He had consulted with Cuestas on the day Cuestas called in MacEachen's supporters, and Cuestas already had obtained Batlle's concurrence when he proposed advancing the Colorado vote. Batlle, as was his custom, accepted the MacEachen group's formal request to move the vote ahead to February 11. It was Batlle's good fortune that Etchegaray's Senate term, like Juan Carlos Blanco's, was expiring. Senator Francisco Soca, an eminent surgeon and another of Don Pepe's old friends, took over the floor management of MacEachen's campaign. Etchegaray was likely to go to extreme lengths to stop Batlle; Dr. Soca was not.

Tension in early February crackled. Batlle, normally somewhat abstracted and given to solitary meditation, had grown worse under the strain. He was constantly weighing his chances; he forgot where he left his editor Arena; he became fearful that spies would overhear his plans, and even imagined that eavesdroppers were hiding behind doors.[23]

The strain on the Nationalists was equally great. On February 2, the Directorio's second delegation returned from Saravia, and that very evening the delegation met with the Nationalist legislators. Saravia seemed to be pro-MacEachen for he had raised objections to all the other candidates,[24] but Saravia would not announce his own choice. This did not help the Directorio, which sent a third delegation out to Saravia on February 5. Its newspaper promised, "It is almost certain that this delegation will bring concrete opinions from the caudillo on the presidential question." [25]

Saravia, though, had gone as far as he cared to go. Saravia did call in Dr. José Romeu, one of the three Nationalist legislators who had joined Acevedo Díaz by not attending the February 2 meeting of the Nationalist legislators. But Saravia contented himself with urging Romeu not to break the Nationalist legislators' agreement and advised him to accept the majority's vote. He did not even tell Romeu it was wrong to vote for Batlle; in fact, he comforted Romeu and said that Acevedo Díaz' support of Batlle helped the Nationalists by keeping the Colorados divided.[26]

When Vidal y Fuentes wrote Saravia to protest the imminent Nationalist jettisoning of Blanco and to ask Saravia's advice on how to vote, Saravia replied: "I am deeply appreciative of the deference you show me in asking my opinion on candidacies for the presidency of the republic, and sincerely lament that, for reasons which you can surmise, I must excuse myself from acceding to your request and from formulating opinions or advising specific attitudes." [27] In short, if the Nationalist legislators were going to follow Saravia's preferences they first would have to divine them.

Cuestas' threat to back Batlle was having its anticipated effect on the Nationalists. The Directorio, left on its own by Saravia, decided to have the Nationalist legislators vote for their presidential candidate on February 9, two days before the Colorados would gather. On the day before the Nationalist meeting, the Directorio newspaper announced the strategy for the next day, strategy brutally damaging to Blanco, transparently promising to Mac-Eachen. Blanco, the newspaper stated, had only six Colorado votes. His low fortunes were due to Acevedo Díaz. Therefore:

Men and scruples must be sacrificed if necessary. Proclaim or eliminate once and for all Blanco's candidacy— . . . by a proclamation we mean a *formal proclamation, with forty-five votes as minimum*. . . .

If this definitive proclamation is impossible, there is no question that we will gain by learning so in *the shortest time possible;* and with this certainty acquired the Nationalist group will then be free to join another solution, one which, within the limits of the possible, best meets the needs of the public. . . .

For example, between the candidacies of Mac-Eachen and Batlle, the party prefers the first based on ample coparticipation as a promise of honorability; while it rejects the second with all its energy, for chaos would be the result of its triumph.[28]

The night of February 9, the Nationalist legislators met in the Club Nacional, on the Plaza Constitución near the Cathedral. A note signed by three legislators, announcing they joined Acevedo Díaz and considered the voting agreement void, was read. Then, thirty-three Nationalist legislators went through the formality of voting for Juan Carlos Blanco as their presidential candidate. A formula was approved which would save the party's dignity, show the party mass that the Nationalist legislators had not voted for the government's presidential candidate MacEachen until there no longer was a safe alternative, and do all this quickly enough to have the party's votes ready for MacEachen before the Colorado legislators came together two days later. A committee led by President Imas of the Directorio would present itself to Juan Carlos Blanco and offer him thirty-three Nationalist votes. It would give Blanco 24 hours to amass the additional twelve votes necessary to achieve the constitutional majority; if Blanco could not amass these votes within 24 hours, the Nationalists would be released from their commitment to him.[29]

The few Nationalist legislators who really wanted Blanco above all other candidates fought to have a motion passed to give Blanco two weeks in which to form the constitutional majority. The motion was overwhelmingly defeated, and even before the meeting broke up lists pledging the Nationalist legislators to vote for Mac-Eachen were being circulated for signature.[30]

The next day was feverish. Cuestas, now that his threat was working, gave up any pretense of abandoning MacEachen; he called two Nationalist leaders to his home and guaranteed that he would furnish the necessary Colorado votes to elect MacEachen, if they secured the Nationalist votes before February 11. According to the provisions of the Colorado agreement, if MacEachen had the Nationalist votes pledged before the Colorado meeting and also could get twenty Colorado votes, Batlle would have to concede the election. All day long the Nationalist leadership put pressure on Nationalist legislators to sign up for MacEachen, and at the same time, the MacEachen forces worked on the Colorados.

The Nationalist legislators reassembled in the Club Nacional that evening, February 10. Blanco had formally advised the Nationalist committee that he did not have the necessary Colorado votes. Those Nationalist legislators who still resisted MacEachen tried desperately to warn their colleagues that MacEachen's Colorado vote total was less than twenty. They reminded the majority that the Nationalist agreement required written proof of a candidate's Colorado vote pledges; they demanded to see the Colorado signatures.

The signatures were not displayed. The majority insisted MacEachen had the twenty votes. As the Directorio newspaper had predicted, men and scruples were sacrificed. The majority voted to pledge the Nationalist votes to MacEachen. Seven Nationalist legislators, furious at Blanco's betrayal, refused to vote for MacEachen; some of the seven even went over to Acevedo Díaz and Batlle.[31]

No matter, the leaders now had twenty-six Nationalist votes for MacEachen and were confident they had stopped Batlle. President

Imas explained the roughshod treatment of the minority in an immediate telegram to Saravia. "This proclamation has been precipitated by reasons of foresight, of imminent urgency to avoid triumph of Batlle which was considered assured." Arturo Berro, who had been one of Saravia's officers, telegraphed: "twenty-six Nationalist legislators proclaimed the candidacy of MacEachen last night twenty Colorado votes pledged to his favor assure his election." [32]

The Colorado vote would come in the afternoon of February 11. That morning, MacEachen had twenty-six Nationalist votes, Batlle had eight Nationalist votes, and the three remaining Nationalists refused to pledge their votes. The furious activity of the MacEachen campaigners disproved their claim of the night before that they already had the needed twenty Colorado votes. They concentrated on the six Colorados who had supported the now dead candidacy of Juan Carlos Blanco, and promised, begged, and threatened these men in exchange for their votes.

Batlle personally tried to counteract the MacEachen offers; he would be satisfied to stop Blanco's men from giving their votes to MacEachen, if they could not see their way to voting for him. The Blanco man closest to joining MacEachen was Joaquín Fajardo, deputy from the frontier department of Rivera. Fajardo was fighting Batlle's follower Julio Abellá y Escobar for control of the Colorado organization of Rivera, and Fajardo had already promised his own faction in Rivera that he would blow his brains out before voting for Batlle. He later reminded Batlle what had happened:

> . . . in that interview I had with you the 9th of February . . . [you] told me textually "Very well, friend Fajardo, you tell me that you can not assure me today whether you will vote for me or not—that you will decide later on; but I need one service from you with which I will be satisfied: will you give me your word of honor not to be visible to anyone today or tomorrow? If you can serve me in this, I promise to help you, and *to remove all obstacles from your way:* as for Julio Abellá—*I'll give him a little job here* [in Montevideo], for example, in the municipal yards, at \$120 or \$150." I, then and there, promised you I would comply with your request, and not only hid myself the 9th and 10th but even until the night of the 11th, as is of public notoriety.[33]

By noon of February 11, it was clear that Blanco's group, still angry at the Nationalist ruthlessness toward Blanco, ruthlessness instigated by the MacEachenites, had refused to change their vote.

MacEachen would not have twenty Colorado votes. The rumor spread that the MacEachenites would not appear for the afternoon Colorado vote, but at 5:30 P.M., with an avid crowd gathered, the Colorado legislators, MacEachenites included, began to file into the Senate antechambers.

Printed ballots were distributed, signed, and sealed. The first vote was counted. Batlle had twenty, MacEachen sixteen! Batlle himself had voted for his friend Senator Capurro, and Capurro had thrown his vote away on a third candidate.[34] There would be two more ballotings for the record, then Batlle would get thirty-seven Colorado votes. With the eight Nationalist votes he already had pledged, his total would reach forty-five—the precious number for victory.

The announcement of the result of the first ballot was Batlle's moment of triumph. Yet it was a strangely near thing. Batlle did not even have a majority of all the Colorado votes to be cast on March 1; actually, at his moment of triumph Batlle's total vote was twenty-eight (twenty Colorado and eight Nationalist) to Mac-Eachen's forty-two (sixteen Colorado and twenty-six Nationalist). Batlle did have a four-vote Colorado edge (six if Batlle's and Capurro's votes were added) over MacEachen; and MacEachen did not have twenty Colorado votes.

Just after the results were announced, a MacEachenite jumped to his feet and started to shout "I won't stand for this." The shout might have sparked a tumult which could have ended with the MacEachenites breaking the agreement and aborting Batlle's victory. Don Pepe, providentially for himself, was close to the man who had jumped up. He put his big hand on the man's shoulder and pressed him back down to his seat. Batlle followed through quietly; he reminded the recalcitrant MacEachenite of the terms of the agreement, and assured him that once he became President he would consider all those who signed the agreement equally his friends, when it came to preferment and patronage. This last bit of information calmed the protestant.[35]

The balloting continued. On the third ballot there were thirty-seven Colorado votes for Batlle. The victorious candidate voted for MacEachen in a gesture of goodwill.

Congratulations were in order; then Batlle responded with a short speech of thanks. He was pleased to see that in spite of a hard campaign all was concord among the Colorados. He was confident that his "well inspired regime would have as its first result the economic resurgence of the country," welcome reassurance to MacEachen's supporters among the business classes. And Don Pepe announced—as he had just assured the protestant—"that he considered all present equally his friends." With much well-wishing the formal pledge to vote José Batlle y Ordoñez, President of the Republic for the period March 1, 1903, to March 1, 1907, was signed by all present.[36]

The crowd outside was now cheering for Batlle and awaiting his appearance. Don Pepe had to get Cuestas' assent and also avoid a Nationalist revolution before he could put on the Presidential sash. The wrong interpretation might be placed on anything he said to the crowd. So, victorious though he was, Batlle and his friends left through a side door.[37]

That night, while Batlle's house was crowded with more well-wishers, two representatives of the eight Nationalists who were pledged to vote for Batlle met with the Directorio-led majority of the Nationalist legislators. Vidal y Fuentes, now one of the eight, reported on his interview with Batlle that morning, when Batlle had renewed his offers to cooperate with the Nationalists. The majority agreed to send a delegation to discuss the matter of majority support for Batlle with the Acevedo Díaz group.

On February 12 and February 13, meetings were held. The minority outlined Batlle's promises; he would cooperate with the Directorio; he promised free elections; he would keep six Nationalist jefes políticos in their departments—the big promise; he would consult with the Directorio before naming individual Nationalist jefes políticos; he intimated that he would give the Nationalists an additional department; he promised to increase the number of Nationalists in his administration.[38] Batlle concluded by predicting that the conciliatory and upright government he planned would make the Nationalists regret having opposed him.

The Directorio toyed with agreeing to support Batlle, but this would have given Acevedo Díaz tremendous prestige. Besides, the Directorio thought it could still stop Batlle, since it knew of his promise made on the 11th, in his moment of triumph, to free those pledged to him if he no longer had forty-five votes on February

27.[39] The erstwhile supporters of MacEachen might still be split away.

The Directorio decided to implement the plan to elect Nationalist Senator Vázquez Acevedo as President of the Senate, but first to consult with the ex-MacEachen Senators.[40] Because of their slowness in seating the new Colorado Senators, the Nationalists had a one-vote majority—if Acevedo Díaz was included. The ex-MacEachen Senators were adamant; they warned the Nationalists, on the morning of February 14, that the only Colorado Senator they would vote for President of the Senate was Batlle. When the Nationalists refused to join the vote for Batlle, Batlle himself hastened to Acevedo Díaz. To his relief he discovered that Acevedo Díaz was prepared to vote for him that afternoon, over Acevedo Díaz' first cousin Vázquez Acevedo. With Acevedo Díaz providing the decisive vote, Batlle was elected President of the Senate, and on March 1 would preside over his own election as President of the Republic.[41]

Etchegaray, who saw his hopes of running the government under MacEachen's nominal leadership disappearing, had tried and failed to get Cuestas to intervene against Batlle.[42] Cuestas' major preoccupation always had been to assure a peaceful change of Presidents, so that he could go to Europe without incident. To join the Nationalists now and overthrow Batlle's election could result in Colorado violence, something Cuestas ever feared. Also, Batlle had been so deferential to Cuestas during the campaign that Cuestas could not consider him an enemy to be kept from the presidency by force.

The old President wrote Batlle on the evening of February 14 and asked him to arrange the necessary legislative approval for Cuestas' trip to Europe. Cuestas ended his note: "I congratulate you on the result of this afternoon's Election which pleased us all." [43] Short of Nationalist revolution, Batlle's candidacy was assured.

The Nationalists seethed; the inevitable delegation was sent to Saravia. The Nationalist Convention would be convoked to judge Acevedo Díaz and his accomplices, who were blamed not only for Batlle's victory but for Blanco's earlier defeat.

Batlle, meanwhile, set about to cement his triumph. On February 15, he met formally with his eight Nationalist supporters and got their signed agreement to vote for him on March 1. In exchange, he signed a secret pledge to carry out all the promises he had earlier made to the Nationalists. He even added a new promise: not to change the electoral laws without previous agreement by both political parties.[44] The eight could now claim, when the Convention judged them, that they had gotten Batlle to give the party greater advantages than the demands made in the original Nationalist legislators' manifesto.

The eight also wanted Batlle to take care of them personally, since they could foresee that the Nationalist authorities would cut them off from power and patronage. What the eight would have liked was to be given the *jefaturas* of some of the six Nationalist departments, but to take departments away from Saravia could provoke him to war. Instead, there was talk of establishing a new Ministry of Livestock, Agriculture, and Industry and entrusting it to the Acevedo Díaz group.[45]

Batlle next moved to get the allegiance of the six Colorados who had supported Blanco. If the eight Nationalist defectors were the prime cause of his victory, the refusal of the six Colorados to vote for MacEachen once Blanco's candidacy had failed, was the second factor. Don Pepe doubtless gave these men the same assurance he had given the MacEachenites, namely, that he would consider all of them equally his friends when it came to patronage. The six also considered themselves the representatives of the Colorado groups outside the legislature, the ones ostracized by Cuestas, and wanted Batlle to promise he would not continue Cuestas' policy of dividing the party. Batlle readily agreed, since he had said many times that electoral liberty would be the great accomplishment of his administration, and only if the Colorados were united could they win an open election.

Batlle proceeded to specify his promises: he would not hold the past against any Colorado group; he would use "competent Colorados of all factions" in his government; he would not try to run the party. "It is my firm resolution . . . to maintain myself aloof from the organization of the Colorado Party and from all which involves its functioning." [46] The six Colorados signed; Don Pepe would receive every Colorado vote cast on March 1.

The Nationalists were frantic in their fury. Their press refused to concede Batlle's victory and hinted at war if he were elected.

The Directorio rejected out of hand the official request of the Colorado delegation that the Nationalists make Batlle's election unanimous.

But Saravia, who had not risked his prestige on any particular candidate, was calm. His secretary prepared a letter to a Montevideo Nationalist deputy.

> In regard to Batlle's triumph, I no longer fear it . . . Now that he is triumphant we will have to await developments. It would neither be wise nor patriotic for us to go to war against him merely because when he was a candidate we expected a bad government from him . . . The conflict would come if he listened to Acevedo Díaz and wanted to change jefes políticos without the previous consent of the Directorio; but I don't think he will dare to do this, for it would be the equivalent of declaring war.[47]

With the return of the Directorio's delegation to Saravia came acceptance of the unavoidable. The Directorio newspaper announced on February 22:

> If this election is consummated, *nobody* would dare make this one event the banner of a revolution. The National Party never overthrows institutions. It would await, prudently and circumspectly, the acts of the new President, to judge him and to define its own role in the new epoch.[48]

On February 25, the Nationalist Convention met and vented its passion. Acevedo Díaz and his three original followers were expelled from the party, the other four who would vote for Batlle were censured, the three remaining Nationalists who had refused to vote for MacEachen were criticized. The Convention could not help noting as well that there had been "errors of procedure" in the conduct of the majority Nationalist legislators.[49]

It was now all over: Batlle would be elected President of the Republic.

A legend has grown up about Batlle's election as President of Uruguay in 1903, a legend which has even reached American textbooks on Latin American history. It pictures a chaotic nation whose people in their despair turn to the most respected among them and ask him to take over the government. It sees an aroused mass calling for social justice, and Batlle heeding the call: Batlle first challenges Cuestas, then the Nationalists, and stands back until the Colorado Party sweeps him to power.[50]

Of course, Batlle's election didn't happen that way. The public was kept out of the presidential election from the acuerdo of 1901 to the morning of March 1, 1903. At his moment of triumph on February 11, Batlle was afraid to appear before the crowds; instead, he slipped out by the side door. Batlle had made promises, political promises and promises to politicians, but he had not advocated social reform. He had parlayed his position as the most Colorado of the candidates acceptable to Cuestas with his personal friendships, and just squeezed through to victory. The proper analogy would be with victory in an American presidential nominating convention where the votes of individual delegates are corralled personally by the candidate.

Those who went through the campaign never endorsed the legend. Years later, Batlle corrected a campaign biography which had him as anti-Cuestas. From the beginning "I was Cuestas' candidate for the presidency to follow his . . . I lost the support of the Nationalists [in 1901] . . . Cuestas thought my candidacy totally lost and looked for another: MacEachen's. His desire was that the citizen who succeeded him be a friend of his." [51] Arena, who saw Don Pepe accept exhaustion and humiliation in his race for the presidency, called Batlle's effort "the most perfect work of . . . intelligence, method, and tenacity." He once asked Batlle during the campaign whether the prize was worth the effort. Even Arena was startled by Batlle's answer that he was not thinking in terms of a four-year presidency but was thinking of the effects for the next thirty or forty years.[52]

Although Batlle's victory was aided by MacEachen's evident mediocrity and the enmity Cuestas had created among the Colorados and some Nationalists, Don Pepe himself contributed two master strokes: one was his handling of the Mendilaharsu opportunity, which enabled Acevedo Díaz to break the Nationalist agreement; the other was his fulsome cooperation with Cuestas and the MacEachen group. On February 11, when Batlle squeezed out his four-vote victory, Cuestas and the MacEachen group, short of admitting that they had no respect for their own pledged word, could do nothing but accept the outcome. Actually, throughout the campaign Batlle had shown exquisite political sense, even to the point of protecting his future in case he lost. A master politician had revealed himself in action.

The same could not be said for the Nationalists, for only their ineptness enabled Batlle to succeed. Most of the blame must rest with Saravia, who did not understand the stakes at issue or acknowledge his own power among the Nationalists. Had Saravia been closer to day-to-day developments, instead of on his ranch, had he been willing to risk his prestige, he could have held all the Nationalists together for Blanco or almost all of them for Mac-Eachen. He could have elected either; by refusing to speak out he elected neither. Without Saravia behind them, the Nationalist leaders first were timorous, then floundered.

V

Y‹‹‹‹‹‹‹‹‹‹‹‹‹r

Dangerous Inauguration

THE day before his election as President, Batlle presented his
program to the nation. In it he reaffirmed what he had said in the
El Tiempo interview, to the eight Nationalist legislators, and to the
six Colorados. The dominant tone was moderation—political, administrative, and economic.

> As for the action of the Executive Power, I believe it should limit it-
> self to carrying out . . . only widely accepted ideas, about whose ad-
> vantages there are no disputes, those ideas which, in every moment of
> history, determine the task which must be immediately accomplished.

There was one novel idea: Batlle was particularly interested in
road- and canal-building because in addition to their obvious advantages,

> . . . they can be built entirely without materials and professional
> services from abroad, and therefore quite the reverse of what happens
> in most public works, without substantial quantities of money leaving
> the country. Considerable sums of money can be allotted to them,
> therefore, without the risk of producing any economic upheaval.[1]

Batlle had already severely restricted his freedom of action by
his political promises: to the Nationalists, continued coparticipation; to the independent Colorados, presidential neutrality in Colorado reorganization. He was, nevertheless, faced by an expectantly
hostile opposition and supported by a Colorado legislative majority
several of whose principal leaders felt privately that Batlle lacked
political stature. The country awaited his first acts.

A great crowd was outside the Cabildo. Don Pepe left home at 3:30 P.M. on his Inauguration Day; shortly thereafter, the procession of horse-drawn coaches reached the Plaza Constitución. Once inside the Cabildo, Batlle as President of the Senate called the General Assembly of the Senate and Chamber to order. The Nationalists, whose convention had met all the previous night and decreed the expulsion of the dissidents, had decided to give their votes to one of their own rather than abstain.

First, the new President's salary—34,000 pesos annually—was authorized,[2] then began the vote. Each time one of the eight Nationalists voted for Batlle the galleries applauded and shouted bravo; when it came his turn, Batlle voted for Acevedo Díaz. Batlle received a total of fifty-five votes—ten over the constitutional majority. Twenty-three Nationalists voted for Enrique Anaya, three for Aureliano Berro.[3]

There was a recess, after which Batlle returned to the chamber and took the oath of office. He spoke briefly, assuring the legislature he would respect its independence. Acevedo Díaz responded for the Assembly, the galleries erupted in enthusiasm. Outside in the Plaza, the crowd took up the rhythmical chant, Bat-lle, Bat-lle, Bat-lle, interspersed with "Viva Don Pepe!"

Inside, the new President and his electors moved to the antechambers where an elegant buffet awaited. The champagne was uncorked, Batlle gave the first toast:

> In the discharge of my functions I will do all I can to justify the confidence of those who voted for me, and to convince those who because of patriotic apprehensions—very respectable ones—have not desired to give me their votes, that they have incurred in error respecting my intentions and my ideas.
>
> If upon descending from this elevated position to which I now ascend, I descend with the affection and respect of all my fellow-citizens, regardless of party, I will have satisfied, so far as I am personally concerned, my greatest aspiration.
>
> I now toast—To the concord of the Uruguayan family.[4]

The press of the crowd around Batlle prevented Vázquez Acevedo from giving the planned toast of the Nationalist legislators, one patterned after the oath given their kings by the Aragonese nobility, which would have concluded:

> We have not voted for you: but faithful to democratic procedures we accept the verdict of the National Assembly. We promise with all

sincerity to second the march of your government, if you carry out your promises and respond to the legitimate aspirations of the country which is anxious for peace, liberty, and progress—and if not—not.[5]

Then, at 5:15 P.M., Batlle left the Cabildo, to walk through the Plaza Constitución up the street to the Plaza Independencia where, in Government House, Cuestas was ready to transfer the presidency. Don Pepe's admirers, sedulously kept out of the presidential campaign, now engulfed him. The mob overwhelmed the police and carried Batlle along; one enthusiast even jumped on him to drape a floral branch over his shoulders.

Still another mob waited in front of Government House. Batlle, big as he was, was disheveled when he finally reached the presidential offices and the select group of guests who would watch him receive the formal sash of office. Cuestas bestowed the presidency with a short speech in which he stressed the government's financial stability and many accomplishments: "I turn the country over to you in peace and order." Batlle thanked him, congratulated him on the success of his government, and added that Cuestas' name would go down in history as one of those "distinguished citizens who have merited well of the Republic." [6]

Batlle then drove with Cuestas up the Avenida 18 de Julio to the ex-President's home, then immediately returned to the still crowded Government House, where he enjoyed the thrill of signing his first decrees as President. Most of the majority Nationalist legislators visited Batlle, either in his office or later in his home, to congratulate him. Just before Batlle left Government House for home, the typographers of *El Día* presented him with a specially embellished manifesto of adherence. He thanked them for their support and told them he especially appreciated the demonstration because it "came from the working class, whose situation he proposed to improve from his post as President of the Republic." [7]

Montevideo was in fiesta spirit that night. Batlle's house was full of visitors and the street outside was packed. Fireworks were shot off. In the Aguada, Don Pepe's old neighborhood where his grandfather had built the flour mill and where Batlle had grown up, there was delirium.

Batlle was full of goodwill. He had rented the house in which Cuestas, soon leaving for Europe, had lived while President; the house had a large salon downstairs where Don Pepe expected to receive visits from politicians of all parties.

He continued Manini Ríos and Arena as nominal editors of *El Día*, although he never really could stop running *El Día*. He stopped the traditional subsidies to *La Nación*, which had lived off monthly payments from the President's office. Without subsidy, the newspaper closed down. Batlle would not subsidize *El Día*, even though Arena was worried about its future—presidential newspapers were notoriously short-lived. As always, Batlle told Arena of his visions for the future: *El Día* would some day sell over 20,000 copies; and, instead of being housed in rented quarters as now, it would be published in its own monumental building.[8]

Having put his personal affairs in order, the new President turned to his most pressing responsibility, the naming of his cabinet and of the nineteen departmental jefes políticos. The Nationalists did not try to complicate Batlle's first days; their Senators joined the Colorados in electing Juan Pedro Castro, Batlle's most eminent supporter during the campaign, President of the Senate.[9] Batlle sent Martín C. Martínez, his future Minister of Finance, to sound out the Nationalists on whether they would rather see Acevedo Díaz' group named to a Ministry or given two departmental jefes políticos. The Nationalist answer was that they would like neither but would tolerate a Ministry. Martín C. Martínez was specifically warned that to take away any departments from Saravia "could lead to serious conflicts." Rodríguez Larreta went so far as to advise Martínez to make his own acceptance of a cabinet position in Batlle's government conditional on Batlle's leaving the Nationalist six departments untouched.[10]

Batlle announced his cabinet on March 5. Martín C. Martínez, considered one of the most brilliant minds of his generation, and Batlle's friend since their Ateneo days, accepted the Ministry of Finance. Martínez, a lawyer, was a non-Colorado Constitutionalist and a bridge to the Nationalists. He was also a conservative, a Spencerian, an admirer of Victorian England; his presence as director of finances would relieve the conservative classes' anxiety over Batlle's financial soundness. José Serrato, the 35-year-old Colorado engineer and economist, grandson of a French volunteer in the Defense of Montevideo, was named Minister of *Fomento* (Development). Dr. José Romeu, a physician, one of Acevedo Díaz' original four, was given the Ministry of Foreign Relations.

Batlle took no chances with the two ministries which controlled the army and the police. Juan Campisteguy, who had written Batlle's campaign biography and had been one of *El Día*'s founding editors, would be Minister of Government—in charge of jefes políticos and police; Campisteguy had also been Cuestas' Minister of Finance for a short time but could not get along with him. The new Minister was reputed to be ultra-Colorado, though otherwise a talented lawyer. An old soldier, General Eduardo Vázquez, Batlle's cousin, was his choice as Minister of War. Batlle had an antimilitarist reputation and the army leadership, constantly rotated by Cuestas, might not be loyal. Batlle decided to overlook the fact that Vázquez had been War Minister for the dictator Latorre; Vázquez had known Batlle since Batlle's childhood, and the new President could rely on him.

In Montevideo, where everyone knew everyone, the cabinet commanded respect, since the Ministers were capable, even brilliant, men. Yet political commentators were disappointed: Batlle had paid his debt to Acevedo Díaz, but had not taken advantage of the opportunity to broaden support for his government by taking an orthodox Nationalist or a pre-'97 Colorado into his cabinet; Batlle's cabinet was made up of members of his own political group and of his personal friends.

Next Batlle would name the jefes políticos, and pulses quickened. Vidal y Fuentes, one of the eight Nationalists who had voted for Batlle, read to the President portions of a letter he had just received from Saravia's private secretary. In the letter, Ponce de León said that the new ministry was not too bad but that everything depended on whether the new Nationalist jefes políticos were appointed in collaboration with the Directorio. Batlle listened carefully and replied:

Look, Vidal, I do not have the aversion to Saravia that is attributed to me since, on the contrary, I have always acknowledged that he is valiant, that he has acted rather wisely in using his influence on his party, and I believe that he together with Lamas [late Nationalist coleader in '97] has contributed in large part to the creation of this political situation within which I have reached the Presidency of the Republic—all of which makes it impossible for me to look at him unfavorably.

Don Pepe went on to explain his problem: the Acevedo Díaz minority was no longer satisfied with only one Ministry, because in their eyes their expulsion from the National Party meant the Party was now divided into two parts and both parts should be represented in the departmental administrations; seven of the Nationalists who had voted for him, all except Vidal, insisted on this. Batlle felt a great debt to the group, while he had none with the Directorio which had refused even to consider his candidacy.

Vidal y Fuentes remonstrated that this would mean war. Batlle interrupted "you are alarmed, but don't worry, nothing will happen, because the citizens I will name are spotless and are tried and true Nationalists." [11]

The Directorio, increasingly preoccupied, kept Saravia advised of developments on the departments. President Imas wrote plaintively on March 10 that the Directorio had met all day and would meet again the next day. Rumor was that the jefes políticos of Flores and San José would be changed: "they are going to keep on taking our positions away from us little by little and then what will we do? Should we wait until this happens or should we act now? It would be good to have your opinion on this, by telegraphic code and under pledge of secrecy." [12]

Batlle tried to appease the Nationalists for his impending nomination of two Acevedo Díaz jefes políticos. He convoked his cabinet and announced that he would send a project to the legislature abolishing the new 6th Cavalry Regiment, which Cuestas had set up to serve as customs patrol; [13] he rescinded Cuestas' veto of the Montevideo trolley electrification concession, a veto supposedly directed against Nationalist leader Rodríguez Larreta, the company's attorney.[14]

On March 13, the appointment of the two Acevedo Díaz jefes políticos was made public. It was even more dangerous than the Directorio had originally supposed, for Batlle was giving Acevedo Díaz the departments of Rivera and San José instead of Flores and San José, southern departments far from Saravia's base, his ranch in Cerro Largo. Rivera bordered Saravia's department of Cerro Largo and bordered Brazil, where there were arms hidden, where munitioneers and allies lived. Saravia would never let Rivera fall into hostile hands.

The Directorio tried desperately to avert war. Although Jorge Arias, Batlle's nominee for San José, agreed to cooperate, Luis María Gil, who was going to crucial Rivera, flatly refused to deal with the Directorio.[15] The Directorio tried, through the President of the Senate, to send a delegation to Batlle, but Batlle felt that after a few days their tempers would cool and suggested they postpone the meeting.[16]

All the goings and comings in Montevideo were irrelevant to Saravia. He acted as soon as he got the Directorio's March 13 telegram announcing the appointment of Gil and Arias. This was not a presidential campaign; this was a military matter, and he was the General. That same day he wired Abelardo Márquez, his jefe político in Rivera, the very Abelardo who had urged Saravia to come out for MacEachen and been told not to talk like a goose, "General Saravia says do not turn over the government to Gil." Abelardo responded, "on Monday the 16th at dawn the Department of Rivera will be armed and ready for war." To Nationalist military officers all over the country went the order, "the 15th or 16th . . . at the indicated point." [17]

Sunday, March 15, was a beautiful day. President Batlle and his family were at the race track as guests of the socially elite Jockey Club. Given the origins of their marriage, Don Pepe and Misia Matilde rarely moved in these circles. All the best people were there, and the President was cheered. Batlle returned home immediately after the last race to learn that the spreading rumor was true: the Nationalists, under Aparicio Saravia, were in full revolt.

Batlle had never imagined that the Nationalists would revolt over a change of the jefe político in Rivera. He had been President only two weeks and did not want war. The army command was not yet organized. Besides, his philosophy opposed bloodshed.

He quickly made a decision. He called Dr. Alfonso Lamas, the brother of Saravia's late co-commander, Diego Lamas, to his office.[18] Alfonso Lamas was very close to Saravia and was also Don Pepe's friend and surgeon. Batlle offered peace to Saravia through Lamas. He would ask for Gil's resignation in Rivera and would name future Nationalist jefes políticos in accord with the Directorio. Lamas telegraphed Batlle's terms to Saravia, and urged Saravia to accept them.[19]

Simultaneously, Batlle mobilized. He named military commanders, and put restrictions on individual movement into effect. He telegraphed the Uruguayan Minister in Rio to ask the Brazilian government to have João Francisco, the caudillo of Rio Grande do Sul and Saravia's source of munitions, interned.[20] Batlle ordered the Uruguayan Minister in Buenos Aires to buy arms from President Roca of Argentina.[21]

The immediate danger of war subsided on the 17th. Lamas was encouraged by Saravia's response to his telegram. He had two more conferences with Batlle, then sent another wire to Saravia:

. . . just spoke with the President of the Republic who agrees that the filling of Jefaturas be done in the form indicated by you. There is a small detail about the Jefatura of San José which personally I do not believe of great importance and about which I will converse with you if, as I expect, you avoid clashes between forces, as will the Government. This afternoon at 5 P.M. I leave in express train for Nico Pérez.

Saravia telegraphed his agreement: "Will order Nationalist forces avoid clashes." [22] So far the only bloodshed had been caused by João Francisco, who led a detachment across the border into the Departmental Capital of Rivera, destroyed two newspapers run by exiles from Rio Grande, and killed several men who tried to stop him.[23]

Lamas left for Nico Pérez, the end of the railroad to the northeast. Before leaving, he had insisted that José Pedro Ramírez, the peacemaker of '97, be brought into the negotiations. Batlle knew that Saravia had wanted Ramírez to be President. Batlle opposed Ramírez' elite politics; his distrust of Ramírez was a family inheritance, for Ramírez had led the doctores' opposition to Lorenzo Batlle. But Batlle desperately wanted peace, so he assented to Ramírez as negotiator.

José Pedro Ramírez remained in Montevideo. He had a long conference with Batlle at which Batlle explained his peace proposals. He would name all the Nationalist jefes políticos after consulting the Directorio except for the Department of San José— Lamas' "small detail." In San José, Batlle would name a Nationalist "who fought in or favored the Revolution of '97." He promised amnesty to all revolutionaries and would let them keep any funds they had taken from public offices during the revolution.[24]

Batlle warned José Pedro Ramírez that these were his final terms, since the President of the Republic could not haggle with revolutionaries. Ramírez boarded the train for Nico Pérez. Once there he would join Alfonso Lamas and both would take the long, dusty trip by horse-drawn carriage to Saravia.

The stock exchange in anxiety-ridden Montevideo closed for 48 hours. The Government called up the National Guard. The news from abroad was bad: the Brazilian government would not intervene in Rio Grande affairs; [25] Argentine President Roca agreed to sell arms only through a third party at exorbitant prices.[26]

A group of young Colorados visited Batlle to assure him of their support and encourage him to stand firm against the revolution. Don Pepe's response to his admirers was sobering:

I can not accompany you in the slogan "Down With Peace" since my duty as President of the Republic is to guarantee peace and concord, because peace means advancement, progress, the well-being of the country, the true slogan of the Colorado Party.[27]

On the 19th, Batlle heard from Ramírez and Lamas. They had reached Saravia in Melo, capital of the department of Cerro Largo, and were now waiting for a Directorio delegation which would join the peace talks.

The next afternoon, in Montevideo, a pro-peace demonstration organized by the Rural Association, the Chamber of Commerce, the Manufacturers' Association, and other business groups filled the Plaza Independencia. The demonstrators had been given a half day off and the column was five blocks long. The young Colorados who tried to interfere were overwhelmed.

The demonstration's distinguished leaders were ushered into Batlle's offices in Government House. He greeted them with: "The vehement desires you bring, are my own desires. I love peace as much as any man!" He outlined all he had done to satisfy the revolution; if peace did not come, it would not be his fault. He wondered whether the revolution had not been planned long before, to take advantage of the military uncertainties during the presidential changeover. He did not like the revolution's delay in answering his proposals. The business leaders were favorably impressed; then Batlle went to the balcony and shouted to the crowd below: *Viva las Instituciones! Viva la Paz!* [28]

That night news came from Melo. The Directorio delegation wired that peace had been made, and at 8:10 P.M. Batlle received this telegram from Ramírez and Lamas: "Proposed bases accepted. We leave tomorrow expecting to settle with you verbally certain differences." [29] Batlle, fearing that Ramírez had given way on San José,[30] put through a telegraphic conversation with the mediators, who explained that Saravia wanted a neutral Nationalist, not an Acevedo Díaz man in San José. Batlle refused, "because I see in this intransigence a very clearly defined effort to weaken the authority of the Executive Power, something which will produce worse calamities than the ones now menacing us." The mediators agreed to overtake Saravia, now on his way to his army at Nico Pérez, and convince him to accept Batlle's original terms. Batlle promised to await their answer all the next day before taking any further action.[31] The Office of the Presidency put out the chilling statement: "Nothing leads to the belief that peace will be made." *El Siglo*, edited by José Pedro Ramírez' nephew, feared war.[32]

The next day, Batlle convoked the Colorado legislators, explained his policy—he was hoping for peace but preparing for war, and asked their support. *El Día* insisted that the '97 peace pact bound only Cuestas, not Batlle. Batlle himself, who had been released from all promises by the Acevedo Díaz Nationalists, wrote in *El Día*, explaining his position on San José: he would not serve as Saravia's weapon against the minority Nationalists, he would rather leave the presidency than keep it at the price of humiliation. Saravia really wanted San José as an advanced base of attack against the capital; to cede would only strengthen "the permanent revolution" with which the country would have to live. If San José was so insignificant, "why does Sr. Saravia, who already has gotten so many concessions to which he had no right, insist on it?" [33]

Batlle's fears of Nationalist duplicity were unjustified. On March 23, the mediators telegraphed the news that Saravia had accepted Batlle's peace terms. Saravia agreed to leave compliance with the terms to Batlle's good faith; he did, though, want time to go through the formality of consulting his officers before giving his final approval. Batlle assented in a telegram praising the mediators for their patriotism.[34] The news spread through happy Montevideo and that night a crowd of thousands, carrying lit matches and led by a military band, passed in front of Batlle's house, cheering as they passed.

The next day, Ramírez and Lamas returned to Montevideo to make the final arrangements with Batlle. Don Pepe insisted that his legal scruples not be offended: the six-clause pact itself would not be signed, since it was outside the constitution, if not unconstitutional; Batlle would make only one legal commitment, to send

an amnesty law to the legislature; the Nationalist jefes políticos
who had revolted against the government must be replaced.[35]
Saravia had already agreed to this replacement, but would turn
over to the Directorio the embarrassing task of asking the jefes
políticos for their resignations.

Several days passed before the revolutionary army assembled
at Nico Pérez. Alfonso Lamas went to join his coreligionaries,
leaving Ramírez in Montevideo. On March 27, Lamas sent Batlle
a message advising him that the Nationalist officers had approved
the peace bases.[36] He sent another wire to Ramírez, one which
would become famous: "Imposing assembly of veterans and young
men of the National Party, with swords at side, have just voted
the peace of the Republic by acclamation." [37]

It was indeed an imposing assembly. The revolutionary army at
Nico Pérez comprised over 15,000 men—a far larger army than
'97—and more were on the way.[38] Saravia's request for a delay to
permit him to consult his officers before agreeing to Batlle's terms
had been designed to give time for what the Nationalists were
now calling "the armed protest" to assemble at Nico Pérez. The
army's size demonstrated that all the Nationalist mass followed
Saravia, that Acevedo Díaz—whom the Nationalists blamed for
the revolution [39]—was a leader without followers. When some of
Saravia's officers asked him why he had made peace when the
prospects for armed victory were so promising, he answered with
what seemed like gaucho shrewdness, "they offered to pay us the
deposit and we had to accept." [40]

The Colorado legislators who visited the immensely relieved
Batlle saw him full of smiles. He even told a joke: "Nothing should
seem strange among us—since we had *Una esquina redonda* [a
round corner] and *un arroyo seco* [a dry creek], it's natural that
we should have had a peace without war." [41] Alfonso Lamas, back
from Nico Pérez, visited Batlle on March 28, for a final conference.
El Siglo reported that Lamas assured the President of the Directorio's good wishes.[42]

President Batlle was Montevideo's man of the hour. *El Siglo*,
organ of the conservative classes, applauded his peace policy; so
did the Catholic press; the English language newspaper, which
reflected the foreign business community's views, also applauded
him. The Chamber of Commerce saluted Batlle with another grand

manifestation. He thanked the demonstration's leaders, denied that the revolution had been justified, but assured the leaders that there would be no cause for another.[43]

Batlle was attracting the same groups which had supported Cuestas. He had given his young Colorado supporters short shrift. In agreeing to consult formally with the Directorio before naming Nationalist jefes políticos, he had gone further than even Cuestas toward conciliating the Nationalists. Many hoped to see Batlle sending emissaries to Saravia's ranch, as in the sensible days of Cuestas.

Saravia dismissed his troops with a proclamation calling upon them to register to vote in next year's general elections.[44] Saravia had also issued a proclamation when he began "the armed demonstration." He had explained then that the Nationalist departments were the party's "positions of force." If the Nationalists let these positions of force be taken away, "they would once more be dependent on the good faith of their adversary in next year's election." [45] Now the positions of force were more secure than ever, and Batlle seemed to be moving, much against his will, to a position where he would be the Colorado President to oversee the historic rotation of parties, the Colorado who would give the presidential sash to a Nationalist.

VI

\<\<\<\<\<\<\<\<\<\<

Uneasy Year

No sooner had the troops on both sides gone home, than Batlle began carrying out the Pact of Nico Pérez. The legislature quickly passed his project for an amnesty law, although not until the Minister of Government had assured a protesting Colorado Deputy that if João Francisco and his men had committed any crimes in Rivera during the revolution they would still be subject to ordinary criminal law.[1] Batlle scrupulously consulted the Directorio before naming the Nationalist jefes políticos. The Directorio, in turn, cleared all these appointments with Saravia. Saravia's personal choice, Carmelo Cabrera, was installed in the danger spot of Rivera; quietly and unnoticed, Gil moved from Rivera to San José.[2]

The Nationalists were encouraged and, as a first step toward the kind of cooperation Cuestas had provided, they suggested that Batlle drop Acevedo Díaz' man Romeu from the cabinet. El Día brought Nationalist hopes down by publishing a statement that Batlle expected to keep his entire cabinet throughout his presidency.[3] When Imas, President of the Directorio, sent a telegram to the interior which intimated there were undisclosed concessions from Batlle in the peace pact, El Día published the bases, "the only written bases which exist." [4]

This rapid cooling of relations between the Government and the Nationalists disturbed the conservative classes. During the third week in April they gave a banquet for Batlle in the *Teatro Solís*,

Montevideo's finest public place. A select audience—except that no important Nationalists attended—heard Batlle give a speech reminiscent of his speeches during the revolution. He explained his belief that politics was a continuous struggle for justice, equity, and progress, and he begged his listeners to support his government, concluding: "I toast, gentlemen, the alliance of public opinion and the government." [5]

But Don Pepe did not intend to rely for support on public opinion alone. He sent a message to the legislature asking that the Southern Military Commandancy and the Fifth Infantry Battalion, both created temporarily during the revolution, be made permanent.[6] He made new army command appointments. Secretly he asked his friend, the surveyor Carlos Burmeister, to draw up plans for a wartime transportation and communications system.[7]

Batlle had begun his administration expecting that by his acts he would win the confidence of the Nationalists. The March revolution had destroyed his interest in winning over the Nationalists. He would not go the way of Cuestas, but he would keep the letter of the peace pact to avoid giving the Nationalists any pretext for revolt. He would strengthen the army so that they would think before revolting; and if the Nationalists did revolt, he would defeat them.

If war were avoided, the showdown would come in the 1904 general elections. The Colorados could win only if they were united. Batlle was in a reasonably good position to encourage Colorado unity: he had led the partisan wing of Cuestas' Colorado supporters; he had not been personally involved in Cuestas' persecutions of pre-'97 Colorados; one of his campaign promises was to support Colorado unity and not try to dominate the party organization.

The first step toward Colorado unification came early in April when Julio Herrera y Obes, still considered a power in Colorado politics, returned from exile in Buenos Aires. Cuestas, the cause of his misfortunes, was now a tourist in Europe. The next step came when Batlle met the terms of General Tajes and the old Colorado military and rescinded Cuestas' decree forbidding political participation by military officers. In late April, after preliminary conversations and to the accompaniment of propaganda in the reactivated Montevideo Colorado clubs, politicians from the various Colorado factions held their first meeting on organizational unification.[8]

The Nationalists also reorganized. The Directorio had wanted to resign ever since its failure in the presidential election. Finally, late in April, after all the jefes políticos were in their departments, resignation was possible. The election of a new Directorio was one of the least contested in memory, in part because the new Directorio would only serve out the old one's term until the end of the year, but basically because now that the once-troublesome Acevedo Díaz group was expelled, there were no sharp divisions in the party.

Under the surface there was some difference of opinion. One faction, mostly from Montevideo, wanted to cooperate with Batlle to avoid giving him a pretext for intervening in the 1904 elections. The other, more aggressive, faction believed Batlle was preparing for war and wanted the Nationalists to prepare as well. But the differences between the factions were not great: the conciliatory group would go to war if Batlle went too far; the aggressive group would try an election if Batlle permitted one. An easy compromise satisfied both factions. Alfonso Lamas, the peace mediator, was elected President of the new Directorio and Carlos A. Berro, the candidate of the more aggressive faction, First Vice President.[9]

Lamas, a surgeon rather than an active politician, at first hesitated then agreed to serve. In his acceptance speech he emphasized that the National Party wanted free elections, and that Batlle, his old friend, "has not delivered a single political speech, he has not written a single article, he has not had a private conversation, in which he had not made free elections the heart, so to speak, of his promises as President." [10] Lamas paid a friendly call on Batlle. At about the same time, Saravia wrote Lamas that he "congratulated you and congratulated myself" on the outcome of the Directorio election.[11]

Batlle and Saravia did not write each other. It was only a month since Nico Pérez, but already the President and the caudillo were being warned by faithful subordinates not to trust the other. Arturo Berro closed a letter to Saravia: "Señor Batlle, I can guarantee you, and his whole group have always hated us, a fierce hate which has increased after the last revolution and which will be translated into aggressions against us, as soon as they think we are weak or indecisive." [12] Batlle received a report that Abelardo Márquez, Saravia's leader in Rivera, was gathering forces: "a Brazilian very closely allied with Márquez guaranteed me, and wanted to bet that there will be a revolution before June." [13]

As a candidate, Batlle had promised to limit his government to the sponsorship of noncontroversial legislation. Since then the political situation had become so much more delicate that even noncontroversial legislation might be questioned as, if nothing else, premature and inopportune. Besides, Batlle did not have a sure majority among the Colorado legislators, especially the Senators. The Colorado legislators believed that Batlle owed his election to them, while they owed him nothing; they felt no obligation to support Batlle's legislative proposals except when these proposals directly confronted Colorados against Nationalists.

The Government's proposals to the legislature, if measures strengthening the army were not included, were so few as not to justify the title legislative program. The Government was especially reluctant to ask the legislature for money, perhaps because of the conservative economic views of Finance Minister Martín C. Martínez. To cover the costs of the March revolution, the Executive asked authorization for only a 500,000-peso loan; the Chamber doubled the authorization, over Nationalist objections, and the Senate concurred.[14]

In administrative acts, where legislative approval was not necessary, Batlle was able to give at least indications of a government policy favoring the lower classes. For the first time, regulations on police procedure during strikes were promulgated. Previously the police had been used to assist employers; now they must remain neutral: they must protect both the right to strike and the right to work. On May Day, again for the first time, labor demonstrators were granted police permits to parade through the center of Montevideo. They sang the Internationale and heard fiery speeches. One speaker exulted that Uruguay now led South America in modern ideas because of its President's liberalism.[15]

Farmers—always on the point of disaster—whose crops had failed were given free seeds, by executive decree not law. In its procurement policy, the Government accentuated Batlle's well-known protectionist views. In another "first," army and police uniforms were required to be made from Uruguayan cloth. The Government also stipulated the piece rate paid the seamstresses who sewed the uniforms. Arguments that locally made uniforms were inferior and expensive did not dissuade Batlle. *El Día* explained:

The President of the Republic is a declared enemy of having things made abroad which can be made in the country. He has been theorizing on this matter for many years. His goal in the government will be to import as few articles as possible, with the commendable aim of keeping in the country the largest possible quantity of money which now goes abroad to pay for these articles, a policy which will favor principally the working classes.

In keeping with these principles he has already ordered that even postage stamps and postal cards, imported up to now, be made in our workshops in the future.[16]

Clearly, whether postage stamps would be printed at home or abroad was of limited importance when present danger faced the nation. Quick constitutional reform, something Nationalist leader Vázquez Acevedo had proposed shortly after Nico Pérez, might change the nation's institutional structure in ways which would diminish party rivalries. Early in May, distinguished intellectuals, important political figures, the President of the Republic himself, met in the Ateneo, scene of memorable philosophical and literary tourneys of their youth, to discuss rapid constitutional reform. The most dramatic proposal was made by Martín Aguirre—a Nationalist out of favor with Saravia. He wanted to abolish the presidency and substitute a six-man government council: [17] four Colorados and two Nationalists on the Council would give Uruguay institutional coparticipation, instead of the anomalous coparticipation the six Nationalist departments presently provided. Aguirre's proposal showed that opening the Pandora's Box of constitutional reform would more likely sharpen party rivalries than dull them, and after a decent interval the Ateneo discussions were suspended.[18]

Batlle attended the Ateneo meetings, but he still held to his own solution of the present danger: a strong army and a united Colorado Party. Army reorganization continued, no matter how loudly the Nationalists protested.[19] The Executive forwarded its project on war claims rising out of the March revolution to the legislature; the bill contained clauses for permanent claims procedures, as if in anticipation of the next revolution. With like foresight, the Bank of the Republic ordered the currency holdings of its branches in the Nationalist departments sent to Montevideo.

It was easier to strengthen the Government's war power than to unite the Colorado Party. Herrera y Obes and Tajes, reconciled after years of political enmity, insisted that they had more popular support among the rank-and-file Colorados than did the "situation"—the group around Batlle's government—and that therefore they, not the situation, should control any united Colorado organization. This, the situation would not accept.[20]

The young Colorados of the *Club Vida Nueva* thought to help party unity by raising the old specter of the Blanco peril, and proposed a great public demonstration against the murders committed by the Nationalists and João Francisco in Rivera during the March revolution. Conservative opinion was aghast; Batlle was urged to forbid the meeting. Batlle, who had refused to agree with these same young Colorados when they urged him to fight in March, would not now prohibit the meeting. He said he considered the demonstration legal but unnecessary since he had just sent a police investigator to Rivera.[21]

Formally, Batlle had sent the proper official to Rivera since he entrusted the mission to the Inspector General of Police, Carlos Travieso. But Travieso, Batlle's very first presidential appointee, was a politician not a professional policeman. He was so deep-dyed a Colorado that he had named his son Rivera, after the Party's founder for whom the department was also named.

The Nationalist jefe político of Rivera, Carmelo Cabrera, was worried that Travieso would find the Nationalist arms caches hidden in the department. Cabrera wrote Saravia that he would refuse to permit Travieso to search the buildings where the arms were stored; if Travieso returned with troops, Cabrera would consider it a violation of the Pact of Nico Pérez and cause for war. Nothing in the published peace pact—and *El Día* had denied the existence of secret clauses—restricted Government troop movements, yet Saravia shared Cabrera's view of the Pact of Nico Pérez: entry of Government troops into Nationalist Rivera would break up the pact and be cause for war. Saravia endorsed the jefe político's plan of operation: "I am in agreement with you on all the points to which you make reference." [22]

Saravia thought it time for the new Directorio to send its first
delegation to him. Montevideo was flooded with rumors that this
was a prelude to war, rumors which Minister of Government
Campisteguy took seriously.[23] Then the delegation returned. President Lamas told the Directorio that Saravia was calm; Lamas also
suggested that the Directorio send a committee, not a delegation,
to Batlle to assure him of the Nationalists' peaceful intent.

Vázquez Acevedo and Rodríguez Larreta visited President Batlle
at Government House and told him that the Directorio wished to
maintain peace. Batlle responded that he never doubted that the
Directorio wanted peace. He admitted he had been concerned
about the Nationalists of the interior, but had come to the con-
clusion there was nothing to the war rumors, even before receiving "such satisfactory information" from the Directorio. The
Nationalists, in turn, asked Batlle why the Government was sending arms to the interior, shipments which alarmed their coreligionaries. Batlle assured them it was a routine change of arms
for the Fifth Cavalry, whose weapons were in poor condition. The
conversation moved to reported Nationalist arms purchases abroad.
The committee was emphatic: "neither before, during, nor after"
the March revolution had the Nationalists bought additional arms.[24]
It was agreed that, to end war rumors, both sides would release
the news of the interview. And, in fact, the Club Vida Nueva
demonstration did take place without serious incident.[25]

Vázquez Acevedo and Rodríguez Larreta had refrained from
telling Batlle that their emphatic "before, during, nor after" denial
of arms purchases would not hold for the future. Saravia's principal purpose in calling the Directorio to him was to have it authorize new arms purchases. Just six days after the Directorio committee's interview with Batlle, Directorio President Lamas wrote
Saravia that the Directorio had agreed to buy 2,000 rifles and
500,000 rounds of ammunition in Buenos Aires.[26]

In spite of ardent Nationalist desires, Travieso continued his
investigations in Rivera. Batlle's April army increase was coming
out of committee; *El Día* explained that before the March revolution the President had hoped to cut the army. "Since then the
government has believed that its first duty was to keep strong
so as to be able to guarantee public order." [27] Debate began on
July 9. Very soon the partisan Colorado galleries had to be cleared.

After three days of debate, Nationalist fury on the floor of the Chamber made it seem wise to put the measure over for later sessions.[28] The Directorio newspaper then came out with the veiled hint that Batlle resign. The Colorado Deputies retaliated by refusing to elect any Nationalists to the Permanent Committee which sat when the legislature was not in session.[29] The Colorado politicians reactivated the lagging plans for party unification.

To this end a gigantic political barbecue with meat, drink, and band music was held on the outskirts of Montevideo. Some 18,000 to 20,000 Colorados, previously warned to give only "Vivas" and no "Mueras" [death to], enjoyed the affair and saw the "historic embrace" between Herrera y Obes and Tajes. The turnout was impressive, the absence of intra-party brawls encouraging. Some had thought Batlle would not welcome the return to prominence of the party veterans Herrera y Obes and Tajes, but *El Día* called the affair "a brilliant party success." [30]

Now the Colorado organizational sessions produced agreement. A provisional national commission made up of eminent Colorados of all persuasions would first be chosen and then elect permanent party officials. The conservative classes and naturally the Nationalists were worried over the increased prominence of Herrera y Obes, who to them represented pre-'97 Colorado intransigence. *El Día* would not share their worries: to leave out Herrera y Obes from a unified Colorado Party would be "to leave out a considerable group in the party." [31]

The Directorio thought another interview with Batlle was in order. It would like Travieso to complete his investigations in Rivera; it might delicately intimate to Batlle that it was concerned about some of the moves within the Colorado Party. The interview took place. The expected statement was issued: the interview had been long and cordial, both sides wanted peace.[32]

The usual sighs of relief were scarcely exhaled when *El Día* took issue with the section of the Nationalist peace statement which suggested that war alarms stemmed from acts of the Government.[33] Travieso gave no sign of leaving Rivera. And 4,000 new Remington rifles for the Government army were unloaded in the port of Montevideo.

On August 1, the President's office issued the pleasing statement that it had turned back to the treasury 864 pesos and 14 cents saved by keeping office expenses below the budgeted amounts. Batlle, the old bohemian, was proving a first-class administrator. He put in long hours, often working a seven-day week; he was good on details; he held up appointments of public employees for weeks or months so that the money for their salaries could be saved. Indeed, he was accused of being somewhat niggardly in providing state entertainments. For the first time in his life he had been able to deposit money in the bank, some four or five thousand pesos saved from his salary.[34]

Government policy, except for a few administrative acts like the organization of night classes for workers by Minister of Development Serrato, continued to be cautious. Batlle was anxious to propitiate Catholics and the conservative classes. During the fatal illness of Pope Leo XIII, a telegram on the stationery of the President of the Republic was sent to the Vatican: "Government and people of Uruguay vitally interested in health of His Holiness and make supplications for his recovery."[35] Businessmen were pleased to see that the timidly increased budget prepared by Martín C. Martínez was not brought out for debate and Cuestas' last budget continued for another year. The Montevideo real-estate tax was also continued without change, even though it was generally admitted that land values were rising and were not being taxed at their true value.

Several Deputies close to Batlle had presented important projects —to increase the capital of the Bank of the Republic; to organize a government alcohol monopoly; to float a loan of three and one-half million pesos which would be used to build roads, canals, and schools—but the Government itself took no stand on these bills. *Diario Nuevo*, the new Colorado unity newspaper, sometimes published radical editorials on fundamental economic issues,[36] editorials written by Julio María Sosa, one of Batlle's young protégés. *El Día*, which had just bought new presses, never expressed such views or even reprinted the *Diaro Nuevo* editorials.

In August, relations between the President and the Nationalists thawed, principally because of an interview Batlle had with two Nationalist Colonels who had returned from a visit to Saravia with Saravia's word of honor that, so long as the pledges made to the National Party were kept, he would keep the peace.[37] Don Pepe valued Saravia's pledge far more than assurances from the Directorio.

Both sides made concessions. Batlle agreed to reimburse the municipal authorities of two Nationalist departments for monies taken in March by the revolutionaries. He also announced that Acevedo Díaz, whose political career was ruined, would be named Minister to the United States, thus removing him entirely from Uruguayan political life. For its part, the Directorio dissuaded Cabrera from resigning as jefe político of Rivera because of affronts produced by Travieso's continuing investigations in the department.[38]

Later in August, Saravia made a trip across the border to see João Francisco, his munitioneer. He returned and agreed to attend the Melo Cattle Fair in November, to demonstrate that rumors of Nationalist revolution were false. His letter of acceptance stated that war could come only "if the Government . . . breaking pacts . . . forces or provokes the National Party to the struggle," and went on to explain that war operations, if they came, would take place close to the capital, so that ranchers in the north could still come to the fair.[39] Saravia's attitude could hardly be called peace-at-any-price. News of Saravia's trip to João Francisco reached Montevideo, and by the end of the month the army-increase bill was back on the legislative calendar.

On August 10, *El Día* reminded the still haggling Colorado factions that during the presidential campaign Batlle had promised that, if the Nationalists won the general elections of 1904, he would respect the result and at the end of his term turn the government over to the Nationalist President the new legislature would elect. The Colorados had better unite or catastrophe could occur.[40] Herrera y Obes still insisted that the nonsituationist Colorados have a majority in the united Colorado organization; the unity negotiations collapsed.

On August 26, *El Día* spelled out what would happen if the Colorado Party failed to unite:

Either it unites, reorganizes and proves once and for all its right to the government . . . or it decides to give up the decision by ballot, taking into account that the lesser evil of a new postponement is preferable to the greater evil of a defeat and the consequent National upheaval.[41]

This was a different Batlle from the one who would reconquer departments, and even a retreat from the Batlle of the presidential campaign. Don Pepe would not go to an election without a united Colorado Party; otherwise he would make an acuerdo with the Nationalists. Among other results, the acuerdo would end the immediate need for Colorado unity; Herrera y Obes' assistance would not be required and, as in the days of Cuestas, he would be without influence in the government.

Colorado tempers began to calm, and new mediators came forward—Colorado businessmen and ranchers who saw civil war as the end result of continuing party division. On September 11, a unity formula was accepted: an ornamental 500-man National Commission would be presided over by a 33-man Executive Committee; 20 of the 33 men were situationist, pro-Government, Colorados. Herrera y Obes had given way, but the election of Juan Pedro Castro, who had represented Batlle in the unity negotiations, as President of the Executive Committee already strained the new-found unity.[42]

Batlle also accepted an invitation to a fair—to the annual one in upriver Paysandú. It would give him an opportunity to further national confidence, and be a preliminary to a second fair visit —to the Melo Cattle Fair where he would have his first face-to-face meeting with Saravia. Arena and Martín C. Martínez were trying to arrange the meeting, in the hope the two leaders might come to trust each other and really secure the peace.[43]

Batlle cooperated, up to a point. He invited the Nationalist legislators to accompany him to Paysandú. The Directorio was peeved that he had not extended the invitation through it; however, after arranging a suitable display of Nationalist political independence in the Senate, the Directorio agreed that the Nationalist legislators should go.[44]

The leading caterers of Montevideo were hired to provide the banquets in Paysandú; a Mihanovich line river steamer would transport the official party. The Executive prepared good news for the upriver citizenry: plans for improving the port of Paysandú, a program for normal schools in the interior.

Just before leaving, Batlle granted an interview to *La Prensa* of Buenos Aires. He confessed that for the time being his entire government program was reduced to assuring the conservative classes there would be uninterrupted peace, so that they would invest in new business enterprises for the good of the nation. Don Pepe professed to believe that the country was settling down and pointed to the accompanying Nationalist legislators as proof.[45]

The overnight voyage to Paysandú was a bit rough. The next day, the fair was opened with appropriate ceremonies. Batlle made the principal speech. Speaking with his usual slow, reasoning style, he urged confidence in the traditional parties.[46] "I am a party man." He saw no enemies in the opposition party, but he called for country over party and an end to revolutions. A political group which puts party first

. . . is converted into a danger to public order, a menace . . . and should be energetically combatted, not only by its adversaries, but by its own component elements, in order to make it enter the path of legality and duty.

He visioned a great future for this land, when human hands would work it and make it produce a hundredfold more than now, then closed with a toast: "To the tranquillity of our homes. To the fertility of our lands. To toil which enriches nature and dignifies and beautifies life." [47]

The Nationalist legislators did not join in the applause. Their leader, Vázquez Acevedo, flatly refused to speak, explaining that his planned speech would have advocated the gradual disappearance of the traditional parties and would appear to contradict the President. He, Rodríguez Larreta, and some of the other Nationalists left the presidential party, on the claim of pressing engagements in Montevideo.

The Nationalists, considering that Batlle's condemnation of revolutions was aimed at them, were offended. That they were excessively susceptible could scarcely be denied. The Directorio newspaper in Montevideo insisted, though, that Batlle had made an inappropriate political speech on a nonpolitical occasion.[48]

With a slightly reduced complement, the presidential party continued its tour. After visiting the fair, Batlle and his First Lady visited the principal buildings of Paysandú. He was escorted through the church and, as he left, the priests who had guided him applauded, as did the onlookers; [49] Don Pepe, the anti-Catholic liberal, seemed to enjoy his reception.

The following day, after a splendid lunch, Batlle spoke again. He marveled at Paysandú's progress. Then, seemingly directing his remarks at his own Colorado admirers who were anxious to fight things out with the Nationalists so that afterwards Batlle's administration could accomplish something for Uruguay, he said:

It is evident that all this progress is tied to the conservation of peace; without peace, there is nothing but disorder and universal catastrophe. Peace must be the goal of all. I have always been a great friend of peace, I have always believed that the worst peace is better than the best war, and I have always believed that when there is the slightest chance of conserving or restoring peace, no calculation of what might be accomplished in the future should stand in the way of directing all our efforts towards the realization of that peace.[50]

The speech had been repeatedly interrupted by applause, applause echoed in Montevideo even by the Nationalists.

The presidential party took six days to return to the capital, stopping at Paysandú's rival, Salto—which never would have forgiven the snub had Batlle passed it by—and other ports of call on the way. At the pier in Montevideo a large crowd greeted Batlle; he told interviewers he considered the trip a success. Still, on October 7, two days after the return from Paysandú, the Secretary of the presidency notified the Melo Cattle Fair that, due to a previous commitment and to a heavy Government work load, the President would have to decline the invitation extended to him.[51] After the Nationalist response in Paysandú, Batlle had no intention of venturing into Saravia's home town.

Now that Batlle and the other Colorado dignitaries were back, Julio Herrera y Obes, joined by Tajes and some of the former Juan Carlos Blanco supporters, resigned from the new Colorado Executive Committee. Their objection was to Juan Pedro Castro as President of the Executive Committee, and in spite of excoriations from *El Día* they would not reconsider.

Within two weeks Castro resigned. Claudio Williman, Rector of the University, a close friend of Batlle's but a sometime victim of Cuestas, was prevailed upon to accept the party presidency. Williman, who had not been involved in the recent party squabbles, promised to be impartial and called for the united Colorado Party to win in 1904. The dissidents, apparently satisfied, withdrew their resignations,[52] and the elusive Colorado unity was finally at hand.

Since the March revolution Batlle had wanted two supports for his government, a united Colorado Party and a strengthened army. The united Colorado Party had been achieved; the strengthening of the army went on. A shipment of Colt machine guns arrived and was tested. On October 17 the army-increase bill was back on the floor of the Chamber. A large gallery expected fireworks, but the Nationalist Deputies put up only token resistance. Probably, they were influenced by a new executive project: the million-peso credit voted to pay the costs of the March revolution would be used for a different purpose—to build public works. There was genuine rejoicing over this, and government bonds went up. The Senate debate on the army-increase bill was perfunctory; the March army units were now permanent.[53]

VII

The Regiments in Rivera

TROUBLE boiled up in the border town capital of Rivera. It all had started when police investigator Travieso implicated one Gentil Gómez in João Francisco's March murders. Travieso asked Cabrera, the jefe político, to arrest Gómez. Nationalist Cabrera refused, until Travieso could produce a judge's order. Travieso got the order; by then Gómez was over the border in Brazil.

On Sunday afternoon, November 1, several drunk members of a Brazilian military brass band were arrested in Rivera after a brawl. While the brawl was going on, Gentil Gómez put in an appearance, even though an arrest order was still on his head. Cabrera, torn between his responsibilities as Nationalist political leader, which were to keep on the good side of João Francisco, and his duties as Police Chief of the Uruguayan Government, opted for the latter and threw Gentil Gómez into jail.

Those Brazilian musician-soldiers who were sober crossed the street over to the Brazilian town of Santa Ana do Livramento, picked up their weapons, their officers, and the Intendent of Santa Ana, Colonel Ataliva Gómez, Gentil's brother. The Brazilians, all João Francisco's men from the army of the State of Rio Grande do Sul, parleyed with their friend Carmelo Cabrera. Carmelo agreed to free the musicians, but because of the court order he could not free Gentil. Colonel Gómez insisted: either his brother was freed by midnight or he, at the head of his forces, would come and get him. Cabrera still refused, barely missed being shot, and retired across the border to Rivera.[1]

A Brazilian-Uruguayan conflict was about to break out. Cabrera started telegraphing Montevideo. He asked his immediate superior, the Minister of Government, for orders. He wired Batlle: "without arms and lacking ammunition I will sustain myself as well as I can . . . I await orders."[2] Influential Brazilians in Rivera telegraphed desperately to the Brazilian Minister in Montevideo to get the arrest order on Gentil Gómez canceled.[3]

It was too late. At about 8:00 P.M., Colonel Gómez moved into Rivera and started shooting. Cabrera telegraphed Batlle: "Brazilians opened fire on my forces they are advancing I have wounded."[4] From Batlle to Cabrera: "Retire toward interior of country taking Gentil Gómez if possible." Another from Batlle: "Advise if need help Cavalry Regiments." Cabrera, afraid the Brazilians would burn and sack Rivera if he moved out, wired back: "I will try to hold out retiring to the interior when can not resist believe help of regiments necessary." Batlle to the previously alerted Colonel Cándido Viera in the neighboring department of Tacuarembó: "Put yourself immediately on march to Rivera with 4th and 5th Regiments, to protect Jefe Político Carmelo Cabrera."[5]

The Brazilians started firing again at 11:00 P.M. Local Nationalists, who realized the situation was becoming disastrous, put tremendous pressure on the Sergeant of the Guard in charge of the prisoner Gentil Gómez. The poor man finally agreed to flee across the border with his prisoner and never himself return home to Uruguay.[6] Gentil reached his brother; Colonel Gómez called his forces back to Brazil; a sort of quiet reigned.[7]

Cabrera was furious. At 12:30 A.M. he telegraphed Batlle:

The guard who should have guarded Gómez whom I planned to send to Tacuarembó with Colonel Leleu fled to Brazil during a new outbreak of firing. I can never be chief of dishonorable men like those I had the misfortune to trust. Therefore I beg Your Excellency to accept my indeclinable resignation from the post with which you had honored me.[8]

Batlle refused:

I do just honor to your conduct which has been as I expected given the integrity of your character and I do not accept your resignation since you are needed to re-establish order in the department.[9]

At first, Batlle feared that the Brazilian foray was a cover for the combined João Francisco-Nationalist revolution about which he had been so often warned. He called his Ministers back from vacation, alerted the jefes políticos, and ordered all railroad bridges guarded.[10]

At 11:00 P.M., Martín C. Martínez visited Alfonso Lamas to ask him for assurances that the Nationalists had nothing to do with the border incident. Lamas didn't like the government's suspicious attitude, particularly Martínez' remark that Saravia had started the March revolution without advising the Directorio and might do so again. Nevertheless, Lamas agreed to send calming telegrams to the interior Nationalists when the commercial telegraph offices opened in the morning.[11]

On November 2, calm slowly returned. Reports from the interior indicated that there was no Nationalist revolution. The Directorio sent Saravia a telegram explaining that the regiments were in Rivera at Cabrera's request. The Minister of Interior advised the jefes políticos that all was well. The Minister of Foreign Relations protested to Rio de Janeiro against the actions of the armed forces of the State of Rio Grande do Sul. Brazilian Foreign Minister Rio Branco assured Montevideo that measures were being taken to prevent any repetition of the "disagreeable events." [12]

Brazilian Federal troops were sent to the border. João Francisco removed Colonel Gómez from his post as Intendent of Santa Ana do Livramento. On November 4, Batlle sent a formal message to the legislature announcing, in effect, that the incident was over.[13]

What about the two regiments now in the Department of Rivera? This was the question Alfonso Lamas asked Martín C. Martínez on November 3. Lamas told Martínez he was speaking as one citizen to another, not as President of the Directorio to a Minister of the Government. He wanted Martínez to know that the National Party had accepted the Peace of Nico Pérez understanding that no army units would be sent to the Nationalist departments. Unless the units were removed once the frontier incident ended, "the militarization of Rivera" would mean war.

Martínez, who had heard rumors that Batlle had pledged in the Pact of Nico Pérez not to send troops to the Nationalist departments, had already questioned the President on this point. Martínez answered Lamas that Batlle had advised him and other Ministers that he had made no such pledge. Batlle had said that he had explained to José Pedro Ramírez at the time of the pact that he would make no pledge which would limit his rights to move units into the Nationalist departments, "even though, as he indicated to Dr. Ramírez confidentially, he did not then have plans to move forces to those departments." Further, Lamas should know this, since Batlle had informed Martínez that he himself had told Lamas what he had said to José Pedro Ramírez, the very day Lamas had returned from Nico Pérez. Lamas acknowledged to Martínez that Batlle had informed him; but, he explained, by March 28, the day he saw Batlle, the Nationalist Army which had formally approved the pact on the 27th was demobilizing, and it was too late to change the Nationalist understanding of the Pact of Nico Pérez.[14]

It developed that on March 27 the Nationalist military officers, just before they were to ratify Peace at Nico Pérez, heard rumors that Batlle planned to send troops to the Nationalist departments. They would not approve the peace pact until they were assured that Batlle would not send troops. Lamas in Nico Pérez and Ramírez in the Montevideo railroad station had a telegraphic conversation. Ramírez later related that, at Lamas' request:

I immediately approached the President of the Republic; I informed him of Doctor Lamas' telegraphic communication, and the President of the Republic told me that he did not have the intention attributed to him, that he told me so confidentially and that I could transmit it in the same form to Doctor Lamas but to warn him that this would not form part of the pact already arranged, nor would it be the object of any other pledge on his part.

I considered that this could and should tranquilize the chiefs of the revolutionary movement and I answered Dr. Lamas in these terms:

"Celebrated conference with President about Nationalist departments with completely satisfactory results, but all this, as he indicated, in purely confidential form and without its being object of pact already arranged or any other pledges whatever. You know that I do not advance or venture in such a serious matter and that all of you can confide in my manifestations and declarations. I believe it advisable not to enter into details by telegraph." [15]

In his anxiety for peace, Ramírez instead of quoting Batlle's exact words had used the phrase "completely satisfactory results," which the Nationalist officers took to mean a blanket commitment by Batlle not to send troops into the Nationalist departments. To them, Batlle's unwillingness to put the commitment into the Pact was merely another of his legal scruples like his refusal to affix his signature to the Pact. The Nationalist officers were satisfied, made peace, and demobilized.

Batlle was not satisfied with José Pedro Ramírez' later recapitulation:

> I told Doctor Ramírez in the most decisive manner that I reserved for myself the power of sending the public force wherever I believed it necessary or convenient and that I would admit no limitation on this power. What I did tell Dr. Ramírez, and he should remember it, was that I would never send the public force to the Nationalist-administered departments to modify electoral situations, and in addition that, for the moment, I would not send them to any of the Nationalist-administered departments because I had decided to put the regiments in other places. But I added that this last declaration should not be taken *as even the shadow* of a pledge.[16]

Alfonso Lamas, in turn, did not like Batlle's version of the conversation he and Batlle had:

> . . . if it is true that several days after peace was made the President told me that he did not accept the imposition which the Nationalist Military Assembly made through Doctor Ramírez as intermediary, he also said to me with complete precision and without any time stipulations that he would not send forces to the departments administered by Nationalists.[17]

It came down to a basic disagreement: the Nationalists felt Batlle had given them assurances he would never send troops to the Nationalist departments; Batlle felt he had not. Unfortunately there were no transcripts or even minutes of the Batlle-Ramírez [18] and Batlle-Lamas conferences.

The Nationalists were fearful of the electoral, not military, effects of the presence of the regiments in Rivera. If war came, the two regiments would be deep in Nationalist-controlled territory and likely to be surrounded. For this reason, Batlle did not send the troops all the way to the capital town of Rivera, which was right on the Brazilian border; instead, he kept them in Tranqueras, a railroad stop halfway into the department of Rivera, where they could be quickly evacuated in case of war.[19]

If, however, the two regiments stayed in Rivera until the general elections of November 1904, they could tip the department's electoral balance in favor of the Colorados. Not many people voted in the interior during an election; one had to sign his ballot, and the opposition remembered. Only those, several hundred in either party, who were prepared to back up their votes with their pistols, voted. Soldiers were forbidden to vote, but officers, sergeants, and corporals voted; Colorado votes from the two regiments might be enough to win the department. There was always the additional possibility that the troops would rough up Nationalist voters; their mere presence in the department might be enough to discourage some fearful Nationalists from voting.

Batlle was angry that the Nationalists could accuse him of planning to keep the regiments in Rivera to win an election. Not only had he given Ramírez explicit assurance that he would not, but his whole political career, he felt, was assurance enough that he was incapable of such an act. He insisted years later: "I had no intention of having them remain and would have removed them had not the Nationalists made an issue of their staying." [20] To remove the regiments now would be to admit that a political motive explained their presence in Rivera. It would be another concession wrung from Batlle by the Nationalists, another boost to Nationalist prestige and blow to Colorado pride. The Government, forced to acknowledge it could not even move troops within the boundaries of Uruguay, would be seriously, embarrassingly, weakened.

Yet Lamas insisted that Batlle remove the regiments from Rivera. He saw Martín C. Martínez again. He warned the brother and the nephew of José Pedro Ramírez: "the permanence of the 4th and 5th Cavalry Regiments would bring civil war as an inevitable consequence." [21] Lamas was trying to save the peace, for he knew Saravia considered that he had an iron-bound commitment from Batlle not to send troops to the Nationalist departments. When Saravia pledged to keep the peace so long as the pledges made to the Nationalist Party were kept, Saravia meant pledges by Batlle not to send troops to places like Rivera.

Saravia insisted on absolute compliance with the Pact of Nico Pérez. There had always been "reserved" or "confidential" clauses in Uruguayan peace pacts and they usually contained the most valuable concessions. For example, Batlle had agreed not to ask the Revolution to return monies taken from public offices, a concession, though publicly acknowledged, not included in the six-clause formal pact. In May, Saravia wrote Lamas about a taxpayer who had paid 2,400 pesos in taxes to the Revolution instead of the government; Saravia insisted that the government consider the taxes paid, under the terms of the concession on public monies. If, as Saravia put it, "the first of the confidential bases," the one on public monies, was not honored, "the pact would be violated and I would be obliged to consider that it had expired." [22]

Since Saravia was willing to consider the Pact of Nico Pérez broken over just 2,400 pesos, what would he do when, in his eyes, the government flagrantly ignored one of the Pact's crucial "confidential bases" and kept the regiments in Rivera? Lamas knew Saravia and knew the answer: either Batlle withdrew the regiments or Saravia would go to war.

The responsible press handled the matter of the regiments in Rivera with great circumspection. *El Siglo* announced the end of the frontier incident on November 5; but its editor, José Pedro Ramírez' nephew, was advised by Lamas of the Nationalist demands on Batlle to remove the regiments, and on November 10 *El Siglo* admitted the country once again was in a very difficult political equilibrium, a situation still preferable to war. *Diario Nuevo*, increasingly the voice of the intransigent young Colorados, tried for a showdown with the Nationalists. It proposed that the legislature abrogate the Pact of Nico Pérez with a "vote for the immediate re-establishment of institutional life." [23] *El Día* stopped this proposition short. It announced that the President of the Republic would resign if the legislature ended the Pact of Nico Pérez. The chastened *Diario Nuevo* restrained itself until the end of November, when it revealed publicly that the Nationalists were claiming that the presence of the regiments violated the Pact of Nico Pérez. *Diario Nuevo* editorialized: "to attempt to deny the Executive Power its right to maintain Army troops in whatever place in the nation it deems convenient is simply wild." [24]

Batlle gave every indication that he wanted no war with the Nationalists. The same *El Día* editorial which warned that he would resign if the Colorado legislators revoked the peace pact also reminded interested parties that the pact would hold only until the end of Batlle's presidency.

Let us leave the re-establishment of full legality to next year's election and to the coming presidential election, and let us live until then as best we can within this anomalous state of affairs, fatally imposed by the most respectable of circumstances, and in which there is raised against the legitimate principle of authority another and abnormal principle foreign to the most elemental notions of constituted government.[25]

That very day, Batlle announced the demobilization of the militiamen added to the regiments before they left for Rivera. But the regiments, with their soldiers, noncoms, and officers, remained where they were, halfway to the border.

Saravia also seemed more interested in elections than war. He made his promised appearance at the Melo Cattle Fair, dismissed rumors of Nationalist revolution, and was reported to be confident Batlle would keep the pact and the peace.[26] Nationalist firebrand Arturo Berro sent another warning to Saravia that Batlle had "the worst possible intentions" toward him and that Batlle "wants an acuerdo, and all his friends, including his Nationalist friends, want an acuerdo: if he is not given an acuerdo he will take or try to take revenge on the Blanco Party." Saravia answered:

Having read your able comments with careful attention I believe . . . that the next electoral struggle must take place on the basis of free suffrage and that, since the National Party can not and does not wish to make a new acuerdo, all the coreligionaries have the moral obligation to inscribe themselves in the civic registers.[27]

As it did when it knew Saravia's views, the Directorio's newspaper echoed them. On November 28, it proclaimed: "The expectations of patriotism center on the general elections of 1904, on which depends the definitive consolidation of legal institutions." [28]

If there was to be an election, Colorado unity must be completed. The party charter called for elections of departmental party authorities, but the times and the provisional nature of present party organization made such formalities troublesome. Instead, the new National Executive Committee would appoint the departmental party officers.

Unity broke apart as soon as the Executive Committee began to name the officers for Montevideo. Herrera y Obes wanted more of his followers represented; Manini Ríos, the young editor of *El Día*—obviously Batlle's agent—refused. Another of Batlle's young followers, Feliciano Viera, proposed that proportional repre-

sentation of the different factions not be attempted. Shortly thereafter, the members of the Montevideo Colorado Committee were
appointed—with the nonsituationists a distinct minority.[29]

Herrera y Obes and Tajes ceased attending the National Executive Committee sessions. They had lost interest in Colorado unity.
Undaunted, the pro-Government Colorados reorganized the other
departments.[30] Batlle had made his last concession to Herrera y
Obes. His tactic now was to leave out the overexigent pre-'97
leaders but to bring in their followers. *El Día* once more announced
that the Government would give patronage to Colorados without
regard to their previous factional alignments.[31]

The young Colorados got up on the stump and warned the
party mass that it was either unity or an acuerdo. If an acuerdo was
impossible, the party might have to abstain, Abstention, a prerevolutionary stance, would be a horrible irony when a friendly
Colorado government was running the election.[32] Yet in spite of
the Colorado excitement, it was by no means clear that the followers were coming in without their leaders. It looked very much
as if one prong of Batlle's post-Nico Pérez strategy against the
Nationalists—a united Colorado party—would be badly blunted.

A sizable crowd had applauded Batlle when he returned from
Paysandú. Don Pepe responded that he had done nothing yet to
justify applause, but that before he left office he would contribute
to "the happiness and progress of the Republic."[33] If he waited
until calm enveloped the Republic before beginning to contribute,
his whole administration would pass with nothing accomplished;
besides, an election was nearing and a program of accomplishments
might be useful.

News spread that Batlle was preparing to submit a bill abolishing the death penalty, a punishment he had opposed since his days
as a philosophy student. Of more immediate concern to the conservative classes, the Executive proposed to raise the rural land
taxes for next year by some 110,000 pesos over the 1,192,313 pesos
collected in 1902–1903. Although the effect on any single property
would be scarcely perceptible, the Executive's accompanying
message had ominous long-range implications, for it asserted that
society, not the landowner, was responsible for rises in land values.[34]

The Chamber of Deputies was reluctant to approve the increases for next year. Now was a bad time to raise assessments; ranchers were already fearful of war; drought and plagues had ravaged the interior; the government did not need more taxes. Minister of Finance Martín C. Martínez appeared on the second day of debate. He, conservative though he was, endorsed the view that society had the right to tax increases in land values which did not come from the labor of the landowner—although, he quickly added, to tax in "moderate proportions." In any event, the present project was unobjectionable: land values had doubled and tripled, yet taxes were still collected on the old assessments; about half the lands in the country were operated by lessees who would not be affected by the tax increase. Martínez closed with some bitterness: "It is well known on whom this tax is to weigh, and the capitalists have much greater strength of resistance than do the great mass of consumers." [35]

Even so, it took a compromise by Feliciano Viera, the shrewd little fat man who had shown his agility in the Colorado unity negotiations, to save the project. Previously, the departmental administrations received all rural land-tax collections which exceeded the amounts collected in 1898–1899; the central government got only the amount collected in that fiscal year. The Executive's project changed this: the basic property tax would remain at 6.50 pesos per 1,000 pesos of assessed value, of which the national government would receive 5.50 pesos and the administration of the department where the property was located 1 peso. Viera got the Executive to agree to a stipulation: if the 1 per 1,000 rate in a department did not produce as much total revenue as the departmental administration had received in fiscal 1902–1903 under the old system, the central government would reimburse the department for the difference. The Deputies, now that they had protected local government, reluctantly approved the increased rural land taxes.[36]

Viera didn't dare rescue another of the Executive's projects, again a moderate project with ominous long-run implications. The Executive had proposed, in the annual business license tax bill, that foreign insurance companies deposit 100,000 to 150,000 pesos in Uruguayan government bonds, as evidence of ability to pay the

claims of Uruguayan policyholders. *El Siglo* was alarmed lest European capital resent such treatment; the Chamber of Deputies quietly
detached this provision from the license law.[37]

It was plain that the legislature would not permit Batlle to let
out many programmatic notches. He could, however, set policy
administratively. Don Pepe was having second thoughts about the
wisdom of letting foreign companies electrify the Montevideo
trolley system. The trolley group needed electric power. Batlle
refused to sell them the government-operated Montevideo plant
and refused them permission to build their own; they must buy
their power from the government plant.[38] Indeed, Batlle was toying
with the idea of having the government power plant operate
trolleys on its own.[39]

Batlle's labor policy was also becoming more affirmative. The
Police Chief, instead of stamping strikes out—and it almost seemed
that Montevideo was going through a strike wave—acted as strike
mediator. Striking cigarette workers paraded in front of Batlle's
house and cheered him. Don Pepe allowed Arena to write a lead
editorial on strike violence in *El Día*. The editorial deplored strike
violence, but answered critics by insisting Uruguayan workers
struck only when driven by desperation.

> . . . therefore we are against the adoption of any repressive legislation.
> Incitement to strike, the right to refuse to work, propaganda to estab-
> lish and affirm the ties of solidarity among workers on strike, all are le-
> gitimate and acceptable rights . . . the freedom to work brings with
> it as a necessary corollary the absolutely unquestionable right to strike
> and, as a result, the freedom of action of strike promoters or initiators,
> so long as they do not violate the rights of others.[40]

The Nationalists were becoming increasingly impatient with
Batlle. Not a single representative of the Government, not even
the Nationalist jefe político, had appeared at the Melo Cattle Fair.[41]
And the regiments remained in Rivera.

Saravia wanted the Directorio to come to him. Lamas tried to
gain time for peace and urged Saravia to delay the visit "because
a feeling of calm is beginning to take the place of the recent agitation and alarm." Saravia insisted that the Directorio send a delegation immediately.[42] On December 13, President Lamas and three
others left for Saravia's ranch; the public was advised that the visit
was about the election of a new Directorio later that month. The

delegation spent a day on the ranch, and was back in Montevideo on December 16. The usual press release went out: there was complete accord between Saravia and the Directorio; they had discussed the party elections and the 1904 general elections. Saravia wanted peace—so long as the Government did not violate the Pact of Nico Pérez.[43]

But it had not been a routine meeting. The Nationalist military commanders did not like the government's arms buildup. The Directorio had dragged its feet on arms purchases; the shipment ordered in July was due to arrive from Buenos Aires on December 31. No war plans could go into effect until after the shipment arrived.

Saravia had to reconcile the war spirit of the Nationalist military with the Directorio's caution. It was decided that Lamas should renew the demand to remove the regiments and couple the demand with a warning that if they remained it would mean war; no deadline was to be attached to the demand for the regiments' removal. Meanwhile the party elections would be held and the registration campaign for the 1904 election continue. Saravia wanted no more acuerdos. He was firm on this.[44]

The day after the delegation returned, the Directorio newspaper printed a blasting editorial ironically titled: "Cuestas 'the Insufferable' and Batlle 'The Good.'" Batlle's government was "the negation of peace . . . a revolutionary government, a declared enemy of party concord and coparticipation in public affairs." Then came the real message: "today it prefers war to transaction with its adversary." The lead and closing paragraphs wondered if the coming year would be devoted to electioneering or to something else: "Does the National Party which represents half the country, does the whole country really have this year of assured peace?"[45]

The blast did not soften Don Pepe. The days when he would call Alfonso Lamas to his office and offer peace concessions were over. Batlle now refused to see any peace mediators personally; they would have to negotiate through Martín C. Martínez.

Lamas tried to get José Pedro Ramírez to carry the message, but Ramírez felt his usefulness was over and refused. Don Pepe had convinced himself that José Pedro Ramírez ought to tell Saravia that President Batlle had given no blanket commitment never to send troops to the Nationalist departments. If Ramírez would do this, Ramírez could save the peace. As Ramírez remained silent, Batlle began to suspect he was playing a devious game: Ramírez wanted war, a war which would end in negotiated peace, a peace which would require Batlle to resign as President and be replaced by the great peacemaker and "neutral" José Pedro Ramírez.[46] Lamas finally turned to Gonzalo Ramírez, José Pedro Ramírez' brother. Gonzalo Ramírez, though on good terms with Batlle, got no favorable response to Lamas' message. Don Pepe felt he was in the right, and in contrast with March he also had might on his side.

Batlle had a war plan ready, in case he had to use it. The army would be alerted, prepared to pounce on local Nationalist military groups before they could leave their departments. If the plan worked, Saravia's army would never assemble.[47] Orders now went out to government military commanders. To Colonel Pablo Galarza, the fiery Colorado of Durazno:

> Without producing any alarm be ready to march at the first command. You will receive a simple marching order, you will move immediately and by forced marches on the Department of Flores, if you encounter any resistance fire on them heavily.—In case the telegraph is interrupted and you note movements by the Nationalists which convince you that a subversive movement has broken out begin march as indicated above, move through the Department of Flores to San José, incorporate the forces of Soriano which will be waiting, round up all the horses, take them with you if possible to the Department of Florida, where you will find General Muniz, under whose orders you will continue.[48]

If there were time, Montevideo would order Galarza to pounce on the neighboring Nationalist department of Flores. If the Nationalists broke out too fast, Galarza would have to be prepared to fight his way South. But Batlle wanted the war to come, if it did, from the Nationalists not the Government. The admonition to Galarza not to move—if out of contact with Montevideo—unless there were Nationalist movements "which convince you that a subversive movement has broken out" was added in Batlle's own handwriting to the previously prepared orders.

The Nationalists had wire taps on the departmental telegraph lines and long since had broken the Government's codes. On December 17, Jefe Político Carmelo Cabrera warned Lamas from Rivera that the Government had sent out military orders. On December 24 he wrote Lamas: "I can assure you that the regiments have orders to be prepared against a blow from Brazil and ready to operate *on a moment's notice in the Department or on Rivera* (textual)." [49]

Saravia began taking the necessary steps for war. His sons started passing out arms on December 22. He called his Nationalist unit commanders to his ranch for a Christmas Day meeting. They came; they analyzed the situation; they prepared war plans; they were alerted. Then they returned to their departments to await orders.[50]

On December 29, Juan José Muñoz, the Nationalist caudillo of the Department of Maldonado, left for home. He would stop over in Montevideo with Saravia's orders for Lamas. That same day, Saravia sent war orders to Cabrera in Rivera, "so that you can make the proper use of them if the march of events so require." [51]

News of the Nationalist military meeting preceded Juan José Muñoz to Montevideo. The rumor spread in government circles that if the regiments were not removed from Rivera a majority of Saravia's officers wanted war on January 1; that day the departmental tax offices would have heavy collections, which the revolution could seize. A minority was supposed to favor delay until February or March; by then, the Nationalists would know whether or not the officers and noncoms of the Regiments had registered in Rivera for the 1904 elections.[52] On December 29, the Government sent Colonel Ruprecht to take command of the forces in Rocha, the department bordering Juan José Muñoz' Maldonado.

War or peace rested on the success of Alfonso Lamas' attempts to get Batlle to withdraw the regiments. Lamas had been re-elected President of the Directorio on December 27. On December 30, he called the new Directorio together. Word of the Nationalist military officers' meeting had been received. The Directorio formally discussed the Pact of Nico Pérez and officially authorized Lamas to negotiate with the Government.[53] On December 31, Alfonso Lamas asked Gonzalo Ramírez to inform Martín C. Martínez, for transmission to the President of the Republic, that "the National Party considered the pact of Nico Pérez violated by the permanence of the 4th and 5th Cavalry Regiments in Rivera and that their withdrawal was required, otherwise civil war was inevitable and imminent." Gonzalo Ramírez tried to get Lamas to tone down the terms of the ultimatum, but Lamas insisted it be transmitted just as he had phrased it. Ramírez, with great misgivings, delivered Lamas' demands to Martín C. Martínez.[54]

It was now Batlle's turn to ponder. The army was ready. The

Nationalist demand that the Government withdraw troops from a part of its own country would appear monstrous abroad, making It difficult for the Revolution to get support in Argentina and Brazil. The young Colorados were spoiling for a fight. War could solve the Colorado unity problem by rallying the party mass around Batlle. But war often turned out differently than anticipated. Borda had been assassinated in '97; some unforeseen circumstance now could ruin Batlle's war plans. More important was the enormity of the decision. Batlle had said in Paysandú that the worst peace was better than the best war. How could he, who opposed the death penalty for murderers, who opposed bullfights because of the bloodshed, oversee the killing of thousands of men in battle?

Before Batlle could authorize war he must satisfy himself that he had done everything possible to save peace. He told Martín C. Martínez to inform the Nationalists that he would not remove the regiments from Rivera but would assure passage of a law which would make it impossible for them to vote there. Instead, the officers and noncoms would vote by absentee ballot in Tacuarembó, where they had previously been stationed.[55] This seemingly should satisfy those Nationalist military officers who were worried only about the electoral consequences of the regiments' stay in Rivera.

Don Pepe had no intention of negotiating army to army, as he had been obliged to do in March. It would be the end of his authority as President. This time, if the Nationalists mobilized, it would be war.

Government mobilization orders were drawn, and arms were shipped. General Benavente went to command the Army of the North. General Justino Muniz, the illiterate old Blanco caudillo from Cerro Largo, who hated Saravia and who had commanded the Government armies in '97, came to Montevideo for instructions. *El Día* warned that the Government would not give in.

Saravia's headquarters in Melo was flooded with requests for orders from the Nationalist military. He telegraphed Lamas: "Alarming news spreading here. Unaware of everything I ask telegraphic information." Lamas answered: "Government taking precautions because it says it has seen suspicious movements in certain departments. We believe all will return to calm. Advisable to wait in order to initiate negotiations with advantages."[56]

Cabrera in Rivera had telegraphed Saravia: "Tell me if I should begin movement." Saravia now answered: "Measures taken by government can be in order to oblige us to precipitate Orlando and avoid responsibility. Advisable to await solution." [57] Orlando was the code name for revolution.

On New Year's Eve the Government started sending troops to the interior. Batlle's home was converted into command headquarters. Telegraphic lines were brought in; reports from the interior were analyzed; military officers entered and left. Batlle and the Ministers of War and Government worked until 1:00 A.M. and Batlle was back at work at 6:00 A.M. on New Year's Day.[58]

In the interior, the police started rounding up known Nationalist military leaders. The Nationalists did not plan to sit at home and be caught. A secret message was relayed to Saravia: "Last night I was informed from Montevideo that Lamas gave orders to tell you to avoid any clashes and that all our friends proceed with energy under alert." [59]

The Directorio wanted time for the revolution to assemble and for pressure to mount on Batlle. Lamas advised Martín C. Martínez that Batlle's offer was unacceptable; Saravia insisted the regiments be withdrawn from Rivera. Martínez returned with Batlle's second offer. Batlle was now willing to withdraw one regiment and to sponsor electoral legislation neutralizing the other.

Batlle also continued mobilization. Early on January 2, the following order went out to all military commanders: "You are ordered to call up immediately the divisions in the department under your command, to break up hostile groups, to gather horses, and to communicate any news." [60] The Nationalists of the interior considered this the equivalent of a declaration of revolution against them by the Government. Saravia gave the order to mobilize but to avoid clashes, and also ordered his brother to bring the arms hidden in Brazil.[61]

Lamas refused Batlle's second offer, but made a counterproposal. If both regiments were withdrawn from Rivera, the Nationalists would raise no questions about their voting elsewhere. Batlle professed to be shocked at this intimation that the Nationalists would let him have the men vote fraudulently elsewhere. He also could see another intimation in the offer: if the Colorados let the Nationalists win the 1904 elections in the six Nationalist departments, the Nationalists would let the Colorados win in the remaining departments. In short, the Directorio would be receptive to a renewal of the 1901 acuerdo.[62]

An acuerdo might not be a bad way out. Batlle had always maintained that an acuerdo was better than war. It could also solve Batlle's Colorado unity problem—the necessity to win over the followers of Herrera y Obes and Tajes—since an acuerdo would do for him what it had done for Cuestas: his Colorado Party would retain all the legislative seats and the pre-'97 group be frozen out. If he made an acuerdo, Batlle could remove the regiments without the removal breaking the Colorado electoral spirit. There would be no electoral contests.

Batlle told Martín C. Martínez to advise the Nationalists that, if they renewed the 1901 acuerdo, he would remove the two regiments from Rivera. But he would not negotiate army to army; if the revolution formed, he would dissolve it by force.[63]

At 10:00 A.M. on January 2, 1904, the Directorio met and decided to negotiate. It put its version of events into the minutes so that posterity could judge:

> Immediately ideas were exchanged on the events of the present. President [Lamas] announced that Minister of Finance Doctor Martín C. Martínez had advised that things could be arranged by dictating a law which would establish that the Regiments could not vote by requiring them to have six months of residence in the Department; that one regiment would be withdrawn and the other subjected to the aforementioned conditions, adding besides that at most only sixty men could vote; that he had advised that another solution could be that of making an electoral acuerdo to tranquilize the Government.
>
> The Minister of Finance also advised that the Government accepted the paralyzation of war operations, and that the Directorio could communicate telegraphically with General Saravia and other Nationalist military officers, and that it could go to Melo to confer with Saravia, to whom the following telegram was sent
>
> "We have bases for negotiation which might prevent conflict. Avoid clashes, Directorio will leave immediately to confer with you, after first having previous telegraphic conference with you to save time and to bring the negotiations already initiated closer to success." [64]

The Directorio had no intention of advising Saravia and the Nationalist military officers to stay put. Lamas was able to get another telegram off to Saravia:

> Directorio in group will leave to confer with you but desires that this does not prejudice operations which the extreme measures of the

government force on you. I await answer. Answer if you expect us, it is advantageous that we leave here, nevertheless continue with preparations.[65]

At 7:00 A.M. on January 3, Rodríguez Larreta, who remained behind, had a final interview with Martín C. Martínez. Martínez gave Rodríguez Larreta a statement dictated by Batlle, a statement phrased to appeal to Saravia:

If the parties celebrate an electoral acuerdo, avoiding the struggle during this presidency, this fact would clear the situation and would cause the reason for alarms and uncertainties to disappear and the President of the Republic would have no need to keep the Regiments camped in the field and would have them returned to barracks.[66]

Rodríguez Larreta telegraphed Melo:

I leave today in express train carrying formula whose acceptance I consider patriotic. Communicate with General Saravia, Drs. Lamas, Berro, Fonseca, asking them to await my arrival in order to decide.[67]

Rodríguez Larreta was still on the train to Melo when General Benavente relayed a telegram to Batlle: the jefe político of Tacuarembó reported that railroad bridges had been dynamited and revolution had broken out. This was the news Batlle had awaited. Now war operations could commence.

General Muniz was in Nico Pérez, of famous memory. To him went this telegram: "Revolution broke out in Tranqueras. You can operate in accord with instructions received—Batlle y Ordoñez." To Colonel Galarza in Durazno (whose original orders Batlle had carefully corrected): "Comply with instructions received, reinforcing yourself conveniently to avoid any mischance —Batlle y Ordoñez." [68] In Maldonado, Nationalist caudillo Juan José Muñoz had received orders to join Saravia, "avoiding all encounters with the enemy." Colonel Ruprecht's Government troops blocked the way; Muñoz broke through. The first skirmish had taken place.[69]

The Government's war strategy was elementary. The Government army divisions in the interior would keep Nationalist contingents from reaching Saravia. General Muniz, with a reinforced army, would rush to Cerro Largo from Nico Pérez and knock out Saravia before Saravia could assemble his army. The revolution would be over.[70]

On January 5, Batlle sent notification to the legislature that a
state of war existed. The Executive, the message stated, was confident that "in a very short time order will be re-established in the
Republic." [71] On January 6, *El Día* changed its headline from "The
Events" to "The Insurrection." On January 7, Muniz moved out
his army. By January 8, Muniz was out of telegraphic communication with Batlle.[72] That afternoon, several Directorio members, including Rodríguez Larreta, returned from Saravia, got off the train
at suburban stops, and came into Montevideo.

The Directorio met at 9:00 P.M. Saravia was willing to make
an acuerdo although he wanted it called by another name. The
Directorio wanted additional assurances from Batlle. Rodríguez
Larreta, entrusted by the Directorio with its message to the Government, feared any further demands would lay the Nationalists
open to blame for war guilt. At midnight, on his own responsibility,
he told Martín C. Martínez that the National Party would accept
Batlle's terms, exactly as Batlle had presented them.[73]

The joyous Martínez rushed to Batlle with the good news.
Batlle told him it was too late. He had made the offer to avert a
revolution, but the revolution had come. He had no intention of
falling into another trap like last March when the assembled revolution had made additional last-minute demands. To negotiate now
would only result in a worse war later.[74] Martínez, crushed, resigned as Minister of Finance. It was war.

The polemic on who was responsible for the War of 1904 still
goes on. Nationalists like to quote Saravia's telegram to Lamas,
"Alarming news spreading here. Unaware of everything I ask telegraphic information." Quoted out of context, the telegram suggests
that Saravia was quietly attending to his own business while Batlle
was plotting his War of Revenge. The Nationalists would do better
if they maintained that Saravia and Lamas in good faith believed
Batlle had broken the Pact of Nico Pérez, and must either remove
the regiments or face the consequences.

The demand to remove the regiments seems so unreasonable to
those who did not live through the uneasy year of 1903 that Nationalists deny it was made or skip over it and emphasize their
acceptance of Batlle's acuerdo offer and his rejection of their acceptance. They blame Batlle's change of mind on General Muniz'

private assurance to him in the interim that Muniz would finish the war within a week. But Batlle's explanation—that Nationalist terms of acceptance might not be final—was closer to the truth than he knew.

In any event, no peace treaty could have foreseen an attack on Rivera by Brazilian friends of the Nationalists and the Nationalist jefe político's willingness to have Government troops enter his department. Yet, had not this development occurred, others were likely. When, after March, Batlle decided conciliation with the Nationalists was no longer possible, when he decided to negate Saravia's power by building up his own, he created a situation in which Saravia's ultimate response would be war.

The fact is that the Nationalists did not trust Batlle to run an honest election. Lack of trust was the basic reason for their March "armed protest" and for their December war ultimatum. Batlle responded to their distrust of his electoral honesty, the cardinal pledge of his twenty years of political life, by insisting on his own rights. Arena tells of a conversation about the forthcoming elections he had with Don Pepe just a few months before the war: "if unfortunately the Blancos triumph, I can be dragged through the streets, but they will get the government." [75] Of course, Batlle would have done all he could to prevent a Blanco triumph. He would have been willing to go to an election only if he thought the Colorados would win; otherwise, he would want an acuerdo. But the Nationalist did not wait to see what he would do to prevent their triumph; they revolted, anticipating that he would use force.

With hindsight, the Nationalists would have been wiser to wait. Either revolution would have been unnecessary or revolution would have had a real banner—Government coercion or use of force. Instead, the Nationalists forced Batlle's hand. Earlier they had underestimated Batlle as a presidential campaigner; if they now underestimated him as a war leader, they might lose everything the party had gained since '97. They might lose much more.

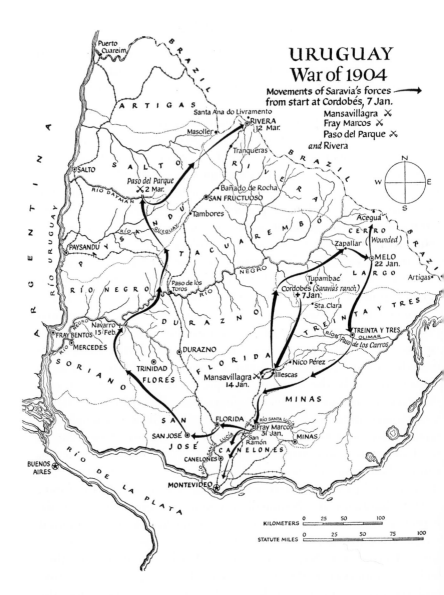

URUGUAY
War of 1904

Movements of Saravia's forces ⟶
from start at Cordobés, 7 Jan.
Mansavillagra ✕
Fray Marcos ✕
Paso del Parque ✕
and Rivera

BRAZIL

Puerto
Cuareim

ARTIGAS

Santa Ana do Livramento

RIVERA
12 Mar.

Masoller

Tranqueras

B R A Z I L

SALTO

Paso del Parque
✕ 2 Mar.

RÍO DAYMAN

R I V E R A

Bañado de Rocha

SAN FRUCTUOSO

Tambores

A N D U

Acegua

CERRO

(*Wounded*)

RÍO ANDU

RÍO URUGUAY

PAYSANDU

T A C U A R E M B O

Zapallar

MELO
22 Jan.

L A R G O

Artigas

RÍO NEGRO

NEGRO

Paso de los
Toros

RÍO

Tupambaé

Cordobés (*Saravia's ranch*)
✛ 7 Jan.

Sta. Clara

T R E I N T A   Y   T R E S

P

R Í O   U R U G U A Y

R Í O   N E G R O

D U R A Z N O

FRAY BENTOS

Navarro
15 Feb.

MERCEDES

DURAZNO

TREINTA Y TRES

RÍO OLIMAR

Paso de los Carros

A R G E N T I N A

NEGRO

S O R I A N O

TRINIDAD

FLORES

F L O R I D A

Mansavillagra ✕
14 Jan.

Illescas

Nico Pérez

MINAS

SAN

FLORIDA

Fray Marcos
31 Jan.

SAN JOSE

SAN JOSE

San
Ramón

RÍO SANTA LUCÍA

MINAS

RÍO LUCÍA

CANELONES

C A N E L O N E S

BUENOS
AIRES

R Í O   D E   L A   P L A T A

MONTEVIDEO

N
W   E
S

KILOMETERS 0   25   50   100

STATUTE MILES 0   25   50   75   100

116

VIII

>‹‹‹‹‹‹‹‹‹‹‹‹‹

The War of 1904

Batlle's house, command headquarters, was crowded with military advisers, Colorado legislators, friends, and friends of friends. Batlle was directing the war. His active military experience was limited to command of a national guard battalion in Montevideo during the one-day counterrevolution against Cuestas, and to several days in the field and then capture at Quebracho, eighteen years ago. Still, Don Pepe was the son of General Lorenzo Batlle, a hero of the Defense of Montevideo, and he was sure he could emulate his father.[1] Usually, Batlle liked to encourage his associates by giving them authority; but when great stakes were at issue, Don Pepe's confidence in his own ability made him run things himself. He had been his own campaign manager; he would be his own commander-in-chief.

There still was no news from General Muniz, who had moved out fast, with only 3,000 men, to catch Saravia. Muniz hated Saravia. Not only had Saravia replaced Muniz as the Blanco caudillo of Cerro Largo, but in '96, Chiquito Saravia, Aparicio's brother, led a filibustering expedition to Muniz' ranch while old Muniz was away and killed Muniz' teen-age son.[2] Since then party affiliation meant nothing to Muniz, whose one military plan was to go after Aparicio, catch him, and thrash him.

The first message from Muniz came on January 11. It was not the expected victory report. Muniz was moving back to Nico Pérez for reinforcements. Batlle's war plan had failed. Nationalist contingents had reached Saravia before Muniz could; Muniz, unaware, had almost begun what would have been a disastrous attack on Saravia's ranch when José Saravia, one of Aparicio's Colorado brothers, warned Muniz that his brother had many more men than Muniz did.[3] Now Saravia, with 9,000 men, was chasing Muniz toward Nico Pérez.

Saravia ordered Juan José Muñoz, who was bringing his division to join Saravia, to countermarch and get between Muniz and Nico Pérez. Juan José Muñoz did not accomplish the mission, either because Muniz had too long a lead or because Juan José Muñoz, jealous at Saravia's being the only Nationalist General, did not hurry.[4] Muniz reached Nico Pérez. Batlle wired him that he would send 7,000 men by railroad within three days. Muniz was confident that when he got those reinforcements, "the Revolution won't last long, Mr. President." [5]

No major battle had been fought, but one was in sight. This prospect, with its destruction of life, property, and Uruguay's credit reputation abroad, dismayed the conservative classes. A group of bankers and businessmen visited Batlle and advised him that the Chamber of Commerce was prepared to help negotiate peace based on an acuerdo. Batlle did not want to antagonize this influential group; he told them he doubted that an acuerdo would be possible but would permit them to interview the Colorado Executive Committee and the Nationalist Directorio.[6] Batlle had also been advised confidentially by Daniel Muñoz, Uruguayan Minister in Buenos Aires, that Argentine President Roca wanted to mediate and had ways of reaching Saravia before battle began.[7]

Batlle wanted victory, not negotiations. His offer to let the Colorado Executive Committee decide was disingenuous, for his supporters on the Committee now voted down—by a narrow margin—a motion to negotiate an acuerdo. To avoid the appearance of outright hostility to peace, the Committee did agree to hear any concrete peace proposals which the Directorio might present. The Directorio refused. It did not want to appear to be suing for peace; it also knew that no proposal acceptable to Saravia would be acceptable to the Colorados.[8]

The Chamber of Commerce peace committee dissolved itself.

President Roca's offer was not made public. Peace would come only after battle.

Saravia pursued Muniz all the way to Nico Pérez. His advisers wanted him to pull back because the Revolutionary army, grown to over 10,000 men, was still only half-armed; the rest carried old gaucho lances or nothing. The Revolution needed time for arms to be shipped over the border. But Saravia, confident that he had Muniz on the run, continued the pursuit past Nico Pérez, toward Montevideo.[9]

Batlle had kept his promise to Muniz, whose reinforced army now had 9,000 well armed soldiers. On January 14, Muniz reversed himself near the railroad town of Mansavillagra and attacked Saravia's vanguard. The Government's new machine guns hurt the Revolution; Muniz captured part of Saravia's already limited arms pack. It was now Saravia's turn to run. His badly shaken army, hard pursued by Muniz, headed back for the home county of Cerro Largo. Muniz exulted in a telegram to Batlle: "in Mansavillagra complete rout of enemy." [10]

Saravia's army could move fast. The men had spent their lives in the saddle; the army had hardly any baggage. By January 21, in spite of rain, they reached Melo. Muniz was right behind Saravia. The Revolution moved north out of Melo, toward Brazil. Muniz was sure the end was at hand, and telegraphed Batlle: "I am following the insurrectionaries who are marching in three columns toward the frontier and I will continue until I dissolve them." [11] *El Día* announced: "the war, as a war of battles, is already over." [12]

El Día was wrong; Aparicio outwitted Muniz. The Revolutionary column which Muniz followed right up to the Brazilian border, where it was temporarily interned, was composed of Saravia's unarmed and wounded solidiers. Saravia's main column had twisted south, eluded Muniz, and left him far behind.[13] For days the Government did not know Saravia's whereabouts. Then the Government realized Saravia had moved deep into the south, perilously near Montevideo. Muniz, his horses exhausted by the chase, was stranded near the Brazilian border. The other major Government army was north of the Río Negro. The Minister of War, General Vázquez, was in the field. All that was between Saravia and Montevideo was the army of General Melitón Muñoz.

Melitón Muñoz, a colorful old man, another of the illiterate caudillos of an earlier era, had been a tough guerrilla fighter in his youth and had for many years been the undisputed Colorado caudillo of Canelones, the farming department next to Montevideo. His army was made up mostly of local farmers who never had been considered good fighting men for cavalry warfare. They should be adequate, though, to block the river passes until reinforcements arrived.

Melitón Muñoz proposed to hold the pass of Fray Marcos on the Santa Lucía River, only some 80 kilometers from Montevideo. Batlle, again making able use of the railroad, sent 2,000 men as reinforcements to San Ramón, the nearest railroad point to Fray Marcos. Batlle also ordered War Minister General Vázquez to move his forces, slowly, to the central railroad line in Tacuarembó in the north. From there, Vázquez could move south quickly if Saravia—barred at Fray Marcos—turned west and headed toward the Río de la Plata, where arms and men from Argentina could reach him.[14]

Melitón Muñoz arranged his forces at Fray Marcos himself and rejected the advice of his professional artillery officer. He wanted the river between himself and Saravia, so he moved his men across the river to the south bank of the pass; by giving up the north bank he put the river between his forces and the railroad at San Ramón, where reinforcements waited. He placed his artillery right on the river bank where it would overawe the revolutionaries, but where it would be vulnerable if the revolution once forded the pass.[15] Muñoz didn't expect the Revolution to ford Fray Marcos. Saravia had already taken a terrible beating from Muniz, had been moving at forced marches, and was reported to have only 2,500 men.

On January 30, Saravia approached the pass of Fray Marcos. He moved to the north bank of the river, effectively cutting Muñoz off from San Ramón and the reinforcements. During the afternoon there were preliminary skirmishes, and the Government forces held well. Melitón Muñoz' confidence remained firm.

That night Batlle, worried that Muñoz would fight without reinforcements, sent him this order: "If you can withdraw early tomorrow to San Ramón, without inconvenience, withdraw."[16] To reach San Ramón, Muñoz would have to cross the river in the face of Saravia's rifle fire. Besides, Melitón smelled victory and wouldn't let the President deprive him of fame. When scouts reported that enemy forces had crossed the river at a pass higher up, Muñoz was sure that the men seen by the scouts were reinforcements from San Ramón on their way to aid him.

Early in the morning of January 31, the Battle of Fray Marcos began. Saravia crossed the river and attacked Muñoz' center. Simultaneously, his brother Mariano Saravia, whose men had indeed crossed the night before, fired on Muñoz' right flank. The farmers of Canelones were sure they were surrounded. Within half an hour they panicked and fled. Their General, Melitón Muñoz, ran with them. Saravia's army had crossed the river, captured Muñoz' artillery and machine guns, and was within a few miles of Montevideo.[17]

Batlle got news of the disaster from Muñoz himself, who was so close to Montevideo he called by telephone. Don Pepe realized immediately that the Revolution had taken on an entirely new outlook.[18]

Saravia was in position to attack Montevideo. Families summering on the outskirts of the capital fled back into the city, a city where people's nerves were so tense that blasting for sewer construction made them sure attack had come. The Government feared Saravia would coordinate his attack with a Nationalist Revolution within Montevideo. Nationalist politicians still in the capital were arrested. Men were dragged off the streets, inducted into the National Guard, and sent to defend the capital; the Montevideo police force was sent with them to the front around the city. Batlle and the Police Chief made public visits to the raw troops to calm them and to assure the public that all was under control.[19]

Batlle regrouped his forces. He telegraphed War Minister General Vázquez: "Nationalists want to make demonstration in front of Montevideo." He moved Vázquez and his men to the littoral by railroad and then by ship to Montevideo. To move them all the way to Montevideo by rail was dangerous, for Saravia might ambush the trains. Batlle sent Muniz to protect General Benavente's Army of the North, in case Saravia headed that way. Batlle's nerves were under control; he told Muniz: "There is much alarm here, but all should go well." [20]

On February 1, Saravia issued an Order of the Day prohibiting pillaging, as though in preparation for an attack on the capital. But Saravia did not attack, though some of his unit commanders favored it. The Revolutionary army, even with the war material captured at Fray Marcos, lacked weapons. Muniz was back on the trail. Batlle, using railroads and ships, was concentrating forces in Montevideo. Saravia could be caught between the defenders of the capital and the first class Government armies moving down from the north.[21]

Instead, Saravia moved west toward the littoral. He encouraged the disappointed: "When I have twelve thousand armed men, then we will turn around and have two or three little battles before entering Montevideo."[22] By February 5, danger to the capital had passed. The troops General Vázquez brought were sent back upriver, although the war Minister himself remained in Montevideo, where his advice might aid the President—whose war direction so far had not been brilliant.

Saravia's confident army headed into the departments of Florida and San José, gathering horses and men along the way. The army was not hurrying, for it would be several weeks before the expedition of men and arms prepared by the Nationalists in Buenos Aires could cross the river. The landing was to take place somewhere between Salto and Paysandú. When the time came for a rendezvous, Saravia would lead his army north across the Río Negro.

Victory at Fray Marcos gave new life to the Nationalists in Buenos Aires, where they had set up a War Directorio under the presidency of Rodríguez Larreta. Funds from affluent Nationalists, hard to get when the Revolution seemed hopeless, now became more plentiful. Money could buy arms, but to ship the arms out of the country required, at the least, the benevolence of the Argentine government.

Rodríguez Larreta and his colleagues were old hands at running revolutions from Buenos Aires. They knew Argentine political leaders; they knew President Roca. They explained their side of the war to Roca, already disappointed by Batlle's refusal to negotiate. They could point out that Fray Marcos had proved how wrong the Uruguayan government was when it said the Revolution could be suppressed by a police action; they, in contrast to

Batlle, wanted Argentine mediation. Argentine customs guards became less vigilant about Nationalist arms shipments.

The Nationalists had a friend inside Montevideo. At the peak of the Fray Marcos panic, Argentine Minister to Uruguay De-María asked an Argentine warship to dock at Montevideo, then called the diplomatic corps together. He seemingly wanted to propose joint foreign intervention to end the war.

Saravia's move away from Montevideo ended any immediate justification for intervention, but one residue of the panic did remain and could give Argentina the opportunity to break relations with Batlle and recognize the Revolution. Colonel Pampillon of the Uruguayan army, a Nationalist once loyal to Acevedo Díaz, had been arrested in Montevideo in the post-Fray Marcos roundup of Nationalists. Upon his release, Pampillon went to the Argentine embassy and asked for asylum. The Uruguayan government had allowed other Nationalists to leave Montevideo, but it would not grant Pampillon safe conduct because Batlle was sure he would join Saravia. The Uruguayan government insisted that Pampillon was an officer on active service and not a political prisoner eligible for asylum. Pampillon remained in the Argentine embassy while the chancelleries of both countries prepared for the next step.[23]

Although the benevolent neutrality of Argentina and the Pampillon case were victories for Nationalist war diplomacy, the Uruguayan Government had all the power advantages. The Government could buy arms anywhere in the world and pay for them with tax receipts. The Government controlled all the ports, all the railroads. The Nationalists had to buy arms in Buenos Aires, or possibly Brazil, needed to rely on voluntary contributions to pay for arms, and then must ship them surreptitiously over the border. If Batlle's spies ferreted out arms, the Uruguayan Government could demand that the Argentine Government seize the illegal shipment.

But the Uruguayan government could use its power advantages only as long as it could command support at home. This was the lesson of '97. At that time Saravia had dragged out the war until peace pressures from the conservative classes caused Borda to agree to an armistice. Meanwhile, dissident Colorados had come out against the government; dissident fury had provoked an obscure youth to assassinate Borda; Cuestas, President of the Senate, took over and made peace. The result, in spite of the Government's power advantages, in spite of Saravia's inability to win in the field, was a Nationalist victory. All these elements were again present in 1904. Saravia was prolonging the Revolution. The conservative classes wanted peace. Dissident Colorados—this time Herrera y Obes and Tajes instead of Batlle and Juan Carlos Blanco —opposed the government.

The War Directorio proposed to repeat the strategy which had been so successful before. Rodríguez Larreta and Rodolfo Fonseca called a press conference as soon as they got news of Fray Marcos. They announced the Nationalist peace program: "the political elimination of President Batlle." Even the Colorado Party would benefit from Batlle's elimination, for Batlle's followers, "citizens of little value," would be replaced by Herrera y Obes and Tajes, the real leaders of the Colorado Party. "The elimination of President Batlle would open the doors to the President of the Senate, Dr. Juan Pedro Castro, whom the National Party considers a guarantee of order and respect for all citizens as he has demonstrated on various and solemn occasions." [24]

Rodríguez Larreta was too experienced to plot against Batlle in public. What he wanted was to alert the dissident Colorados and stir them to action. He had also given the Nationalist soldiers a simple war aim: Batlle's elimination. Later, when the conservative classes put their inevitable pressure on Batlle to make peace, the Nationalists could withdraw this extreme demand as proof of their own willingness to sacrifice for peace.

Batlle was not Borda. He had no intention of giving the dissident Colorados any leeway to undermine his government; he would not let the conservative classes demonstrate for peace. Batlle had used the leeway Borda permitted to overthrow Borda, but he would not permit another to do the same to him. After all, Borda was immoral, corrupt, and politically evil; to undermine Borda was to strike a blow for liberty. Don Pepe felt that Batlle stood for the right. To undermine Batlle was a crime against legality.

Don Pepe put a tight censorship on newspapers at the very beginning of the war, causing the Directorio newspaper and even Acevedo Díaz' *El Nacional* to cease publication. After Fray Marcos, the Interdiction Law, which authorized the Executive to freeze the assets of supporters of the Revolution, was pushed through a secret session of the legislature. Batlle put hundreds of names on the Interdiction List, to stop funds from reaching Saravia. This was the first time such a ruthless—in Nationalist eyes—violation of property rights had ever been attempted during a Uruguayan revolution.[25]

Juan Pedro Castro must cease being President of the Senate. Castro had been Batlle's most influential supporter during the presidential campaign, and had been on Batlle's side in the party struggle with Herrera y Obes. But the Nationalists had invoked Castro as Batlle's successor. Nationalists and public opinion must be made to realize that they would be unable to convert Castro into a Cuestas. Castro was obliged to decline re-election as President of the Senate; Batlle's very close friend, the ailing Anacleto Dufort y Álvarez, from whom the Nationalists could expect no duplicity, was elected in his stead.[26]

Some of Don Pepe's advisers wanted him to use the traditional Colorado Generals instead of relying on Muniz, who though full of fight could not catch Saravia.[27] Don Pepe didn't trust Colorado Generals. They had ties with Tajes, and might betray Batlle in battle to let Tajes benefit from a negotiated peace. General Benavente, a line officer, did command the Army of the North, but Batlle never could bring himself to let the Army of the North do battle. Benavente, though not a comrade of Tajes, had connections with Herrera y Obes.

Batlle's house, still command headquarters, had settled down to a routine. The telegraphist passed the messages to Batlle, who went to his maps and moved the pins in accord with the received information. Batlle spent hours poring over those maps, trying to pin down Saravia. Don Pepe's sixteen-year-old son, César, a sublieutenant in the Montevideo National Guard, became a war casualty, wounded in a roundup of conscriptees.

Batlle's most immediate preoccupation was to keep Saravia from crossing the Río Negro and making his rendezvous with the men and arms about to leave Argentina. Once more, Batlle entrusted Muniz with catching Aparicio. Benavente's Army of the North was ordered to cooperate with Muniz' Army of the South.[28] On February 15, Saravia reached the pass of the Río Negro he had expected to ford to the north. Luck was against the revolution; the river was too high. Saravia could not wait for the river to come down; by then Muniz would be on him. The contingent from Argentina had crossed from Monte Caseros. For the moment, they would have to hold out by themselves.

Saravia retraced his path to the south. Muniz and Batlle debated whether Saravia was heading back to Cerro Largo or would turn back north and try to cross the Río Negro at another place. Batlle ordered Muniz to Paso de los Toros, a rail center on the Río Negro, to be ready to face Saravia when he appeared. But Saravia had once more outfoxed the Government. He had turned back north, passed near Paso de los Toros, and crossed the Río Negro at an unguarded pass—all this days before Muniz reached Paso de los Toros.

Saravia planned to capture Salto, set up a provisional government, and get recognition of belligerent status from the government of Argentina.[29] He sent part of his forces toward Paysandú, in the hope that the Government would send the Salto garrison to reinforce the city. He sent a powerful force, his rearguard, back to Paso de los Toros, to blow up the railroad bridge and keep Muniz from following.

Muniz' forces were too strong; they drove off Saravia's rearguard, crossed the bridge at Paso de los Toros, and were after Aparicio. Saravia's rearguard warned him the Army of the South was on his trail. Saravia thought the rearguard was claiming it was Muniz' whole army to justify the failure at Paso de los Toros. He was sure the forces on his trail were only the units guarding Paso de los Toros. Muniz himself must be days away.[30] Saravia let his vanguard go on ahead and rested the main force of his army, which was preparing to ford the Río Daymán at Paso del Parque on the southern boundary of the department of Salto.

At 8:00 A.M. on March 2, Muniz finally caught up with Aparicio, whose army still was south of the river. Muniz didn't bother to plan a battle. He just threw his men, as many as he could move, into a frontal attack. Since Muniz did not try to envelop the Revolution, Saravia, who by now realized his rearguard had been right, was able to hold him off until the Nationalist army crossed the river. The Revolution's rearguard put up a desperate fight. Saravia, pistol in hand, risking death, stayed in the midst of the

battle urging his demoralized men to resist. Though the army got
across, Saravia had to leave the arsenal behind.[31]

The Revolution was not yet out of danger. The river passes
ahead were too high. Saravia looked over the terrain, doubled back,
recrossed the Daymán within a league and a half of Muniz' victorious army, and sped east to safety in the department of Rivera.

Muniz never suspected that Saravia slipped by him. He sent another victory telegram to Batlle: he had recaptured much of the
material lost at Fray Marcos, 12 wagons of ammunition, a cannon;
the enemy had 100 dead and 300 wounded; he had lost 70 men;
unfortunately, his horses were exhausted. For the moment he could
not pursue the enemy.[32] It was March 12, ten days after the battle,
before the Government realized that Saravia was safe in Rivera.

Montevideo was shaken by the sight of the wounded coming
in from Paso del Parque. First Fray Marcos, now Paso del Parque,
and still the war went on. Just before Paso del Parque, Batlle had
discouraged a distinguished Argentine group which wanted to
mediate peace.[33] Perhaps now, when he ought to realize that victory really was impossible, Batlle would be more sympathetic to
negotiation.

The Archbishop of Buenos Aires personally led the peace mission to Montevideo. The Archbishop carried with him an offer
from two well-known Argentine citizens who asked Batlle to
authorize them to visit the Revolution and propose peace to it.
Batlle received the Archbishop and his colleagues, who also carried President Roca's approval of their undertaking, and promised
a formal reply to their authorization request the next day, though
his remarks left little room for hope. He told the Argentines he
would accept no return to the prewar situation: "peace now could
no longer be a truce but must be based on real submission, not to
the will of a man, but to the laws of the Republic." [34]

The next day, the Archbishop said a Mass for peace, visited
dignitaries in Montevideo, and in the evening came for Batlle's
reply. Batlle told the peace mission he would not authorize delegates to discuss peace with Saravia; he would not negotiate with
the Revolution, from it he would hear only offers of submission.
The written reply, on which Don Pepe had worked carefully,

contained a memorable phrase: "I do not have the peace. It is in the hands of those who ripped it from the niche of legality in which it reposed." [35] The delegation returned to Buenos Aires, where it announced that henceforth it would restrict its activities to assisting the Uruguayan war wounded.

The war would go on, but how much longer could Batlle hold back peace sentiment? [36] The Colorado legislators had supported Batlle's opposition to a negotiated peace—this time. But they had caucused first. Just as he refused to give army commands to the Colorado Generals, Batlle refused to take the pre-'97 Colorado political leaders into his government. Instead of expanding his cabinet, he was contracting it; only unconditional followers were left. Serrato had taken over Martín C. Martínez' Finance portfolio and kept the Fomento Ministry. Minister of Government Campisteguy was on a leave of absence. He seemed to have a nervous condition, but insiders believed he had opposed Batlle on the Interdiction Law freezing Nationalist assets. Dufort y Álvarez, recently elected President of the Senate, died. His successor, the loyal Canfield, had been elected only after a coin toss solved a tie vote.

When *El Día* claimed that the absence of public peace demonstrations proved public opinion wanted the war to continue, *El Siglo* braved closing by the censor to point out that the reason there were no demonstrations was that the Government had forbidden them.[37]

IX

No Peace

THE war was not going well for the Government. Saravia's army was in the city of Rivera, but Muniz, still exhausted from Paso del Parque, could not get together enough horses to attack the Revolution. Benavente, his Army of the North at Tambores, 155 kilometers from Rivera, wanted to go in after Saravia, but Don Pepe couldn't bring himself to commit him to action. He told Benavente that Saravia might be preparing a trick, and moved his army back to Paso de los Toros on the Río Negro. Benavente offered his resignation, but Batlle dissuaded him with the promise he would soon see battle.[1]

The Revolution made good use of its freedom from pursuit. The men and arms from Argentina, left on their own by Saravia's failure at Paso del Parque, rode into Rivera by themselves. A second arms shipment from Argentina reached Saravia by way of Rio Grande do Sul, with João Francisco's assistance. Colonel Gregorio Lamas, brother of Alfonso and Diego, a professional soldier who headed the Government Military Academy in Montevideo and had refused to revolt against Borda in '97, resigned his post and joined Saravia as Chief of Staff. On March 23, the revolutionary army, in its best shape since the beginning of the war, moved out of Rivera and headed for Saravia's home country of Cerro Largo.[2]

In Montevideo, it was rumored that Batlle was on the point of nervous breakdown. He was interviewed by a Buenos Aires

URUGUAY
War of 1904

Line of movement of Saravia's
forces – Rivera to Melo to
        Paso de los Carros ✕
Zapallar
- - - ►Abelardo Márquez
     convoy, Santa Rosa to
     Guayabos   Government
                  forces from
                 •Tambores

newsman who found him the same as ever. Don Pepe had shaved his beard, but still was the big, heavy, apathetic-looking man, still spoke slowly, harshly, and with conviction. Batlle was confident. The Government had been held back by a shortage of horses, he told the interviewer, but it was now buying horses at higher prices than the Revolution could afford. Soon the Revolution would be short of horses, especially when oncoming winter exhausted the few horses it yet had. Then, the superiorly armed Government armies, 36,000 men strong, would easily catch Saravia's 9,000 men. The Revolution's claim of having 12,000 to 15,000 men was an exaggeration.[3]

The interview was not well received in Argentina, where Batlle was accused of being oblivious to the fact he was not winning the war and indifferent to the suffering he had caused. Buenos Aires opinion was particularly incensed at his refusal to give Colonel Pampillon, two months in the Argentine Embassy in Montevideo, safe conduct to leave Uruguay. Argentine Minister De-María wanted an Argentine naval squadron to make a demonstration in Montevideo harbor. To forestall this, Batlle gave way and let Pampillon leave, though he did get official assurances from the Government of Argentina that Pampillon would be interned to prevent him from joining Saravia.[4] President Roca also gave Batlle private assurances that, once Pampillon was out of Uruguay, Argentine customs authorities would give more scrutiny to Nationalist arms shipments.[5]

Campisteguy, his nerves still not rested, resigned as Minister of Government. Here was the second most important post in the Executive and the traditional steppingstone to the presidency, but no politician wanted the job. It was likely to be the end of a career, for the Minister of Government had to administer the interdictions on Nationalist property. Once the war was over and the Nationalists recovered their political influence, Batlle's Minister of Government could have no political future.

Batlle offered the portfolio to Claudio Williman, Rector of the University and Don Pepe's choice as President of the Colorado Executive Committee. Williman had turned down the Ministry of Government before, at the beginning of Batlle's term when it was a plum. Now, upon the advice of friends, he declined again; others also declined to serve. Finally, out of loyalty to his old friend

Batlle, Williman agreed to be Minister of Government.[6] After all, he had never been greatly interested in a political career.

El Siglo, with the war bogged down, came out openly for a negotiated peace. The censor immediately advised the newspaper's publishers "the President of the Republic had resolved that the propaganda in favor of peace initiated by *El Siglo* must stop, on penalty of indeterminate suspension if continued." [7]

El Siglo's propaganda had effects. On April 11, the principal ranchers of Uruguay met in the salon of the Asociación Rural; over 80 million pesos of the nation's wealth were represented in that room—a sum five times greater than the Government budget. Ostensibly, the meeting was called to discuss recommendations to the Government and the Revolution on how the warring armies could minimize damage to ranches. The real hope was that the group could also bring the contending parties to agree on peace.

A special Ranchers' Committee was named and visited Batlle, who listened with "marked attention" to their recommendations on minimizing property damage. He assured the ranchers that the Government had already isssued such orders, but in addition would order its armies to follow the Committee's specific recommendations. The Committee, pleased with this reception, asked Batlle for permission to visit the Revolution—ostensibly to deliver the damage recommendations.[8]

The War Directorio in Buenos Aires also began explorations to see if Batlle was now prepared to make peace short of Nationalist submission. On April 17, Rodríguez Larreta arranged an interview with Daniel Muñoz, the Uruguayan Minister to Argentina. Muñoz wrote Batlle:

Doctor Rodríguez explained his project to me as follows: The basis for peace would be the constitution of a truly representative cabinet, which would be the guarantee for a policy of concord.—You would name the Blanco jefes políticos in departments you yourself chose, the Blancos would trust you to make these nominations in the proper spirit, by picking well-known citizens from the nationalist majority.— The disarmament of the revolution would be complete and would be carried out honorably, without subterfuge or mystification. The law of interdictions would be derogated.—The Government would contribute a sum to be fixed to pay for the demobilization of the revolutionary forces.—The nationalist majority would prefer the elimination of the nationalist minority from the cabinet to its own representation in the cabinet, and Dr. Rodríguez told me this would be one of the conditions least susceptible of modification.[9]

Rodríguez Larreta's peace outline in no way resembled his public peace aim—the political elimination of Batlle. He was suggesting a return to the prewar situation, camouflaged with concessions to satisfy the rank and file on both sides. The Nationalists would let Batlle choose the departments to be administered by Nationalists and no longer require him to consult formally with the Directorio on nominations of Nationalist jefes políticos, but Saravia would still control one-third of Uruguay. Batlle, in turn, would drop Romeu—the Nationalist minority long since had disappeared as a political force—and change his cabinet, but no Nationalists would enter. The proposed Nationalist concessions were a shade more substantial, and Rodríguez Larreta's mention of modifications was an intimation that the Nationalists might give up something more.

Batlle did not respond to Rodríguez Larreta. Batlle did not give the Ranchers' Committee permission to visit the Revolution (it could get to Saravia anyway). Direct negotiations or publicly authorized mediation would put the Revolution on a par with the Government. There would be bargaining, demands for an armistice, pressures on Batlle to compromise. Once more, *El Día* called for peace by submission.[10]

Don Pepe and his generals had a new plan to end the war. Muniz, whose army was still reorganizing, would start after Saravia, now in Melo, and force him to move south. Benavente's fresh army would be in the south waiting for the Revolution. It would block Saravia, force him to fight, and defeat him.[11]

Saravia's army was about to move southward out of Melo when Dr. Nin and Colonel Mascarenhas, the President and Secretary of the Ranchers' Committee, arrived. In their honor, disciplinary prisoners were released. Saravia readily agreed to their damage recommendations; then, Nin and Mascarenhas asked Saravia about peace. He reiterated the War Directorio's public war aim that Batlle's government must go, but he also told the ranchers, according to *La Nación* of Buenos Aires, that "he was in favor of peace and would always be willing to enter into agreements which would end the war." [12]

Nin and Mascarenhas felt that Saravia had authorized them to begin serious peace negotiations. They interviewed the War Directorio in Buenos Aires, whose proposals Batlle had ignored. The War Directorio was still waiting for Batlle's views; Nin and Mascarenhas returned to Montevideo. If Saravia really had enough of the war and wanted to make peace, Don Pepe was interested.

Mascarenhas, after conferring with Batlle, returned to Buenos Aires. He took Uruguayan Minister Daniel Muñoz with him to a meeting with the War Directorio. Mascarenhas proposed a possible peace plan. He began by impressing on the Nationalists that the Pact of Nico Pérez was dead and that the Government would accept no such restrictions in the future. He proposed an acuerdo giving the Nationalists the same representation they had before the war. The War Directorio agreed, provided that they got the seats now held by the Nationalist minority. Then came the heart of the matter—the departments. Vázquez Acevedo demanded the same departments the Nationalists had before the war—"the only real guarantee for the party." At this, Daniel Muñoz, in spite of his diplomatic experience, lost his temper and mutual recrimination followed.[13]

A second meeting was held that night. No better understanding emerged. On May 8, Mascarenhas sent written peace bases to the War Directorio. The Directorio formally advised Mascarenhas on May 9 that it "did not find in them suitable terms on which to begin negotiations." [14]

Undaunted, Mascarenhas returned again to Montevideo. He interviewed the Nationalist minority. Then he and Nin prepared new bases for submission to Batlle and the Revolution. The bases contained the usual provisions on amnesty, derogation of interdictions, and war claims. There could be an acuerdo, if the parties wanted one. The key to the new bases would be a statement by the Nationalist minority saying that Batlle's promises to it on coparticipation, given in February 1903, would henceforth apply to the Nationalist majority.[15] Nin and Mascarenhas carefully explained to Batlle:

. . . in respect to either general or departmental administration you will continue your policy of coparticipation without that meaning anything more than your better exercising of your institutional functions without limitations or renunciations of your full power.[16]

Batlle endorsed these preliminary bases, for they meant that the Nationalist jefes políticos would be his agents, the departments would no longer be Saravia's. The War Directorio flatly turned them down. Rodríguez Larreta wrote Nin, on May 16, that Batlle, "the one responsible for the war . . . wants only a peace solution which would mean the nullification of our party as an effective force in the politics of the nation." [17]

Mascarenhas decided to deliver the bases directly to Saravia. *La Nación* of Buenos Aires, whose Montevideo correspondent was an old colleague of Batlle's, reported:

. . . rumors of new peace attempts by persons close to the President of the Republic. It is said that momentarily an extra-official agent will leave here for the revolutionary army, carrying with him propositions for an agreement whose acceptance by Saravia would end the war immediately, before the bloody struggle which is to take place in Minas occurs.

In accord with these propositions, the revolutionary army will submit, handing over its arms and receiving $200,000 in payment. In addition, the interdiction on the property of the insurrectionary leaders and their accomplices will be lifted, a loan of five million pesos to pay war damages will be issued. Once the revolutionary forces are dissolved, the President of the Republic will reorganize his ministry in a form capable of satisfying a really national policy, eliminating Dr. Romeu. As a complement to all the foregoing, the parties will celebrate an acuerdo for the forthcoming elections in which the nationalist minority will not participate . . . Finally, the Government will have exclusive rights, without limitations, to name the jefes políticos of all the departments of the Republic, it being left to its own desires, if it considers it just, to give some of them to the party now in arms.[18]

Don Pepe was giving Saravia a decorous way to surrender. The origin of the peace proposals was in Rodríguez Larreta's original proposition to Daniel Muñoz. But the heart of Rodríguez Larreta's proposition—the departments—had been removed.

Batlle made sure no public pressures would force him to make a more attractive offer. The censor again warned *El Siglo* not to advocate a negotiated peace. Simultaneously with Mascarenhas' departure, *El Día* synthesized Batlle's official peace program: *one law, one government, one army.*[19]

Mascarenhas reached Saravia, and Saravia turned down the proposals. The War Directorio had kept him advised of its negotiations with the Ranchers' Committee;[20] the War Directorio's demand for real jefes políticos, not camouflaged departments, was Saravia's own. Saravia was not about to surrender. His southward-moving army had more attractive alternatives.

Muniz was not carrying out his mission. Instead of forcing Saravia into Benavente's path, Muniz was hanging back. The old man no longer seemed up to commanding a major army; he was especially inept at regrouping his army after battle. Batlle sent War Minister General Vázquez to the Army of the South, to ask for Muniz' resignation; Colonel Galarza, now in charge of the army's vanguard, would take command.[21]

Batlle was uneasy at the prospect of seeing Benavente do battle, for he had heard that Benavente's friends in Montevideo had written the General that Batlle was making a fool of him.[22] This information had come at the same time Don Pepe had been warned about dissident Colorado-Nationalist plots against his life,[23] and Batlle feared Herrera y Obes was behind the letters to Benavente. Saravia solved Batlle's problem. He did not want to fight Benavente. He had started south from Melo to Minas; now he reversed himself and headed northeast. This meant he was moving toward Muniz, and Muniz—as always when there was a chance to catch Aparicio—dropped his lethargy and took on speed.

Muniz caught Saravia at another river pass, Paso de los Carros on the Olimar River in the northeastern department of Treinta y Tres. This time Saravia avoided the errors of Paso del Parque. He moved his army across the river in orderly fashion and headed back to Cerro Largo.[24]

Muniz had punished Saravia's rearguard and thought he had almost finished off the Revolution. He planned a final blow in conjunction with Benavente. But within a week he confessed to Batlle that his army had no horses, no ammunition, no clothes; there were heavy desertions and many sick. Batlle finally decided to carry out Muniz' removal from command of the Army of the South and to let Galarza take over. Muniz would be given a new and smaller Army of the East, to be formed near Montevideo.[25]

Saravia's slow move to the southeast and then back to Cerro Largo had not been purposeless. Its purpose was to attract the government forces away from the littoral so that the Revolution could land the largest arms shipment of the war in the northwest corner of Uruguay. And the stratagem worked.

The War Directorio had crossed the arms to Santa Rosa del Cuareim, a tiny port at the very northwestern tip of Uruguay. Saravia's army, back in Cerro Largo, controlled the passes of the Río Negro through which the arms would come. Abelardo Márquez, the ex-jefe político of Rivera, was on his way to bring in the shipment. Saravia's orders to Márquez were to form a convoy at Santa Rosa and transport the arms, taking a route which would hug the Brazilian border. If trouble came, the arms could be deposited with Márquez' many friends in Brazil.[26] The Revolution had become expert in this technique, although never before with such large quantities of arms.

Batlle, at first, was not sure whether Márquez was coming by himself, or as the vanguard of Saravia's whole army. Benavente's army was recalled from the southeast and ordered embarked for the railroad town of Bañado de Rocha at the north of the central department of Tacuarembó. Here, Benavente could be between Márquez and Saravia.

Batlle's best information had it that Saravia was moving west to attack Salto. Batlle sent reinforcements to Salto, and urged speed on Benavente, who was still embarking his army. On May 29, word came of the attack on Salto. It was not Saravia, only Márquez. Márquez had assumed that the Salto garrison would be weak because it had sent forces to support the government's unsuccessful pursuit of Saravia in the southeast. If he could take Salto, he would achieve one of the Revolution's principal aims—a provisional capital and the opportunity for Argentina to accord the rights of a belligerent to the Revolution.[27] But Batlle, using the Government's abundant reserves and control of the railroad, had reinforced Salto.

Márquez attacked Salto all day. Then he gave up and moved east with his arms convoy. The futile attack had taken him far from the protection of the Brazilian border. The Government, if it moved fast, was now in position to intercept the convoy. Benavente's army had reached Bañado de Rocha in Tacuarembó. Batlle encouraged Benavente: "You can take the convoy, Márquez thinks that you are still in Rivera. I believe that if the convoy is taken it will give a death blow to the insurrection."[28]

Saravia might bring his army west to save Márquez; if he did, he would put himself squarely in front of Benavente. Batlle was excited. He gave Benavente freedom of action and urged him to concentrate on Saravia, not Márquez. Don Pepe even got Benavente on the telegraph line at 4:00 A.M. to go over the opportunity, apologizing: "I regret awakening you on such a cold night, but my desire that this operation be successful prevents me from sleeping well." [29]

Saravia did not appear. But Benavente's vanguard, commanded by Colonel Feliciano Viera, father of the young Batllista deputy from Salto, was in position—at Tambores about 55 kilometers south of the main body of the Army of the North—to intercept Márquez and his arms convoy. Batlle and Benavente decided to give Viera a chance to capture the convoy.

At Guayabos, six leagues from Tambores, Viera caught Abelardo Márquez unsuspecting and encamped. Viera's forces surrounded the convoy and attacked. Márquez couldn't move the wagons. He held out for two hours, then tried to burn the munitions. Viera's outfit wanted its prize; it pressed in and Márquez fled.

Viera reported exultantly that he had captured 24 vehicles with 58 cases of arms and 162 cases of ammunition, and still more to be counted. He took his trophies to Salto, instead of to Benavente, to parade them before the hometown folks. Batlle wanted to reproach Viera, but Benavente suggested that Viera deserved his day of glory.[30]

For the first time since the war's beginning, the Government had carried a mission through to complete victory. The Revolution had been deprived of the arms it so badly needed if it were to do more than run away from battle. When Saravia's soldiers learned of this disaster, what little morale they still had left from Fray Marcos would disintegrate.

Those who hoped the Nationalists would give up were encouraged by Viera's feat. In the legislature, Angel Floro Costa proposed peace based on Saravia's exile for five years. Don Pepe continued to oppose public peace efforts, efforts whose end results could never be foreseen. Floro Costa withdrew the project, explaining that Batlle "considered it inopportune at this time to raise the fantastic hopes of the enemy, who by exploiting our magnanimity and courtesy would still prolong the duration of the war." [31]

Batlle, though, had heard that Saravia was tired of the war and disgusted with the Directorio.[32] Even before the convoy's capture,

Batlle had sent Mascarenhas to Saravia to renew his decorous surrender terms.[33] As part of the peace effort, the Uruguayan Minister to Brazil journeyed to Rio Grande do Sul, got the Governor to call in João Francisco, and advised João to tell his Nationalist friends to make peace without insisting on jefes políticos.[34] On June 5, the very day the convoy was captured, Mascarenhas crossed the Brazilian border and headed for the revolutionary camp on the Zapallar River in Cerro Largo.

The War Directorio would not stand by and let Batlle try to split Saravia away from it; nor would it let Argentina think that just because a convoy had been lost the Revolution was over. The War Directorio issued another public peace proclamation. Peace base number one was "the resignation and absolute separation of don José Batlle y Ordoñez from the government of the Republic." Rodríguez Larreta followed this up with an interview in which he announced that General Tajes would make an acceptable President, once Batlle was gone.[35]

If the Revolution would not submit, ranchers and businessmen wanted once more to try to build up public sentiment to force Batlle to negotiate reasonable peace terms. Dr. Nin, President of the Ranchers' Committee, on its behalf formally petitioned the legislature to formulate acceptable peace terms, even while Mascarenhas was away [36] renewing Batlle's offer to Saravia. The legislature was, *de facto*, all Colorado since the Nationalist members no longer attended; it did not act on Dr. Nin's petition.

Nevertheless, some Colorado legislators were dissatisfied with Batlle's refusal to use Tajes and Herrera y Obes. Only a few legislators were prepared to stand up and be counted in favor of a negotiated peace, but a larger number, especially in the Senate, were prepared to open the way for peace negotiations by attacking Batlle at his weakest legal point, his censorship of peace propaganda. Batlle's general war powers were the only legal basis for his censorship since there was no specific law restricting freedom of the press.

Already, Setembrino Pereda, a nongovernment Colorado deputy, had introduced a free-press bill. On June 14, the day Pereda's project reached the Chamber floor, the Executive sent its own bill. The Executive's project gave the sanction of law to what Batlle had been doing up to now by Executive decree. The short accompanying message, signed by Batlle and Williman, explained:

> . . . the executive power desires the most ample freedom of the press,
> it recognizes the transcendental importance of the press and considers
> press criticism indispensable in times of peace; but the abnormality of
> the present moment makes compliance with this aspiration both impossible and dangerous to public order, and the executive power sees
> itself obliged, much to its own regret, to maintain, only for the period
> absolutely necessary, some of the restrictions previously decreed.

The bill ended previous censorship but forbade publication of nonofficial news of war operations and criticism of the military acts of public officials, on penalty of suspension for an indefinite period by the Executive. Sections III and IV of Article 2 forbade:

> The directing of disrespectful, personal, or offensive criticisms at
> the Chief of State insofar as they refer to the general conduct of the
> war and affect his authority and prestige.
> The advocacy of peace on any basis other than unconditional surrender to the constituted authorities.[37]

The project's bluntness gave a wonderful opening to deputies critical of the government. They attacked Batlle as a traitor to his profession of newspaperman, as a man who had used press freedom against Borda but would not now permit it. Several deputies publicly aired their belief in the necessity for a negotiated peace, the first such public statements since the beginning of the war.

Then the illustrious philosopher-essayist Rodó—originally a supporter of Juan Carlos Blanco and now a borderline supporter of the Government—used his great personal prestige to introduce a compromise proposal which prohibited "propaganda in favor of pacts which imply a violation of the constitutional order insofar as these pacts break the political unity of the country and limit any of the incumbent faculties of the public power."

Minister of Government Williman was present but could give no opinion on the compromise until he consulted the Executive Power—Batlle. The bill was sent back to committee. The Executive Power accepted Rodó's compromise—with alterations. The committee reported out the altered compromise: an apparently redundant additional clause, "or diminish its legitimate authority," had been added.

The addition was not redundant, for Rodó had intended to

permit peace agitation calling for the resignation of the President of the Republic. Ricardo Areco, formerly Rodó's colleague in support of Juan Carlos Blanco and since the war floor leader of the Batllista bloc in the Chamber, informed Rodó and the Chamber that the addition outlawed such agitation. Rodó protested. A voice vote was taken; Areco's interpretation won. Any newspaper which called for Batlle's resignation would be closed.[38]

Once more Batlle had halted an attempt to build public peace pressures. But the debate revealed a restive Colorado majority. If the war went on much longer, Don Pepe would be hard put to avoid a negotiated peace.

A basic reason for Batlle's success, even after six months of war, in holding down peace pressures was that the conservative classes could find no fault with the government's war finances. Borda's corruption and excessive spending in '97 had convinced businessmen he must go, but Batlle and his Minister of Finance were scrupulously honest. The Executive was also able to announce in mid-June that, even though it had organized the largest army in Uruguay's history, the fiscal year 1903–1904 would not be appreciably worse than 1902–1903. The expected deficit would be only 287,000 pesos.[39] This achievement was appreciated by the financial community; Uruguay's Consolidated Debt Bonds, which had been quoted at 40.60 in '97, were now at 54.80.

Economies in government offices and postponements of already budgeted expenditures played some part in the government's secure financial position, but the principal explanation was that tax collections, especially the crucial customs taxes, were holding up. Total tax collections would be some 15 million pesos, compared to the 16.1 million of the previous year.

The economy, in spite of cries of woe, was not at a standstill. Merchants were still importing and ranchers were still sending livestock to market. In fact, ranchers were sending as many livestock as they could, to keep the animals out of the hands of hungry army units.

This close-to-normal economic year, in the midst of civil war, was not due to war industry, which scarcely existed, or to the stimulating economic effects of government war spending, which went mostly for purchases abroad. The absence of large-scale destruction was the reason. The armies would take cattle to feed themselves, and all the horses they could find; soldiers dug up fence posts to burn in campfires; but there was no wholesale destruction, no scorched-earth policy.

Saravia tried to blow up railroad bridges; they were too well guarded. The Revolution did rip up a few kilometers of rails. Beyond this it did not want to go. The revolutionary army was made up of volunteers from all over the country, officered, in good part, by landowners. To destroy the countryside might in the long run weaken the government; the most immediate result would be to make the Revolution unpopular. The government armies were under strict orders to keep destruction down to a minimum. Destruction would immediately hurt tax revenues; more important, it would alienate the nation.

For no one was fighting in enemy land. This was a national, not a sectional, war. When in the first days of the war Muniz chased Saravia to Melo, Colonel Buquet, Muniz' artillery officer, proposed they bombard the town. Muniz was astounded: Why, Melo was as much his home as it was Aparicio Saravia's!

X

From Tupambaé to Masoller

MASCARENHAS returned to Montevideo. He was laconic, limiting himself to the statement that Saravia had accepted some of the peace bases and rejected others. Batlle reported to Benavente: "A rancher from Cerro Largo was with Saravia at Zapallar five or six days ago and found him very disgusted with the Directorio, saying that they had made him enter into a risky adventure and that he would have already gone to Brazil if it were not for the many people who had involved themselves because of him."[1] But it also appeared Saravia had told Mascarenhas he would not make peace without consulting the War Directorio.[2]

João Francisco appeared in Buenos Aires accompanied by Dr. Assis Brazil, prominent Rio de Janeiro politician. The Uruguayan Minister to Rio had advised João Francisco to tell the Nationalists to make peace, but he was, instead, advising them to buy arms. Assis Brazil's presence in Buenos Aires led to renewed rumors of a combined Argentine-Brazilian intervention to end the Uruguayan revolution. To counteract this, sources in Montevideo spread stories that the Uruguayan government had appealed for assistance to the United States.[3]

The War Directorio was straining its resources to make up an arms shipment to replace the one lost by Abelardo Márquez. Uruguayan Minister Daniel Muñoz had tracked the shipment's assembly point to Concordia, across the river from Salto, and he was sure it was the last shipment the War Directorio had the funds

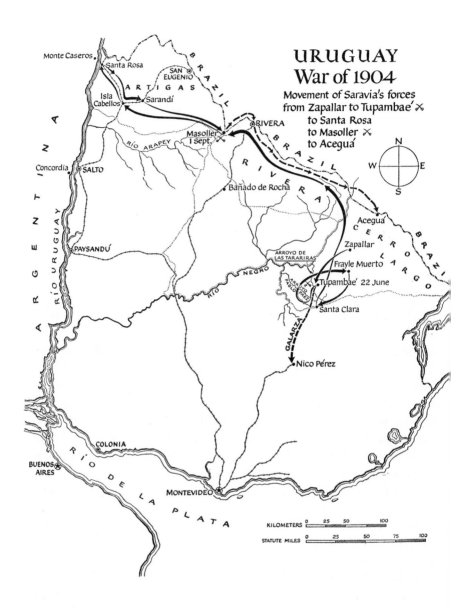

URUGUAY
War of 1904
Movement of Saravia's forces
from Zapallar to Tupambae' ✕
to Santa Rosa
to Masoller ✕
to Aceguá

to buy.[4] Batlle wanted to catch Aparicio before the arms could reach him. Saravia's army should be low on munitions and demoralized by the loss of the arms convoy. Once more, official circles announced that the war was as good as over.

Colonel Pablo Galarza was now in command of the Army of the South, his first army command. He was a younger and more cultured man than Muniz; in peacetime, he was a surveyor and published a local newspaper. He was close to the Government; Manini Ríos, the *El Día* editor, acted as his war secretary. But above all, Galarza was Colorado. At war he wore the party colors, not just a red ribbon, but red trousers, red shirt, and red hat. He accepted command "with the object of being useful to the Government and to my Party and to pursue and combat the enemy, regardless of how numerous he may be." [5]

The Army of the South, camped at Pablo Páez Creek, five leagues north of Nico Pérez, was down to 6,500 men; there had been considerable desertion and dissatisfaction with Muniz' leadership. Galarza wanted to move down to the railroad at Nico Pérez for refitting, but Batlle vetoed the idea. He would send convoys from Nico Pérez to Galarza, to prevent "the bad effect" exposure of the army's real condition would have on the public.[6] Once refitted, Galarza in combination with Benavente would move in and end the Revolution.

Benavente, at Bañado de Rocha in Tacuarembó, was eager to start east; Batlle, as always, hesitated about using him in battle. After numerous countermanded orders from Batlle, Benavente lost patience: "In a word, Mr. President, after so many different orders please tell me categorically in which direction I am to move." [7] Finally, Batlle let Benavente go toward Saravia. Then he called him back to Bañado de Rocha and ordered his army embarked for Florida in the south. Saravia, instead of running, was moving on Galarza. Batlle wanted Benavente's army near Montevideo in case Saravia broke through.[8]

The news of Abelardo Márquez' disaster had been kept from Saravia's soldiers, but soon they would find out and, unless something were done, begin deserting. The War Directorio's new arms shipment was on the way. This time the whole revolutionary army would go and get it.

Saravia called his division commanders together and outlined the situation. It was most unlikely that the Revolution could reach the littoral without encountering a government army. Should the Revolution head west and attack Benavente? Saravia had more respect for Benavente's fighting power than Batlle did, for he warned his commanders that Benavente's army recently had been reinforced. Or should they attack the Army of the South? Saravia let his commanders think that old Muniz, not the fiery Galarza, was in command and got the answer he wanted. The commanders decided to battle the Army of the South.[9]

Galarza's army was not entirely refitted but when he learned that Saravia was coming for him, Galarza lived up to the promise he made when taking command. He moved his army to the Tarariras River, squarely in Saravia's path. Galarza placed his army at the river and on Tupambaé Hill, which dominated the river, with the vanguard out in front of the hill.

Saravia was ready. He brought his army up in parallel columns, divided into left, center, and right. He personally commanded the center. Battle came on the afternoon of June 22. Saravia's cavalry charged, forcing Galarza's vanguard back to the Government's main positions on Tupambaé. The Revolution tried to take the hill, fighting desperately, first on horse, then on foot. Galarza's machine guns and artillery held them off until nightfall.[10]

During the night some of the revolutionary forces moved back. Galarza doled out the ammunition he had left—forty rounds per man. The Revolution, with even less ammunition, did the same. In the morning the Revolution attacked, attempting to retake the positions given up during the night. By mid-morning, the Revolution was so low on ammunition that it ordered a charge by lancers, as in old gaucho days. In the face of the charge, Galarza moved his machine guns, placed his artillery on the crest of the hill, and forced the Revolution back.

By afternoon both sides were out of ammunition, except for Galarza's artillery, which still fired. The Revolution, in spite of its numerical advantage, had failed to break through. Its troops moved back and left Galarza master of the field.

Galarza telegraphed Batlle in triumph:

. . . battle renewed today at 8 A.M., our forces fighting bravely until 4, at which time the enemy defeated on all the line, began retreat towards Melo, we are unable to pursue them more than two leagues for lack of horses, because of which today's battle fought completely on foot.[11]

It had been the bloodiest battle in the whole bloody history of Uruguayan wars. In two days, some 20 percent of the effectives on both sides had been killed or wounded. On Tupambaé, as elsewhere in the world, machine guns proved superior to cavalry charges.

The morning of the third day Saravia held a solemn meeting with his division commanders. Chief of Staff Colonel Gregorio Lamas advised that the Revolution was over from the military point of view, for it had no more arms. Many of the division commanders were willing to quit. Saravia felt otherwise. He had been fighting gaucho wars for a long time and knew Galarza's army was in little better shape than his own. Benavente, had he been near, would be in position to finish off the Revolution, but Batlle had moved Benavente far from the chance of battle. Galarza, Saravia expected, would move back to Nico Pérez for supplies. Saravia proposed to lead a small force—the troops of his brothers, sons, and those of Basilio Muñoz, Jr., his friend from Cerro Largo—and harass Galarza down to Nico Pérez. The bulk of the Revolution would escape to the north, yet it would look as if Saravia were pursuing the fleeing government army.[12]

It was risky. If Galarza realized that Saravia had only a handful of men with him, he could turn back, capture him, and end the Revolution. If Galarza were deceived and thought Saravia's whole army was pursuing but still was able to fight, the result would be equally disastrous.

Galarza was deceived and did not choose to fight. When scouts advised that Saravia was following, he ordered his men to stop smoking, lest their lit cigarettes give away the army's location.[13] Saravia harassed Galarza all the way to Nico Pérez, then rode back to his revolutionary army, which once more was safe in Cerro Largo.

On June 29, Saravia issued a victory proclamation. Alfonso Lamas telegraphed Rodríguez Larreta: "Hard battle 22nd and 23rd in Tupambaé. Galarza army retreated to Nico Pérez, pursued by our vanguard. 2,300 casualties estimated between both armies. Our army enthusiastic. Accept our congratulations." [14] The telegram was meant for the Buenos Aires newspapers.

Tupambaé had been a Government victory. Saravia's plan to break through Galarza and head for the littoral and new arms had failed. But Batlle exaggerated the extent of the victory. As late as June 25, while Galarza was being followed to Nico Pérez by Saravia, Batlle telegraphed Benavente: "although it is possible that after this action the insurrectionaries will begin to disband, it is also possible that they will try to continue their movements." [15]

Batlle wanted Benavente to block the passes of the Río Negro, through which Saravia could escape to the northwest. Benavente opposed this strategy, which had repeatedly failed. Benavente wanted to let Saravia cross the Río Negro. The Army of the North would be waiting and would finish off the Revolution.

This conversation occurred in the morning of June 25. Batlle thought over the question. He could not be enthusiastic: if Herrera y Obes had corrupted Benavente, Benavente might let Saravia through to the littoral. At 3:00 P.M., Batlle was back on the telegraph wire:

> I can not accede to your desire to permit the insurrectionaries to ford the Río Negro. On the contrary, you will immediately send a division to the Melo pass to prevent this. It is necessary to end the insurrection without loss of time, and to allow it to pass to the North, now that it is trapped in a zone which offers it no resources of any sort, would be to give it new probabilities of prolonging its existence. The army at your command will accomplish a considerable objective in keeping the extensive zone of the north free of the enemy, if it develops that in the course of its operations no opportunity to destroy the enemy presents itself. The battle of Tupambaé has been hard fought and it must give its fruits.[16]

Benavente replied that he was sending 1,000 men to the pass. Simultaneously, General Benavente telegraphed his resignation to the Minister of War.[17] This time it was accepted.

Batlle chose Muniz to replace Benavente. His friends in Montevideo and followers serving in the Army of the North didn't want the illiterate, old, Blanco caudillo to command the Army of the North.[18] But Batlle trusted Muniz who had no ties with dissident Colorados. He was sure Muniz, who hated Saravia, would never betray the government, and sent the old warrior up north to redeem his tarnished military reputation.

Justino Muniz

Saravia's Army crossing at Fray Marcos

Saravia leads his army into Minas

Pablo Galarza

Batlle's present war plan was the one he had favored since the beginning of the war. The Army of the North would keep Saravia from crossing the Río Negro. Galarza's Army of the South, now being refurbished at Nico Pérez, where Galarza had received a hero's welcome, would pursue, catch, and defeat the Revolution.[19]

The wounded from Tupambaé, a sobering sight, were coming into Montevideo. Batlle told Galarza: "I have been deeply saddened . . . My conscience, nevertheless, is clear, it keeps telling me that I gave no cause for this war, nor have I been able to avert it." [20]

Even the Colorado press bent before the sight. *El Día* redefined what it meant by "one law, one government, one army."

. . . within these principles, thus synthetically expressed, there fit more than peace based only on the absolute submission or the spontaneous dissolution, or the collective emigration of the rebels. On the contrary: a peace arranged on certain conditions and assured by various guarantees can fit perfectly.[21]

A grand opportunity for pressing Batlle toward peace existed. The Senate had been debating the Chamber-passed bill on wartime press restrictions. Before Tupambaé it had been hard to raise a quorum; now the sessions were well attended. With the Nationalist Senators absent, the Senate was down to ten members. For a week, voices were raised in favor of the right to agitate for peace, for mediation, for free travel by peace mediators to the Revolution. Not a single one of Batlle's former Colorado Senate colleagues cared to speak in favor of the censorship bill. Finally, on July 5, after Batlle had exerted all his influence, a reluctant majority approved the project, not on its merits but because, the majority explained, censorship under law was preferable to censorship without law.[22]

The law went into effect on July 7. On July 8, the censor closed Mendilaharsu's independent Colorado *El Tiempo* for five days, explaining:

. . . this organ of publicity, by classing as barbarous and sterile the defense which the government is making of its legal authority and of legality, and by maintaining that peace should be made at any price, tends to bring into disrepute that defense and thus contradict, in its letter and spirit, article 3 of the law on restrictions of the liberty of the press.[23]

On July 9, Rodó interpellated Minister of Government Williman in the Chamber of Deputies about the closing of *El Tiempo*. Williman went through the errors of the offending editorial line by line, and to the cheers of the gallery concluded:

. . . The Executive Power probably desires peace for the Republic more vehemently than those who preach it daily, but not being in favor of the egoistic formula—after me the deluge—it must look ahead and proceed in such a way that once order is re-established it will last long enough to prove that a formula has finally been reached which means real peace and not a mere truce with all its dismal consequences.[24]

Even with the clear indication that Batlle was opposed to outside peace negotiations, the conservative classes of Montevideo could not stand aside, after Tupambaé, and once more offered themselves as mediators. The Chamber of Commerce and the Manufacturers Association sponsored a general meeting pro-peace, attended by businessmen and independent politicians, including Herrera y Obes, Tajes, and José Pedro Ramírez.

The President of the Chamber of Commerce publicly called for peace by transaction. An executive committee was then formed, with Batlle's obvious political enemies left out. Possible peace bases were prepared. Pablo De María, a distinguished member of the now nonexistent Constitutionalist Party, presented the bases to Batlle, and Eduardo Acevedo carried the same bases to the War Directorio in Buenos Aires.[25]

For the moment, Batlle was asked to examine, not approve, the bases, which called for amnesty, an acuerdo, the end of interdictions, and disarmament of the Revolution. On Jefaturas in the departments, the bases were intentionally imprecise. Batlle would be asked to announce that at the war's end he would give

. . . to citizens of the revolutionary party the same participation in the departmental administrations they had before the war. This should not be interpreted to mean that there are regions in the country belonging to one party and regions belonging to another, nor in any way to impair the integrity of the government or the unity of the nation; but it should be recognized that, after a bloody struggle like the one whose patriotic end we are seeking, it is a sound political principle not to designate as delegates of the Executive Power persons who are separated, by political reasons, from the great majority of citizens who inhabit these departments.[26]

Batlle heard De María out, consulted with his cabinet, and announced that permission to publish the peace bases was denied.

Acevedo returned from Buenos Aires with the War Directorio's approval of the bases, subject to consultation with Saravia. However, the War Directorio wanted Government authorization to send its delegation to Saravia by way of Montevideo. De María and Acevedo visited Batlle to secure his consent. Batlle refused, though his written refusal was far less categorical than his statement to the Archbishop of Buenos Aires in March:

The President of the Republic persists in his resolution prohibiting transit through Montevideo to the revolutionary army by delegates of the Revolution; but explaining that he does this purely for military reasons, he adds that he looks with favor on the efforts being made in favor of peace, and that he would not be opposed to an acuerdo made under acceptable conditions. Nevertheless, he recognizes that the arranging of such an acuerdo would not enter into his attributes. Neither would he be opposed to a policy of coparticipation, so long as the form in which it would be made effective would not present a danger to peace.[27]

The War Directorio, advised of Batlle's refusal to authorize free passage, offered to send a delegation to deal directly with the Government. The War Directorio's goal was obvious: it wanted Batlle to acknowledge, in one way or another, that the Revolution was an organized force which must be treated on a government-to-government basis. The peace mediators would not transmit the War Directorio's proposition to Batlle. They urged it to consult directly with Saravia, without free passage through Montevideo. This the War Directorio refused to do.[28] Another attempt to negotiate peace had failed.

As Benavente had foreseen, the plan to keep Saravia penned up in Cerro Largo until Galarza could fall upon him failed. Galarza could not move. Muniz did not block off the Río Negro.

Galarza's army, weary from Tupambaé, started into Cerro Largo, but by July 17 Galarza confessed to Batlle:

I communicate to your excellency that as a result of the two forced marches made with the objective of catching the enemy, many horses were worn out . . . I consider it impossible for me to approach Melo and remain in condition to follow any movement of the enemy. I have been obliged to put corps of the line in with men of many divisions who have been deserting taking arms with them.[29]

Muniz' Army of the North was still at Bañado de Rocha on the railroad at Tacuarembó. The old Blanco caudillo could not get cooperation from his disgruntled Colorado staff officers. Muniz sent forces to cover the passes of the Río Negro, but the forces moved with inordinate slowness, seemingly out of spite for Muniz. As a result, the Revolution crossed the Río Negro, over a bridge specially constructed by Carmelo Cabrera. The whole Revolution, hugging the Brazilian border as Abelardo Márquez was supposed to have done, was heading toward the littoral and the War Directorio's arms shipment—the same objective which had caused Saravia to fight Tupambaé.

Muniz was still in an excellent position to stop Saravia from reaching the littoral. On August 2, Muniz assured Batlle that he had blocked off all the fordable river passes between his army and Saravia. That remained to be seen.

What could be seen by anyone who would look was the big arms shipment the War Directorio had assembled in Concordia, Argentina, on the River Uruguay, a shipment the War Directorio would send across the river when Saravia arrived to receive it. Batlle even got word a battery of six Krupp cannons had left the Buenos Aires arsenal for shipment to the Revolution.[30] Such transparent complicity could mean only that Argentine President Roca was throwing his support to the Revolution.

Batlle had to do something. On August 2, Acevedo Díaz, Uruguayan Minister in Washington, asked Secretary of State John Hay for an immediate private audience with President Theodore Roosevelt "about a transcendant matter which admits no delay." [31] Roosevelt saw Acevedo Díaz and passed him on to Hay. What transpired at the Acevedo Díaz-Hay interview was not recorded. Years later Batlle explained:

. . . the Uruguayan Minister in the United States was asked to advise the government of that country that ours would be pleased to see the presence of American ships and the influence it was willing to exercise in the Plata, so that the countries there would observe the neutrality required of them.[32]

Secretary of State Hay noted, of his interview with Acevedo Díaz: "I declined all his requests for cause." [33] The United States was not disposed to intervene between Uruguay and Argentina.

Word of the Uruguayan appeal reached Argentina. On August 4, the American Minister in Uruguay, William Rufus Finch, complained to Washington that he had been quoted in the Montevideo and Buenos Aires press as saying the United States would not permit outside intervention in Uruguayan affairs. "These publications have had the effect their authors desired, but they do me an injustice, and would have been publicly repudiated except for my dislike to go into the newspapers to confirm or deny publications I am unable to trace to official sources." [34]

Batlle had put Argentina on notice that he was advising foreign chancelleries of President Roca's embarrassing complicity with the Uruguayan revolutionaries. And Batlle was also telling Argentina that he would try to widen any attempt at forced mediation by bringing in the United States. The last thing Argentina wanted in the Plata was direct American influence.

The arms, though, were waiting for Saravia if he could break through Muniz, and, should he get them, he would be formidable. After Tupambaé, Batlle had bent before the public peace pressures of the Chamber of Commerce group. To avoid another Tupambaé, he decided to renew the peace terms Mascarenhas had taken twice before to Saravia; but this time Batlle was offering more than decorous surrender. Mascarenhas could offer three or four real departments.

Batlle would have liked someone besides the unsuccessful Mascarenhas to carry the new offer to Saravia. Don Pepe twice asked Ramón de Silveyra, a well known Rio Grande do Sul rancher, to serve. Ramón de Silveyra declined, for he felt that anything short of the old jefaturas in the old departments would be unsatisfactory to Saravia. Mascarenhas, ever willing to bring peace, agreed to try once more. After Tupambaé, he was no longer an extra-official mediator; now he was going as Batlle's direct representative to the Revolution.[35]

In spite of his cares, Batlle continued his practice of showing himself publicly, as a visible sign the war was going well. Don Pepe, in the company of Matilde and their two youngest children, took his regular afternoon ride on August 6. It was winter, so they used a closed coach. They were traveling slowly on their usual route through suburban Montevideo. Then there was an explosion. Cobblestones, trolley rails, and dirt flew up in front of the horses; fortunately, the coachman kept the team from bolting.

Until the coachman advised that the explosion was serious, Don Pepe thought that a child must have been playing with gunpowder. Someone had exploded a mine, but because the mine had been poorly made or detonated too soon it went off before the coach was on top of it and did no harm.[36] The plot against Batlle's life, about which he had been repeatedly warned, had come and failed.

The family returned home. Batlle calmly explained the details to his aides. Actually, he was rather pleased, for he could feel he had taken direct part in the war. When his son César had been wounded, Don Pepe told Arena he felt relief that some of his family's blood had been spilled. Now Batlle answered Galarza's congratulations on his escape: "proud of sharing the danger, even if in minimal part, of the defense of legal institutions with the valiant soldiers who sustain it." [37]

The police rounded up the obvious suspects, and quickly found the perpetrators. The War Directorio, at first suspect, was not involved. The man behind the plot was Osvaldo Cervetti, who had been implicated in the 1902 plot against Cuestas' life. Cuestas had suspended Cervetti from his job in the customs house for dishonesty. Batlle just recently had refused to reinstate him.

Cervetti had hired an "expert" to make the mine. The expert hired an Italian immigrant, who was oblivious to Uruguayan politics, to hide in a rented house and detonate the mine when the President's coach passed over it. Cervetti assured the expert that once Batlle was out of the way Tajes would become President and he, Cervetti, would be restored to his rightful place in the bureaucracy.[38]

No one higher up than Cervetti could be connected to the plot. Tajes testified that he scarcely knew Cervetti. The police kept watch on Tajes, Herrera y Obes, and their followers, but no ramifications developed.[39] The matter was now one for the criminal courts.

August 6 might have been for Batlle what August 25 was for Borda. Had the mine succeeded, it could have exploded Uruguay's future into a different direction. As it turned out, the abortive assassination plot was just an incident. Batlle was back directing war operations that evening.

Muniz failed again. Saravia was near the city of Rivera, within easy reach of the Army of the North, but Muniz' vanguard, commanded by Colonel Rodríguez, just wouldn't catch up with the Revolution. On August 13, Muniz telegraphed Batlle that Rodríguez' delay was inexplicable. "I fear political tricks from circles hostile to Your Excellency." [40]

The truth was out. Saravia had gone right through Muniz' army —just what Batlle had feared Benavente might let Saravia do. Saravia was now on the way to the littoral, new arms, and new hope. Muniz, his army half on foot, was painfully trying to catch up with the Revolution. Muniz offered Batlle his resignation.

The Revolution captured a railroad train at Isla Cabellos junction in the department of Artigas, and Saravia invited his vanguard to take a ride. The vanguard appeared before and easily captured Santa Rosa del Cuareim, the same tiny port in the extreme northwest where Abelardo Márquez had assembled his ill-fated convoy. The arms were sent across the river and landed without difficulty. The Revolution recorded the distribution of 1,344,650 rounds of ammunition and 1,906 rifles.[41] Three cannon and three machine guns also came across the river.

It was a glorious moment for the Old Corporal, the troops' name for Saravia. He had kept the Revolution going for eight months. He had just come through two Government armies in the middle of winter. The Revolution, finally, was ready to give a good account of itself in battle.

Batlle prepared his response to Saravia's success. Galarza's army, in a remarkable movement, was sent from Nico Pérez to Salto by way of Montevideo in one day. The next day, August 22, Batlle entrusted War Minister General Eduardo Vázquez with the embarrassing task of once more accepting Muniz' resignation. Vázquez himself—there was no one else who could be trusted—would have to take command of the Army of the North.

American presence could make Argentina less willing to let future arms shipments through to Saravia. On August 23, at the request of Uruguayan Foreign Minister Romeu, American Minister Finch advised Washington:

> Uruguay confident revolution would not have lasted two months except for assistance from contiguous Republics, and confident of ability to crush it within a month if this were cut off. Uruguay does not ask or expect help. Sufficient resources available. No peace negotiations are pending. Moral influence of United States expressed in some form or shown in some way would, President thinks, be effective in stopping further aid from border neighbors to insurrectionists. Light draft vessel could make friendly tour of observation and offend nobody.[42]

Alvey Adee turned the dispatch over to Secretary of State Hay with the notation: "Remembering the Uruguayan minister's visit to you, I send you this. The Navy tells me there is no ship of any kind nearer than the Cape of Good Hope, but that some ships will be on the South Atlantic coast about September 3rd." Hay answered: "I declined all his requests for cause. But if a vessel could look in there sometime, it might do no harm." [43]

Minister Finch must have expected a favorable reply, for on August 19 the American Consulate in Montevideo announced the impending arrival of a naval squadron.[44]

On August 21, Batlle moved Galarza to Salto. On August 22, Batlle sent General Vázquez to the Army of the North. On August 23, Finch wired Washington. On August 24, Mascarenhas, Batlle's peace emissary, accompanied by Dr. Nin, reached Saravia's camp, near the railroad stop of Sarandí in the department of Artigas.

Mascarenhas and Saravia conferred in Saravia's tent. Batlle had authorized Mascarenhas to tell Saravia that if the Revolution made peace without fighting another battle, he would give the jefaturas of three or four departments to the Nationalists, although he would not formally consult with the Directorio on nominees. The departments could not be on the Brazilian frontier and Batlle would feel free to send army units into the new Nationalist departments. The

Acevedo Díaz Nationalists could have two departments, so that, ostensibly, there would still be six Nationalist departments.[45]

Saravia, as always, listened courteously. Batlle had come around to accepting the heart of Rodríguez Larreta's proposal to Daniel Muñoz, made in April. Still, if Saravia made peace now, he would have to turn in all those new arms. Batlle had given much after Tupambaé, he would give more after another Tupambaé. If Saravia beat one of Batlle's armies in battle—quite possible with the new arms—Batlle would give very much more. Saravia told Mascarenhas that the government would have to disband the new army units formed in 1903 before he could make peace. The revolutionary army was breaking camp, ready to move out. Saravia saw Mascarenhas off with the words: "Continue working . . . don't be discouraged . . . peace must come and will come."[46]

The Nationalist officers knew that Mascarenhas had come about peace but Saravia kept Batlle's specific offer to himself, lest his officers urge him to accept it. Saravia did tell his son Nepomuceno that the deal was "to divide the orange in half"—which sounds like three jefaturas. Saravia told his son it was a pretty good offer but that he wanted to move to Rivera before making peace. In Rivera, they could pass over a good many of the new arms "to our friends in Brazil" instead of turning them over to the government.[47] The arms would be waiting in Brazil for the next revolution.

By the time Mascarenhas reached Montevideo, events had dated Saravia's answer to Batlle's peace terms. The reaction in Montevideo, though, was that Saravia had rejected them outright. *El Día* bristled:

> We are aware, as are all those persons who have intervened in the peace efforts, that the President of the Republic has been prepared to make various concessions, and that the good will of all those involved has been dashed against the criminal obsession of Saravia, who does not want to hear of anything unless he is given the six jefaturas he had before, *exactly the same ones as before;* if the jefes políticos are not named after previous Consultation, if the urbana military companies [militarized prison guards used as Nationalist cadres] are not left in those same departments, and if it is not clearly stipulated that the armies of the government under no circumstances can violate Saravista territory.[48]

Saravia was moving from the littoral to Rivera, taking the same route by which he had come. The Army of the North, on the railroad line in Tacuarembó and Rivera, would almost have to retreat to avoid meeting the now well-armed Revolution. The Army of the North had never fought a battle. General Vázquez, its new commander, arrived on August 27, and took over 7,500 poorly armed men from Muniz.[49]

Batlle demanded of Galarza that he hurry his army out of Salto and rush to the aid of the Army of the North:

> In the current state of affairs, my greatest preoccupation is the possibility of a conflict between the army of the North and Aparicio and I expect that you will be alert to see that it does not come to pass without the presence of the army at your command or a considerable part of it, because the change of generals and other circumstances like the present dispersal of its forces make me fear that it may not be in condition to combat with complete certainty of success.[50]

Vázquez moved his army west to the Arapey River to meet Galarza. Instead of Galarza, Vázquez saw—with his own eyes—Saravia moving east. Vázquez notified Batlle:

> I am moving back but I believe I will not catch him because he is reasonably well mounted and I mostly on foot. I know nothing of Colonel Galarza, but I suppose he will make himself felt by tomorrow . . . I found only 200,000 rounds of ammunition in the arsenal. There remain 25 in reserve for each soldier. As I was far away from communications with you, I asked Colonel Galarza for another 200,000 rounds, which I now believe it will be impossible for him to send me because of the direction he is taking.[51]

Batlle really preferred that Vázquez not catch up with Saravia for, as Batlle had admitted to Galarza, he didn't think Vázquez' army was in condition to win. Batlle wired a message to Vázquez, to be carried into the field by courier:

> It is advisable that you let Galarza proceed with the most independence possible. It occurs to me that if Aparicio comes south leaving you behind and you are unable to use the Central Railroad because it is intercepted, perhaps the shortest route of return would be to move your army to the Railroad Station at Arapey [in Salto], in order to take the railroad to Paysandú and from there to Montevideo by river. You could, nevertheless, take another route if you consider it more convenient.[52]

Batlle's message, with the intimation that Vázquez get out of Saravia's way and let Galarza carry the pursuit, was sent out at

1:00 A.M. on September 1. It would not reach the Army of the North for several days. The burden of decision rested on Eduardo Vázquez, a veteran soldier and a brave man, but no fool. Only five days ago, Vázquez had taken over a dissension-filled army. As Minister of War, Vázquez knew that victory by Saravia, or even another Tupambaé, could mean peace on Saravia's terms. But if Vázquez let Saravia through to parade in front of Montevideo, the Government's cause would be as deeply hurt.

On August 31, Vázquez reported to Batlle. The Army of the North was near Cuchilla Negra on the Rivera border. "My scouts have advised me of the location of the enemy. I will march on him as best I can." [53]

In Montevideo, those in the know were tense. There was danger in the North, there was danger at the Capital. From Argentina, breaking his promise to President Roca, Colonel Pampillon—the man whom Batlle had tried to keep from asylum in Argentina— had embarked in launches with the southern Uruguayan port of Colonia his destination. Pampillon planned to harass Montevideo.[54] Part of Pampillon's plan seemed to be a plot on Batlle's life, for the Montevideo police uncovered a plot to cut the electricity to Batlle's house, simultaneously with Pampillon's landing, as a prelude to assassination. Nationalist Deputy Joaquín Silvan Fernández, the suspected organizer of the plot, fled to asylum in the Argentine Consulate.[55]

Batlle's agents in Argentina had been following Pampillon, and had bribed the captains of his launches, who allowed the launches and their supplies to be captured.[56] Pampillon eluded capture and landed, but was reduced to hiding in the hills. All had been foiled in Montevideo, but what of Vázquez?

Vázquez' vanguard got to Cuchilla Negra ahead of Saravia. The vanguard was arranged behind a curving, four-kilometer long, double line of rocks at Masoller, the very tip of a deep triangle made by the Brazilian border and Rivera. Saravia's route was blocked, but he made no effort to dislodge the Government's vanguard. If Eduardo Vázquez wanted a fight, he could have it.[57]

The morning of September 1, Vázquez brought up the bulk of his army, practically on foot. He had time to place his men and artillery in good positions. The Revolution's problem was to flank or overpower Vázquez. The terrain made it impossible for Saravia to use all his men. Instead, he used half his army, leaving the other half in reserve.

Saravia began the attack at 3:00 P.M. The fighting was more bloody than Tupambaé, for this time the Revolution had artillery too. Saravia tried to flank Vázquez and failed. Then came the frontal attack. Vázquez held.[58] By late afternoon, firing had slackened off.

Saravia was confident that he would win when fighting resumed in the morning, for he had fresh reserves and ammunition, while Vázquez did not. To encourage his forward elements to maintain their positions and not move back after nightfall, Saravia was inspecting the front lines. A group of Government soldiers were taking long shots at the enemy. Saravia's horse was hit. So was Saravia, who gripped his leg. His son rushed up to him: "Is it your leg?" "No, damn it, it isn't." [59] He had been hit in the chest. They took him off his horse; a stretcher was fashioned. They brought him back behind the lines.

Colonel Gregorio Lamas, Chief of Staff, approached Saravia, who ordered him to use the fresh divisions the next day. It was impossible to keep secret the news that Saravia had been wounded. Colonel Lamas came back with word that the division commanders wouldn't fight without Saravia.

Saravia had been the only General in the Revolution. Although jealous of others, he also knew the men had come to fight under him, not some other General. Saravia regularly did things foolhardy for a Commanding General to do: he risked his life in battle; he led the vanguard; he inspected the front lines. His foolhardiness caught up with him at Masoller, but until then it had made his volunteers feel the Old Corporal was looking after them.

The division commanders were mutually jealous. Many of them had only tolerated Saravia. They didn't like the way he kept all his plans secret, the fact that he always picked members of his own family to lead battles; they had little respect for Saravia as a strategist. Eight months of war, distress, failure—and now this. The division commanders would not fight under the technician, Colonel Lamas.[60]

Instinctively the Revolution moved north into Brazil, out of the way of Vázquez and Galarza's arriving army. Saravia had seen the same thing happen when his brother Gumersindo, Chief of the revolutionary forces in Rio Grande do Sul, was killed. He told his son:

The Army is going to dissolve; don't accept any post of command; stay with them and try to save five hundred rifles, and we'll win later with those.[61]

They carried Saravia to Brazil, to the ranch of João Francisco's mother. Dr. Lussich, an eminent Montevideo physician serving with the Revolution, tried to save Saravia's life.

On the morning of September 2, General Eduardo Vázquez, doubtless relieved, watched the last of the Revolution cross into Brazil. He moved his forces to the positions which the day before had been held by the Revolution. Vázquez realized he had won the victory which should end the war.

Batlle got his first information on the battle from Antonio Bachini, editor of *Diario Nuevo*, who had left his newspaper to head the garrison guarding the city of Rivera. Bachini telegraphed on September 2: "If the news have just received is correct, the war is over." [62] He went on to tell Batlle that the Revolution had been defeated and had moved into Brazil, taking along the wounded Saravia. On September 3, Vázquez wired news of his triumph to Batlle. By September 4, rumors that Saravia had died reached Montevideo.

Batlle took no chances. He ordered the garrison at Rivera reinforced, in case the Revolution tried to take the city. On September 5 and 6, the Revolution was reported coming out of Brazil and entering the department of Rivera. Batlle ordered Galarza, whose army finally had arrived on the scene, to pursue the enemy.

On September 7, Batlle received confirmation of Saravia's death. Don Pepe's friend, the painter Pedro Figari, in charge of medical assistance to the Government armies, was with Batlle when the news came. Figari saw tears in Batlle's eyes, and heard Don Pepe say: "Poor man! Political passions have driven him to the sacrifice, and he is *un gaucho bueno*." [63]

The revolutionary army could scarcely be called an army any longer. No one had taken responsibility for the march into Brazil, and once there the men began to desert. The division commanders met, tried to name a Commander in Chief, but could not agree; João Francisco got them to accept a temporary triumvirate. They moved back to Uruguay, undecided as to what the army should do. As they crossed the border, entire divisions took off. They turned into Brazil, coming out again at Aceguá in Cerro Largo. There Basilio Muñoz, the only one of the triumvirate still nominally in command, made the bitter decision which none of the other commanders could bring himself to make. Basilio Muñoz began to sue for peace.[64]

On September 10, emissaries of the Revolution came to Comandante Machado in Rivera with a written request that Machado, a Government officer respected by the Nationalists, ask Batlle for an armistice. Machado conferred with Batlle by telegraph:

BATLLE: I would like to suspend operations immediately so that not another drop of blood be shed. You, who know me well, know that I am not a man with party hatreds and that I am one of the most ardent and convinced friends of peace. All my ideas and all my feelings would make me order the immediate suspension of hostilities. But such a suspension if not effected on the basis of previously known and accepted bases of agreement would be very imprudent and instead of diminishing could greatly increase bloodshed. Transmit these bases to me and if they are acceptable I well hasten to have hostilities cease.

MACHADO: They tell me that they do not know the bases on which Saravia negotiated with the [Mascarenhas] commission; by the conversation I had with them I know that peace is a certainty; they want it. If Your Excellency authorizes me, I could go to their camp, since they do not ask for jefaturas or the lifting of interdictions. They ask general amnesty. They talk of an electoral acuerdo for the coming elections in order to tranquilize the country. They promise to turn over all their arms and arsenal and not move from the place they are in until everything is settled . . . the only thing that they will ask is that the jefatura of Cerro Largo go to a Colorado, not to one of the Muniz faction. I believe, Mister President, that these negotiations could be completed in two days while your army halts; I could promise to leave tomorrow at dawn and the day after tomorrow Your Excellency would have the definitive bases.

BATLLE: I have to consult and think. The night is long and we have all of it to arrange this matter . . . Stay close because I will have to talk with you.

At 12:45 A.M., Batlle was back on the line:

The bases I would accept are these:

    1st. General Amnesty.

    2nd. Electoral legality: acuerdos would depend upon the deliberations of the party directive commissions.

    3rd. Lifting of interdictions.

4th. Acceptance of the legal authorities by the forces now in arms against them.

5th. Complete and effective handing over of their arms and arsenal by those forces to the Minister of War who will go to the place of disarmament for the purpose.

6th. If these conditions are accepted, the forces in arms will camp in the place where acceptance occurs and will communicate the location to the commander of the Army of the South which will camp a league's distance away, from that moment hostilities will be suspended.

7th. During the entire time before disarmament, the forces in arms against the Government will not receive incorporations of men, or arms, or munitions, or horses; the approach of these elements of war will be sufficient cause for declaring that hostilities have broken out.

8th. The forces in arms against the Government will not be allowed to move camp or begin to march for any reason without the approval of the general in command of the Government army.

In addition, you can advise Señores Vincente Ponce de León and P. Soria [the Revolution's envoys] that, according to their indication that a Colorado and not a member of the Muniz faction be named Jefe Político of Cerro Largo, a Colorado who will give guarantees to all will be named.

Machado said that the Revolution would want a little money to pay passage home for its soldiers. Batlle preferred that the Government transport the soldiers: "It has always seemed demoralizing to me to give money to the insurrectionaries at the end of a war." [65]

Bachini was with Machado at Rivera and thought Batlle's terms too generous. He was confident the Revolution could be wiped out militarily and feared the negotiations were just a stall for time. Batlle advised Bachini to reread his concessions: "you will see that they are limited to general amnesty and lifting of interdictions." [66] Vázquez had been plugged in on the Batlle-Machado telegraphic conference. He, quicker than Bachini, realized immediately Batlle's terms "meant practically submission." Batlle had really given the Revolution nothing: no departments, not even an acuerdo, for he had said it would be up to the Colorado organization to make an acuerdo if it wished. Nevertheless, to assure that the peace negotiations could not be used to gain time, Batlle instructed Machado to add a ninth clause: disarmament must begin within 48 hours after acceptance of these terms.

The envoys left for the Revolution, followed by Galarza and Vázquez at the head of their armies. The envoys asked for more time. It was granted. The War Directorio, ignored in the peace negotiations, called for continuation of the war; [67] the Revolution moved in and out of Brazil. Batlle began taking precautions.

Then peace news started coming in. Telegrams on September 19 and 20 announced a meeting of the revolutionary commanders. On September 21, Basilio Muñoz, for the Revolution, accepted Batlle's terms in principle but advised that the Revolution would propose additional bases.

The eleven additional bases demanded everything from constitutional reform to jefaturas and concluded with a requirement that the War Directorio approve all peace terms; but these bases were merely for later propaganda purposes.[68] Basilio Muñoz advised Batlle "you can discard or modify whatever you judge convenient in the amplified bases proposed by the revolutionary commanders with the certainty that I will accept everything. Peace is a great and patriotic accomplishment and we will accomplish it." [69]

On September 23, Batlle formally rejected the additional bases and informally thanked Basilio Muñoz for his telegram. Galarza, in charge of negotiations on the scene, was authorized to assure the Revolution that the Red Cross, at government expense, would transport its soldiers to their homes and give them spending money. Galarza advised Batlle that the Revolution had accepted his terms. All it asked was that instead of the Red Cross—a humiliation—some mixed commission oversee the trip home. Batlle agreed.[70]

Montevideo went wild in jubilation. Batlle had not permitted victory celebrations during the war, out of respect for the dead on both sides, but today was different. In the morning, a crowd of students cheered Batlle; at night a large demonstration marched by his house. Batlle improvised a response to the demonstrators:

Fellow Citizens: Peace is on the horizon of our country, accompanied by its splendid court: liberty, legality, progress, civilization!—The blood of our compatriots no longer is shed—I understand your aspirations, I share your joy.—I have been able to feel the weight of our misfortunes, of our sorrow.—Let us vow that this sorrow may be a great lesson for us: that no longer shall we settle our disputes on the battlefield, that we shall always settle them at the ballot box, on the field of the law.

Accompany me in giving a Viva for the soldiers of legal institutions.

In giving a hurrah, as sorrowful as enthusiastic for those who have fallen in their defense.

And in deploring the fate of those who, fighting for what they believed to be a patriotic ideal, have also fallen, gone astray on the not always clear path of duty.[71]

Vivas rang out. Don Pepe had scarcely remonstrated the soldiers of the Revolution, "gone astray on the not always clear path of duty."

For a while it seemed that jubilation was premature. Stories spread that the surviving Saravias refused to surrender, that Basilio Muñoz, the peacemaker, had been killed. Vázquez and Galarza were sent back into action. Soon it developed that everything would be all right: some of the Revolution's commanders had been unable to allow themselves to be sent home by the Red Cross as charity cases; when assured that the Red Cross would not be in charge, they reconsidered.

On October 3, Batlle authorized a new armistice and new disarmament terms. A mixed commission, instead of the Red Cross, would send the defeated troops home. The Government agreed to contribute 100,000 pesos to the commission and to allow a public subscription of another 50,000 pesos. Individuals who had collected taxes on behalf of the Revolution would be included in the amnesty. The Revolution would not have to suffer the additional humiliation of giving up its arms to General Eduardo Vázquez, the embodiment of the disaster at Masoller; instead, Galarza would be in charge.[72]

On October 5, by way of Nico Pérez, renewed good news came. The Revolution, except for Saravia's brother Mariano, who was emigrating to Brazil, had accepted Batlle's revised terms. The Chamber of Commerce Peace Committee gave the War Directorio an opportunity to assent to the peace, and so salvage its formal authority.[73]

On October 15, amnesty and the end of interdictions were approved by the legislature and became law. Those revolutionaries who were willing to go through the shame of it turned over what rifles they could not hide, got their money, and went home. In Montevideo, there were parades and proclamations. The arrival of four American warships was scarcely noticed. The Argentine Minister to Uruguay was recalled and replaced. Uruguayan Minister to Argentina, Daniel Muñoz, whose son had been killed at Masoller, no longer would have to protest Nationalist arms shipments. The War Directorio quietly shut its offices in Buenos Aires. Don Pepe closed down the telegraph lines in his house. It was all over.

The compelling conjecture about the War of 1904 is what would have happened had not Saravia been hit that first afternoon at Masoller. The Nationalist version was that Vázquez had prepared telegrams for Batlle announcing he would have to retreat if the Revolution attacked on the second day.[74] Batlle, years afterward, asserted: "The insurrection was finished with Saravia or without Saravia. The long-awaited moment had come when the forces of the government had more mobility than the insurrection, because of the shortage of horses in the country." [75]

What-might-have-been can never be known with certainty, but the most likely end to the War of 1904, had Saravia lived, would have been a peace with the Nationalists in a political position resembling their prewar stance. Had he won at Masoller, Saravia doubtless would have demanded more departments than he had in 1903, or, as he liked to put it, stronger Nationalist positions of force. But Vázquez did stop Saravia, a point the Nationalists forget. Saravia was killed, the Revolution dissolved. Batlle, the director of war operations, imposed a victor's peace. Batlle was now the war hero of a victory-proud Colorado Party. Batlle had reestablished unquestioned Colorado control of Uruguay.

Batlle contributed to the victory. He and Serrato were first-rate quartermasters; the Government armies were well equipped, and Batlle made very effective use of the railroads. Batlle's greatest contribution to the victory was his ability to withstand the pressures for a negotiated peace, and, in withstanding, bring the Government's superior war powers to bear on the Revolution. Batlle did not do well as a strategist. His misplaced trust in Muniz and misplaced distrust of Benavente prolonged the war and, before Masoller, endangered its outcome.

Saravia was a poor battlefield commander, but a magnificent guerrilla. He kept the war going for eight months; time after time, he outwitted stronger Government armies. There were only two major battles—Tupambaé and Masoller—in 1904. They were fought because Saravia wanted to fight; they came when new government army commanders were not ready for battle. Had a less tough opponent than Batlle been President of the Republic, Saravia long since would have won a negotiated peace. The military power of the Government was so much greater than the Revolution's that a negotiated peace would have been a victory for Saravia.

It is sometimes claimed that the War of 1904 represented a struggle by the urban proletariat led by Batlle, against the feudal landowners of Saravia. To see the war this way is to use warped hindsight. Batlle's armies were better supplied than the Revolutionaries, but other than that, there was little difference between them. Both sides were made up mostly of men from the interior, both had contingents of peacetime police. The Government also had the regular army units. Saravia had fewer line officers and more rancher-caudillos than the Government; still, the head of the Military Academy, Colonel Lamas, was Saravia's Chief of Staff. The Government had its own set of rancher-caudillos, topped by its principal General, Justino Muniz. Both sides had their contingents of university students and older politicians. Some of Saravia's own brothers fought on Batlle's side.

The war was not a sectional war, and it was not a class war. Anarchist and Marxist leaders of the Montevideo labor unions could see no dialectic significance to the war; during the fighting, all the Montevideo unions signed a manifesto calling for a negotiated peace.[76] The one thing the unions wanted was to keep workers from being caught in the National Guard dragnet.

At bottom, Colorados were fighting Blancos. This traditional reason was enough for the troops. Batlle and his followers were fighting, as they put it, for legal government, for laws not pacts, for elections not acuerdos. Their opponents were not so much fighting against these ideals as they were fighting to make sure that these ideals would come about under trustworthy auspices.

XI

Elections

Triumphant Colorados were in the streets. The regular Directorio, almost silently, reopened its sessions in Montevideo. The stock exchange was shooting up, now that a stable peace was in prospect. The conservative classes hoped Batlle would take the meaning of the war to heart and conciliate the Nationalists; *El Siglo* reminded Batlle of the old postwar slogan of Plata politics: "No Victors and No Vanquished."

Batlle was not taking part in the victory celebrations. His moral code forbid it; he never had enjoyed formal banquets; and since August he recognized the danger of assassination. But Don Pepe knew the real meaning of the war: he was the victor, the Blancos were the vanquished. The war had wiped clear the promises he had been obliged to make as a presidential candidate.[1] There would be no more coparticipation, no more presidential aloofness in Colorado politics. The time had come when Batlle was in a position to put his cherished political ideas into effect. Not to do so would be to waste the blood and sacrifice of 1904.

The Directorio's first act was an exchange of letters with the Nationalist military leaders, to heal the breach caused by the army's separate peace. Minister of Government Williman immediately called in Carlos A. Berro, the Directorio's First Vice President, and told him that in the event of repetition of such acts "the Executive Power was prepared to take the necessary measures even including the dissolution of the Corporation and action against its individual members." [2]

The Directorio met and voted to disregard the admonition because what it had done was legal in peacetime. But Batlle had given the Nationalists notice that the days when the Directorio was treated as something like a co-government were over. From now on, the Government would treat the Directorio as a potentially subversive organization, to be dealt with by the police and the courts.

Next, Batlle quickly took the major step to ratify the war victory: he sent the legislature a message proposing general elections for January 22.[3] The postponement from November to January would give time for voter registration and still permit the new legislators to take their seats on February 15, 1905, the constitutional date. Batlle could have postponed the election for a year. The conservative classes would have preferred time for war passions to calm, but Batlle was determined to end the era of electoral acuerdos and postponements. He wanted the new legislature to have full legal status. Don Pepe also knew that quick elections would favor the war-victorious Colorados.

The Nationalists were in a strange vise. They had gone to war because they feared Batlle would negate the electoral advantages of "their" departments. Now they had no departments. They could abstain. However, to abstain without being able to overthrow the election results by war—their present situation—would be to concede to Batlle the next legislature and the choice of the next President of the Republic. There still were many Nationalist voters on the registry lists. Herrera y Obes and Tajes were still hostile to Batlle.[4] If the Nationalists could elect a sizable number of legislators and the dissident Colorados do the same, the anti-Batlle Nationalist and Colorado legislators could combine and elect their own choice for President in 1907. With cautious hope, the Nationalists accepted the January 22 date and prepared to organize the campaign.[5]

The old legislature, still in session, had accomplished little in its nearly two years under Batlle. Yet Batlle did not plan to push through a pre-election legislative program. It was not necessary. The electorate was small; only those deeply involved in politics

voted. To the Colorado electorate, Batlle's accomplishments were
unbeatable: he had turned back the seemingly almost certain Nationalist movement toward taking power; he had restored Colorado
total control of the government, to an extent scarcely imaginable
when he took office.

Batlle continued the cautious, sound financial policy which partially reconciled the conservative classes to his political intransigence. The rural land tax was kept at prewar rates with no increase. Batlle and Serrato explained:

. . . the Executive Power, taking into account the abnormal situation
in which the country finds itself, does not believe it opportune to make
modifications . . . this is not the most propitious occasion.[6]

The budget was still the old Cuestas budget. The legislators
would have liked to do something for the government workers,
who by the nature of things would do the voting and get out the
vote, but Batlle said no. Minister of Finance Serrato did promise
that a new budget would be presented in six or seven months, a
promise which could be dangled in front of government employees.[7]

Two significant changes, neither of which cost money, were
made in the budget. The urbana military companies were abolished.
These companies, ostensibly departmental prison guards, had been
Saravia's cadre in his six departments. Two new regiments would
take their place. The total number of regiments in the army was
raised from twelve to fifteen; the complement of soldiers in each
regiment was reduced.[8] The total cost would be the same, but
the changes had their advantages: the Nationalists were deprived of
their urbanas; the new units would provide billets for National
Guard officers who, because of war service, were being given
regular commissions; a larger number of units would make army
expansion in wartime easier. Batlle was looking out for the army,
which had done so much for him and might have to fight for him
again. Yet the changes were also in line with one of his old antimilitarist ideas: the more army units there were, the more difficult
it would be for a few unit commanders to get together in a barracks
uprising and overthrow the government.

The other budget change cut the annual subsidy to the Catholic
Seminary down to 4,000 pesos a year instead of the previous 8,000

pesos.[9] Before the war, Batlle had leashed his and his government's anti-Catholicism. During the war, Don Pepe became convinced that the Uruguayan Red Cross, run by Catholic women, was pro-Saravia. He then set up the nonreligious Central Assistance Agency under Figari to care for the government armies. Now that Batlle's political situation was secure, government anti-Catholicism was growing.

Anti-Catholicism pleased the young Colorados, just out of the University. Batlle also aided the University's building and autonomy programs, again to the pleasure of his young Colorado admirers. Army officers were being looked after. Government workers had the promise of a pay increase. Businessmen and ranchers were satisfied to know their taxes would not go up. Add the great war victory, and the Colorados should sweep the January elections.

Every logical expectation was that the Colorados would win overwhelmingly, but Don Pepe was not a man to take avoidable risks. In November 3 the Executive sent to the legislature a bill reapportioning seats in the Chamber of Deputies. The project was designed to increase the Colorado majority in the Chamber and would go into effect for the January elections. As a presidential candidate, Batlle had promised the Acevedo Díaz Nationalists not to introduce such legislation—he was identified with the scheme before the 1901 acuerdo—but that was another promise wiped out by the war.

A storm of protest broke. The Nationalists had only a token representation now sitting in the legislature. All the Nationalist Deputies had been expelled for nonattendance during the war; only three Nationalist Senators, and these alternates, were left in the Senate.[10] It was unjust to pass a law inimical to Nationalist interests without giving the Nationalists a chance to resist it in the legislature. The Executive had not changed the rural land tax because it felt this was not the time. Was it time to change the electoral law, just before elections and within weeks after a revolution? Batlle had expected this storm and proceeded to add to its fury, by calling Deputies to his home to tell them how much he wanted the bill passed—something presidents never openly did.[11]

Batlle's and Williman's Executive message accompanying the

bill was not particularly inspiring. It pointed out that the Constitutional requirement of one Deputy for each 3,000 inhabitants had been made obsolete by population increase. Reapportionment had several times been authorized, most recently in 1890, when the Chamber's membership was set at the present sixty-nine Deputies. Montevideo elected twelve Deputies, Canelones elected six, the other seventeen departments elected three each.

The Executive considered this apportionment unfair to the more heavily populated departments. Flores, the least populated department, elected one Deputy per 5,291 inhabitants, while in Montevideo one Deputy represented 22,361 inhabitants. To rectify this inequity, the Executive proposed to follow Salterain's 1901 suggestion and elect representatives on the basis of one Deputy for each 12,000 inhabitants of a department. This would raise the total membership of the Chamber to seventy-five instead of sixty-nine. Montevideo would have twenty-two seats instead of twelve, Canelones seven instead of six, the next three most populated departments four instead of three. Seven departments still would have three seats each. The next six departments would lose a seat, dropping to two seats instead of three. Flores would be given only one seat.

Colorado Montevideo most obviously benefited, but since it was the intent of the Constitution that the Chamber reflect population, and since each department would still have only one Senator, it was hard to raise outright objections to Chamber reapportionment on the basis of population. However, Batlle had stacked the project with several pro-Colorado devices. Before '97, the party which won a majority in a department got all the department's seats. One of the reforms resulting from Saravia's '97 revolution was minority representation. Now the majority got two-thirds of a department's seats, the minority one-third.[12] Batlle's project used the figure one Deputy per 12,000 inhabitants intentionally, for it gave departmental representations of twenty-two, seven, four, three, two, and one. In only seven departments could the seats be divided by three. In the seven least populated departments the majority would get all the seats; in the five most populated departments, the majority would get more than two-thirds of the seats. Batlle put in another change beneficial to the Colorados. At present a minority had to get at least one-fourth the vote to win a department's minority seats. Batlle's project raised the minority minimum to one-third the vote, although the majority still needed to get only one vote more than the minority to win a department's majority seats.[13]

The opposition was quick with numerical examples to show the project's unfairness. For example, Viera's department of Salto would have four seats up for election. If the Colorados got 2,001 votes to the Nationalists' 999, the Colorados would get all four seats. This would mean that the Colorados of Salto got one Deputy for each 500 votes, while 999 Nationalists would be without representation in the Chamber. Luis Alberto de Herrera, young editor of the new Directorio newspaper *La Democracia*, dubbed Batlle's project "the law of the wrong third." [14]

A young Nationalist hothead like Herrera could be expected to oppose any electoral law sponsored by the government. But a respected figure, Martín C. Martínez, Batlle's former Minister of Finance, a man famous for his prudence and rectitude, also criticized the measure in a series of articles for *El Siglo*. Don Pepe felt obliged to answer Martínez personally, in *El Día*, using his well-known pseudonym Néstor.[15]

Martínez did not base his case on hypothetical arithmetical examples, for on that ground Batlle could, as he did, produce an even more convincing hypothetical case. Don Pepe demonstrated that under the present law it was possible for a party with a minority of the national popular vote to elect a majority of the Chamber, "a revolutionary situation, whose very possibility demonstrates the urgency of the reform." [16] Martínez concentrated on the practical, not hypothetical, results the project would bring. It would reduce the Nationalist representation to one-fourth of the new Chamber instead of the one-third of the present Chamber the Nationalists now had.

Martín C. Martínez maintained: "ten thousand bayonets and twenty thousand dependents of the State, almost always pledged electorally to whoever is governing, should be enough without touching the electoral law." [17]

Batlle refused to admit this:

When a regime based on fraud governs, the political color of the agent of the Executive Power in a department assures the triumph of the party to which he belongs. In a regime of liberty and electoral legality, the only thing which can assure the victory of candidates who support the policies of the government is the prestige which that government has won by its actions. Certainly, an unpopular government would be constantly defeated.[18]

Martínez feared that the project would intensify party rivalries, while the present law "permits the extension of the grand projections of tolerance and political coparticipation to all the Republic." [19] Don Pepe was tired of the words tolerance and coparticipation:

It is time we stopped fooling each other with empty phrases. There is no more solid basis for conciliation in politics than the increasingly perfect application of ideas of law to the actions of everyone. At first it may produce resistance, but it imposes itself in the end and pacifies men's spirits.[20]

Batlle made clear what he meant by this:

The evil for doctor Martínez is that the revolutionary faction of the nationalist party, without its caudillo, without control of any departments, anarchized by its recent fall, perhaps will not obtain more than the minority in each department but . . . this is not a very great evil, and on the contrary, it should be considered a positive good that a party which has committed grave errors, feels the consequence of them in the diminution of its political power.[21]

Only once in the debate, when Martín C. Martínez said that if the electoral law were changed it should be in the direction of proportional representation, did Don Pepe obliquely reveal his real reason for insisting on passage of the project. He too favored proportional representation, "the last word in science," as an ideal. But, "committed as the presidential election is to the Legislature, that reform would immediately lead us to the very situation which just produced so many misfortunes." [22]

Batlle was trying to prevent a recurrence of the 1902 presidential campaign, when a sizable Nationalist minority, had it played its hand well, could have combined with a Colorado faction and elected a President to its liking. Batlle wanted to make sure the Colorado majority in the next legislature would be so large that in 1907 it would elect the next President by itself—under his guidance. Don Pepe did not confess this until 1911, when in the course of another polemic he admitted:

The 1904 law tended to give representation to the minority, but not a proportional representation. On the contrary, its purpose was to separate the minority from the majority, so as to avoid the possibility that the minority might be converted to a majority through the will of a small group of people when the Legislature functioned as electoral college of the President.[23]

Martín C. Martínez had scored debater's points, but Don Pepe had the votes in the Chamber of Deputies. Only Colorados were there, all of them were up for re-election, and all of them knew that Batlle would have a decisive voice in making up the departmental Colorado tickets for deputy. In the course of one session, on November 16, the project was debated, approved, and sent to the Senate, where it could expect a rougher time. Even Rodó made only perfunctory objections.[24]

The Colorado organization, dormant during the war, was reactivated. Herrera y Obes' and Tajes' resignations from the Executive Committee were accepted, and Williman was replaced as Executive Committee President by Antonio M. Rodríguez, a professional politician. The Montevideo Colorado clubs revived.[25] New executive committees were named in the departments.

Herrera y Obes and Tajes took their supporters to Victoria Hall and set up a dissident Colorado organization. But the veteran leaders no longer constituted a threat, for the war had brought the Colorado mass to Batlle. *El Día* dismissed the dissidents as "the microscopic coterie."[26]

Traditionally, the line between the party organization and the departmental jefe político could be drawn only with the greatest difficulty. After the war, Batlle named trusted Colorado jefes políticos to all but two departments. These two he gave to Acevedo Díaz Nationalists.[27] Batlle's jefes políticos were honest men. He scrupulously kept his promise to the Revolution and named Machado, who had transmitted the Revolution's armistice request, as jefe político of Cerro Largo. He named Basilisio Saravia, one of Aparicio's Colorado brothers, jefe político of Treinta y Tres. But Batlle's jefes políticos, except for Machado, were also his old lieutenants.

With devoted jefes políticos in the departments and with the Colorado organization functioning efficiently, Colorado registration went swimmingly. Army officers brought their sergeants and corporals in to register; government workers were reminded that under law they must register. Policemen were registering, though legally they could not vote. An old political trick was in prospect: policemen would be discharged the day before elections, rehired the day after; on election day they would vote as private citizens. When Batlle was reminded that government workers, policemen, and soldiers were beholden to the government and could not vote freely, he dismissed this blandly by saying they were citizens and should vote.[28]

In his polemic with Martín C. Martínez, Don Pepe predicted that henceforth the political color of government agents would not influence the outcome of elections. Instead of carrying out this prognostication by neutralizing the political activities of government officials, Batlle went the other way. He had stated in his 1903 pre-presidential *El Tiempo* interview, that the President of the Republic could not be denied the right of advising friends of his political opinions, "thus exercising a moral influence." He now reinterpreted, and extended to others, this moral influence:

. . . it consists in recognizing the right of the President of the Republic and of all government employees to exercise their personal influence in elections in favor of candidates of their sympathies, so long as they do not use any official authority or equipment.[29]

Voting would be public. The parties would print ballots and distribute them to voters. The voter would take his ballot to the polling place, put it in an envelope, sign and seal the envelope, and then deposit the signed envelope in the ballot box. Every voter's ballot could be identified. There were enormous opportunities for "moral influence." When the army officer marched his sergeants and corporals to the polling place he would know how they voted. When the head of a government office decided on promotions he would know how his subordinates had voted. When the rural police chief decided whether to go after cattle thieves, he would know how both the ranchers and the rustlers had voted.

Galarza wrote Batlle that he was having his troops register.[30] Miguel Lezama, jefe político of Rocha, one of Batlle's oldest associates, wrote the President that registration was going well:

Nevertheless, we feel the absence of the 3rd and 6th Cavalry corps which were formed with men from the department whose votes are

considered to be lost. There is a real need for one of these corps to return to guard the prison. . . . Because of the exigencies of good government service, I expect a favorable resolution in the indicated sense.[31]

An old gaucho proverb on politics said: "The police chief's
horse always wins the race." Who would bet against Batlle's candidates when they were everywhere riding on the police chief's
"moral influence"?

Things were going so well that Don Pepe decided to go ahead
with his most daring postwar venture. One of the Revolution's
presurrender propaganda counterproposals was constitutional reform. The Revolution had in mind reforms which would institu-
tionalize coparticipation and weaken the power of the central
government. Of all the counterproposals, Batlle accepted only constitutional reform. When he sent the amnesty and end of interdictions projects to the legislature, he included a notice that the
Executive shortly would authorize the legislature to consider constitutional reform. At the time, it seemed a meaningless concession,
like the one leaving acuerdos up to the party organizations.

On November 23, Batlle sent the promised project to the
legislature. It adopted Nationalist leader Vázquez Acevedo's 1903
proposal which would get around the constitutional requirement
that three successive legislatures approve reform by considering
that the 1894 legislature's approval constituted the second step.
Batlle's bill asked that the legislators to be elected in January be
empowered to approve the proposal pending since 1894: to amend
the enabling provisions of the Constitution and permit the immediate popular election of a constitutional convention. The
project pointed out that a majority of the distinguished jurists who
in 1903 met in the Ateneo on constitutional reform had approved
this procedure.[32]

The Nationalists wanted no part of this kind of constitutional
reform. *La Democracia* stormed:

. . . the only motive which moves President Batlle to propose constitutional reform is the bite of insane, guilty ambition, the dictatorial
desire to prolong himself in power by arranging that his adulators make
possible his re-election.[33]

The Senate took up Batlle's electoral reapportionment bill, while
the Chamber began debate of Don Pepe's constitutional reform

proposal. The Senate did not like the reapportionment project. There had been joint meetings of the Senate and Chamber legislative committees, consultations with Minister of Government Williman—all to no avail. The only way for the Senate to kill the project was to vote it down. An amended project would go to a joint session of Chamber and Senate in General Assembly, and Batlle had more than enough Chamber votes to assure the two-thirds majority needed to get his version through. However, the terms of one-third of the Senators were expiring; they could not be re-elected, but they could be appointed to some government position or run for the Chamber. Batlle's goodwill was essential. The Senate saved its principles and gave up on the substance, by amending the Chamber-passed reapportionment project. The Senate restored the old total vote minimum necessary to win a department's minority seats, one-fourth of the votes cast, instead of the new requirement of one-third the votes cast.

The Chamber rejected the Senate amendments, "believing that the modifications prejudice . . . the equitable distribution between the parties," and demanded a meeting of the General Assembly. The General Assembly met on December 27, and passed Don Pepe's original project into law.[34]

The Chamber gave every indication of being just as cooperative on the constitutional reform project. Batlle's motives in presenting the project were understandable. He had, as Serrato put it, "an authentic ambition for greatness." [35] Don Pepe knew that the non-political accomplishments of his presidency were negligible. Two years of tension and war had gone by. Batlle wanted more time than the two years he had left to do the things for Uruguay that he wanted done.

But Don Pepe was beginning to doubt the advantages of sponsoring immediate constitutional reform. The Nationalists and dissident Colorados could campaign in the election as the defenders of democracy against Batlle's dictatorship. Batlle's agents were alerting him about possible Nationalist prerevolutionary effervescence.[36] A revolution against his maintaining himself in office beyond his original term would make Don Pepe look like the standard power-hungry Latin American despot. Batlle was worried that if he stayed as President beyond four years, Uruguay's reputation and credit abroad would be hurt.[37] *El Siglo* was polling the opinions of prominent members of the conservative classes: they opposed immediate constitutional reform.[38] Finally, Don Pepe's skin was not yet so thick that he could tolerate letting an inconsequential young firebrand like Herrera call him—with his long years of democratic preaching—insanely mad for power.

Batlle decided to give up immediate constitutional reform. He used another of his well-known pseudonyms, Nemo, in *El Día* to explain:

. . . the President, who initiated the reform before the legislature in compliance with the pledge he contracted when the revolution submitted, would have been very satisfied to see the reform go through, because he believed that the introduction of some modifications in the constitution would be of great advantage to the nation. Once the reform was completed, he would not have been brokenhearted if the extension of his term or the possibility of his re-election resulted from the reform, because he wants to do good and is not insensible to the flattery of a high personal position. The President now thinks, in view of the attitude of *La Democracia*, of the resistance of those who solicited constitutional reform when they declared their obedience to the law, of the opinions of certain distinguished citizens whose sincerity he can not doubt, and of the fact that certain incorrect procedures which would easily be overlooked if the reform had a general consensus of opinion in its favor might increase in importance without this consensus, the President thinks, we say, that perhaps it would be convenient to postpone the reform to a better opportunity.

Besides, the President feels repugnance lest certain individuals, who if they were in his place would sell their souls to the devil, might suspect that he was like them.[39]

Instead of quick constitutional reform, the plan now was to go through the protracted procedures outlined by the Constitution. The next legislature would announce itself in favor of reform; so would the two subsequent legislatures. It would be nine years, at the earliest, before any reform could be effected.

The constitutional prohibition against immediate re-election of the President of the Republic still stood. Don Pepe could try to pick a successor who would permit Batlle to be elected again as President in 1911. Previous Presidents had attempted this, but none had succeeded in returning to the presidency.

Batlle kept his long-term strategy to himself, but early in January he got the Colorado Executive Committee to require all candidates to sign this secret pledge: "Not to vote for any candidate for President of the Republic who has not been proclaimed in a declaration published in the press by at least twenty-five electors affiliated with the Colorado Party." [40] The reapportionment law had cut Nationalist chances to elect a sizable minority; the pledge would prevent any Colorado splinter group from complicating the next presidential election. Precautions had been taken against all foreseeable dangers. It was time to name the candidates.

Voters would not vote for individual candidates; they would vote for a list of candidates equal to the total number of Deputies to be elected by the department. If the Colorados won a majority of votes in a department, the candidates on the top two-thirds of the list—or a little farther down where the new arithmetic held—would be elected. If the Colorados won more than three-quarters of the votes, all the candidates would be elected. If the Colorados won only one-third of the department's votes, just the top third—or less—of the list would be elected. In short, the candidate who headed the list was almost certain of election, while the candidate at the bottom would win only if the Colorados swept the department.

The departmental Colorado organizations made up the lists, but these organizations had little freedom of action. All candidates had to be cleared with Don Pepe, who had spent twenty years in this business. Batlle filled the lists with his young supporters. Manini was to run from Durazno; Arena from his former home of Tacuarembó. Still, there was a limit to the number of men from the capital a local politician could put on his department's ticket; he had his own candidates.

There were intradepartmental rivalries. All claimed to support Batlle; yet if Batlle could not settle the dispute there might be two Colorado tickets in a department, a situation which could result in the Nationalists' winning the department's majority seats. Don Pepe's hardest job was to find places for the Acevedo Díaz Nationalists. He had promised this to them when he gave them only two jefaturas instead of the six they had hoped to inherit at the end of the war. The Colorado departmental politicians balked at this, for they considered Acevedo Díaz Nationalists electoral poison.

Various problems emerged. Batlle sent his brother Luis, can-

José Batlle y Ordoñez, 1907

Afternoon in the country
(seated left to right: Manini, Antonio M. Rodríguez, Serrato, Batlle, Juan
Pedro Castro, Williman, Arena, and Viera)

Batlle and his family
(left to right: sons Rafael and César, Matilde, daughter Ana Amalia, Don Pepe; son Lorenzo on floor)

didate for deputy in Río Negro, to Fray Bentos to straighten out difficulties there. From distant Artigas, Amaro F. Ramos reported to Batlle: "the list which Your Excellency had the goodness to recommend to me personally, when I was in Montevideo was proclaimed by the majority of the commission." [41] Ramos, though, was having difficulty deciding on a candidate for Senator. Batlle wired back a name. A telegram from Artigas confirmed receipt: "In accord with telegram Your Excellency, commission proclaimed candidacy Dr. Vidal." Ramos, in his haste to answer, had forgotten the rules of the moral-influence game; instead of signing his own name, he simply signed with the words jefe político.[42]

The ugliest problem was in Cerro Largo. Jefe Político Machado, in an attempt to win the support of Nepomuceno Saravia, Saravia's son, sponsored one Gallardo as candidate for Senator. Gallardo was unacceptable to Batlle. Machado resigned, and Don Pepe replaced him as jefe político with Dámaso Vaeza. Vaeza, with Batlle's blessing, sought and got the support of Justino Muniz, shifting the political balance in Cerro Largo to Muniz, something close to what Batlle had promised the surrendering Revolution would not happen. Jefe Político Vaeza then sent Batlle this coded telegram: "[Colorado Departmental] Commission asks you for candidate for first titular [as Senator] today." [43]

El Día saw the best of all worlds emerging:

The news coming in from the interior assures that the Colorado Party will ballot entirely united, voting for the candidates proclaimed by the respective departmental party authorities.
This unity of views and procedures is bound to give it victory in the elections, assuring its majority in the National Legislature, and will demonstrate definitively that its permanence in the government is the result of the desires of the great majority of the country, who belong to the party and share its patriotic ideals.
The proclamations of candidacies announced so far by the departmental committees have come about through the frank democratic cordiality of the committee members and are the best omen of the victory which the Colorados will give their candidates in the ballot boxes.[44]

The most important ticket would be in Montevideo, where a candidate for Senator and twenty-two candidates for Deputy had to be selected. Ex-Minister of Government Campisteguy, his health restored, returned from Europe. When Williman decided he would rather remain in the cabinet than run for Senate, Campisteguy was nominated for Senator from Montevideo. This had been Batlle's post, and the rumor went around that Campisteguy was Batlle's candidate for next President of the Republic.

What was holding up things in Montevideo was Don Pepe's insistence on including Acevedo Díaz Nationalists in the list for Deputies. Montevideo politicians would not go along and could argue that inclusion of Nationalists on a Colorado ticket violated Batlle's long avowal of one-party government. Batlle found a way out. Emilio Frugoni, young lawyer and poet, who had fought for the government during the war, announced that the Socialist Party was thinking of running its first candidate. *El Día* proposed a progressive Montevideo ticket of Colorados; Socialists; nonparty, anti-Catholic liberals; and Acevedo Díaz Nationalists:

> Colorados would vote for Socialists, for Liberals, for minority Nationalists, not just as a favor but precisely because these candidates, in the Parliament, would represent the same tendencies, ideas, principles, and great ideals as the Colorados, either because immediate political circumstances or a community of final goals tie them to the Colorados.[45]

El Día was notably vague, especially on the specific measures which this disparate group advocated in common. No matter what *El Día* said, politicians knew that the Socialists had no registered voters, the anti-Catholic Liberals very few, and the real beneficiaries of the alliance, the Acevedo Díaz Nationalists, would probably lose votes for the ticket.

But Don Pepe insisted. Manini got the grumbling Montevideo Colorado Committee to put one liberal and six Acevedo Díaz Nationalists in as the bottom third of the ticket. Manini promised his coreligionaries the minority Nationalists would bring 2,000 votes with them. If they didn't, the Colorado Party would lose nothing, for it would still win the majority seats in Montevideo, and the Colorado candidates on the top two-thirds of the ticket would sit in the Chamber of Deputies. Frugoni, the new Socialist, was yet a Colorado to his old comrades-in-arms. They put him on as an alternate near the top of the list and went out to the neighborhood political clubs to explain to the rank and file why six Acevedo Díaz Nationalists were candidates of the Colorado Party.[46]

The Montevideo ticket was not completed until four days before the election. The final adjustments in some departments took place even later. This extremely late announcement of candidates was normal. In all Uruguay, the registered voters totaled only 71,000.[47] Local political leaders knew who they were and how they voted. As long as the ballot was printed by election day and the voter followed his leader, it made little difference who was on the ballot.

The Directorio, as familiar with this kind of electioneering as the Colorados, was engaged in the same task of compromising the desire of interior politicians to run local candidates with the necessity of placing men from the capital on the departmental tickets. The Nationalist spirit was low. Registration had not gone well, and financial contributions were hard to get.[48] To improve the party's chances, two distinguished non-Nationalist Constitutionalists, José Pedro Ramírez and Martín C. Martínez, were nominated—Ramírez as Senator from Flores, Martínez as Deputy from Minas. Both were highly thought of by the conservative classes and might bring money as well as votes to the party. The Colorados countered by nominating Pablo De María, lawyer, intellectual, and Constitutionalist, for the Rocha Senate seat.

Off and on since the war, the Directorio had been negotiating with the Herrera y Obes-Tajes Colorados over a coalition ticket in Montevideo.[49] There was a possibility, in the party's present state, that unless this was done the Nationalists would not get the necessary one-third of the votes cast and would lose the seven minority seats from Montevideo. Herrera y Obes assured the Directorio that Batlle would not win more than thirty of the seventy-five seats in the new Chamber, and promised 4,000 votes to a coalition ticket if he were nominated for Senator from Montevideo. The Directorio vetoed this arrangement, for it never could get its people to accept Herrera y Obes, the Colorado ex-intransigent.

Herrera y Obes proposed a less embarrassing solution. Minas would elect a Senator. Since the voters elected an electoral college which in turn elected the Senator, Herrera y Obes suggested that a coalition ticket run for the Minas electoral college. The coalition would announce no candidate; once it won, it would elect Herrera y Obes Senator. In exchange, the dissident or, as they preferred to be called, Independent Colorados in Montevideo would vote a coalition ticket for Deputies.[50]

The Directorio debated. Vázquez Acevedo was opposed:

> It seems to me that a small number of *possible* allies in the legislative chambers will not appreciably help our situation there; for the big presidential question of 1907, no matter what precautions Batlle takes, we will succeed in forming a majority against him, with or without the six independents.[51]

The other members of the Directorio still felt the need of additional votes in Montevideo. Besides, a Nationalist-Colorado ticket against Batlle would sound like a national movement against an unpopular government.

The Directorio negotiators wanted proof that the dissidents could deliver the promised votes. General Tajes told them he had 2,000 voter registration certificates in his possession, and offered to display them if asked.

Possession of registration certificates was an old political practice and not of itself illegal. A registered voter could give his certificate to another, as a sign of support or for safekeeping. But the practice was open to all sorts of fraud. Batlle had always opposed the amassing of certificates. It was undemocratic; also, the political leader holding certificates owned an independent personal capital with which he could bargain for advantages.

The Nationalists, though they were attacking Batlle's moral-influence techniques, had no hesitation in accepting Tajes' more blatant and crude device for electoral manipulation. They could not very well question Tajes' word, so they accepted his claim without asking for his certificates.

At 3.00 A.M. on January 20, just two days before election, the Montevideo coalition and the Minas arrangement were approved. The Nationalists got the lion's share in Montevideo—the first seven places on the ticket. Three Colorados were put in the middle of the list, where they would reach the Chamber only if the coalition won the majority.[52] The Nationalists were now certain of winning the seven Montevideo minority seats, but Herrera y Obes and Tajes had gotten nothing for themselves in Montevideo unless, veteran politicians that they were, they were right when they said the coalition would defeat Batlle in Montevideo.

Don Pepe made no public speeches during the campaign. It was not customary for the President of the Republic to give political speeches, and this was one presidential custom which Batlle had no desire to break.

The young candidates for Deputy took the train to the capital of the department they hoped to represent, introduced themselves to the local organization, and before undertaking the more serious purpose of their trips—the overseeing of electioneering on election day—made a few fiery speeches. In Rocha, Eugenio Martínez Thedy thundered: "The fortunes of war, which are really caused by the power of the people, have given to the Colorados the glorious task of orienting the country toward progress and to the Nationalists the mystical consolation of repentance to redeem themselves from their ancient sins." In Canelones, the candidate closed with, "Viva the Colorado Party! Viva the President of the Republic! Viva Our Chief and Caudillo Colonel Acuña!" Julio María Sosa and Florencio Aragón y Etchart, in Montevideo, called for cheers for "our great red banner." *El Día* summed up the Colorado electoral message: "these elections are nothing else than the continuation of the recent war on peaceful, institutional, and useful terrain." [53]

Groups of men were forming in the departments. With their leaders they would ride their horses to the polling places, just as they had ridden together to the war. In Montevideo the clubs were busy and offered barbecues for voters. Some 500 policemen had taken the one-day discharge and would vote. The Nationalist press was warning against expected Government fraud, while justifying the coalition to the Montevideo Nationalists. For the first time in thirty years there was going to be an election whose results were not known in advance. A new pre-election atmosphere was in the streets; even the conservative classes were caught up in the excitement.

On election day, Sunday, January 22, saloons were closed by government order. In Montevideo, soldiers patrolled the streets as replacements for the "discharged" policemen. Batlle had given strict instructions that the polls be kept open and potential voters not harrassed; Williman and the Police Chief toured the polling places to oversee that all went well. The parties provided carriages to bring voters to the ballot box in style. There was a large turnout, but not a single fist fight. All Montevideo was proud of its new, adult, election-day behavior.[54]

In the interior, where election-day quarrels traditionally ended with pistol shots, it was almost as easy to vote as in the capital. Batlle had ordered the jefes políticos to assure free voting and the jefes had passed the command down to the rural police chiefs. There were tricks in some places—early opening of polls to slip voters in before they could be challenged, dubious voters elsewhere, intentional miscounting—whose results would be challenged in the Chamber. There was only one real incident: in Treinta y Tres, a cavalry officer hit a local Nationalist leader with the flat of his saber.[55] Otherwise, the same feeling of self-congratulation at having achieved free elections which so exhilarated Montevideo passed through the interior.

The election results demonstrated that Batlle need not have insisted on reapportioning the Chamber. It was a Colorado landslide. The Party had won the majority in all but three or four departments; the Nationalists had failed to reach even the minority in two departments. The Colorados did well in Saravia's Cerro Largo, getting 482 votes to the Nationalists' 536. In Montevideo, the Colorados won a majority in 20 of the city's 21 polling districts. The Montevideo Colorado vote was 8,869; the Nationalist coalition, 5,452. Over the whole country, the total Colorado vote was 26,705, the Nationalist vote was 16,871.[56] The Colorados would have fifty-four Deputies to the Nationalist twenty-one; Colorados had won five of the eight Senate seats, the Senate would be made up of thirteen Colorado Senators and six Nationalist Senators.

A stunned Directorio met and entertained motions that "it resign in mass in view of the results because the coreligionaries had not obeyed the exhortations of the Directorio." Carlos Berro, who as Vice President had been running the Directorio under the nominal leadership of Alfonso Lamas since the war, agreed: "having presided over the war and the elections with the known results, he believes it is a matter of personal delicacy to resign." [57]

In public, the Nationalists blamed their defeat on the reapportionment law and police voting. This convinced no one, since everyone had seen the Colorados rally to Batlle, while the Nationalist voters stayed home.

For Julio Herrera y Obes, the first modern Colorado civilian politician to become President, defeat meant the end of his political career. The results also confirmed that the Acevedo Díaz Nationalists had no following; they too were finished. Neither dissident group had contributed votes, and from now on politics would be based on votes.

The election did ratify the results of the war. Batlle was now undisputed leader of a Colorado Party united as never before. Throughout Uruguay the Colorado organization was headed by men completely in control of their departments and completely obligated to Batlle. Batlle was accompanied by a swarm of bright young Colorados, fresh out of the University, whom he had put into office ahead of their time. Some, like Manini, were sons of immigrants; some, like Sosa, came from old Colorado families. All looked to Batlle. He had led them to victory, he was right, he was wise, he was BATLLE.

The Nationalist prospects were appalling. They could not win a war; they could not stand up to an election. Saravia in death did not win the victories of Saravia alive. The chance to stop Batlle from choosing his successor had disappeared; the Nationalist party organization was collapsing. The Party's very future was at stake.

Before, the conservative classes had urged the Government to mollify the Nationalists and so keep peace. The conservative classes still thought Batlle was politically obstinate but they now recognized that he was in charge of a stable peace. Hereafter they would remind the Nationalists that power was on the Government's side, that peace brought prosperity, that revolution was unthinkable.

At most, only 45,000 voted, a pitifully small figure in a population of 1,000,000. More than 150,000 men were eligible to vote,[58] so that only 30 percent of the possible electorate had voted. Yet the election began a new era; men were willing to abide by its results. The Nationalists still looked to their rifles, but more with nostalgia than premeditation. Batlle, with all the advantages he set for his party, believed in elections. In his ruminations, he visioned masses of voters casting secret ballots under proportional representation in immaculate elections, casting them always for Colorados who would make Uruguay the world's model state.

XII

‡‡‡‡‡‡‡‡‡‡‡‡

New Situation

STATISTICS were cold reminders that Batlle's half-over administration had done little in the way of physical improvements for
Uruguay. In reports prepared for inclusion in the President's annual
February message, minister after minister was forced to admit that
needed public works—post offices, prisons, asylums, schools—had
been postponed because of the war. Minister of Finance Serrato
estimated that the war had already cost the government two million
pesos. Six to eight million pesos in war claims would still have to
be paid, while tax collections for calendar 1904 were 1,745,946
pesos less than 1903.[1]

The war, while not ruinous, had done the country no good.
Property sales had declined, marriages dropped from 4,787 in
1903 to 2,622 in 1904. Immigration, ever welcome, fell to 3,652
arrivals in 1904, from 9,880 in 1903. Even postal correspondence
went from 72 million pieces in 1902, to 70 million in 1903, to 55
million in 1904. Statistics on livestock holdings, if one trusted
ranchers' estimates, showed the same pattern: 18,559,106 sheep in
1903, 13,915,796 in 1905; 6,947,936 cattle in 1903, 6,028,980 in
1905. Blooded breeding stock, whose number was an excellent
barometer of rural prosperity, had fallen from 450 bulls and 123
rams in 1903 to 398 bulls and 56 rams in 1904, and about the
exactness of these numbers there could be no doubt.[2]

Yet the economic future was extremely encouraging. Herds and
breeding stock could be built up. Money was available; interest

rates were low because businessmen had been reluctant to invest profits ever since the economic disaster of 1890 and had instead increased their bank deposits.[3] With peace and the now rising prices for meat, wool, and hides, ranchers could get loans. Symbolically, the Frigorífico Uruguayo, the country's first refrigerated packing plant, began operations in December 1904.

Foreign capital was also available. These were England's peak years of investment in Latin America, and German and French capital was also interested in the area. News that concession rights to electrify Montevideo trolleys had been sold in London for £350,000 [4]—rights which Rodríguez Larreta lobbied through the legislature, rights given to the concessionaire gratis—amazed Uruguay. Railroad building in the country had ceased in recent years; now the British companies were again interested in extending their lines.

Mortgages which had been close to worthless since 1890 were taken out of strongboxes; promoters began to show themselves. Uruguay had political stability, a rising market for its exports, and available capital. It might expect great things.

Don Pepe bought a house in Piedras Blancas on the outskirts of Montevideo. It was an airy place, with a lot of land, vineyards, and trees. He paid for it with 16,000 pesos saved from his presidential salary.[5] Batlle kept the house he was renting in the capital, but stayed in Piedras Blancas most of the time. Since the war he had given up public appearances and attendance at official functions. It was not only because of concern over assassination. The war's tragedy, the sleepless nights, the casualty reports, were still with him. At Piedras Blancas only invited visitors reached the President, and regular office hours were not needed; a telephone connected him with Montevideo and *El Día*. Security measures were less obtrusive. Don Pepe could spend more time with the friends who had stood by him during the war, more time with his family. At Piedras Blancas, Batlle could take his long solitary walks, then sit under a favorite tree, and plan.

There were many young, new faces in the Chamber of Deputies. The leader of the young Colorados was the forthright Manini, elected Deputy for the first time. Arena was there too, a strange sight with his flowing locks, huge ties, his language colorful with *lunfardo* (street slang). Arena had a good head, though, and no enemies, and everyone knew he could speak to and for Don Pepe. Several of the new Deputies brought favorite projects. Gabriel Terra, just a little suspect of ties with Herrera y Obes, presented a bill inaugurating progressive inheritance taxes. Julio María Sosa, enthusiastic Colorado and Batllista, wanted to regulate foreign insurance companies. Carlos Oneto y Viana had a divorce project.

Ricardo Areco would again be Colorado floor leader. Areco could not walk and his hands shook too much for him to write, but his mind was sharp. During the war, he had countered a Catholic Sunday-rest proposal by introducing an eight-hour-day project—for the record. He had some more surprises ready. Areco and the shrewd Viera, a Batllista before 1903, worked as a team rounding up votes.

Some older men remained on the Colorado side of the chamber— the grandiloquent Angel Floro Costa; Gregorio Rodríguez, who had been Cuestas' Minister; Julio Muró, prominent Paysandú rancher. Rodó sensed this legislature would not be to his liking, resigned, and was in Europe.

The Nationalist contingent was too small to influence passage of many bills, but it would make itself heard. Former Senators Rodríguez Larreta and Vázquez Acevedo were the minority leaders. Martín C. Martínez, on the point of officially becoming a Nationalist, could use his prestige to criticize government financial measures. Young Luis Alberto de Herrera, another first-time Deputy, was prepared to start any kind of scandal on the floor, partly for fun, partly to embarrass Batlle politically.

The new legislature organized itself expeditiously. Antonio M. Rodríguez, President of the Colorado organization, was elected President of the Chamber. Campisteguy, on whom Batlle seemed to be bestowing his mantle, was elected Senate President.

Don Pepe anticipated his annual February message with a bill making it a crime to address nonmembers of the army with military titles. He didn't want to hear any Nationalist called "General" or "Colonel." The annual message was harsh and the forewarned Nationalist legislators did not attend when the clerk began to read it. Batlle blamed the war on the Nationalists:

Civil war vented its rage on us and our land was devastated. There was an outpouring of blood, on the one side of the brave soldiers of the law, who, conscious of their duties offered it with high and patriotic spirit; on the other side, the blood of the soldiers of subversion who, separated from the path of duty by error or passion, seemed to put what they considered to be the interests of their political collectivity ahead of the general and permanent interests of the Republic.[6]

The words resembled those Don Pepe had used at the war's end, but the spirit was the prewar Paysandú spirit, hardened with recrimination.

The Directorio, "in the desire not to provoke debates and animate passions, which patriotism advises be quieted," decided to postpone publication of its prepared reply to Batlle's message. Simultaneously, it resigned.[7] Batlle was worried lest the goings and comings of Nationalist leaders, ostensibly over the election of a new Directorio, were a cloak for war preparations. Supposedly, Mariano Saravia was preparing revolution from his self-imposed exile in Brazil. The Directorio knew the party was in no shape for war—finances were so low that Nationalist legislators were required to contribute up to 20 pesos monthly to the party treasury—and wanted to forestall any mass arrests of Nationalist leaders, something Williman had threatened shortly after the war. It sent Basilio Muñoz, who signed the peace of submission, to see Batlle.

Muñoz, made the scapegoat for disaster by his fellow Nationalist military commanders, had been treated with great deference by Don Pepe as a man who had sacrificed personal interest for the nation. Batlle and Muñoz sipped *maté* and talked for three hours. Muñoz told reporters that he had advised Batlle that those who were agitating for war had neither the prestige nor the capacity to start a revolution.[8] Then Muñoz went home and wrote Batlle a letter:

I told Your Excellency that I would not rise in arms against your government and that is in fact the case; I could not proceed in any other way since my prestige disappeared when I made the peace . . . my name would not raise a man . . . but what I did not dare tell you personally is that what is being said about a forthcoming uprising is true. Yes; it is very true that the National Party will make itself felt very soon if Your Excellency does not change his government program.[9]

Don Pepe had no intention of changing his program. On the back of Muñoz' letter, Batlle penciled a telegram for Muniz, Galarza, Colonel Viera, and all jefes políticos: "I recommend great vigilance and caution."

From April 1 to April 5, the Nationalist Electoral Congress— one delegate from each department—met and named a new Directorio. Carlos Berro, President of the previous Directorio in all but name, was elected President of the next one; Rodríguez Larreta and Vázquez Acevedo were back.[10] A strange newcomer, Martín Aguirre, who had brought Justino Muniz to the Colorados, was also elected. Saravia had despised Aguirre, but Saravia was dead and Aguirre was making a comeback as leader of the "radicals"— the faction trying to win over the Nationalist military.

The new Directorio, though, was decidedly "conservative." The "conservatives" opposed allowing the party to undertake any fore-doomed escapades. The party leadership was increasingly identified with the interests of Nationalist ranchers and businessmen. *La Democracia*, the party newspaper, boasted that, although the Colorados were supported by those who lived off the government, the National cause "monopolizes the majority of private fortunes and has the sympathy of the productive elements."[11] The productive elements wanted peace above all. Vázquez Acevedo walked in to a Directorio meeting as a draft of its first public manifesto was being read aloud. He observed that "in his opinion it would be well to accentuate the peaceful purposes and tendencies of the party a little more," and the Directorio agreed.[12] The Radicals wanted the party to abstain from the 1906 Senate elections; the manifesto, when re-leased, called for the party to go to the ballot boxes in 1906.[13]

Alarms quieted. Within a month, *El Siglo* gave the delighted report: "thank God, calm begins to reign in politics."[14]

Before the war, Nationalist organizational problems were simple, while the Colorado organization was chaotic; now the situation was reversed. The Colorado organization was finally to be organized in accord with the party charter. Antonio M. Rodríguez, simultane-ously President of the Colorado Executive Committee and of the Chamber of Deputies, called a joint meeting of the committee and the Colorado legislators. At the meeting, Areco moved that, as called for by the charter, elections of officers in the Montevideo Colorado clubs and in the departments be held in September.

A small group favored postponing these elections until 1906 or, even better, 1907. They left their real reason unexplained: if the elections were held soon, Batlle's followers would swamp the party offices; if elections could be held off until the end of Batlle's administration, men less enthusiastic about his leadership might get footholds. But the great majority of those present were already enthusiastic about Batlle's leadership and they voted for Areco's motion with gusto.[15] There would be Colorado party elections in September.

Optimistic postwar economic forecasts were being borne out. Land values were rising; pedigreed breeding stock imports were up; the first shipload of refrigerated meat left for Europe. Government bonds rose. In fact, the special Montevideo port-construction bonds with which the Government paid the French construction company, bonds whose price was tied to the Consolidated issue, were transferred to the company at over par, and the company protested against this Uruguayan government windfall. The English electric trolley company was preparing to invest two million pesos to construct its new line, and proposals for additional trolley electrification concessions were pending. Tax receipts also were up. The Executive marked its second anniversary by sending a three-million-peso road-building project to the legislature, with universal approval.

Batlle refused another offer to sell the government-owned Montevideo electric power plant; instead, he expanded its board of directors and authorized them to plan an enlarged system. The new board was a refuge for several Acevedo Díaz Nationalists, but Batlle also named an engineer and a communications expert as directors. He had followed the same policy during the war with the Bank of the Republic when he named a banker as President; Finance Minister Serrato had then promised that the government would make no political demands on the bank. The outlines of an established policy for government-owned enterprises were emerging: they should be encouraged, expanded, and as far as possible have professional, not political, management.

Don Pepe made some public appearances. He partook of the

shipboard luncheon honoring the departure of the first cargo of refrigerated meat. He dedicated a bridge over the Santa Lucía, the river Saravia had forded at Fray Marcos. Don Pepe's speech, reported in the third person, was short:

... his principal desire since taking office had been to endow all the Republic with means of communication which would facilitate its progress and development. He was confident that in the two years still left him to govern—with advisers like the Minister of Fomento and with the cooperation of the many young engineers who had already begun to give obvious indications of competence and activity—projects like the one just inaugurated would frequently be undertaken and opened to public service.[16]

Improved transportation facilities would be sponsored by governments of any ideological persuasion. Since the war, though, a Batllista persuasion—religious liberalism and government-owned enterprises—had been increasingly apparent. New views were also especially noticeable on land taxes where, although Batlle kept his ultimate purposes unrevealed, he was beginning the foundations of a system which could eventually end profit in landownership, urban and rural, and encourage more intensive land use.

Diario Nuevo printed an article by "X," with the editorial note that it did not entirely agree with the author. "X" insisted that several hundred ranchers owned two-thirds of the total area in the nation and were a privileged class who exploited a semislave rural proletariat; the solution was to break up the *latifundias* (large landed estates). *El Día* reprinted the article.[17]

Later, *Diario Nuevo* proposed its solution to the latifundia:

... a gradual and continued progressive tax on land value, a tax which will fill all our social needs, will reduce their present costs, and will give an enormous surplus which will help that same land by obliging it to produce.[18]

El Día did not reprint this editorial. It was Don Pepe's newspaper and Batlle did not want to frighten ranchers, now busy restocking herds, or urban landowners now planning new buildings.

Serrato had been having long talks with Batlle, during which Don Pepe explained his visions for Uruguay's future. Serrato issued a decree authorizing a long-needed house-to-house property reassessment in Montevideo; the decree required land to be evaluated separately from improvements. In the course of a Senate debate,

Serrato was half-jokingly questioned as to whether this decree meant that the Executive followed the land-tax ideas of the American Henry George. Serrato knew Don Pepe agreed with George that society not the individual was responsible for rising land values and that the tax power should be used to force land into efficient use. He also knew that Don Pepe was not ready to disclose all his views and so he parried the question: "A reform which is already coming into effect in the world. The distinguished Senator ought not think that it would be a novelty if it should be implanted in our country. I say this without expressing an official opinion on the matter, naturally." [19]

When it came time for the annual Montevideo land-tax bill, the Executive proposed that the property tax reassessment with the separate valuation of land and buildings, which Serrato had established by decree, be made a permanent part of the tax law. The Executive also wanted to collect more data:

Property taxes, not all that are due, are collected, but nothing has been done to prepare material on this and other taxes, concerning the social problem relative to the seat and distribution of taxation, which is of such great interest today in all the civilized world, as a result of the new economic ideas which are discussed in some places and applied in others.[20]

The Executive expected "interesting revelations" to emerge from the reassessments, revelations which would be useful for future land-tax projects.

After Martín C. Martínez got agreement from the chamber that the project's second reform proposal, to shift the school tax from tenant to landlord—another straw in the wind—be postponed, it approved the permanent reassessment program.

Don Pepe was anxious to use the time left to him. The divorce proposal would soon be coming out of committee and on to the Chamber floor. Originally, Batlle had planned to introduce his own divorce bill, but when he learned that one of his young admirers— he always liked to encourage them—Oneto y Viana had the same idea, Don Pepe decided to back Oneto's bill. Batlle had so many other bills under preparation: he was about to submit one, announced before the war, abolishing the death penalty; he had asked the Senate for authorization to negotiate a treaty with Argentina for the reciprocal ending of lotteries on both sides of the Río de la Plata. The Executive had already set up the *Diario Oficial* to print government notices, decrees, and parliamentary debates. The budget of this official daily needed legislative approval; the Nationalists, fearful that it would become a political journal of the government, refused to vote funds.

Batlle felt the need to exercise some more moral influence on the Colorado legislators and to take another step in the organization of Colorado party discipline. On May 8, *El Día* announced:

> The President of the Republic has decided to offer periodic receptions to the legislators. The first of them will be held next Friday evening.
> The receptions will not have a fixed objective. There will be no personal invitations to them. Naturally, it is understood that all legislators who are friends of the President can attend.
> The Ministers of State will also attend the aforementioned receptions.[21]

The best people were upset: sensible political leaders didn't do what Batlle was doing, flaunting his authority, making public distinctions between friends and enemies. *El Día* tried to protect Don Pepe's prospective guests by assuring the world that men "with the most unshakable independence of character" would attend.[22]

The receptions went on as planned. After the second one, attended by 32 Colorado legislators, *El Día* explained: "Sr. Batlle wanted to have an opportunity to exchange ideas on political questions with his friends from the Chamber and there is a predilection for these questions at the receptions." [23]

The receptions helped Batlle's projects in the legislature. The Chamber readily approved the *Diario Oficial* budget. Next, it took up the Executive's bills for the electrification of two new trolley lines in Montevideo.

Batlle was not enthusiastic about seeing foreign companies make profits from the trolley riders of Montevideo, but local capital was inadequate and neither treasury finances nor public opinion were ready for government-operated trolleys. So Don Pepe tried to make the concessionaries accept the stiffest terms he could impose. He had justified his rescinding of Cuestas' veto of the first trolley electrification concession by saying that the working class would be able to build homes in distant neighborhoods where land was still cheap and ride the new trolleys to work in the center of Montevideo. Now, he insisted that both new concessions build their lines beyond the heavily populated districts. The concessionaires objected, claiming that the extensions would be unprofitable since there would be few riders; they preferred to build when traffic justified new lines. But Batlle, who had read of the huge unearned profits made in the transfer of the rights to the first electric trolley line, was adamant. He announced that all future concessions would require building ahead of traffic. The Chamber supported the Executive's position, and the concessionaires finally accepted Batlle's terms, for they still were getting 75-year concessions and paying nothing for them.[24]

On May 23, the Chamber began to debate the Executive's three-million-peso road-building project, its second anniversary gift to the nation. In the interior, roads still followed the old paths, rivers were forded not bridged. Under Cuestas, a road engineering department was established; however, it had only limited funds. Batlle and Minister of Fomento Capurro proposed to spend 2,750,000 pesos for immediate building of roads, bridges, ports, and river improvements and 250,000 pesos to plan a long-range road network.[25] The sum was small in comparison with the 60,000,000 to 150,000,000 pesos needed to build a first-class road system, but it was the largest yet appropriated in Uruguay for road-building.

Everyone was enthusiastic, except about the project's financing. The Executive proposed to finance construction with a bond issue, the bonds to be serviced by raising the export tax on hides. Road maintenance would be paid for by an annual 25-cent tax on each horse in the country—really a chance to discourage owners from keeping excess horses and so deprive any future revolution of the mobility Saravia had enjoyed.[26]

Ranchers opposed the hide tax; the horse tax, it was generally agreed, would be a nuisance to collect. With Serrato's consent, a compromise emerged: an additional 50-cent tax per 1,000 pesos of assessed property valuation, which would bring in 100,000 pesos a year, about half the bond service costs, would be levied on rural lands; the balance of the costs would be paid from general revenues.

A small license tax on carts would pay for maintenance. After debating the measure from various angles, the Chamber approved the modifications.[27]

The compromise was not unwelcome to Batlle, for he expected to have rural land assessments raised soon. Then the 50 cents per 1,000 pesos would bring in more revenue. The new law also had two interesting provisions. In one, land expropriated for right of way would be paid for at assessed value plus 20 percent. The practical effects were unimportant; actually, ranchers frequently donated land, for it was to their interest to have roads on their properties. The precedent, though, could mean something later, when valuable lands were expropriated for public buildings. If the principle became permanent, either the government would get land at bargain rates or landowners, to protect themselves against the future, would be willing to pay taxes on true land values—in which case land tax revenues would rise. The other interesting provision gave the Executive the option of putting road construction projects up for bid by private contractors or of building the roads with government equipment and workers. As in other postwar projects, Don Pepe had slipped in a few seeds for the Uruguay of the future.

In June, Cuestas died in Europe. MacEachen, practically unnoticed, had died during the war. Cuestas' death produced a spate of newspaper editorials but, from the day he left the country, Cuestas had counted for nothing in Uruguayan politics. The years when Batlle had been one of many politicians, while other men dominated the scene, were almost forgotten. Now politicians speculated on whom Batlle would choose as his successor; Williman, Serrato, and Campisteguy were his rumored favorites.

Batlle made no mention of his preference. His Buenos Aires agents were again reporting Nationalist prerevolutionary effervescence. The Nationalists must be forcefully reminded once more that the Cuestas era of conciliation was over, that Nationalist appeals to force would be efficiently smashed.

The Chamber elected five Colorados—President Antonio M. Rodríguez, Areco, Viera, Manini, and Fleurquin—all stalwart Batllistas, to the Permanent Committee which sat when the legislature was not in session, ignoring the traditional courtesy of including minority members. The distinguished Nationalist candidates, Martín C. Martínez and Vázquez Acevedo, were defeated. However, the Senate, where Batllista influence was not so strong, preserved the amenities and elected Nationalist Senator Berinduague along with Senate President Campisteguy to the Permanent Committee.[28]

There was not much the Nationalists could do about the Chamber snub except protest in the newspapers. The Directorio knew that former Nationalist contributors would not finance a revolution by Mariano Saravia and his malcontents, a revolution foredoomed to failure. Directorio President Berro met secretly with Mariano Saravia and Abelardo Márquez in Buenos Aires to dissuade them from action.

Antonio Bachini, now Uruguayan Consul General in Buenos Aires, and Daniel Muñoz, still Uruguayan Minister there, learned of the meetings and interpreted them as preliminaries to war. Bachini also warned Batlle about assassination attempts.[29] In Uruguay, an informant advised Batlle that Uruguayan army Colonel Carbajal had been invited to join a barracks uprising which would be combined with Batlle's assassination.

Batlle took immediate action. He alerted the jefes políticos and moved troops to the interior. He discovered that there was nothing to the Colonel Carbajal story, but he had the informant arrested, as a precaution. Justino Muniz reported from Cerro Largo that everything was quiet. The new President of Argentina assured Batlle that Argentina would cooperate with the Uruguayan government against any Argentine-based Nationalist revolution.[30]

Batlle's precautions had exceeded the danger. To the extent that he himself created alarm, Batlle was delaying the achievement of one of his basic goals—the creation of a stable political situation which would encourage the conservative classes to invest in the economy and bring continued prosperity to Uruguay. The Nationalists explained Batlle's actions as a device to keep his hold on the Colorados by parading the Blanco peril before them; but it was not that simple. Men like Antonio Bachini and Daniel Muñoz were experienced at smelling out revolutionary plots and their information could not be disregarded. Directorios before had opposed revolution, only to discover their orders ignored by the Nationalist military. Much of the explanation was inside Don Pepe. Several thousand men had been killed or wounded in 1904. If Batlle could convince himself, and the nation, that the Nationalists were perpetual conspirators and professional revolutionaries always on the point of revolting for the pleasure of it, he could project this conviction back to 1903, and feel himself a moral man forced to fight by the primitive, bloodthirsty opposition. The dead, instead of being on his conscience, as they were, should be on Nationalist consciences.

Batlle was doing more than just watching Mariano Saravia. He presided over the laying of a cornerstone of the new university buildings, on land his government had donated. On September 8, *El Día* advised public employees that the government was planning to give them a raise.

Don Pepe also finally decided to let the English railroad company extend its line from Nico Pérez to Melo—this should open Saravia's old domain to progress. Batlle wanted to make sure the contract protected Uruguay's interests. He scrutinized the railroad's proposals, called Ministers Serrato and Capurro to his home on Sunday for consultations, asked Sudriers, a railroad specialist, for advice on the extent of the government's profit guarantee to the railroad, then refused the railroad's terms and made a counterproposal. Batlle, the old Bohemian, had turned into a conscientious administrator. The new Batlle had a new name. His friend, the Catholic poet Zorilla de San Martín, christened him "a fanatic for legality."

In August, the terms of seven members of the National Charity Commission, which ran public hospitals, asylums, and the like, expired. Batlle named seven new members, all anti-Catholic liberals. Nuns did most of the hospital work, because respectable women did not become nurses. They were paid only a nominal wage, which kept down the public budget, but the nuns used "moral influence" on patients to get them to go to Mass and confession. The new majority on the Charity Commission issued an order which forbid requirements that the sick take part in religious practices. *El Día* congratulated them: public assistance "must go on losing its active religious character." [31]

The major anti-Catholic move was Oneto y Viana's divorce project. Batlle believed in divorce—he and Matilde had personally experienced the anguish indissoluble marriage ties could cause—and was sure women would be benefited by divorce laws. They would no longer have to live with unhappy marriages; divorce would also make men less fearful of entering into marriage. Don Pepe explained to Arena that divorcees would be better off than old maids: "At least they would have exercised the supreme function for which they come into the world, and legally. And, who knows, the divorcee when she returns to loneliness might take a son with her, who could be a material help; and who always would be a help spiritually!" [32]

Most Uruguayan women feared that divorce would enable men to use and then abandon their women. A petition in opposition to the measure, signed by 10,000 Catholic women, was presented to the Chamber. *El Día*, in a long series of editorials, tried to convince women of the advantages of divorce. Batlle, at his receptions for Colorado legislators, pressed them to get the divorce bill out of committee.

The bill's chances were uncertain. Deputies on both sides of the question were preparing for what promised to be the longest and best debates of the session by going back to their law books, philosophy texts, and statistical yearbooks. The Colorado majority in the Chamber was made up of religious liberals, but whether they were liberal enough to pass a divorce law was uncertain. The Senate, as presently constituted, was very doubtful.

After much pressure, the committee reported out the bill to the Chamber on September 9, by a vote of four to three. Even this narrow majority was fictitious, for some members of the majority wanted to amend the project. In such a case, normally the committee would present its own revised bill; but, since the majority could not agree on revisions, it reported out the original bill, accompanied by a perfunctory committee report which noted that some committee members would propose amendments on the floor.

The Nationalists took no party stand on the bill, although almost all the Nationalist deputies opposed it either because they denied the need for divorce, considered the moment inopportune, or were Catholics. Rodríguez Larreta was one of the three committee members who had opposed the project, and knew the majority could never agree on a committee version. He moved that the bill be sent back to committee for further study, maintaining that it was too important a piece of legislation to be reported out in so perfunctory a manner. He reminded his colleagues, "it is not enough that an idea has a majority in a Legislative Assembly, for this majority to arrogate to itself the right to impose this idea on the country."

Manini and Arena led the opposition to Rodríguez Larreta's motion, insisting that it was only a dilatory tactic. Deputies' tempers rose; the President of the Chamber had to plead for calm. Then came the vote. The motion was defeated, a sign that Batlle had the votes to pass some kind of divorce bill through the Chamber.

The project before the house was cautious. It limited the causes of divorce to three, and specifically excluded mutual consent by the spouses as a cause. The first cause was adultery, although the bill went along with local prejudice and Roman Law and made adultery of any sort by the wife a cause, while the husband had to commit adultery under the family roof, with a mistress, or as part of a public scandal to give grounds for divorce. Criminal attempts on the life of a spouse constituted the second cause. The third cause, "grave acts of violence or frequent and grave injuries, and bad treatment of the wife by the husband, sufficient to make life intolerable," would have to be defined during the course of debate. Interpreted narrowly, it meant wife-beating; interpreted broadly, "bad treatment of the wife by the husband, sufficient to make life intolerable" would offer grounds like mental cruelty to wives looking for divorce.

One day a week was set aside for the divorce debate. Under Uruguayan parliamentary rules, a project was debated, then voted on in general. If this vote was favorable, then each article was debated and voted. Months were certain to go by before the final version of the bill emerged from the Chamber.

The Catholic women's petition against divorce, augmented to 93,000 signatures, was presented; then arguments began. Both sides pointed to Uruguay's high illegitimacy rate. Those favoring divorce claimed that, by making marriage less forbidding, divorce would encourage marriage and reduce illegitimacy. The opponents were sure that illegitimacy would rise because divorce would encourage extramarital sex relations. Smoldering beneath the surface and frequently bursting into the arguments was the real issue: for Catholics, by God's will marriage was indissoluble; divorce threatened the foundations of the family. For religious liberals, freedom of conscience was at stake; marriage was a human relationship, a contract entered into by two parties, dissoluble when the partners no longer could live together.[33]

About the same time the Chamber took up the divorce bill, it began debate on the Executive's project for a bond issue of eight million pesos to pay the 1904 war costs—the budget deficit, bills still owed by the Government, war claims against the Government armies. Claims against Saravia's army would not be paid. Had Saravia accepted the terms brought him by Mascarenhas, payment for requisitions and damage done by the Revolution would have been included in the war debt bond issue. Now, Batlle would not pay Nationalist war claims, even though third parties might suffer, for to honor these past claims would be to encourage ranchers to supply and tolerate any future Nationalist revolution.

Usually, a debate on war claims would be disheartening, but government finances were improving so steadily that the Executive's message was optimistic. No new taxes would be needed to pay the interest and amortization on the bonds:

> The gradual increase of government income, as a result of the economic improvement of the Republic and of progress made by the organizations in charge of collection and fiscalization of taxes will surpass this sum by several times . . . It would be easier for the Government if it had more income; its action would, perhaps, be more brilliant, but it would not meet the real desire of the country which still needs some time to repair the losses produced by the commotion of 1904.

The message had been written in June; by September, tax receipts, especially customs taxes, had risen to the point where the June optimism was now overcautious.

Areco, the first speaker, announced an amendment on behalf of himself and his colleague Viera, an amendment already approved by the Executive. Tax receipts had risen sufficiently to service a nine-million-peso instead of an eight-million-peso debt issue. The additional million would be disbursed as follows: "One million pesos for the construction of school buildings throughout the territory of the Republic." [34] With this move, Areco had shifted debate from retrospective regret at the wastes of war to expectations of a better future.

The Uruguayan school system had stagnated for many years.

Even Cuestas had found no funds for new schools. Up to now, Batlle had done nothing to build schools; there had been 615 schools in 1902, there were 618 in 1905.[35] During the present debate it was revealed that in the interior three-quarters of the children of school age did not go to school (90,378 out of 120,236). The Areco-Viera amendment meant new hope for them. Vázquez Acevedo, a bitter enemy of the government but a famous educator, was moved to remark:

> The project of Doctors Areco and Viera has awakened in my spirit the enthusiasm which in earlier days filled all my civic ideals, and which, I say with frankness, was almost extinguished by unhappy disenchantments.[36]

The Chamber passed the project to the Senate, which quickly concurred.[37]

The new legislature had accomplished more in its first months than the previous legislature in the last two years. During these same months, Batlle had demonstrated that his government had firm control over the country. He had taken steps to consolidate his leadership of the Colorado Party, he had begun to implement his plans for a transformed Uruguay. The new situation was well under way.

XIII

Reform

DURING these successful months, Batlle suffered some defeats —defeats in two or three not too important questions before the legislature and in Montevideo's greatest labor strike. The defeats indicated how difficult reform of Uruguay really was going to be.

One of the new Chamber's first acts was to take up the pending request of Liebig's meat company of Fray Bentos that the export tax on its product be reduced. Liebig's famous meat extract and meat products were sold all over Europe. The English company was considered to be a great boon since it provided a market for livestock and popularized the name of Uruguay in the world. Liebig's recently had begun operations in Argentina, where it paid no export taxes, and threatened to transfer operations across the river unless the Uruguayan tax was lowered.

Now Liebig's had an extraordinary and well known record of profitability: its dividend rate for the twenty years ending in 1903 averaged over 19 percent annually, plus additional stock dividends; and its profits were rising.[1] M. E. Tiscornia, the Catholic Batllista, insisted that a company with this kind of profits, profits which it was sending abroad, needed no tax relief. Tiscornia's views startled many Deputies, for they went counter to two widely accepted economic axioms: foreign capital investment should be encouraged by beneficent legislation; and export taxes were harmful. Gregorio Rodríguez, Cuestas' old Minister, could see no relation between taxes and profits. The Nationalists shared this view. Carlos Roxlo, the young coeditor of *La Democracia*, didn't care if Liebig's made 30 or 40 percent profits annually, it still should not pay export taxes.

Accinelli, one of the new Colorados, agreed with Tiscornia. In general, he was dissatisfied with:

> . . . those foreign companies, whose acts are inspired by cold and calculating egoism . . . They are interested purely or almost exclusively in squeezing out the greatest possible advantages here. They send the largest part of their profits far from here, without associating themselves affirmatively with the progress and permanent interests of our country.[2]

The Batllistas were asking only that the existing legislation remain unchanged; the burden of proof was on the opposition. The vote was close, 25 to 23, but Liebig's won and the Batllistas lost. Batlle let advice get out that if the Senate—where his influence was much weaker, for only 5 of the 13 Colorado Senators were beholden to him for their election—approved the Liebig's request, he would veto the change.

Batlle had chosen the Colorado candidates for deputy with as much freedom as any political leader would ever have. However, the candidates had campaigned as Colorados, not social reformers. The limited electorate had expressed no concern about the profits of foreign companies in Uruguay. There was no Colorado position on the role of foreign capital; there was no Colorado discipline which required legislators to follow anybody's ideology—not even Batlle's.

Labor union activity increased after the war. In December, the railroad workers formed a union. In January, the union made demands: an eight-hour day six months a year and a ten-hour day the other six months; wages of 80 pesos a month for locomotive engineers, one peso and twenty cents a day for manual laborers; two days off with pay each month; dismissal payments to men over fifty who were discharged. The railroad rejected these demands, and the workers struck.

Batlle sent Williman, the railroad's former attorney, to offer himself as mediator. Anxious to extend its line from Nico Pérez to Melo, the railroad wanted the usual government subsidy. It knew

Batlle's pro-labor sympathies, verified by Williman's presence, and accepted most of the strikers' demands. It drew the line at recognizing the union, but promised to take back the strike leaders in due time—a remarkable concession. The jubilant strikers returned to work.[3]

In May, an anarchist labor leader expelled from Buenos Aires was refused entry when his ship docked at Montevideo. Though there was no law prohibiting the entry of anarchists, the Montevideo police made it a practice to cooperate with the Buenos Aires police by keeping out undesirables. When Don Pepe heard of the case, he wired the ship's next port of call and offered the anarchist permission plus passage money to return to Montevideo.[4] This sort of legalism hardly endeared Batlle to employers but it reminded the unions, anarchist-led, that they had a friend at the top.

On May 23, the men who unloaded the ships in the port of Montevideo struck. The consoling fiction Uruguayan public men usually invoked during strikes—that local workers were better off than European workers—could not easily be invoked here. The men had to go out on launches and lighters to load and unload cargo. They worked night and day when the job required—frequently sleeping on the launch decks—and were paid by the job not the hour.

The strikers demanded more money, an eight-hour day, fixed numbers on work gangs, and union recognition. The employers felt that the men were earning enough—37 to 42 pesos a month. Employers blamed the strike on the Anarchist union leaders, "elements foreign to daily labor, who came with deceitful words to perturb the workers' tranquillity."

The harbor was at a standstill. The port construction workers joined the strike. Some 11,000 men were involved—it was the largest strike in Uruguayan history.[5]

Batlle gave the police his usual instructions: they were to protect the right to strike, as well as the right to work. The stevedoring companies were going to bring men in from the interior, where there were always idle hands except at sheepshearing time. The companies advised Williman they wanted no mediation and would have nothing to do with the union. If it came to a test of endurance, all the advantages lay with the employers. Some of them were English stevedoring companies; the largest single employer was the

Uruguayan Lussich family—Catholic, Nationalist, and very wealthy. The union's entire strike fund was 1,200 pesos, or about eleven cents per striker.

Batlle did not like the companies' intransigence; *El Día* warned that if the strike was not settled the Government might have to intervene. On May 29, Batlle named Benjamín Fernández y Medina, one of his few Catholic supporters, as official fact-finder. The employers had insisted the strike was a private matter between individual employers and their workers; the Government, by appointing a fact-finder, converted it into a public question, between employers as a group and workers in a union.

The strike, now in its second week, inevitably had political overtones. *La Democracia*, the Nationalist newspaper, blamed Batlle for the strike. *El Día* answered that the Nationalists were "the most genuinely aristocratic, conservative, and reactionary party in the Río de la Plata." [6] *La Democracia*'s two young editors, Herrera and Roxlo, were Deputies and had introduced a labor reform bill at the opening of the legislature.[7] As the strike went on, their pro-labor sympathies wore thin, and the two presented a new bill which would require unions to register with the government and permit only citizens and workers employed in the industry represented to be union officers. The provisions restricting union officers came from a proposal just approved by the Manufacturers' Association.[8]

Fernández y Medina, the fact-finder, presented his report, which indicated that the strikers deserved better conditions and advised the Executive to arbitrate the strike. Batlle consulted with Williman, Serrato, and the Socialist Frugoni. The Executive had no legal power to arbitrate strikes or compel employers to deal with unions. Batlle could order the army to unload ships, but he would really be acting as strikebreaker if he did. Frugoni told Don Pepe the strikers, some of whom had already gone back to work, would be willing to settle for a wage increase and give up all their other demands.

On June 14, Batlle met with Lussich and urged him to settle on the terms suggested by Frugoni. The President of the Republic had put his personal influence on the scale. Lussich promised to consult the other stevedoring companies.

To encourage the strikers, to counter the hostile attitude of the Montevideo press, and to educate the public, Batlle let Arena write a series of lead editorials on strikes in *El Día*. Arena's unsigned editorials, which distilled years of his conversations with Don Pepe, were to become famous.[9] Arena defended professional labor leaders: "These so-called agitators" were to workers what attorneys were to employers. The fact that labor leaders were foreigners should not be held against them, for it gave them experience with labor conditions elsewhere and enabled them to judge the possibilities of success before striking. It was unjust not to rehire strike leaders and strikers must not allow their leaders to become "expiatory victims."

Exploitation of workers, not the machinations of agitators, caused strikes:

. . . generally, what the worker earns, in the factory, or the quarry, or in the field, is the minimum he needs to sustain himself—and this minimal amount is not, and can not be, the value of his labor! [10]

Arena was close to Marxism here, but he went on to deny the existence of any class struggle. Employers should favor higher wages, which could be passed on to the consumer in the form of slightly higher prices.

It is for this reason that in our judgment good employers should not look with disfavor on industry-wide strikes since these strikes tend to put manufacturers of the same product under the same conditions by making all unfair competition impossible.[11]

The most famous of the editorials was titled "Agitators."

. . . to limit, in general, the action of agitators, is not only to limit liberty, it is to limit progress . . . every new idea, however perturbing it may appear at a given moment, can ripen in a more or less distant future, urged on and propagated by agitators.

"The great new ideas of all times" were launched by agitators. Socrates and Christ were agitators. Today's advances were yesteryear's absurdities.

Let us remember that Socialism, for example, whatever may be its errors and utopianisms contains a great and unanswerable truth when it tells us that there are multitudes with the most perfect right to life who languish in hunger; when it reminds us that three-quarters of humanity works laboriously without rest, without more recompense and without any hope other than a slow and painful exhaustion; when it makes all of us, men of good will of every doctrinal position, feel that grave chronic evils are perpetuated within the existing social system, evils which must be alleviated, if not ended, by looking for the remedy wherever it may be found. And since the evil is felt and the remedy is not found, at least let these propagandists work, however much they are believed to be dreamers, however much they are considered to be misguided, even if only for the both distant and magnificent goal they seek![12]

Arena's editorials may have provided spiritual consolation to the hard-pressed strikers, out of work for a month; but that was all the help Arena could contribute. A group of strikers caught a band of strikebreakers who were being escorted by the police. The strikers attacked, the police fired on them, killing one and wounding five others, to the macabre pleasure of the non-Batllista press.

Batlle's request to Lussich did not bring results. The employers insisted on their original position: the men would have to come as individuals and ask to be rehired, no strike leaders would be taken back; the employers would have nothing to do with the union. The Executive did what it could within the law to help the strikers. It tried to keep strikebreakers from running the launches by requiring that only licensed maritime mechanics operate the boats; it refused to permit the launches to work on holidays. But the companies were able to unload cargo, and the strikers, in spite of bold talk of a general strike which would halt the economy of the entire city of Montevideo, were at the end of their resources.

By the last days of June, practically all the strikers were back at work. Lussich, angry at being accosted by strikers, told his men they must choose between their jobs and their union. The strike had failed; the union was shattered. The men won an increase of a few cents a day but had lost over a month's pay. *El Día* wrote the strike's epitaph: "It has been a submission rather than a transaction, so that the only ones who can celebrate are the employers." [13]

The strike had demonstrated that the Montevideo unions were not strong enough to stand up to employers, regardless of the justice of their case. Batlle's policy of benevolent neutrality could not make the weaker defeat the stronger. Only in exceptional situations—situations like that of the railroad, when employers needed to get some special concession from the government—would the government's pro-labor sympathies make an employer willing to treat with a union.

The working man could not help himself. If his position was to be improved, the Government must help him. The strike had shown that the leaders of public opinion had no real sympathy for unions, or even for workingmen's aspirations. How could Don Pepe get labor legislation passed, when the unions were too weak to make themselves felt politically, and when there was no formed public opinion calling for such legislation?

One of the things Arena did during the strike was to cosponsor a bill in the Chamber to set up an experimental colony on a plot of government land in Tacuarembó. The experiment would attempt to discover whether those shiftless sons of the gauchos displaced by the fencing of ranches in the '70's, the present denizens of the pueblos de ratas in the interior whose number was estimated as high as 100,000 able-bodied men, could be transformed into hard-working farmers. Arena hoped that if these men had permanent employment they would no longer work as strikebreakers. Beyond that, Arena was one of the many who wanted to encourage agriculture, with its settled family life and productive use of land.

Ranching was progressing, but agriculture remained stagnant. Only 400,000 to 500,000 hectares were under cultivation, while 16,000,000 to 17,000,000 hectares were still pasture—pasture that was fenced in, but otherwise left untouched in its natural state. Ranchers, making good profits, were unwilling to subdivide their lands, and farmers were even emigrating to Entre Ríos in Argentina, where farm land was available at prices farmers could afford. Muró, the deputy from Paysandú, proposed that the Executive be authorized to expropriate some land in Paysandú and resell it to farmers.

In due time, the Muró and Arena-Canessa projects came out of committee. The committee report of the Muró bill was full of the usual hopes for agriculture, but the committee had stripped the project of all of its innovations. The Executive would have to go through the ordinary drawn-out process of expropriation. Once it got the land, the Executive would have to subdivide it and sell the plots to farmers at prices which would repay the cost of the whole operation. No credit could be extended; only farmers able to pay the entire price at once would benefit. In this form, the bill was approved.[14]

The Arena-Canessa experimental colony faced an absolutely hostile Chamber. Canessa assured the Deputies that the project would cost only 13,000 pesos. Arena invoked Don Pepe: "When my colleague Canessa spoke to me about this colony, just then the

President of the Republic was taking measures to try something similar in the department of Tacuarembó."

The Chamber was still not convinced: all past government agricultural colonies in Uruguay had failed. If the men in the pueblos de ratas were worthless, it was their own fault. As Martín C. Martínez put it: "Let them begin as peons in ranching establishments and learn." When Arena suggested there were no ranch jobs, Martínez answered that such an assertion—that 100,000 Uruguayans could not find work—would injure the country's reputation abroad. Arena compromised. "Make it 50,000."

The Chamber would not compromise. Even Areco's manipulatory talents could not get the bill passed. After months of parliamentary maneuvering, it was "temporarily" taken off the calendar.[15]

The Arena-Canessa experimental colony never went into operation. The Chamber had been willing to help Liebig's, already making substantial profits, but it was not willing to help the helpless Uruguayans of the interior. The Chamber majority in both cases was consistent: Government intervention with what the Deputies considered to be the natural working of the economy was undesirable, whether this intervention meant impeding the free flow of exports with taxes or trying to save the shiftless. The debates, though, did reveal an already considerable legislative concern over the role of foreign capital—Liebig's had won by only two votes— but also very great legislative doubts about the wisdom of rural reform.

On September 8, *El Día* ran this notice:

The President of the Republic is occupying himself with the making up of an extensive labor law designed to resolve many of the questions which today cause conflicts between employers and workers.
The President of the Republic intends to formulate several laws on labor matters in order that the various questions be treated separately.
This procedure not only will tend to facilitate the study of these most important matters but also is designed to avoid the dangers which large projects run: they are postponed because of their very magnitude.[16]

The Chamber's action in the past few months had given little reason to believe that Batlle's projects would have easy passage. Don Pepe was not perturbed. For the short run, he had his receptions for Colorado legislators; for the long run, he had many plans. To educate the Uruguayan people to his reform ideals, to give the Colorado Party an ideological program, to organize the party in such a way that elected Colorado officials would be required to put the party programs into effect—these Batlle conceived of as the work of the rest of his life.

XIV

ⲧⲧⲧⲧⲧⲧⲧⲧⲧⲧⲧ

Preparing the Way

THE September Colorado Party elections showed how far the party was from having an ideological program and how indifferent the members were to matters of internal party organization. The Colorado Executive Committee and the Colorado legislators entrusted Manini to draft a pre-electoral manifesto which could serve as a party program. Manini summed up the Colorado accomplishments in forty years of power, and then outlined a five-point program: constitutional reform, concern for labor, economic self-sufficiency, increase of rural population, and reduction of taxes on consumption. None of the points proposed anything specific. For example, the labor plank invoked the standard consoling fiction: "It is an exaggeration to present these problems in our society in the almost dreadful terms in which they are agitated . . . in some European societies." [1]

Manini's caution mirrored the views of most young Colorados. Manini, Don Pepe's protégé, could follow Batlle enthusiastically on political questions and against Catholicism; beyond this, his attachment was to the man, not to his advanced views.

The Colorado Party elections themselves were disappointing. In the interior, politicians went through the forms and announced that elections had taken place in which these same politicians were named to lead the departmental organizations. In Montevideo, a big turnout for the election of Colorado club officers was expected. But the Colorado clubs were mostly paper organizations which became active only before general elections. The Colorado rank and file did not care who was elected to preside over the clubs and did not bother to vote. So few voted that in over one-third of the clubs less than the minimum number of voters required to validate an election appeared. The problem was solved in classic fashion: a second set of elections was held at open-air free barbecues; this time, the aroma of roasting meat attracted the requisite number of Colorado voters.[2]

Still, by early October 1905, the Colorado Party organization throughout Uruguay was no longer provisional. It had been elected, more or less, in accord with the party charter. Men loyal to Batlle were continued in their posts and would run the party in the future.

Don Pepe was now ready to take another step. On October 15, *El Siglo* printed a scoop: "The President of the Republic has told his friends among the legislators that the candidacy of Doctor Claudio Williman for future President of the Republic is the one which he prefers." [3] Visitors to Batlle's house in Montevideo were much in evidence. Within three days more than enough vote pledges were secured from the Colorado legislators to assure Williman's election as the next President.

Things were going so well that it was decided to proclaim Williman's candidacy publicly and immediately. At a meeting of Colorado legislators on October 24, Manini moved:

. . . that the Assembly designate a committee from its midst to plan a norm of conduct to be followed on behalf of the candidacy of Doctor Claudio Williman as successor of Sr. Batlle y Ordoñez as President of the Republic.[4]

Don Pepe went to his country place at Piedras Blancas. He was not needed in Montevideo. Viera, Williman's manager, could operate the smoothly running machine.

On October 30, the formal proclamation of Williman signed by 53 Colorado legislators—more than the constitutional majority— was published.

Those who sign below, members of the Legislative Assembly which must elect the citizen who will succeed Sr. Batlle y Ordoñez as President of the Republic, in the belief that they correctly interpret the aspirations of the country, resolve:
To proclaim as their candidate for the future presidency of the

Republic the citizen Claudio Williman, in whom they see the necessary conditions and aptitudes to continue the fruitful and moralizing policies of the present government.[5]

What old Cuestas had connived at and failed to do—get his Minister of Government to succeed him—Batlle had done effortlessly. Batlle quickly defended himself against the charge that he had imposed his will on the Colorado legislators:

> To anyone who knows the least bit about the thinking of the members of the legislature it is evident, most evident, that Sr. Williman had such a large number of supporters in the legislature that by themselves they are sufficient to form the constitutional quorum.[6]

Months later Batlle admitted he had already picked Williman as his successor before the legislature convened (a choice very likely made when Don Pepe gave up the plan for immediate constitutional reform), but cloaked the disclosure with his usual sophistry:

> The President always announced to friends who questioned him about it that his inclination was toward Williman's candidacy, and even before the new Legislative Assembly was constituted, the President was already of the opinion that Dr. Williman, because of his many and close ties with the young university graduates who would form part of the assembly, and because of his political ideas, would be the most probable candidate.
> But, to think, to have preferences, is that to impose?
> Nobody can claim that the President combated any of the other candidates then being mentioned. On the contrary, he always announced that the problem of the presidential election did not disturb him, because he was sure that, in one way or another, it would be well resolved.
> Is that to impose?
> If Dr. Williman's candidacy triumphed rapidly and invincibly, it was because there was a great unity of viewpoints in the Assembly and because divisions which are not based on divergent and opposed aspirations are absurd.[7]

By settling the presidential succession early, Batlle had forestalled possible unpleasant surprises, and had also gained time for his own administration. Usually, legislators devoted the last year of a president's administration to politicking over his successor; now they could devote the next year to approving Batlle's projects. The accomplished succession was also designed to impress upon the Nationalists that they had no chance to influence the choice of the next President. Even if they assassinated Batlle, his successor was already chosen.[8]

Why had Batlle picked Williman, rather than Serrato or Campisteguy? Serrato, younger and more talented, had never been on the political firing line. In the face of revolution or the threat of revolution, he might give way and conciliate the Nationalists. Williman's "political ideas" (Don Pepe's phrase) were forged during the War of 1904, when he administered the interdictions on Nationalist property and publicly defended Batlle's anti-negotiated-peace policy. Batlle was confident that Williman would never give way to the Nationalists.

Campisteguy was an experienced and popular politician, who, if president, might try to build his own political organization. Williman, in spite of Batlle's sophistries, had no real personal political following. Even better, from Don Pepe's viewpoint, Williman preferred university life and the practice of law to organization politics. Williman could be expected to leave the Colorado Party in the hands of Batlle's followers.

For the conservative classes, Williman was assurance that Batlle's radicalism would die down in the next administration. Williman was of the conservative classes; his nickname was "The Englishman." He had been a railroad lawyer, and was now lawyer for the electric trolley company. Businessmen knew that, however often Williman countersigned Batlle's rash legislative projects, however frequently Batlle sent Williman out as strike mediator, at bottom "The Englishman" was one of them.

Batlle had chosen Williman because Williman was the most likely to continue the existing political situation. To secure this continuation, Don Pepe had sacrificed quick ideological change. Put succinctly, Williman in the presidency was the best assurance Batlle could have of his own re-election.

Williman was virtually unknown to the country at large. Senator José Espalter, now a Williman enthusiast, proposed to ignore this embarrassing feature of Williman's candidacy. Espalter maintained that the election of President of the Republic was a private matter for decision by the legislators. The general public, which under the Constitution did not vote for President, must trust the judgment of the men elected Deputies and Senators.[9] Such a solution was not congenial to Batlle. If Williman was not now well known, he would become known in the year or so left before the next presidency.

The campaign to popularize an already victorious candidate, another of Don Pepe's innovations, began. Biographies of Williman were circulated. In his youth, he had been a philosophy student at the Ateneo, together with Batlle, and had fought alongside his friends against Santos at Quebracho. Thereafter, Williman left militant politics to become a successful physics professor and lawyer; his career culminated in election as Rector of the University. Williman refused Cuestas' offer of a ministry and, at the outset of Batlle's administration, the Ministry of Government; both times he claimed political inexperience. His respectability and lack of political stature made him an acceptable compromise President of the Colorado Executive Committee during the abortive 1903 unity effort. Aside from serving as Minister of Government since 1904, his only other public service had been in the Montevideo municipal government from 1899 to 1901.[10]

There was nothing about Williman which could be used against him. He was a self-made man. Like so many of Vázquez y Vega's former philosophy students, Williman had a reputation for honesty and morality. He had married well. He was a very competent administrator and an intelligent, if not brilliant, man. Yet, when his record was added up, Williman had done nothing to justify election as President except secure Batlle's blessing.

The Williman popularizers made the most of the candidate's strong points. Throughout the country, committees were formed to explain his virtues. Local newspapers in the interior came out for Williman. All the new Colorado departmental organizations formally announced their support. The Treinta y Tres statement was typical:

> The Departmental Committee believes itself to be interpreting the will of the coreligionaries of the department who see in Dr. Williman the surest guarantee that his government will carry on in the progressive currents ably sown by the present administration.[11]

Williman himself made no speeches, and refused to comment on men or issues. To speak could expose him to rifts with Batlle or could alienate some segment of his supporters. In this the Batlle-Williman strategy coincided, perhaps unconsciously, with the Cuestas-MacEachen strategy of 1903.

The reception given Cuestas' remains, when they arrived in Montevideo, disabused anyone who still might not have recognized the great political changes which occurred since 1903. Batlle had praised Cuestas to the point of obsequiousness when Cuestas bestowed the presidential sash. Ex-Presidents normally were accorded a state funeral and buried with honors, but Don Pepe did not ask the legislature to approve the customary presidential burial. Batlle's young Colorado supporters in the Chamber were prepared to castigate Cuestas for his persecution of Colorados and compromises with the Nationalists. Batlle did not care to exert any moral influence to restrain his followers. Instead, he contented himself with saying that personally he favored funeral honors for Cuestas but, in the interest of avoiding "a heated discussion," had decided not to forward the enabling project to the legislature.[12]

The Nationalists had not really expected to be influential in the presidential election, but the abruptness with which they were shut out galled them. It was the manner in which Williman's candidacy had been managed more than the candidate himself which bothered the Nationalists.[13] Actually, the businessmen who had assumed control of the Directorio after Saravia's death knew and trusted Williman, as did his Nationalist former students.

These Nationalists wanted the Nationalist legislators to vote for Williman in 1907, and not repeat what had turned out to be the ghastly mistake of refusing to vote for Batlle even after his victory was assured. It was common gossip that Batlle would go to Europe at the end of his term and then try for re-election. Once Williman was freed from Batlle's baleful influence, his political views might soften, especially if the Nationalists voted for him. Many a successor had broken with a predecessor—as Batlle's contemporary, Theodore Roosevelt, would discover—and the group around the Directorio wanted to encourage a break between Batlle and Williman.

The radical Nationalists intuitively doubted that Williman, who had been willing to become Minister of Government when the war was going badly for Batlle, could be won over by any Nationalist tactics. Almost simultaneously with Williman's proclamation, reports reached Batlle that Mariano Saravia and João Francisco had brought arms across the border. Saravia's widow, the rumor went, had pledged her fortune to finance the upcoming revolution.[14]

Batlle had Uruguayan Minister Daniel Muñoz inquire at the Argentine army arsenal about purchasing a battery of ultramodern pon-pon cannon, but not even the Argentine army was equipped with these weapons. The Directorio, as usual, tried to calm alarms, though it also decided to publish its long-postponed answer to Batlle's war guilt message. Foreign Minister Romeu, one of the original Acevedo Díaz Nationalists, was sure this publication was part of a plan for a new revolt. He had information that the Directorio would combine the revolt with a revolt by the Radical Party in Argentina. Williman relayed to Batlle a report of Nationalist arms caches in Treinta y Tres.[15]

Batlle had sent his friend Carlos Blixen, with the title of Inspector of Customs Houses on the Northern Frontier, to uncover Nationalist plots. From Santa Rosa on the Argentine border, Blixen reported:

Ochotorena, without adding or changing a word of what he had previously said, continues to predict your assassination, as a fatality already decreed by destiny. Now, just as a few months ago, you are to be killed with the previous consent, if not with the collaboration or by the hand of Colorados . . . already pledged to a future political combination. The movement must break out before the renovation of the presidency of the Senate because, according to Ochotorena, if the movement is postponed beyond that date the election of a radical Colorado addicted to you could destroy everything. He has also spoken of Campisteguy in terms which invite one to open his eyes or to think that they want to harm him.[16]

Batlle's police spies in Montevideo advised that the Directorio was trying to dissuade Mariano Saravia from a revolution but that the Directorio was not altogether sure it would succeed.[17] On December 5, the Directorio published an official and categorical denial of any Nationalist plans for revolution,[18] and alarms died down. Within a few days Romeu told Batlle that the revolt had only been postponed: the new date was to be either March or April. He relayed a message from an informant: "alert the authorities in the interior so that they can apprehend all the Nationalist commanders and officers on the day I indicate."[19]

The legislature, once it settled down from the excitement of approving Williman's candidacy, went back to work. On December 7, the Chamber began debate on two related Executive projects: one would raise the take-home salaries of the lowest paid government workers; the other would finance the additional cost of the pay raises by increasing the tax on rural landed property.

Government workers and pensioners were subject to various deductions from their nominal salaries. The most onerous deductions, dating from the 1890 crash, were 10 percent on gross income and an additional 5 percent on net income. Now that government finances were improving, Batlle and Serrato proposed to end the 10- and 5-percent deductions for all government workers and pensioners who earned less than 360 pesos a year. Some 15,000 individuals would benefit, individuals whose salaries and pensions would still be pitifully low—30 pesos a month or less. The message promised higher paid employees that their deductions would be ended later.

The bill had been timed to coincide with the start of the Williman popularization campaign. Since much of the Colorado organization was made up of government workers, the good news made this campaign easier. The estimated cost of ending the deductions would be 380,000 pesos annually; government workers would get this rough equivalent of a 15-percent pay raise only if the cost was met by increased rural-land-tax assessments.

By now Batlle's interest in land taxes was widely known. The message reminded the legislature that:

To maintain the existing valuations is knowingly to maintain strong favoritism for the rural tax contributor, when what should be done is to strive for greater tax proportionality based on economic and social concepts.[20]

The method of rural-land-tax assessments was still somewhat primitive. Each property was taxed at the rate of 6.50 pesos per 1,000 pesos of assessed value, but individual properties were not separately evaluated. Each department was divided into zones; within each zone the assessed value per hectare (2.471 acres) of land was the same. The project asked for a 25,000-peso appropriation to continue statistical work leading to eventual individual property assessments. The Executive also wanted two immediate changes: an increase to over 140 zones instead of the 100 zones now used, and a new method of tax assessment. Assessment would be based on the average price of property sold within the zone in the last ten years minus 10 percent.

Indignant ranchers protested. The legislators, torn between their landowner constituents and their political friends, the government workers, compromised. The Chamber Committee changed the assessment base to sale price minus 20 percent. It wrote in a requirement that the assessments on any single property not be raised more than 50 percent. The committee stated that its compromise bill would bring the treasury an additional 200,000 pesos in tax receipts, instead of the 380,000 pesos proposed by the Executive, but that the reduction would still permit the end of pay deductions for low-paid government workers.

The Nationalists seized the opportunity and pictured themselves the friends of the oppressed ranchers.[21] Martín C. Martínez estimated that the compromise would bring in 350,000 pesos, not the 200,000 claimed by the committee. He tried very hard to keep the tax recently voted to finance road-building—50 cents additional to the 6.50 per 1,000 pesos of assessed valuation—at the old assessment rates. The Colorado legislators held firm; the Committee's compromise passed.[22]

The Chamber wanted to encourage agriculture and agreed to have assessed values on small agricultural plots cut by 50 percent. Martín C. Martínez objected, explaining that the tax rates, even under the new system, were so low that a 50-percent reduction would not induce a latifundist landowner to subdivide his huge properties. Martínez was really answering his own protests that the new valuations oppressed landowners, for the new annual land tax would still average about ten cents per hectare.

Serrato, nevertheless, was satisfied that the land-tax measure had prepared the way for the future. In his section of the annual presidential message for February 1906, he pointed out:

The day is not far away when rural property will be assessed individually, at that same time fiscal lands usufructed unlawfully at the present moment will pay taxes; but until this day arrives, we accomplish this purpose in part by increasing the number of zones and altering their prices in accord with a scientific criterion.[23]

The mention of fiscal lands, government lands occupied under cloudy title by individuals, raised an unsettled question. If the Government pushed its claims to fiscal lands in an extreme form, it could alter the whole landholding structure.

During the war, Serrato had announced plans for debt conversion. There had been debt conversions before, but they really had been bankruptcy proceedings to enable Uruguay to resume payment on defaulted bonds. Serrato's postwar debt conversion project —a contract with the Bank of Paris and the Low Countries—was different: it was designed to take advantage of Uruguay's improved credit rating and lower the interest rate on Government bonds; it also would relieve the strain on the Montevideo money market caused by the bond issues authorized by the legislature since the war.

The contract, which called for the issuance of 32,488,300 pesos in new 5-percent bonds to replace 31,110,550 pesos in 6-percent bonds, required legislative approval. Three classes of bonds would be converted: 12 million pesos authorized since '97, already issued locally, whose owners would be given the option of conversion to the new bonds or redemption in cash; 12 million pesos authorized since the war but not yet issued; 7 million pesos in new bonds to pay the French company constructing the port of Montevideo (the company was delaying construction because it did not want to accept payment in port bonds at over par).

Success of the issue depended on whether most holders of present bonds preferred conversion—for each 100-peso 6-percent bond they now owned they would get a new 5-percent bond plus a bonus of 3 pesos in cash—to redemption at 100 pesos cash. The Bank would provide the funds to redeem bonds and in exchange the Bank would receive from the Uruguayan government new bonds for sale in Europe. It would receive the new bonds at 90, which meant that the Uruguayan Government had to give roughly 111 pesos in new bonds to redeem 100 pesos of old bonds, but to convert old bonds it would give only 103 pesos in new bonds. If enough bondholders converted, there would be some new bonds remaining at the end of the transaction. The Executive proposed to use these remaining bonds to finance the building of a School of

Veterinary Medicine, a School of Agriculture, and secondary schools in the interior—up to now secondary schooling was restricted to Montevideo.

Martín C. Martínez felt that Serrato could have made a better bargain. He objected to the guarantees Uruguay had given the French bankers: 24 percent of the Uruguayan customs tax receipts would be pledged to pay the interest and amortization of the bonds; Uruguay promised not to float any new foreign loan for two years; Uruguay promised not to attempt any new debt conversion for eight years. All these guarantees, designed to make the 5-percent bonds attractive to European investors, meant that the bankers did not yet consider Uruguay a Class-A credit risk. Martínez also feared that owners of present bonds would redeem, not convert. The only ones who would then profit would be the bankers, for the bankers would receive the bonds from the Uruguayan government at 90 and sell them in Europe at 97 or more. Martínez acknowledged that neither Serrato nor anyone else in the government had been corrupt: "I know that it is the same government of probity of which I had proof in ten months in its administration." Still, he urged "the honest government" to contain the bankers' usury.[24]

Serrato insisted that he had made a good bargain. The customs-receipts guarantee was merely a bookkeeping device because the funds would be deposited in the Bank of the Republic. He was optimistic about the future of the country and was sure the present bondholders would convert, not redeem, in which case bankers' profits would be reasonable.[25]

The legislature approved the contract,[26] and the new bonds were issued. Of the 12,323,850 pesos in bonds eligible for redemption, only 6,001,560.67 pesos were redeemed; the rest were converted. Serrato later exulted, "As a result of this satisfactory result, which exceeded expectations," there would be 691,109 pesos left over for building the veterinary, agricultural, and secondary schools.[27]

Yet the 1905 Debt Conversion demonstrated the difficulties of financing economic development in even a solvent South American country. Local private capital, the Montevideo money market, could absorb only relatively small quantities of government bonds; the government could not supply much capital on its own and had to go abroad for funds to finance large-scale undertakings; European capital demanded protection against future bond over-issues and insisted on respectable underwriting profits. Whether it looked to itself, local capital, or foreign capital, the Uruguayan government could find only limited aid in carrying out expansion of the nation's services.

This explained why Don Pepe, with all his reluctance to see foreign companies run Uruguayan public services, allowed the British railroad company to extend its lines from Nico Pérez to Melo instead of trying to have his government build and operate the line. In the hope the extended railroad would connect southern Brazil with the new port of Montevideo, Batlle required the company to build beyond Melo to Centurión on the Brazilian border within three years—ahead of traffic, just as in the Montevideo trolley concessions. He also insisted that a new formula for computing the government's usual 3.5-percent profit guarantee to the railroad be written into the contract.[28]

In the year or so since the war there had been solid achievements: schools, university expansion,[29] roads, and now 340 kilometers of new railroad. Last year the annual ministers' reports spoke of postponements; this year the reports listed construction projects scheduled and already under way. Don Pepe was even experimenting with specially built riverboats on the Río Negro, a river most people considered unnavigable most of the year.

XV

The Nationalists Humbled

The Montevideo business community, the Rural Association, and the Manufacturers' Association joined in sponsoring a grand banquet honoring Williman, a banquet not reported in *El Día*. Martín C. Martínez, by now one of the leading Nationalists, and José Pedro Ramírez, whom Batlle regularly denounced as responsible for the War of 1904, were there. Williman, continuing his policy of making no speeches or statements, did not attend. After the banquet a delegation visited Williman, who had not expected them and was caught in a state of semidress. He limited himself to saying he was delighted such an eminent group supported his candidacy.[1]

The conservative classes intended the banquet as more than a gesture of good will toward Williman. They intended it as a warning to those Nationalists, who were supposedly plotting a revolt to come after the February election of Senate President, that the substantial element of Uruguay was satisfied with Williman, was counting the days until Batlle's term expired, and would give neither material nor moral support to any Nationalist revolution. Elements within the conservative classes were also trying to ease tension by bringing the Colorados and Nationalists toward conciliation —a term whose political meaning was Nationalist participation in the government.

This was not the direction in which Batlle wanted Williman to go. *El Día* first ignored the conciliation campaign, then rejected it:

Why, therefore, talk of conciliation? The government must be presumed *a priori* to be conciliated with all the inhabitants of the country, regardless of their political affiliation, whom the government is obliged to respect so long as they comply with their responsibilities. For these reasons, it must be granted that the Nationalist Directorio, so long as it does not leave its legitimate orbit, is naturally conciliated with the President of the Republic, without the necessity of processes of negotiation. And if the Directorio should decide to leave that orbit the solution would not be to seek more or less platonic cordial relations but to give intervention to the judges, to the other legal authorities whose function is to punish those who disobey laws and constituted government.[2]

Batlle had written the editorial; he had decided to proclaim boldly what he had been practicing since the war—one-party government. During the last two weeks of January 1906, *El Día* ran a series of editorials extolling one-party government and condemning coparticipation or bipartisanship. The first one, a bombshell titled "The Utopia of Coparticipation," insisted that coparticipation was the method bad governments used to "make their great faults tolerated." Coparticipation, however begun, ended fatally in war, as recent experience had demonstrated.[3]

The next day *El Día* tried to answer the argument that one-party government might make sense abroad, where the parties rotated in office, but was inapplicable to Uruguay, where the Colorados had kept the government for forty years. Rotation itself was not a positive good; the positive good was that the majority elected the government.

The reciprocal duties of those in power and those out of power are therefore fixed. The one fully complies with the mission the voters have given it. The other should resign itself to obtaining at the ballot box what up to now it has been unable to achieve either by its arrogance or its hatreds.[4]

Don Pepe soon entered the polemic. The basic reason for one-party government was that men with common principles must guide the government and determine its policies.[5] How far down did one-party government go? That depended:

The doctrine of one-party government applied to government positions involves, mainly, executive and political posts. For example, it would be absurd to seek candidates for the departmental jefaturas from the ranks of the opposition, since the departmental jefaturas have to reflect an exact image of the Executive. But the same does not hold for technical or judicial posts . . .

Nor does one-party government mean that citizens of the opposition, in greater or lesser numbers, should not be found among the great mass of public employees. We recognize that in certain countries, countries which certainly are not characterized by lack of liberty, it is an almost absolute principle that the party which takes over the government does not allow even a single adversary to remain in any post; but we believe that such a system would be too harsh to apply in a new country like ours where the lack of industries makes public employment a common livelihood. Therefore, we consider it perfectly legitimate among us that public employment be distributed equitably among all citizens, based principally on the individual's aptness for the position and his personal conduct, as assurances that he will perform well in his respective position, without putting great emphasis on his political coloration.

This being so, why does the present government ignore saravista [6] citizens when it fills vacant positions? Simply because the government feels that, so long as the saravista party does not renounce its aggressive policy, does not demonstrate clearly and convincingly that it has forever abandoned warlike aspirations in order to take its place tranquilly in the ranks of those whose only aspiration is to make their rights count in the wide field of labor and law—that party can not provide really useful men for public positions.

A man who has his bags packed ready to revolt at the first subversive cry, and who places the authority of his party above every other authority . . . can not be a good servant of the nation . . . To place men of war in public positions is to hand over the nation, handcuffed, to its enemies. Those who were in the army and police would think only of disrupting these forces; those who were in the telegraph offices, at the opportune moment, would destroy the equipment; those in the Customs House would have no thought other than to facilitate war contraband. And so on everywhere. But we are sure that some day, more or less distant, the saravista faction must change its conduct, must think and act as the other political factions of the nation think and act, and then the government will be able to cease making the disagreeable distinctions with them that circumstances impose on it today.[7]

Batlle was thrashing the Blancos, but he offered them a distant consolation. Once they reconciled themselves to being a perpetual minority they would be included when subaltern government jobs were distributed.

El Siglo announced that it would survey the opinions of a distinguished group of citizens on the advantages of coparticipation. A similar *El Siglo* survey on immediate constitutional reform after the war had contributed to Batlle's decision to give up the plan. Since then he had won an overwhelming electoral victory and felt secure; he would not give up one-party government. Don Pepe had intentionally proclaimed one-party government in violent fashion because he wanted the conservative classes to know he would not allow them to try and win Williman away from him. He wanted to crush any hopes the Nationalists might have that they could gain concessions by threatening revolution.

The risk was that Batlle, by his virulence, would make it impossible for Nationalist moderates to restrain Mariano Saravia's revolutionary intent. Batlle's informants again announced plots for a March revolution, to come after Campisteguy's re-election as President of the Senate and to be coordinated with Batlle's assassination.[8]

If the Nationalists planned revolt, it was to their advantage to revolt soon. In November, six Senate seats would be up for election, and the Nationalists, in their present apathetic state, were likely to lose all or almost all these contests. The new Senators would be Batlle's personal choices; together with the five Senators he had elected in 1905, they would secure the Senate against duplicity. The Nationalist revolutionary strategy, if it existed, was to get another Cuestas elected President of the Senate in February, while Batlle's Senate majority was uncertain, and then revolt.

Don Pepe prepared against this eventuality. On January 12, the same day *El Día* came out against conciliation, the Colorado legislators signed a secret pledge: in the event the presidency of the Republic became vacant they would immediately vote for Claudio Williman as President for a term to end March 1, 1910.[9] Normally, Williman would take office on March 1, 1907, and serve to March 1, 1911. The pledge had a grisly purpose. If Batlle were assassinated now, Williman, not some accomplice of the Nationalists, would take his place and remain in office for four years. The pledge also had a less ominous purpose. Batlle was toying with the idea of resigning six months early and having Williman elected for a three-and-a-half-year term.[10] Batlle's early departure would be welcomed by the Nationalists and the conservative classes. The plan would also gain a year for Batlle for, if all went well, he would be re-elected President in 1910 instead of 1911.

Don Pepe also got ready to put down any Nationalist uprising.

On January 20, he sent the following order to Colonel Américo Pedragosa, an able officer he had installed as Jefe Político of Cerro Largo once the electoral need for a malleable politician as jefe had passed:

> If a subversive movement breaks out and your communications with the government are interrupted, you should assemble the departmental division to carry out departmental policing, holding on to Melo and Artigas.
>
> In case you do not have sufficient forces to remain in Melo, you can retreat to Artigas or wherever circumstances make it necessary.[11]

Batlle worked hardest to prevent Campisteguy's re-election as President of the Senate. He did not believe that Campisteguy, one of his closest political and personal friends, was plotting with the Nationalists. Nationalist plotters were using his name to convince potential revolutionaries that a vast conspiracy was afoot, and Batlle wanted to shatter the conspiracy. That Campisteguy himself would appear to have been jettisoned as a potential traitor was just part of politics; Don Pepe felt that he should understand this. In 1913, Batlle complained: "Doctor Campisteguy, who had been Minister of Interior of Sr. Batlle y Ordoñez, and was at that time President of the Senate felt himself to be offended because of some unimportant incidents and Sr. Batlle y Ordoñez has not had the pleasure of seeing him again from then until now." [12]

It was not easy to stop Campisteguy's re-election. All the Nationalist Senators would vote for him, as would José Pedro Ramírez, elected Senator by the Nationalists. Several Colorado Senators saw no reason to insult Campisteguy and would also vote for him. At first, Batlle tried to win a majority for Blengio Rocca, one of the new Colorados, but the senior Colorado Senators would not accept him. Then Don Pepe turned to Dr. Francisco Soca, leader of the MacEachenites in 1903, who long had urged himself for the presidency of the Senate as reward for his cooperative attitude during the last weeks of the 1903 campaign.

Batlle called Senators to Piedras Blancas and asked them to vote for Soca. Juan Pedro Castro had suffered in 1904 what Campisteguy was to suffer now, yet he agreed that "it was not good politics" to keep him as Senate President.[13] Espalter had promised Campisteguy his vote, but now that Williman's election as President of the Republic was involved, he broke his promise. It boiled down to one doubtful vote, that of Senator Rodolfo Vellozo, a Nationalist out of sympathy with the Directorio, and an old friend of Soca's and Batlle's.

Don Pepe asked Soca to bring Vellozo in for a visit. In a long interview, Vellozo told Batlle that he would give his vote to Soca and ask nothing for himself in return. He did feel he had the right to ask Batlle to use Nationalists in the government; this would consolidate peace. Don Pepe responded with his soft version of one-party government:

He does not exclude even ministries and departmental jefaturas from the positions which can be filled by members of other political parties. Although it must be understood that in the future these positions will not be given to a political party so that the party, in accord with its interests and viewpoints, can fill the positions with its delegates. Rather these positions will be given to individual members of that party so that they can sincerely and usefully collaborate in the shared goals of the government. It will therefore be necessary that insofar as these positions are concerned these men must be in accord with the program of the government.

Since the war, Don Pepe acknowledged, he had been unable to use Nationalists in his government because of "the heat of their passions and their violent opposition to the present political regime." But, sooner or later, "administrative correctness and respect for all rights and every liberty" would calm the Nationalists.

Dr. Williman who will take over the government without any promises or obligations—I can assure you and I do not doubt that you will honor my word—without any promises or obligations except those which his conscience as a party member and as a citizen, and the laws of the Republic impose, will be able to judge, in a more tranquil situation, the proportion of citizens from all parties who will be called to aid in the work of his government.[14]

Batlle's disclosure that he had exacted no pledges from Williman —for example, to support Batlle's re-election—was designed to strengthen the moderate Nationalists against those who wanted a revolutionary solution. Let the Nationalists wait for Williman, Don Pepe was saying, then they will get jobs and perhaps more. Still, he had been careful to note that Williman would follow "his conscience as a party member."

Vellozo's vote gave Soca nine votes to Campisteguy's eight, and he was elected President of the Senate.[15] Batlle's mind was not yet at rest. José Saravia, the Colorado Saravia who had saved Muniz from disaster at the beginning of the war by warning him that Aparicio had more men than he did, visited Batlle. He reportedly warned: "Take care, Mr. President—my brother Mariano is going to try a filibustering expedition against you in March." [16] On February 24, Julio Abellá y Escobar, whom Batlle had made Jefe Político of Rivera after the war, wrote Batlle that Mariano Saravia had scheduled horse races across the border for March 4.[17] Horse races were the traditional gaucho disguise for assembling a revolution. The men would ride in, ostensibly for the races, and, once gathered, raise the banner of revolt.

Batlle was so concerned that he held no reception on March 1, the third anniversary of his government. On March 2, Secundino Benítez, Jefe Político of San José, sent a coded message to the Minister of Government:

> For your information I transmit the following data which have come to my knowledge: the so-called Colonel Marin and other revolutionary leaders addicted to him have been inviting people to join an armed movement to take place soon, advising them to be ready to leave from the 4th to the 5th.[18]

The Directorio also was concerned. It sent Basilio Muñoz (who had taken command after Saravia's death and accepted Nationalist defeat in 1904) to see Mariano Saravia and talk him out of any foolishness.[19] The government interpreted Basilio Muñoz' mission differently: he must be the Directorio's war envoy to the revolutionary army. Concern mounted; the Directorio wanted to keep the Nationalists of the interior from joining Mariano should he invade. It issued a public manifesto, dated March 2, calling on party members to concentrate on party reorganization and future elections. The manifesto concluded:

> While the Directorio dedicated itself to these civic activities, alarmist reports once again came to the ears of some of its members. The Directorio believes that this time it should not wait until this new wave of uncertainty spreads, causing its pernicious effects. Believing that the condemnation of the efforts to renew a bloody and sterile struggle, which perhaps are being attempted in the present circumstances, will

be a worthy corollary to its efforts at civic reorganization, the Directorio judges such efforts to be entirely anti-patriotic and contrary to the political interests of the party.[20]

The manifesto had an unexpected effect. Batlle seized upon it as proof the Directorio had failed to restrain Mariano and that he would, in fact, invade on March 5. Don Pepe did not wait to see if his surmise was correct. On March 3, he telegraphed the jefe político in every department to arrest all known Nationalist military officers. The jefes relayed the order to the rural police chiefs, who jailed as many as 1,000 Nationalists.[21] In Montevideo, all Radical Nationalists except those with legislative immunity were imprisoned, including Basilio Muñoz, who had returned with the information that Mariano was quiet. Nationalist political clubs were closed and searched for evidence; the press and telegraph lines were put under censorship.

Colonel Cándido Viera's regiment moved to the Brazilian border to await Mariano's invasion. War Minister General Vázquez held a telegraphic conversation with him and Jefe Político Abellá y Escobar. For the moment, all was quiet; João Francisco had sent his second in command over to say that this time he would give the revolution "no aid of any sort." Abellá did report that Basilio Muñoz "had come on a revolutionary mission on behalf of the directorio and that the revolution would come at the end of March or the beginning of April." [22]

Mariano held his races and nothing happened. The Nationalist prisoners were taken before judges who, in the absence of any evidence, began ordering their release. On March 5, Batlle and Williman sent the constitutionally required message to the legislature asking it to approve the action taken by the Executive. The message presented the evidence on which the Executive had acted: the coded message from the Jefe Político of San José on March 2; year-old minutes of a Directorio meeting; a secret code found on Dr. Morelli, an arrested member of the Directorio and one of its emissaries to Mariano; and the Directorio manifesto.

The Executive explained that "the Republic could not remain at the mercy . . . of the first brazen individual who judges himself authorized to throw it into turmoil." The Directorio manifesto had alerted the government to the danger. If the Executive had waited to see whether a revolution broke out, "it would in fact have made itself an accomplice in the revolution which was being prepared against the tranquillity and order of the State." [23]

By the time the Executive sent this message, all reports agreed that no revolution was being prepared; the whole affair had been a false alarm. Manini delayed legislative debate on the Executive's action until March 9. On that day, a second Executive message, ending all extraordinary measures but announcing that the released Nationalists would be required to remain in the departmental capitals for several days, was sent to the legislature. The Executive had heard that the invasion was to be postponed until the Nationalist officers were released and it wanted to keep them under surveillance.

The second message took urgency off the legislative debate and the government supporters were able to get a further delay. Finally, on March 12 and March 13, the legislators debated the legality of Batlle's acts. The Nationalist position was that the Executive had no basis for action. The only specific piece of evidence, the message from San José's Jefe Político that Cicerón Marin was gathering men, was denied by Marin in a sworn statement read by a Nationalist deputy. This did not satisfy the Colorados. Magariños Veira, friend of Don Pepe's youth, shouted at the Nationalists: "You are all revolutionaries . . . what you want is to stop don José Batlle y Ordoñez from governing another day, for the crime of having conquered you in a bloody struggle you yourselves provoked." [24] Every Colorado, Campisteguy included, voted to approve the Executive's message: the final vote was 48 to 16.

On March 14, the Nationalist military officers were given full freedom of movement. Batlle's fears, over the last two months, had been unjustified; yet the government was strengthened by the March commotion. It had been a kind of fire drill; *El Día* put it this way: "the government wants not only to demonstrate, as it has demonstrated, that any struggle against public order is impossible, but that even an attempt at revolt is becoming more impossible every day." [25]

For the Nationalists it had been another humiliation. Men who once had been proud officers of Saravia's army had been thrown in jail like common criminals. Dr. Morelli, released from prison, resigned from the Directorio, saying that the manifesto had been both unnecessary and a mistake. Rodríguez Larreta tried to post-pone collective resignation as long as possible because "today there is no attractiveness whatever in being a member of the Directorio, and it would be difficult to make up one willing to bear the burden of responsibility which events keep creating." [26]

XVI

Onward

THE Directorio made a determined effort to regroup rather than resign. It planned to send delegations to encourage registration in the six departments where Senate elections were scheduled for November.[1] There was brave talk of Nationalist coalitions with dissident Colorados to sweep the officialists to electoral defeat.[2]

On April 5 and April 6, Directorio President Carlos Berro met in Buenos Aires with Mariano Saravia, Basilio Muñoz, and other Nationalist military leaders. It seems that Berro advised them to wait and see how Williman's administration acted before considering revolution. The conference participants assured interviewers of their peaceful dispositions, although Basilio Muñoz did say, "we have not come here to make war, we do not intend to make war, but war will come inevitably, sooner or later, if Sr. Batlle's political regime, with its hatreds, its persecutions, its arbitrariness, continues." President Berro was more explicit: "I can assure you that the immense majority of the party thinks as the Directorio does . . . that peace should not be disturbed." [3]

The Uruguayan government's agents in Buenos Aires relayed a different version of the Nationalist conference. Foreign Minister Romeu advised Batlle of plots against his life and reported:

One of the informants communicated to me that the junta of officers headed by Basilio Muñoz bought 800 rifles in Buenos Aires destined for San José and the Directorio bought 850,000 rounds . . . the officers want to revolt next month but the Directorio wants to postpone it until September so that it can be a powerful revolution.[4]

Police spies watched the Nationalists. A shipment of machine guns, the newest available, "those which by their precision and destructive power won the Transvaal war by making Boer resistance impossible," arrived and was tested in Batlle's presence.[5]

Don Pepe once had been described as a man with resigned valor who, if told that an assassin was waiting for him up the street, pistol in hand, would walk on. That was before the mine exploded in front of his coach; since then, assassination attempts seemed more likely than revolution and Batlle had himself carefully guarded.[6]

Late in April, the young Nationalist editors of *La Democracia* described Batlle's walk home after ceremonies honoring the war dead of Tupambaé and Masoller:

Several policemen headed the presidential escort. . . .

The President of the Republic gave his arm to the Minister of Government doctor Williman, keeping his aide-de-camp, Colonel Domingo Romero on his right.

Behind them came the chief of the investigative police señor Levratto and another person . . . Further behind, a group of soldiers, still further behind a group of agents of the investigative police. Next to the sidewalk curb, two carriages followed the presidential retinue, at a slow pace.

On the sidewalk across from the one His Excellency was walking went Colonel Bernassa, the jefe político of the capital, Colonel Barriola, commanding officer of the presidential escort, and behind them a platoon of guards and secret police.

Needless to say, the trajectory followed by the President was rigorously guarded by active and sagacious agents, who did not miss a single detail of everything which transpired on the main Avenue while the official parade went on.

After this, no one will be able to say that His Excellency does not appear on the streets, does not go to Government House, but locks himself within his fortress at Piedras Blancas because he is afraid.

Who said afraid? [7]

Don Pepe was sure the incorrigible Herrera had written the piece. Without waiting to confirm authorship, Batlle aimed in Herrera's direction with his own "Who Said Afraid?"

La Democracia in today's number tells us that last night the President was in the General Staff building where the remains of those who fell at Tupambaé and Masoller were honored, and it adds that when he left he did so on foot, followed by an army of policemen and investigative agents.

It is possible that the President, although he had advised no one that he would return home on foot, for the simple reason that the idea did not occur to him until he left the General Staff building, was followed by the army of which *La Democracia* speaks or in fact by three or four police agents. Actually, we find nothing wrong in this because the security of the President of the Republic is closely tied to the keeping of peace, of order, of all the public fruits which the flourishing of the current situation is beginning to produce.

But because of this, *La Democracia* plants a problem which places us in the most profound uncertainty: Who said afraid?

To resolve it we will make a funereal incantation:

Oh you, most beautiful and heedless girl, you who did not have at your side a strong male in the days of danger, though you had a weak one in the days of error, rise from your forgotten slab of stone and tell us who said afraid! [8]

Batlle was raking up a tragic scandal. Everyone knew Herrera, the lover of the "beautiful and heedless girl," had not interceded to save her. Herrera, who was not the author of the *La Democracia* editorial, sent his seconds to *El Día* and demanded satisfaction. Román Freire, Don Pepe's former secretary, appeared at the *La Democracia* office and informed Herrera that Batlle, the author of the *El Día* answer, "was not disposed to withdraw even a comma of what he had said," and would put himself completely at Herrera's disposition once his presidential term ended. The rules of dueling did not permit ten-month postponements; Herrera's seconds declared his honor vindicated.[9] Another storm of criticism descended on Batlle for his making the office of President look ridiculous. Don Pepe himself felt satisfied he had finally put Herrera in his place "with three well chosen words." [10]

Batlle was pressing to take advantage of the months left to his administration. The Executive sent the legislature a project nationalizing and expanding the municipally owned Montevideo power system. Batlle urged government engineers to prepare their plans for roads more quickly. When the plans were forwarded to him, he sent them back with instructions to reduce the period allowed contractors for completion.[11] No sooner had the legislature appropriated funds for the Legislative Palace than Batlle demanded plans, and he wanted something "really monumental." [12]

The legislature worked hard. It approved the first of the long series of steps which would bring constitutional reform—over Nationalist objections. The Chamber voted the divorce bill in general, by a vote of thirty-seven to thirteen, with five Colorados and eight Nationalists opposed. This meant only that the Chamber approved the general principle of divorce; it would now proceed to debate each article of the bill.[13]

Gabriel Terra's progressive inheritance tax project came out of committee. The existing inheritance tax, whose proceeds went to education, was widely evaded and produced only 200,000 pesos annually. Terra's original project, though it introduced progressive taxation, was moderate: on estates of over 1,000,000 pesos, children would pay but 2.5 percent while relatives six times removed would pay 18.5 percent. Even this was too steep for the committee, whose revised version levied the tax on the individual inheritance not the estate (if four heirs inherited a 1,000,000-peso estate, each would be taxed in the 250,000 bracket) and cut the highest bracket—on relatives six times removed to 14 percent. The Chamber passed the project in general. Martín C. Martínez, not surprisingly, considered it dangerous and announced that he would offer amendments when the bill's individual articles were debated.[14]

Batlle's young disciple, Julio María Sosa, was now editing *La Prensa*, a newspaper founded to popularize Williman's candidacy. Sosa felt that Terra's original project was too timid. Modern society was beset by high prices and low wages; the multitudes were in misery while potentates squandered "vast sums they have not produced."

> Taxes should rest almost exclusively on inheritances and latifundia, so that this mass of capital and land now concentrated in a few hands, once divided would return to the national patrimony. It would then spread its regenerative force on all forms of labor, which once free from restrictions, will double production, reduce the cost of living, and because of the constantly expanded demand for the force supplied by human muscles will increase wages.[15]

Don Pepe could not yet let *El Día* say such things, things which, at the very least, frightened investors. He wanted investors to buy Uruguayan government bonds, especially now that so much public building was under way. He knew that investors liked sound finance, and in this he agreed with them. Batlle, though a tax visionary, was a believer in hard money and balanced budgets. He remembered that paper money and budget deficits had helped ruin Lorenzo Batlle's presidency.

On May 10, the clerk read the Executive's annual financial message to an attentive Chamber. When the clerk finished, the entire Chamber, Colorado and Nationalist, broke into spontaneous applause. Serrato had announced a budget surplus! The message gave details: the previous deficits, the war costs, the postwar building projects—yet for fiscal 1905–1906 there would be a budget surplus "of some four-hundred-thousand pesos." [16]

A four-hundred-thousand-peso budget surplus—there was a figure to roll around on one's tongue, especially in view of Uruguay's tragic financial history. General prosperity had resulted in substantial imports; customs revenue had risen more than two million pesos. This rise, rather than any special financial wizardry, explained the surplus. Even so, businessmen had to admit that, whatever dangerous schemes Batlle had in the back of his head, he and Serrato had handled finances brilliantly.

The Directorio's efforts to stir up support in the interior and stave off resignation were unsuccessful, and it resigned. A new Directorio had to be elected to fill out the unexpired term ending in December. The electoral process was a shambles. One newly elected Directorio resigned. A special party convention, whose only accomplishment was a paper party program,[17] was assembled. Finally, a more or less acceptable interim Directorio was elected. Carlos Berro again would be President; Martín Aguirre, the Radical leader, moved up to First Vice President.[18]

The election had returned the cautious Conservatives to control, but had given the Radicals a greater voice in the Directorio. The protracted series of elections showed that the party mass was indifferent to both sides: the Conservatives could not get them to vote; the Radicals, to revolt. Actually, the Radical bellicosity was mostly verbal. Martín Aguirre, the civilian leader, had been ostracized by Saravia; Basilio Muñoz, the military chief, was the scapegoat of 1904. Tough talk was the way back to political importance for them, but the Nationalist military officers would not really fight under the Radical leadership. *El Día* gleefully announced the imminent disintegration of the "Saravista" party.

Batlle's informants, though they continued to report Nationalist plots, did so with a reduced sense of urgency. Bachini, Consul General in Buenos Aires (who had heavier responsibilities now that Acevedo Díaz, an indifferent diplomat who wanted to be closer to home, was Minister to Argentina), advised Batlle that a vast plan for revolution had been postponed: "My informant affirms that for the moment you can be calm; there is nothing going on." [19]

Nothing could halt Williman's candidacy. A movement to run Galarza, the hero of Tupambaé, as presidential candidate was stopped by Galarza himself. He wrote Manini, his wartime secretary: "I am a servant of the present situation; I am an adherent of Williman's candidacy and I am a supporter and personal friend of Sr. Batlle y Ordoñez." Manini published the letter.[20]

Williman consented to an interview by *La Nación* of Buenos Aires. He refused to announce a program but he did say,

> . . . that in political matters he shared the opinions announced by the President of the Republic to the Nationalist Senator Rodolfo Vellozo in February of this year. . .
> —When talking about the possibility of conciliation between the parties, Dr. Williman was optimistic . . . even though he doesn't say so, he is convinced that his candidacy does not provoke real opposition among the Nationalists and that, therefore, his government will begin under the best auspices. In administrative matters Dr. Williman proposes to see through to completion the improvements begun by the present government, considering it a great honor for himself to complete the many and valuable improvements already undertaken rather than to begin new ones.[21]

Conciliation was almost a technical word in Uruguayan politics, defined as bringing the opposition into the government to keep them from revolting against the government. Such an inference from Williman's interview would encourage the Radical Nationalists; both *El Día* and the Williman campaign newspaper, *La Prensa*, printed an immediate retraction:

> We understand that Doctor Williman has not used exactly this word which has been attributed to him. In his interview with the editor of our Buenos Aires colleague he could only have referred to possible modifications in the conduct of the Nationalists, without entering into an evaluation of the consequences such modifications might produce in the future political situation.[22]

Don Pepe was already preparing the list of candidates for the November election of six Senators, all of whom, since they served six-year terms, would vote for his re-election—if his plans succeeded. Batlle's first concern was for his cabinet members: no department would run Romeu, the Acevedo Díaz man, but safe seats were assured Serrato and Capurro (the Minister of Fomento). Viera and Areco were to be promoted to the Senate from the Chamber. Tiscornia, the Catholic Batllista, would run in his home department of Río Negro, and Martín Suárez was Batlle's candidate for Rocha.[23]

Usually, Senate candidates were not settled upon until immediately before election. Batlle's ability to write the ticket months in advance was a striking demonstration of his control of the Colorado Party. His mind had eased considerably since February and March, and he had given up thoughts of cutting short his presidency. His friends spread the news that he would leave for Europe just as soon as his term ended. In Europe, Don Pepe would be out of Uruguayan politics and could avoid giving cause, or seeming to give cause, for any quarrel with Williman.

Batlle continued to work his government hard. All sorts of projects were being prepared—additional railroad expansion, plans for a new port on the Atlantic, the end of salary deductions for higher paid government employees, the long-announced labor law. Don Pepe was particularly captivated by the idea of a Grand Avenue, which would cut through the center of Montevideo to connect the Legislative Palace, not yet built, with the Executive Palace, not yet even authorized. Word got out that Batlle planned to finance the Grand Avenue by taxing "the increased value" which would be given to property by this monument to his administration.

The Chamber worked hard too. It began debate on the budget for 1906–1907, the first full-dress budget revision of Batlle's administration. The Executive proposed an 18,200,000-peso budget, which would include all the postwar salaries and the annual cost of the new bond issues. The 400,000-peso budget surplus already announced would go for road-building, as would 500,000 pesos left over from the amounts budgeted for war claims.

Fixed costs still consumed most of the tax revenues and greatly

limited the Executive's ability to carry on new activities. Of the
18.2 million-peso budget, 7.8 million would go for debt service and
railroad guarantees, 1.4 million for pensions, 2.2 million for the
army, and 2.1 million for the police and Ministry of Government—
all told, this was 74 percent of the budget. The Executive had been
extremely cautious in estimating revenues. It budgeted for only
10.7 million pesos in customs receipts, though it had collected 12.3
million pesos from customs last year. Even with the underestimated
tax receipts, the budget still showed a 109,000-peso surplus.

The Colorado Deputies knew the overcautious revenue estimates
were designed to curb legislative spending proposals, and they began approving pay increases for government workers. The Executive stepped in and proposed to end the 10 percent deduction on
gross salary for public employees earning over 360 pesos a month.
The Executive wanted to stop here, but the Deputies had already
made some promises and a few individual pay raises were also authorized.

Serrato appeared before the Chamber, warned against the assumption that tax revenues would inevitably rise, and advocated
seeing the surplus in the treasury first, then appropriating it:

. . . surpluses should be used only partly to lower taxes. Rather we
should use them to stimulate economic development, which increases
production and not only gives employment to native sons but also
solves the great national problem of attracting immigrants to these
shores.[24]

The very words "stimulate economic development" had a new and
unusual ring.

On the whole, the Deputies restrained themselves. The young
Colorados ended the annual subsidy to the Catholic Seminary (previously reduced to 4,000 pesos) over the objections of their elders.
More rural police were authorized. The budget, as approved and
sent to the Senate in September, called for expenditures of slightly
over 19,000,000 pesos—20 percent more than the current budget.

Serrato, who was about to resign as Minister of Finance to be
legally eligible to run for the Senate, told the Chamber that the
Executive would accept the budget. He advised that the exact
budget surplus for 1905–1906 was 453,110 pesos, somewhat larger
than originally estimated, and concluded with an optimistic prediction: "The Executive Power expects that this surplus will be but

the first in a continuous series." The enthusiastic Chamber voted that broadsides of the speech be printed and circulated throughout the country.[25]

Serrato had talked of stimulating economic development. A congenial opportunity was at hand. The English and German electric trolley companies needed electric power; they wanted either to buy out the government-owned plant which now had a legal monopoly or to build their own plants. Don Pepe did not intend that the foreign companies do either. He preferred to settle the involved question of ownership between the Montevideo municipality (the legal owner) and the national government (the actual operator) by nationalizing the power system, and to meet the need for increased power by expanding the plant.

The municipality wanted better terms from the national government and refused to agree to nationalization. The trolley companies needed power immediately, for their concessions required them to go into operation very soon. Batlle solved the problem by asking the legislature to appropriate funds for immediate expansion while leaving the question of nationalization for later settlement. The Executive accompanied its bill with a message in which it explained its general view of the role of government-operated economic enterprises:

The experience of those nations which have taken over the furnishing of electric light and power, whose supply it is always dangerous to delegate to private individuals who sacrifice the needs of general interest to their own interest, demonstrates that only operation by public administration can meet the needs of this public service . . . whenever private initiative is lacking, or the class of public service constitutes a natural monopoly, it is the State, safeguarding the interests of society, which must take over ownership and operation. . .

Neither official industrialism with strictly business aims and fiscal profits nor the carrying out of any Socialist doctrines is behind this preference: . . . rather, higher motives of a social and economic order and interest in the widest diffusion and distribution of all classes of services which are presently considered necessary for the general welfare, comfort, and hygiene.[26]

The enunciated doctrine was far-reaching: the State should provide all classes of services needed for the general welfare, comfort, and hygiene, not just the usual public services; the State's industrial goal should be service not profit.

Whatever Batlle's ultimate goal, his immediate project—electric power expansion—was welcome. The Chamber Committee, with support from above, raised the Executive's original request for 400,000 pesos to 1,200,000 pesos. No new taxes were needed and the financing was delightful: the State would issue mortgage bonds on the power plant and pay them off with the increased profits of the expanded system.

The bill passed both Chamber and Senate easily, although there was some concern about government ownership. Gregorio L. Rodríguez, who had been Cuestas' Minister of Fomento, explained:

> I do not believe that this type of service, in countries like ours, should be administered and operated by public corporations . . . exploitation on behalf of the State always means higher costs and lower income than operation by private companies.

Cabral, one of the young Colorados, who had written the committee report, answered:

> . . . the justification of a State monopoly rests, precisely, in the suppression of the avidity and voracity of private individuals, and in the cheapening of the service or product, which results in general welfare.[27]

Batlle had moved quickly to expand the electric power system, even before its ownership was settled, because otherwise the English and German trolley companies could not be denied the right to build their own plants. Although he was reluctant to admit it, he was much more concerned with stopping voracious profit-making by foreign companies than by Uruguayan capitalists. Foreign companies sent their profits abroad, de-capitalizing Uruguay; Uruguayan capitalists spent their profits in Uruguay, and created demands for products and more jobs. Besides, when Uruguay became the model state Don Pepe envisioned, Uruguayan capitalists, through stiff inheritance taxes at their death, would turn their fortunes back to society.

Liebig's, as expected, won Senate approval of its request for reduction of the export taxes on its products. Batlle, as he had warned, vetoed the reduction. He wanted to explain his position, but as President did not want too public an identification with the doctrine behind his veto, so he wrote a long *El Día* editorial,

"About Liebig," and instead of signing it with one of his well-known pseudonyms like Nemo or Néstor, he signed it "N."

N. began by insisting that the Senate had given Liebig's a gift of 35,000 pesos because Liebig's was a foreign company, and had justified this gift "on the popular thesis that we must attract foreign capital."

Very well. But there are two classes of foreign capital: one which comes to our country with its owner, establishes itself in the country, leaves its profits here, and identifies itself and mixes in with local capital, forming an integral part of the national wealth; and the other which comes to the country alone, and, leaving its owner abroad, sends its profits far away, and at the end when it feels like it leaves our country.

The first class of foreign capital should be "embraced with open arms"; the second presented problems.

As a new country we need capital; as an inexperienced country we need those who manage it. Therefore we should not be too upset that capital comes from abroad and is administered from abroad. Nevertheless, we should aspire to administer it ourselves and to create sufficient funds of our own for the development of our economic life.

The second class of foreign capital also was divided into two parts. One was capital coming in at fixed interest rates, like the money borrowed by the government at 5 percent on its new bonds. The other was capital coming in without any fixed rate, like Liebig's, which was earning 20 percent.

There is no doubt that it is to our country's advantage to import capital at 5 percent, so long as this capital is employed in productive tasks. Right now, roads, bridges, canals, ports, etc. are being constructed with funds taken at 5 percent and there is no question that over and beyond this 5 percent, there will remain in our country a profit of 5, 10, 15 percent, and perhaps more. But is it equally unquestionable that capital which extracts 20 percent leaves us real profits?

Liebig's, in addition to its factory, owned land and cattle. It could buy more land and raise all the cattle it needed for its factory. From the economic viewpoint, part of Uruguay would be foreign territory: "Thoughtless protection of foreign capital could lead us to these extremes."

Liebig's promised to print "Made in Uruguay" on the labels of its meat extract sold in Europe, if the tax reduction were approved.

The consumers so alerted will know that here is a people of shepherds, owners of vast herds—herds which a company located in Berlin exploits, because these shepherds neither know how or are able to exploit them. And the consumers will not be able to help wondering at our primitive simplicity and generosity if they come to discover that, even though that company takes out of our country every five years a sum even greater than all the capital employed, we insist, full of gratitude, that it take out even more.[28]

Batlle surprised even his close political followers with his economic ideas, ideas he had not preached before becoming President. He always had preached moral ideas, from his days as a philosophy student under Vázquez y Vega in the Ateneo; he himself had written the Executive's message which accompanied the bill ending the death penalty. A year had gone by but the bill still was in committee. Just recently, Don Pepe had commuted a death sentence by ruling that a murder had not been premeditated. He wanted no additional burdens on his conscience.[29]

On June 18, Arena rose in the Chamber to ask that the bill ending the death penalty be put on the calendar:

Public works are already under construction; the country's finances are in perfect order. Therefore, we can discuss this important matter without fear of prejudicing interests of another order. For my part, I declare in the most formal fashion that I am always ready to give preference to laws of a moral character; and that if I had to choose this very minute between a road-building law or the law abolishing the death penalty, I would choose the latter without hesitation, because I consider it the best sort of civilizing law.[30]

Arena's outlandish garb and the project itself evoked some macabre humor, but the Deputies knew that behind Arena stood Batlle; they scheduled debate for June 25.

Batlle's reading of Ahrens' "Course on Natural Law" as a young man doubtless influenced him when, as President, he wrote the bill's message. The message stated that the death penalty was antiquated:

. . . execution has to be hidden more and more inside penitentiaries because it is repugnant to public sentiment . . . It is true that for certain authors this penalty is a punishment suffered here on earth as a means of tempering the punishment which should be received in heaven . . . But positive law can not have as its object the settling of religious questions, but rather the common good, and more or less terrible punishments can not be imposed for religious reasons.

In primitive societies, where there were no prisons, the death penalty might be justified. More advanced societies killed men when such a society was obliged to resist an invading army or put down revolution. "These mass executions are legitimatized by the imperious and supreme reason of social conservation."

But, once order is re-established . . . no civilized society needs to do away with the delinquent to protect itself against his attack . . .

He who is about to commit a crime is detained and always will be detained by the powerful instinct in our organism which prevents us from inflicting physical harm on a fellow human being, and even more violently stops us from shedding his blood, than by all the preventive and repressive measures that might be taken.

The death penalty conspires against this protective sentiment and tends to weaken and extinguish it. The prolonged legal process to which the culprit is submitted and the calculated coldness with which he is judged and executed, can not but familiarize us with acts of this nature; can not but make us more and more insensible to another's suffering and to deaden the horror which the taking of human life by violence produces in us.[31]

The bill proposed to replace the death penalty with an indeterminate prison term of thirty to forty years. No prisoner could be released before serving thirty years; whether he served all or some of the remaining ten years would depend on his good behavior during the last half of his sentence.

Nationalist leader Vázquez Acevedo, author of Uruguay's criminal code, opposed abolition of the death penalty because he considered Uruguay still in the group of nations where life and property were not entirely secure. He concluded by voicing the increasing concern in respectable circles over the variety and radical nature of Batlle's recent manifestations: "Nations achieve good repute more by the prudence of their laws and the good sense of their procedures than by their advanced initiatives." [32]

Nationalist strategist Rodríguez Larreta found a way to get the bill sent back to committee. Batlle, at Arena's request, had included in the bill a provision ending the death penalty in military law as well as under civil criminal law. Rodríguez Larreta moved that soldiers be subject to the death penalty in wartime; Arena refused. The upshot, as Rodríguez Larreta had hoped, was that the Chamber sent the bill to its Military Committee for an opinion on the advisability of ending the military death penalty.[33]

Batlle's message on abolition of the death penalty tied executions to religion. Most of Don Pepe's moral preoccupations sooner or later involved anti-Catholicism, just as his interest in government-run business enterprises stemmed from his reluctance to see foreign companies take money out of Uruguay. Since the war, the anti-Catholic campaign had taken on considerable momentum: divorce proposals, the anti-Catholic Charity Commission, the end of subsidies to the Catholic seminary.

This Easter, Batlle wrote for *El Día* an "exposé" of The Resurrection, using the pseudonym "Judas," which was not one with which he could be publicly identified. In a style he made famous in later years with his series, "Reading the Bible," he outlined the physical impossibilities of the literal version of Jesus' resurrection.

Therefore, the resurrection appears to be nothing else but a gross lie plotted by the malice of some and accredited by the simplicity and superstition of the rest. Only one other, also Catholic, can be compared with it: the one which Mary put over on the simple Joseph about her relations with the Holy Ghost.[34]

The new Charity Commission kept busy expanding public assistance and cutting Catholic ties. On July 6, after fierce debate, it ordered removal of all crucifixes from sickrooms under its jurisdiction. In sign of protest, the Society of Catholic Ladies voted to wear crucifixes around their necks for a year, and they were supported by the Archbishop of Montevideo.

An influential non-Catholic also opposed the removal of crucifixes. Rodó, the religious liberal, in one of his most brilliant pieces, "Liberalism and Jacobinism," affirmed that Christ was the father of charity. To remove His Image from sickrooms was to cross "the frontier which separates the just from the unjust." It was Jacobinism not Liberalism.[35]

In this, as in his reactions to Batlle's other policies, Rodó revealed the views of his generation. He was a religious liberal in the elitist sense, as proof of his superior sensibilities to the common run of men. Religion, he now put it, is "a powerful means of suggestion . . . for the education of the masses." [36] Rodó himself was a lifelong bachelor, but men of his class married Catholic women in church, allowed their children to be brought up within the Church, and all the while wore a sardonic smile of superiority. When Batlle and his followers attempted to convert religious liberalism into a mass creed, as Batlle was also doing with organization politics, Rodó's generation became frightened.[37] Liberalism and political participation for the elite were sensible; liberalism and political participation for the masses were dangerous.

The Charity Commission had discussed removal of the crucifixes with Batlle before issuing the order, and Don Pepe leapt to the Commission's defense. In *El Día*, he answered Rodó's central contention. Batlle did not believe "in the possibility of full liberalism under the shadow of Catholicism."

> Does not that liberalism seem . . . more complete which permits the most complete liberty relative to religious beliefs to every patient, which does not force the inmate to ask for help under the protection of images in which he does not believe, which does not brutally force the unfortunate to seek aid in a room which officially displays objects of cult contrary to his faith, than the liberalism which requires all who implore the benefits of charity to contemplate the symbols in which only the affiliates of a given religious sect believe.[38]

In the hubbub which followed, *El Día* came out for complete separation of Church and State in the future constitutional reform.[39]

Batlle announced a Catholic plot against his government. It appeared that two Monsignors of the Church, taken in by rumors, offered General Tajes 250,000 pesos to finance a revolution, and Tajes had refused. All parties to the supposed plot, from the Archbishop down, dismissed the story as false,[40] but now the Catholics had been labeled, along with the dissident Colorados and the Nationalists, as avowed opponents of Batlle's regime.

XVII

†‹‹‹‹‹‹‹‹‹‹‹†

Tidying Up

On the second anniversary of Saravia's death, in September, the Nationalists placed a plaque on his tomb, across the border in Brazil. The Directorio sent a delegation; Mariano Saravia and other Nationalist military officers were present. Some of Batlle's informants advised that the Nationalists had come together to plot an October or November revolution. Other informants had it that the Nationalists would wait and watch how Williman governed.[1]

Only one hundred or so—a disappointing number—attended the ceremony at the tomb. Peace sentiment seemed to outweigh war talk. Batlle was notified, though, of a spreading rumor that to pacify the Nationalists he had offered Basilio Muñoz two departmental jefaturas.[2]

Such rumors must stop. While the memorial meeting was still going on, Batlle sent a revised army budget to the legislature. The revisions continued Batlle's postwar army policy: more units; more higher echelon command organizations. The country was to be divided into three military zones instead of two; a medical company and an army physical education school were established. Six new infantry battalions and six new cavalry squadrons were created by cutting the size of all infantry battalions to 250 men and all cavalry and artillery units to 200 men. The ostensible reason was that discipline would be improved if entire units, instead of detachments, served as departmental prison guards—the old compañía urbana function. The real reasons were the same as before: more units meant more officers who had fought in 1904 on active duty at full pay; more units would make it even harder for any handful of discontented unit commanders to stage a successful barracks uprising.

The expanded army budget arrived just as the Chamber was about to forward the entire government budget to the Senate. The Chamber paused long enough to hear Nationalist objections over the waste of money the army changes would involve—Martín C. Martínez estimated the increased cost at 280,000 pesos annually, Serrato put the increase at 90,000 pesos—and to the dangerous militarization of Uruguay it portended. Then the Chamber approved the army increase, included it in the general budget, and sent the budget on to the Senate.[3]

Serrato, Minister of Finance, and Capurro, Minister of Fomento, the heads of the two most active ministries, were on the point of resigning, to be candidates for the Senate; projects and decrees must be completed now. Conservative opinion had already called out against Batlle's "veritable rain of projects," but more projects descended: concessions for an irrigation canal, veterinary inspection of newly arrived livestock, assistance for newly arrived immigrants, prizes for cattle fairs. *El Día* explained that Batlle's administration needed to make up for the two years it lost putting down the revolution.

Don Pepe had given up his home in Montevideo; he and the family would stay in Piedras Blancas until the end of his administration. Micelli, an Italian freethinker, visited him there, and Batlle "affirmed his full sympathy for the proletarian class, agreeing that its betterment went hand in hand with the development of republican institutions." He told Micelli that before his term expired he would present his long-delayed labor project to the legislature.[4]

Late in September, Batlle, Williman, Serrato, and other friends went horseback riding along the beaches which extended up the Atlantic coast from Montevideo. All enjoyed the outing, but Don Pepe did not restrict his attentions to pleasure. He returned convinced, as was Williman, that a paved shore drive would be a great asset to Montevideo and a magnificent tourist attraction.

One of Batlle's favorite projects, which authorized government financial aid for annual track and field contests, reached the Cham-

ber floor. Don Pepe wanted a yearly 50,000-peso subsidy. He had
given the project an anti-Catholic twist by proposing that the days
when the contests were held be legal holidays; two religious legal
holidays would be canceled to balance the calendar. The Chamber
revised the bill, leaving out the holiday change, and, over Martín
C. Martínez' almost inevitable complaint that the idea was a waste
of money, passed the bill to the Senate.[5]

The three controversial bills—divorce, abolition of the death
penalty, and the progressive inheritance tax—had all been approved in general and then sidetracked. On October 25, Manini
got the divorce bill put back on the calendar. The death penalty
abolition was brought out of committee, and, after intricate parliamentary maneuvering, the Chamber approved the bill and sent it
to the Senate. Arena's desire to end the death penalty under military
justice was compromised: the military death penalty would be
ended in peacetime and "even in wartime, for crimes committed
outside an army unit, besieged or militarized zone." [6] The inheritance tax, which took money away from important people, had a
difficult time. It was briefly debated in October and again in November, but whether it would get the Chamber's ultimate approval
was not yet clear.

October 29 was the first anniversary of the proclamation of
Williman's candidacy. Even though the candidate himself had made
not a single speech or political appearance and had carefully refrained from announcing a program, for an entire year his name and
qualifications had been broadcast throughout the country by a maze
of committees. Anniversary day was duly celebrated. New biographies of Williman appeared; all the Montevideo business houses
signed a presentation album which was delivered to the candidate;
the Colorado legislators' pledge, now signed by 58 future electors,
was republished.[7]

Williman represented Batlle at the inaugural run of the Montevideo electric trolleys, and his presence was doubly welcome for
he was also the company's attorney. Don Pepe had already bought
tickets on the March 28 sailing of the Royal Mail liner *Araguaya*.
Manini was going along on his honeymoon; Colonel Bernassa y
Jerez, Police Chief of Montevideo, would look after Batlle's safety
during the trip. Once Don Pepe was settled in France, Manini,

Bernassa, and the rest of the party would return to Uruguay. It was expected that Batlle and his family would stay away for three years.

One outstanding matter—the election of six Senators, one-third of the Senate—had to be settled before Batlle could leave for Europe assured that all was in good hands. The present Senate had given Don Pepe considerable uneasiness, especially the election of its President who was always a potential focus for conspiracy. Batlle wanted to be sure that Williman's Senate cooperated with Williman and supported Batlle's re-election. Batlle also wanted a Senate more sympathetic to social and moral legislation. One reason why Chamber debate on divorce and kindred bills had been allowed to drag was the certainty that the Senate, as presently constituted, would not be disposed to their passage.

The Senate elections presented few difficulties. The Directorio had polled the Nationalist organizations in the departments where elections would be held. Most departments wanted to abstain, not as a symbol of protest but because there was no chance of victory. The Nationalists put up candidates in only two departments, where the dissident Colorados were expected to run rival Colorado candidates to Batlle's candidates and so split the Colorado vote.[8]

The organization Colorados, as *El Día* had announced months before, nominated Batlle's six followers: Serrato, Capurro, Areco, Viera, Suárez, and Tiscornia. Tiscornia's Catholicism brought him under attack when the time came for the Colorado National Commission to approve the candidates. Still, he was Batlle's choice and the only man in his home department of Río Negro who could win against both the Nationalists and the Colorado dissidents. Arena and Tiscornia's other supporters got his candidacy approved by explaining that since the party charter did not yet require candidates to be religious liberals it was unfair to discriminate against him because of his Catholicism.[9]

In Rocha, the dissidents put up Gregorio L. Rodríguez, Cuestas' minister, even though Areco was sent to dissuade them. Then the "moral influence" of the whole government from Batlle, who announced, "the candidate of his sympathies is Doctor Martín Suárez," down to the tax collectors in Rocha, was thrown behind Suárez.[10] In Río Negro the dissidents did not put up a candidate, but called for Colorado abstention. Shortly before the election, a hostile judge imprisoned the Colorado caudillo of the fifth district in Río Negro. The Colorado-dominated elections board postponed the elections in that district for a week; [11] by then, the caudillo's release would be arranged by his lawyers. The Río Negro election promised to be close, and the postponement would enable the fifth district's caudillo to know how many votes he must deliver to overcome any Nationalist lead won the Sunday before.

Election day, just as in January 1905, was without incident. Batlle had received reports that Mariano Saravia might try something during the elections and had sent out alerts, but all went well.[12] In Rocha, because of the Colorado split—1,398 for Suárez, 739 for Rodríguez—the Nationalist Ros, with 1,735 votes, won. In Río Negro the Nationalists got 444 votes to Tiscornia's 438, but the fifth district delivered the needed votes the next week.[13]

In 1900, these same six departments had elected five Nationalist Senators to one Colorado and precipitated Batlle's reconquest-of-the-departments speech; in 1906, it was five Colorados to one Nationalist.[14] No wonder Nationalists were ashamed to gather before Saravia's tomb!

Once the elections were over, there was a noticeable slow-down in government activity. Batlle decided not to appoint new Ministers of Finance and Fomento, and simply left the portfolios vacant. One of the last pre-election decrees had authorized the establishment of secondary schools in the interior, another of Batlle's favorite projects. It would be up to Williman to implement the decree. Williman would have a number of projects which he could implement or pigeonhole, and the most momentous was a message Batlle himself wrote, Williman countersigned, and the Executive sent to the legislature. The message and accompanying bill made up Don Pepe's frequently announced and long-delayed labor project.[15] In a post-election interview with Micelli, Batlle explained why he had held the bill back so long:

I have worked to prepare a plan of social reforms, all designed to look after and to liberate the working classes. But you must realize that up to now we have had a Senate composed of good patriots, but conservatives. The new Senate, on the other hand, will be entirely liberal and will not put obstacles in the way of the reforms. The workers already know that they will find protection in the government. I believe—in effect—that in countries like ours, where the problem of liberty is already resolved, it is necessary to begin to resolve social problems.[16]

As the interview indicated, the December 1906 labor project was a testament, a guide for the future. Batlle left it for his followers to enact in his absence, if they could.

The bill provided for a workday of eight hours and for one day of rest each week. These "most natural and legitimate demands" were made in every strike, and almost always disregarded,

> . . . not because the capitalist does not consider this aspiration to be just, but because under the system of industrial competition only establishments which have outdistanced their competitors and which make substantial profits can make concessions of this sort. In most cases, even the minimum amount of repose which the worker requires to resume his tasks with renewed energy is sacrificed to the compelling necessity of low cost and plentiful production, with the result that the health and life of the worker is prematurely destroyed. . .
>
> But this very minimum amount of repose . . . is not the only repose to which man has the right. The worker and, in general, all laboring men, members and important factors of civilized society, must be granted the right of the life of civilization, to the life of sentiment, of affection, of the family, of society, and therefore the right to dispose of the time necessary to participate in these benefits. When they have devoted the necessary time to the alimentation and repose of their organisms they should dispose of some more time to talk with their friends, to harmonize ideas with their wives, to get to know their children and to fondle them, and to broaden their moral and intellectual culture.

The State was involved because most of the national population were workers:

> Individualist theories, today happily almost completely rejected by social science, in the name of freedom of contract oppose any official intervention in the relations between workers and capitalists, and these theories look with indifference on the submission of an enormous mass of population to homicidal labor conditions. These same theories accept the prohibition of slavery contracts, basing this prohibition on the fact that these contracts destroy liberty, yet they do not consider the fact that agreements which destroy health and life debase something more precious than liberty itself, something which is, besides, the very condition and basis of liberty. In any event, the supposition that any real liberty can exist in the relations between worker and capitalist is sadly

derisive when the former, driven by hunger, is obliged to accept any situation which satisfies hunger, without any thought for the future, while the latter, obliged by competition or blinded by speculation, demands annihilating efforts from the worker.

In almost all the legislation of the most advanced countries the necessity of protecting women and children has been recognized, and if this protection, except in very few cases and very inadequately, is still not given to adult males, who are just as weak and incompetent as women and children in the face of the power of employers, it is because the industrial struggle between one nation and another makes the adoption of measures of this nature almost impossible. This situation has not yet developed in our country which has not yet fully entered the industrial era, and we should hasten to regulate labor, basing ourselves on elevated principles of justice, before the magnitude of the interests involved makes this task more difficult.

Our Republic should take advantage of still being in its formative period, during which it is easy to correct incipient vices and defects, as well as to implant new institutions, and should prepare itself to occupy a distinguished place among civilized nations, not because of its armed might, towards which it should not aspire and could not because of its small territory, but because of its rational and advanced laws, its ample spirit of justice, and because of the physical, moral, and intellectual vigor of its sons.

The fact that a reform has not yet been accomplished in another country or is not generally accepted, reasons frequently advanced during your legislative debates, should not be invoked except very parsimoniously, because our condition as a new people permits us to put into effect ideals of government and social organization which could not be made effective in other countries with old organization without overcoming enormous and tenacious resistance.[17]

The last paragraph was Batlle's answer to Vázquez Acevedo's cautionary exhortation that nations achieved their reputations through prudence rather than advanced legislation. The whole tone of the message was dramatic proof of the changes in the last four years. When he took office, Batlle agreed to limit his projects to "generally accepted ideas"; now he was confident that Uruguay was ready to occupy a distinguished place among nations, among other reasons because of its advanced laws and spirit of justice.

The message justified the advantages of the eight-hour day, in part on experience abroad which showed that production did not fall when the workday was reduced because the per-hour production went up, in part on studies of the harmful effect of long work hours on health. Batlle's fundamental justification, though, was not pragmatic. He did not base the need on the evils of Uruguayan working conditions; he based it on a philosophical concept of man. All men, including working men, had the right to "the life of civilization." Workers needed time away from work "to broaden their moral and intellectual culture."

The bill made various concessions and did not call for a rigid eight-hour day. A ten-hour day would be permitted where work, by its nature, was interrupted and gave workers time "to distract their attention and to rest." During the first year of the law's operation, this latter group could work eleven hours, while the general run of workers could work nine hours a day. Children under 13 years of age would not be permitted to work; children 13 through 15 could work a half-day; children 16 to 18, a three-quarter-day. Working mothers would get a month off—without pay—after giving birth. Batlle let his plans for old-age-pension legislation be known, when he said:

> This disposition can be completed, when a Pension Fund for all workers is created, by insuring a woman who has given birth for the salary or wages corresponding to the four weeks of compulsory rest.[18]

Under the bill, all workers would get a day off every week. Batlle could not resist combining this provision with an attack on the Catholic Sunday. An employer might close his establishment on Sunday and give his workers the day off, but, if he wished, the employer could keep open seven days a week and have one-seventh of his work force off every day. Batlle advocated this second option. He maintained that Sunday would be a dull day for workers if everything were closed; Sunday shutdowns would also keep machines and capital idle, a tremendous loss to the nation.

Press reaction to the bill was cautious. In theory, everyone favored labor legislation, but when specific laws were proposed reasons for opposition invariably emerged. *El Siglo* advocated more study. *La Democracia*, whose editors had written the eight-hour-day plank of the Nationalist program, called Batlle's project "exaggerated." [19] The Catholic newspaper would have preferred a bill on accident compensation. Actually, after a flurry of comment, the newspapers moved on to more pressing matters, for it was apparent that the bill would not receive serious consideration until well into Williman's administration.

The Chamber still had to consider the progressive inheritance tax and the divorce bill. Gabriel Terra, author of the inheritance-tax bill, proposed a new algebraic formula, but Martín C. Martínez and Vázquez Acevedo counseled further prudence. The Batllistas decided to send the bill back to committee, in the hope they could get a stronger measure approved under the next administration.[20] *El Día* excoriated opponents of the progressive inheritance tax with a vigor that was another revelation of how far Batlle now felt it was safe to go.

> The conservative spirit—as we said the other day about the labor question—cedes ground but beats a strategic retreat: for example, in this particular case it accepts the principle of the progressive tax, because it can not help but accept it because it is a principle which today constitutes the a.b.c. of economic science . . . but it wants, with all the means at its command, to limit the effectiveness of its application and reduce its application in law to the minimal extent possible.
>
> Society as it is constituted today benefits the rich almost exclusively . . . the poor, on the other hand, pay most of the taxes . . . why not compensate for this evident and irritating inequality, by applying a rigorous progression on inheritances, which would fall on the least sympathetic and least respectable way of gaining property, since inheritance represents neither labor nor effort, and frequently the recipient does not deserve it? . . .
>
> For example, among us, each of our departments of the interior, except for a few holdings, is made up of eight or ten latifundia; the police of the interior, who cost the State vast sums, have as their almost exclusive mission the protection of the lives and estates of these great latifundists . . . Why should the conservative and retrograde spirit oppose requiring that the estate left by one of these latifundists pay a much higher tax than that left by a poor farmer, who has not received the same benefits from the State, either in quality or quantity? . . . tax reform is one of the most felt needs in our country and will be one of the campaigns our Party must carry out.[21]

On divorce, which involved the young Colorados' religious liberalism, the Batllistas did much better. The article-by-article Chamber vote was proceeding uneventfully when the alert Areco proposed a new legal cause for divorce: "mutual consent by the spouses." To prevent coercion by one spouse of the other, Areco was willing to stipulate a six-month waiting period when mutual consent was invoked. Areco said he was sure that mutual consent would be the most used cause; the other causes would discourage couples from seeking divorce, "for fear of exposing publicly the troubles or the shame of family life."

Against the formula I propose, Mr. President, no religious sentiment can object.

I am also convinced that sincere Catholics, believers in good faith, will never use divorce however grave the causes which separate the spouses, because, as I have just said, when religious sentiment is sincere this sentiment is going to contain the couple, is going to prevent them from using the courts to destroy what they consider to be indestructible.[22]

Areco's motion was not favorably received. Even Pérez Olave, who was heading the floor fight for the bill, felt it was "quite radical" and needed further study. The vote on mutual consent was 21 opposed, 18 in favor.[23]

Batlle realized that if he could get a few absent Deputies to vote for mutual consent it would win on reconsideration;[24] the difficulty was that a two-thirds vote was needed to move reconsideration. Vázquez Acevedo, old parliamentarian though he was, unwittingly provided this opportunity. He wanted the legal cause on cruel treatment of the wife by the husband to be reconsidered and defined to mean only physical mistreatment. His motion to reconsider was approved, but his narrow definition of cruel treatment was voted down. Then Areco, carried into the Chamber as always, reintroduced mutual consent.

Manini supported mutual consent as a divorce cause, even though some older deputies suggested that his concern was a bit premature since he had not yet married. Areco spoke from his seat:

I, who have thought over the formula I propose . . . for many hours, am convinced that it has no other purpose and object than to assure the liberty of the woman; even further: that it tends to give the woman equality with the man, something for which humanity has been struggling for centuries.[25]

This time mutual consent won. Drama went out of the debate; the rest of the articles were voted, and on February 21 the whole bill was sent to the Senate where Areco, who had been sworn in as Senator the week before, could guide it through to ultimate passage.[26]

XVIII

Departure

A NEW Directorio was elected in January—the last one had been only an interim Directorio. The balance tipped to the Radicals; Martín Aguirre, First Vice President of the last Directorio, was elected President, while Carlos Berro, the previous President, was now First Vice President.[1] The Directorio's first manifesto maintained that the Nationalist legislators should not vote for Williman unless he previously indicated that he would change Batlle's policies.[2]

This disappointed most Nationalist legislators who, backed by the conservative classes, wanted to vote for Williman in the hope that this act of goodwill would dispose him favorably for the future.[3] Ten Nationalist legislators, led by Martín C. Martínez, Rodríguez Larreta, and Vázquez Acevedo—these last two no longer Directorio members—sent Herrera to arrange a joint meeting with the new Directorio. At this meeting, the legislators maintained that the Directorio's opinions were merely advisory.[4] Events seemed to be shaping up as in 1903, with a group of Nationalist legislators breaking away from the Directorio to vote for the winning candidate. But now it could be only an incident, not a Nationalist catastrophe.

Batlle and his family moved from Piedras Blancas on February 1, to stay in Montevideo until their ship sailed. Arena and Manini announced the formation of a joint law partnership. Williman, still silent, was rumored to have asked General Vázquez to remain as Minister of War.

The first step in the changing of administrations, the election of President of the Senate on February 14, gave little hope to those who wanted Williman, sooner or later, to break with Batlle. Feliciano Viera, the newest and youngest Senator, was elected.[5] "El Indio" Viera, known for his political loyalty, a Batllista before 1903, had served as Batlle's behind-the-scenes campaign manager for Williman.

The new Senate worked efficiently. José Pedro Ramírez had been holding up approval of the budget; the new Senate passed the budget—19,160,547 pesos and 39 cents, the sum to the penny of the budget sent by the Chamber.[6]

Once the budget was law, Batlle was able to make a number of appointments before leaving office. Muniz, Galarza, Feliciano Viera, Sr., all Generals now, were appointed commanders of the three military zones. Colonel Bernassa y Jerez, who would accompany Don Pepe to Paris, was named to the Supreme Military Tribunal. Juan Pedro Castro was made Minister to France, where he would be with Batlle; Castro's vote against Campisteguy had been rewarded. Juan Carlos Blanco was promoted to President of the Bank of the Republic, and Foreign Minister Romeu was named to the bank's board of directors.

On February 15, the clerk read Batlle's last annual message, a bulky sixty-page document. Each ministry reported its achievements and Batlle contributed a triumphant introduction:

> It can be stated without hyperbole that our country has never enjoyed a prosperity superior to the present one or more complete civil and political liberty, from the time it was organized constitutionally. The national energies have been developing with increasing vigor in all economic fields, and for its part the Government has put all its zeal for the public interest into intelligently aiding the progress of the nation. Public works have received a considerable impulse; higher education is moving toward new and fruitful orientations which will widen our general culture and make our principal industries, ranching and agriculture, more scientific. Government income has increased in unprecedented fashion, permitting us to end the financial period with a *budget surplus* which by itself says more in honor of the Administration than any propaganda could.[7]

The budget surplus about which Don Pepe was so proud was not the 450,000 pesos of last year, but the one for 1906–1907—no less than 2,143,921 pesos.

Solid citizens had to admit to themselves that, though they knew Batlle was a mad radical, he was leaving the country in much better financial shape than even their paragon Cuestas. *The Montevideo Times*, which spoke for the foreign business community and spoke with that certain condescension which so endeared Englishmen abroad, remarked:

> We asked a shrewd friend recently what verdict he would pass on Sr. Batlle as President. The reply was, "He should be granted 50,000 pesos out of the public money in recognition of his good works, and then be banished to Europe for ten years to atone his errors and to learn the true meaning of the word institutions." We think that hits the mark very fairly.[8]

Williman granted another interview to a Buenos Aires newspaper. His discussion of his relations with Batlle raised somewhat the hopes dampened by Viera's election as Senate President:

> The president has observed an attitude with me that reveals the most scrupulous delicacy. We are old and good friends; I have collaborated in his government for three years. In conversation, when this or that matter of common interest, involving future projections of his government, was discussed, he could have indicated to me desires or expectations which his successor should carry out. He has never said a word which could be considered as a recommendation or an insinuation. I understand that some people have gone to talk with him to interest him in a certain candidate for this or that post in the next administration; he has never told me anything. His evident purpose is to do nothing, to make not even the slightest statement which could in any way limit the liberty of his successor in the government. This has been his attitude ever since my candidacy was proclaimed.[9]

The Colorados, busy with plans for demonstrations in favor of Batlle and Williman, already were in festive mood. Government workers had taken up a collection for Batlle and Serrato, in thanks for the end of pay cuts. Batlle would not accept the 16,000 pesos— a substantial sum—they had collected, and suggested, with Serrato's concurrence, that they find some worthy cause for the money.

The Colorado convention opened on February 23, to endorse Williman, write a program, and join in the tremendous send-off planned for Batlle. It met, went through the cheers, heard motions for charter and program reform, and adjourned until later. The 250 delegates, among whom *El Día* was pleased to see prominent ranchers, were now free to enjoy the preinaugural festivities.[10]

The important Colorados, who before the convention had met at Areco's house to plan strategy, continued to work. They prepared charter changes in line with Batlle's frequently stated preference for large-sized Colorado departmental and national committees; large assemblies, he said, prevented control by small cliques. The fact that these important Colorados—a steering committee, not a clique—were controlling a large convention with great ease did not make the steering committee doubt the correctness of Batlle's proposal. José Espalter, Williman's friend, was given the task of drawing up a party program which would include constitutional reform, separation of Church and State, municipal autonomy, and labor legislation. Batlle asked that proportional representation also be mentioned.[11]

Espalter's program reflected his own and the Colorado organization's caution, and the void created by Williman's silence. It called for constitutional reform, if possible without waiting the entire period required by the Constitution. These constitutional reforms were needed: direct popular election of President of the Republic, proportional representation for legislative elections, municipal autonomy, and separation of Church and State. The program favored reduction of consumption taxes and the enacting of progressive taxation, not of the magnitude which would despoil private fortunes, rather "a limited and moderate progression, whose rate oscillates between certain limits." The State had the right to intervene in labor questions but, "It is a matter for elevated inspiration and exquisite tact." [12]

The delegates were not excited about the charter changes or the program. Many delegates did not attend the convention's second session. After all, it was convened two days before inauguration, when everyone was occupied with flags and bunting. The quorum had to be lowered before the session could begin. Then letters of thanks from Batlle and Williman were read and the program and charter given preliminary approval. The convention's next session, scheduled for after inauguration, would consider the changes in detail.

The only uncertainty about the presidential election was the portending Nationalist split. Rodríguez Larreta and Martín C. Martínez did not want to follow Acevedo Díaz out of the party, and tried to convince Directorio President Aguirre to allow Nationalist legislators to vote without Directorio instructions. When Herrera printed an account of the secret meeting between sixteen legislators and Aguirre, the Directorio lost patience. It published a manifesto calling on the Nationalist legislators to vote for Colonel Guillermo García, an old Nationalist war hero and Saravia's successor as Honorary President of the Directorio, for President of the Republic.[13]

Eleven Nationalist legislators—the majority of the Nationalist bloc—led by Vázquez Acevedo, Rodríguez Larreta, and Martín C. Martínez, replied with a statement that they would abstain from voting in the presidential election. To vote for Williman would be an insult to Colonel García; to vote for García would acknowledge the Directorio's authority.[14] Worse times, not better times, were ahead for the National Party.

Everything was ready for the inauguration. Visiting warships from Argentina and Brazil were in the harbor. The hotels and *pensiones* were filled with visitors from the interior.

On the day—March 1—a crowd stood outside the cabildo, in spite of the heat; inside, the galleries were packed. At 3:10 P.M., Viera called the session to order. The votes were cast: seventy for Williman, nine for Guillermo García.[15] A committee was appointed to escort Williman to the legislative chamber. When Williman arrived in front of the cabildo, the bands in the plaza played, fireworks were shot off, the crowd cheered. At 3:45 P.M., the new President of the Republic appeared before the legislature and took the oath of office. Then he spoke and the speech was carefully listened to, for it was the first time he revealed his program:

I believe that the party to which I belong, whose distinguished representatives in the Legislature have just decided my election, and the great majority of the people of the country, who have supported my candidacy, have wanted in so doing to confirm the conquests and fundamental policies of the Government which is ending, and of which I will always have the honor of having formed part. A government which leaves pages of unquestionable merit written in the history of the Republic, by its absolute honesty and correctness in the management of the treasury, by its scrupulous respect for political liberty and individual rights, by its noble and just preoccupation with the betterment of the humble, by its inspired foresight in public works and in initiatives related to education and the development of the country's productive economic forces; and principally for its decision to face up to the gravest difficulties, in order to impose respect for the law upon all, to re-establish unity in the exercise of national authority, and to secure peace and order on solid bases.

These characteristics and tendencies of the Government of the illustrious citizen who today leaves the presidency amidst the acclamations of justice, to remain consecrated as a brilliant statesman deserving of national gratitude, should be maintained and continued; and the people, who do not want a policy of retrogression but one of advancement, have so sanctioned it with eloquent expressions.

I assume the Government with anger towards no one. I am prepared to have individual and political rights respected as well as to maintain unbroken the principle of authority.

The political parties can be sure that they will enjoy the most complete and absolute electoral liberty, and that observing due impartiality, I will surround suffrage with all guarantees. I will respect its verdict and will make this verdict respected.

This part of the speech was punctuated by applause. Williman had announced himself solidly behind Batlle's policies; in fact, his praise of Batlle was framed in language usually reserved for funeral eulogies.

Williman was fundamentally an administrator and he devoted most of his speech to describing the administrative reforms he would undertake: intendencies in the interior departments, the establishment of the Supreme Court, new law codes, a population census, a geological survey, regulation of corporations, a government labor office, reorganization of public charity, and a new Ministry, that of Public Education. He promised to see through to completion the public works now under construction and to undertake new ones, especially sanitation in the interior and the physical improvement of Montevideo. He would expand education, maintain the army, and build up the navy.

The new President saw much to be done on the economic front. The national or municipal governments should take over "many public services or services of great public interest which are in private hands." The Government should bring harmony to the relations between workers and employers, and should preoccupy itself with social questions. It was imperative "to resolve the prob-

lem of populating the interior, which in the midst of great prosperity remains half deserted, since it is not the existence of a handful
of great fortunes which constitutes the wealth of a nation." [16]

This last sentence got a great round of applause, and the whole
speech sat well with the Colorados. It almost seemed that Batlle's
ideas had infiltrated Williman.

The speech over, all participants adjourned to the antechambers
for the traditional champagne toasts. Carlos A. Berro explained the
Nationalist position and wished Williman good luck. Williman then
left the cabildo and walked to Government House, where Batlle
awaited him. The two exchanged formal speeches. Batlle was now
a private citizen.

Don Pepe wanted to go home. He went out of the building to
his coach. A huge crowd was there. They wanted to unhitch the
horses and pull the coach themselves. Batlle could not accept so
servile an homage. He decided to walk. The crowd, delirious, overwhelmed him. They wanted to shake his hand, to embrace him.
Manini was on one side of Don Pepe; Varela Acevedo, Batlle's
secretary, on the other; both were badly pummeled. Don Pepe, big
as he was, could not touch ground: he put his hands on the shoulders
of those closest to him, straightened his arms, and let the crowd's
momentum carry him home.[17]

Finally home, he escaped inside. The crowd cheered, demanding
a speech. Batlle came out on the balcony to thank them. He insisted
that the success of his government came from the contributions of
the many men who had helped him in peace and war.

I am almost the past—Doctor Williman is the future—a future which
is assured because the new president has a firm hand and a calm head
to lead the nation ever forward toward progress.[18]

That night there were the official receptions and inaugural ball;
Don Pepe attended in the company of his friend Eduardo Iglesias,
with whom he had gone to these same functions four years before.
The culmination of the day, though, had been the afternoon mob
of enthusiasts who saw Batlle home. The Colorado clubs were preparing several later public demonstrations, but this one was unexpected. It answered those who said Batlle was an ogre who hid
in his cave in Piedras Blancas and would be forgotten the day he
left office.

The Colorado convention had to be postponed, as the delegates could not be assembled for a meeting. It was not just frivolity which kept them away. They were planning two gigantic demonstrations: one in honor of Batlle and Williman, and the other to see Batlle off to Europe. There was a purpose behind these demonstrations, really more serious than that of the convention. They would demonstrate the power and popularity of the Colorado Party and the close relations between Batlle and Williman and leave a stunning memory of Batlle's departure, so that, as Constancio C. Vigil—once editor of the Directorio's prewar newspaper, and now an enthusiast for Batlle—expressed it: "We shall bring the genius back from France for his second presidency." [19]

The day before the first demonstration, Batlle was visited by the Colorado departmental delegates. Don Pepe uncorked the champagne and spoke. Once more he emphasized his confidence in the future and the help he had received during his government; he announced a toast for the one who had done the most, raised his glass, paused, and toasted: "To the Colorado Party." [20]

The March 3 demonstration for Batlle and Williman, sponsored by the Colorado departmental organizations, the Montevideo Colorado clubs, and the Montevideo business community, was magnificent. Twenty thousand demonstrators marched with their flags, brass bands, and noisemakers. First they went to Williman's house, where Williman and Viera greeted them. Williman bid them go to Batlle:

... to the upright man of government, to the one who for twenty years as a propagandist preached principles which he converted into reality as a statesman, and with your applause compensate him for his noble struggle for the greatness and unity of the Republic and for the days of pain which filled his heart in days of sorrow.

The solid crowd moved up the 18 de Julio Avenue. Batlle, surrounded by distinguished personages of Montevideo, was awaiting them on his balcony. There were cheers, vivas, and speeches. Then Don Pepe began to speak. The crowd quieted; men took off their hats.

Your applause more than meets my aspiration on the day I ascended to the presidency of the Republic and it is the best medal which could be offered me, had I done something worthy of a prize.

It is grand to ascend to power on waves of popular approval but it is grander still to descend surrounded by its cheers and applause.

For it means that the functionary descends unblemished; that he has struggled for right and liberty; that he has thrown all his force into serving the general welfare, since although people frequently keep silent before extortionists and despots in dark days they never, be it said in honor of humanity, congratulate and applaud them.

Thank you! I needed this act of popular approval. Many of the days of my government were dark and dangerous. During it the worst of national tragedies occurred . . . Mothers still cry for their sons . . . wives for their husbands . . . The red daisies of our countryside still seem drops of blood . . . The country was devastated and darkened from end to end.

You would not be here if the responsibility for that great national misfortune rested on me.

And your civic conscience does not deceive you. I did everything I could to avert catastrophe: first I gave in to subversion; I submitted to it; I accepted its conditions; I complied with these conditions with all the sincerity of which I am capable, for almost a year.

My tolerance was considered weakness; my effort to avoid bloodshed, an inclination to submit easily to impositions. And the tide of subversion rose and broke through all barriers and finally it was necessary to resist it with arms in hand, to cut down even greater evil than was already menacing us.

The arteries of the Nation were opened and her blood gushed out . . . the blood of soldiers and citizens who offered it generously and with abnegation to re-establish the reign of law and the exercise of all rights, and also the blood of citizens on the other side who thought they too were fighting for their liberties and their rights but who were deceitfully dragged to an obscure and meaningless sacrifice by the fully conscious promoters of that great tumult!

Now, in the zenith of our country's sky there shines in splendor something like that smiling sun, which after storms encourages the flight and singing of the birds, caresses the young birds, brings flowers to flaming colors, and diffuses the love of life over everything; that shining light of hope which dawned on our horizon with peace and re-establishment of order, which shone with more brilliance in the two following years of labor, of moral and material progress in the Republic, that light of hope has now reached its high point with the election we are celebrating, which promises, because of the qualities which distinguish the man elected, a period of government with new and great progress.

Let it be that in days to come reality comes ever closer to our most beautiful hopes and let our country be great because of its spirit of liberty and justice and because of the increasing felicity of its sons.[21]

Batlle had almost broken down while speaking. He dwelt on the war because it was politic—the war had united the Colorados behind him—but Don Pepe also had to talk of the war. The war was always with him. He wanted to free himself from blame for it and, when he tried, the poetic and Biblical in him came out.

The crowd wanted more speeches, less somber speeches, and Manini obliged. He told them Batlle had been too modest, had not given himself enough credit for the accomplishments of his administration. Other speeches followed. The holiday spirit took over. For two hours the marchers, bands and all, passed in review. As each contingent passed Batlle on his balcony, the men cheered.

On March 4, the legislature approved Batlle's request to leave the country without waiting the year specified by the Constitution. He explained his reason for going abroad in reasonably straightforward fashion:

> It being absolutely necessary for him to absent himself from the country, in order to remove himself from political life, in which he has acted for more than twenty years, and thus give his organism some time to repose.[22]

The legislature, that same week, also approved changing the legal name of Nico Pérez to Batlle y Ordóñez. Batlle had helped the villagers in a lawsuit involving their lands and they wanted to show their appreciation. Don Pepe had not wanted the name change approved while he still was in office—it was unseemly—but it was a great solace that the place where the ignominious peace of 1903 had been ratified would henceforth be called by his name.[23]

Williman's ministry, when he announced it, was another disappointment to those who hoped for conciliation with the Nationalists. First, it was all-Colorado. Second, Williman had continued General Vázquez as Minister of War and named Varela Acevedo, Batlle's secretary, Minister of Foreign Relations. Third, the rest of the Ministers, while not of Batlle's inner circle, were bright young ex-students of Williman. There was no one in the cabinet with political prestige, no figure who could be built up into a rival for Batlle in 1911. Still, it was early; once Batlle had left and Williman began to feel himself President in his own right, things might change.

Batlle auctioned off his furniture and moved with his family to a hotel until the ship left. Manini had just married and would take his bride along. Though they had been married in church, Manini had told the priests he was a sworn enemy of their faith and refused to have his children brought up as Catholics. He conceded only one restriction, that his wife's beliefs not be molested.

Batlle and his party would stop over in Rio de Janeiro, on invitation from the Brazilian Foreign Minister. Six special trains were bringing Colorados from the interior to help see him off.

March 23 was a fine day. Beginning early in the morning, visitors came to the hotel. At 11:00 A.M., coaches hired by the committee on honors came to take the voyagers to the harbor. Crowds lined the way. Lunch was served in the Customs House, then Juan Carlos Blanco, Batlle's erstwhile rival for the presidency, spoke. Batlle answered, again emphasizing the theme of his recent speeches—that he was but one of many who had made his administration a success.[24]

Williman and his Ministers arrived. Toasts were drunk. The band struck up; fireworks went off; medallions with Batlle's image were passed out. There was a tremendous crowd on the pier—20,000 to 25,000—and another 10,000 rabid Colorados in small boats in the harbor.

At noon the party moved to the dock. Williman took Matilde by the arm; Don Pepe escorted the new first lady. Batlle and his party got into the launch which would take them to the liner. As the launch pulled out, Batlle shouted, "Viva the President of the Republic!" Williman answered, "Viva the great citizen, José Batlle y Ordoñez!" The small boats followed the liner out to sea until it outdistanced them. Batlle and his party, as long as they could still see the boats, waved their handkerchiefs.

XIX

t‹‹‹‹‹‹‹‹‹‹‹‹f

Conclusions: The Sources of Leadership

Batlle's presidency was of decisive importance to Uruguay. It was during this period that armed politics lost out to electoral politics. The resultant political stability permitted the rapid upgrading of livestock ranching and the undertaking of previously postponed business ventures. Prosperity produced rising government income and budget surpluses. The government was able to begin long-desired public works and to take advantage, within limits, of the country's improved external credit position. The solidity of the political situation allowed Batlle to move Uruguay in new directions—toward concern for working-class well-being; the moralizing of personal life; an expanded government role in the economy; and the popularization of political action.

Four years is a short time; the basic life processes changed little. One out of every four births was illegitimate; illiteracy was still over 45 percent. But the increased attention to primary and advanced education begun under Batlle, accentuated by Williman, and continued thereafter have ended illiteracy as a major problem and produced free university education. A similar start was made on road-building; roads cost more than schools and the results have been slower. Schools, roads, and railroads were—and are—narrowing the gaps between rural life and Montevideo.

The years of Batlle's presidency secured the supremacy of ranching over agriculture, though it was not realized at the time. The post-1904 stable peace and the opening of refrigerated packing plants encouraged ranchers to invest in improving and expanding their herds. In 1902, there were 283 pedigreed cattle and 38 pedigreed sheep in Uruguay. By 1907, the number of blooded cattle had increased sixfold, the number of blooded sheep was 34 times greater than in 1902. The 1908 livestock census counted over 8 million cattle and 26 million sheep, the largest number ever pastured in Uruguay. That same year, exports reached a record physical volume. Landowners, having made such a success in ranching, would not subdivide their plots for the plow.

The post-1904 years were prosperous. Total foreign trade went from 57 million pesos in 1902 to 72 million pesos in 1907, and continued upward until World War I. The proportion of capital goods among imports rose; the country's economy was becoming more diversified. Generally everyone benefited for there were higher profits and more employment. Workers, though, did not improve their relative economic position because they were too weak to dispute successfully with employers over the division of the increased prosperity. This was why Batlle wanted the state to intervene and secure a reduced workday.

Batlle's administration was laying the groundwork in many areas, trying especially to expand the state's role in the economy and to reduce the importance of foreign companies. Batlle and Serrato were among the earliest economic development planners, and they learned what later planners are still discovering: affirmative government in underdeveloped areas is not easy. The opportunities for government action then were more limited than at present: government debt absorbed too much revenue; new capital was costly and scarce. World prices for Uruguayan exports, world willingness to invest in and lend to Uruguay, were far more influential in producing the post-1904 prosperity and consequent budget surpluses than any of Batlle's economic policies.

These years made the greatest immediate impact and produced, ultimately, the most far-reaching changes in Uruguayan politics. In 1902, it seemed that the Nationalists would soon take over the government. Instead, Batlle solidified Colorado control and pushed Uruguayan democratic development into a new course. He made many compromises with the ideal; "moral influence" was an enormous sophistry. But Batlle moved the ordinary Uruguayan toward electoral politics, as he hoped to move him toward intellectual preoccupations and religious skepticism. Today in Uruguay, better than in most places, the common man counts and his vote is counted.

The key to Batlle's success was his use of the Colorado tradition and the Colorado organization. He was elected President as the most partisan candidate acceptable to Cuestas. The War of 1904 made him a Colorado hero and united the party behind him. He ratified his war victory with the 1905 electoral victory which put his supporters into the legislature and his lieutenants in control of the party organization all over Uruguay. Having secured his position, he was ready for reform.

Support by specific interests was a subsidiary factor in Batlle's strength. Urban labor was weak; the middle class or classes, especially the professional men who are usually considered to be the middle-class leaders, were dubious about the direction he was taking. The most powerful interest group in Uruguayan politics, the conservative classes, considered Batlle an intransigent politician and an increasingly dangerous radical. To counteract the influence of the conservative classes, Batlle did not organize a rival class coalition; instead, he united the Colorados.

Batlle is commonly explained as being "ahead of his times." He was more than ahead of his times. Batlle created his times. His success reminds us that a man's ideals can lead other men.

Bibliography
Notes
Index

Bibliography

Batlle's private papers, which I was the first to use, head the bibliography. The Nationalist Party papers are valuable, though the Directorio minutes, written with the possibility of government seizure in mind, avoid giving details. The Colorado Party papers for these years were later burned.

Newspapers—each political group had its own—are the liveliest sources for the narrative. Uruguayan parliamentary debates are not the rubber-stamp affairs which Latin American legislative debates are supposed to be. The debates and committee reports are necessary sources on a wide variety of questions. Of the books, pamphlets, and articles, the most useful are the few first-person accounts, like *Apuntes-Cuestas,* and Vidal y Fuentes, *Verdades.* The *Memorias de Saravia* stand out in importance.

I interviewed a number of principal figures of the era or, in their absence, their sons. Recall of events fifty years past is necessarily uncertain; yet, to talk with Alfonso Lamas about the Peace of Nico Pérez, or with Serrato about Batlle, was to feel very close to the Uruguay of not so long ago.

Primary Sources

Manuscripts

Batlle Archive, Batlle Pacheco family, Montevideo.

Partido Nacional Archivo: *Actas de las Sesiones Celebradas por el Directorio del Partido Nacional,* I–IV to I–VI, April 25, 1899—February 6, 1907; *Notas Recibidas por el H. Directorio del Partido Nacional,* II–VII to II–XVI, January 11, 1900—December 30, 1907; *Notas Enviadas por el H. Directorio del Partido Nacional,* III–IV to III–VI, May 15, 1899—April 4, 1907; *Notas de la Convención del Partido Nacional,* VI–V to VI–VI, August 9, 1900—December 26, 1903; *Actas del Congreso Elector de Directorio del Partido Nacional,* VII–I to VII–III, March 30, 1900—February 4, 1932; *Documentos Diversos. Revolución de 1904,* XII–I. There is a catalogue, Directorio del Partido Nacional, *Catálogo del Archivo del Partido Nacional* (Montevideo, 1949).

United States Department of State: *Diplomatic Dispatches, Uruguay,* Vol. 17; *Diplomatic Instructions, Uruguay,* Vol. 2; *Diplomatic Post Records, Uruguay; Notes from Foreign Missions, Uruguay,* Vol. 2; *Notes to Foreign Missions, Uruguay,* National Archives, Washington.

Newspapers

(All published in Montevideo unless otherwise noted)

La Democracia, 1904–1907.
El Día, 1902–1929.
El Día de la Tarde—El Ideal, 1919–1929.
Diario Nuevo—El Diario, 1903–1905.
The Montevideo Times, February–March, 1907.
La Nación, 1902–1903.
La Nación (Buenos Aires), 1904.
El Nacional, 1902–1903.
La Prensa, 1902–1903 [Directorio newspaper].
La Prensa, 1906–1907 [Williman campaign newspaper].
El Siglo, 1902–1907.
El Tiempo, November 1903.
El Uruguay, 1905.

Public Documents

Banco Hipotecario del Uruguay, *25 Años Banco Hipotecario del Uruguay.* Montevideo [1937?].
Banco de la República Oriental del Uruguay, *1896—24 de Agosto—1917.* Montevideo, 1918.
[Blanco, Juan Carlos] *El Puerto de Montevideo.* Montevideo, 1912.
Diario de Sesiones de la H. Asamblea General, Vols. IX–XI. Montevideo, 1905–1914.
Diario de Sesiones de la H. Cámara de Representantes, Vols. CLXV–CXC, CCXXIII. Montevideo, 1902–1907, 1915.
Diario de Sesiones de la H. Cámara de Senadores, Vols. LXXIV–LXXXIX. Montevideo, 1901–1909.
Diario de Sesiones de la H. Comisión Permanente, Vols. XI–XII. Montevideo, 1914–1937.
Dirección General de Estadística, *Anuario Estadístico de la República Oriental del Uruguay,* 1901–1915. Montevideo, 1902–1917.
Jefatura Política y de Policía de la Capital, *Memoria . . . Administración: Coronel Juan Bernassa y Jerez 1903 á 1906.* Montevideo, 1907.
United States Department of Commerce and Labor, *Report on Trade Conditions in Argentina, Paraguay and Uruguay by Lincoln Hutchinson.* Washington, 1906.
United States Department of State, *Papers Relating to the Foreign Relations of the United States,* 1902–1907. Washington, 1903–1910.

Interviews

Luis Batlle Berres	March 12, 1951
César Batlle Pacheco	1951–1952
Rafael Batlle Pacheco	1951–1952
Ovidio Fernández Ríos	April 11, 1952
Emilio Frugoni	September 24, 1952
Luis Alberto de Herrera	September 20, 1952
Alfonso Lamas	September 25, 1952
José Serrato	September 21, 25, 1952

Jacobo Varela Acevedo   April 18, 1952
José Claudio Williman   September 1, 1952

Books, Pamphlets, and Articles

Abad, José T., *La Candidatura Williman, Los Ataques de "El Siglo."* Montevideo, 1905.

Acevedo Díaz, Eduardo, *Carta Política.* Montevideo, 1903.

Albístur, Víctor, *El Problema Presidencial de 1907 y el Manifiesto Nacionalista*, prologue by José Enrique Rodó. Montevideo, 1907.

Almada, Amadeo, *El Divorcio Ante la Razón, El Derecho y la Moral.* Montevideo, 1905.

—— *El Problema Nacional.* Montevideo, 1905.

Anales del Ateneo del Uruguay, vols. I-X. Montevideo, 1881–1886.

Aragón y Etchert, Florencio, and Julio María Sosa, *Conferencia Política. Club Colorado "Francisco Tajes," Noviembre 21 de 1904.* Montevideo, 1904.

Ardao, Arturo, "La Sección de Filosofía del Ateneo (1879–1881)," *Revista de la Facultad de Humanidades y Ciencias*, IV (June 1950), 129–144 (minutes of the Sección de Filosofía).

Arena, Domingo, *Batlle y los Problemas Sociales en el Uruguay.* Montevideo, 1939.

—— "Escritos y Discursos del Dr. Domingo Arena Sobre el Señor José Batlle y Ordóñez," *Biblioteca "Batlle,"* vol. I. Montevideo, 1942.

—— prologue to Luis Batlle Berres, *El Batllismo y el Problema de los Combustibles.* Montevideo, 1931.

Arlas Buccelli, Rafael, *El Carácter Nacional Consolidado por El Hogar, La Escuela, El Trabajo, El Ideal.* Montevideo, 1903.

Bases de Unificación del Partido Colorado. Montevideo, 1903.

Betelú, Francisco C., *La Lucha Electoral, Conferencia Política Pronunciada la Noche del 21 de Enero de 1905 en el Club Colorado "Marcelino Sosa."* Montevideo, 1905.

Biblioteca del Club Colorado "Defensa de Montevideo," *Proceso de la Gran Asamblea de Villa Colón, Julio 19 de 1903.* Montevideo, 1905.

Biblioteca del Club Vida Nueva, *Protesta Contra el Crimen.* Montevideo, 1904.

Buela, Avelino G., *Conferencia Política Sobre la Candidatura del Doctor Claudio Williman . . . Octubre de 1906.* Montevideo, 1908.

Cabrera, Carmelo L., *Masoller.* Montevideo, 1939.

Callorda, Pedro Erasmo, *Evocando el Pasado. Batlle.* Habana, 1928.

Capurro, Federico E., *Una Memoria Más, 1898–1948.* Montevideo, 1950.

Carta Orgánica del Partido Colorado. Montevideo, 1901.

Carve, Amaro, *Contra el Divorcio.* Montevideo, 1905.

Un Colorado, *La Proclamación Contra el País. Réplica al Dr. Espalter.* Montevideo, 1905.

Comité Defensa Nacionalista, *Contra la Calumnia. Gestiones de Protesta por las Invectivas del Club "Vida Nueva."* Montevideo, 1903.

Cosio, Pedro, *Crónica de los Sucesos de Rivera.* Montevideo, 1903.

Costa, Ángel Floro, *La Cuestión Económica en las Repúblicas del Plata.* Montevideo, 1902.

Cuestas, Juan L., *Páginas Sueltas.* 3 vols., Montevideo, 1897–1901.

Documentos Relativos á las Gestiones del Comité del Comercio en Favor de la Paz. Montevideo, 1904.

Eirale, Alberto, *Memorias de un Médico que Actuó en el Ejército del Sur Durante Toda la Guerra Civil de 1904.* Montevideo, 1951.

Ejército Nacionalista, *Campaña de 1904: Colección Completa de Órdenes Generales Dictadas por el Estado Mayor General del Ejército.* Montevideo, 1905.

Espalter, José, *El Problema de la Actualidad.* Montevideo, 1904.

—— *El Problema Nacional.* Montevideo, 1905.

—— *Una Base de Pacificación: Proyecto de Ley y Exposición de Motivos.* Montevideo, 1904.

Etcheverry, Venancio Guillermo, *Guerras Civiles de 1897 y 1904. Campañas del General Benavente; Páginas de mi Diario.* 2nd edition, Montevideo, 1935.

Falcao Espalter, Mario, "La Presidencia Williman," *Revista Nacional*, XIII (February 1941), 193–207 (prints Williman letter).

Fernández Prando, F., *Escritos y Discursos de Prudencio Vázquez y Vega, 1875–1882.* Montevideo, 1958.

Fernández Ríos, Ovidio, *Un Libro Más.* Montevideo, 1949.

Fernández y Medina, Benjamín, *Leyes Electorales de la República Oriental del Uruguay.* Montevideo, 1907.

Figari, Pedro, *El Momento Político 1910–1911.* Montevideo, 1911.

—— *La Pena de Muerte.* Montevideo, 1903.

Gómez Arias, Marcelino, *Revolución Uruguaya de 1904. Sus Operaciones en el Sud.* Buenos Aires, 1905.

González, Ramón P., *Aparicio Saravia en la Revolución de 1904.* Montevideo, 1949.

Grunwaldt Ramasso, Federico, "Apuntes de Don Juan L. Cuestas. La Elección del 1o. de Marzo de 1903," *El Día—Suplemento*, February 28, 1954.

—— *Páginas Sueltas Sobre la Personalidad y Obra de Don Juan Lindolfo Cuestas al Celebrarse el Cincuentenario del Puerto de Montevideo.* Montevideo, 1951.

Guastavino, Santiago, *1904: La Revolución.* Montevideo, 1904.

Las Jornadas del Civismo. Tupambaé y Masoller. El Caudillo y sus Glorias. Montevideo, 1905.

Manini y Ríos, Pedro, *La Culpa de la Guerra.* Montevideo, 1905.

Martínez Thedy, Eugenio, *Conferencia Política . . . a Propósito de la Organización Partidaria la Noche del 29 de Octubre de 1905.* Montevideo, 1905.

Martínez Vigil, Carlos, *El Problema Nacional.* Montevideo, 1905.

Melián Lafinur, Luis, *El Problema Nacional y su Solución Immediata.* Montevideo, 1905.

Muñoz, Juan José, *Apuntes Históricos.* Montevideo, 1952.

Muñoz Miranda, J., *Milicias Nacionales, Escalafón Militar del Partido Nacional.* Montevideo, 1902.

El Nuevo Samaritano, *Folletín Histórico de la Actual Guerra Uruguaya.* Buenos Aires, 1904.

Oneto y Viana, Carlos, *El País y la Vida Institucional.* Montevideo, 1904.

Partido Nacional, *Exposición. El Directorio Saliente á la Nueva Corporación. Abril, 1905.* Montevideo, 1905.

Pérez Olave, Adolfo H., *Conferencia Política*. Montevideo, 1903.
—— *El Problema de la Instrucción Pública*. Montevideo, 1904.
El Programa de la Revolución, Las Verdaderas Bases de Paz. Montevideo, 1904.
Rahola, Federico, *Sangre Nueva; Impresiones de un Viaje á la América del Sud*. Barcelona, 1905.
Revista de la Sociedad Universitaria, vols. I–IV. Montevideo, 1884–1885.
Riestra, Solano A., *La Paz*. Montevideo, 1904.
Rodó, J. E., *Liberalismo y Jacobinismo*. 1st edition, Valencia, n.d. Montevideo, 1906.
Ros, Francisco J., *La Feria de Melo; Reflexiones Económicas Sobre los Departamentos de Cerro Largo, Treinta y Tres, Rocha, Minas y Maldonado*. Montevideo, 1902.
Sánchez, Florencio, *El Caudillaje Criminal en Sud América*. Montevideo, 1914.
Saravia García, Nepomuceno, *Memorias de Aparicio Saravia*. Montevideo, 1956.
Sosa, Julio María, *Deberes Partidarios*. Montevideo, 1903.
Suárez, Luis, *De Tupambaé al Apa; Expedición de Auxilios a los Heridos de Tupambaé*. Montevideo, n.d.
Viana, Javier de, *Con Divisa Blanca*. 2nd edition, Buenos Aires, 1921.
Vidal y Fuentes, Alfredo, *Verdades*. Montevideo, 1903.
Zubillaga, Juan Antonio, *La Prensa Independiente en la Época de José Batlle y Ordóñez*. Montevideo, 1907.

Secondary Sources

[Acción] *Batlle, Su Vida, Su Obra*. Montevideo, 1956.
Acevedo, Eduardo, *Anales Históricos del Uruguay*. 6 vols., Montevideo, 1933–1936.
—— *Economía, Política y Finanzas*. Montevideo, 1903.
—— *Manual de Historia Uruguay*. 3rd edition, Montevideo, 1943.
—— *Notas y Apuntes; Contribución al Estudio de la Historia Económica y Financiera de la República Oriental del Uruguay*. 2 vols., Montevideo, 1903.
Acevedo Díaz (h), Eduardo, *La Vida de Batalla de Eduardo Acevedo Díaz*. Buenos Aires, 1941.
Ahrens, E., *Curso de Derecho Natural ó de Filosofía del Derecho*. 6th edition, 5th printing, Paris and Mexico, 1880. 1st printing of 6th edition, 1868. Translated by Pedro Rodríguez Hortelano and Mariano Ricardo de Asensi.
Álvarez Vignoli, Juan Ángel, *Evolución Histórica de la Ganadería en el Uruguay*. Tesis. Montevideo, 1917.
—— *Tratado de Economía Rural*. Montevideo, 1922.
Araújo, Orestes, *Historia de la Escuela Uruguaya*. Montevideo, 1911.
Ardao, Arturo, *Batlle y Ordóñez y el Positivismo Filosófico*. Montevideo, 1951.
—— *Espiritualismo y Positivismo en el Uruguay*. Mexico, 1950.
—— and Julio Castro, *Vida de Basilio Muñoz*. Montevideo, 1938.
Blanco Acevedo, Pablo, *Estudios Constitucionales*. Montevideo, 1939.
Boerger, Alberto C., *Investigaciones Agronómicas*. 3 vols., Montevideo, 1943.

Buzzetti, José L., *La Magnífica Gestión de Batlle en Obras Públicas (Proceso Evolutivo de las Obras Públicas en el País)*. Montevideo, 1946.

Castro, Juan José, *Estudio Sobre los Ferrocarriles Sudamericanos y las Grandes Líneas Internacionales*. Montevideo, 1893.

Cosio, Pedro, *José Serrato*. Montevideo, 1922.

Criadores del Uruguay, *Cincuentenario de la Fundación de los Registros Genealógicos de la Asociación Rural del Uruguay*. Montevideo, 1937.

Diario del Plata, *Uruguay—1930*. Montevideo, 1930.

Díaz, José Virginio, *Historia de Saravia*. Montevideo, 1920.

Dondo, Pedro, *Los Ciclos en la Economía Nacional*. Montevideo, 1942.

[El Día] *El Día. 1886–Junio–1961*. Montevideo, 1961.

Fernández Saldaña, José María, *Diccionario Uruguayo de Biografías 1810–1940*. Montevideo, 1945.

Fernández y Medina, Benjamín, *La Imprenta y la Prensa en el Uruguay (1807–1900)*. Montevideo, 1900.

Fitzgibbon, Russell H., *Uruguay: Portrait of a Democracy*. New Brunswick, N.J., 1954.

Gálvez, Manuel, *Vida de Aparicio Saravia*. Buenos Aires, 1942.

Giúdici, Roberto B., and Efraín González Conzi, *Batlle y el Batllismo*. Montevideo, 1928.

González, Ariosto D., *José Serrato: Técnico del Estado*. Montevideo, 1942.

—— *Los Partidos Tradicionales*. Montevideo, 1922.

González, Florencio César, *Ejército del Uruguay*. Montevideo, 1903.

Grompone, Antonio M., "La Ideología de Batlle," introduction to *Batlle: Sus Artículos*. Montevideo, 1943.

Guarnieri, Juan Carlos, *Nuestras Industrias Madres; Síntesis de su Evolución Histórica y Perspectivas del Futuro*. Montevideo, 1946.

Gutiérrez, Fernando, *Paso del Parque*. Montevideo, 1921.

—— *Tupambaé*. 3 vols., Montevideo, 1915–1918.

Hanson, Simon G., *Utopia in Uruguay: Chapters in the Economic History of Uruguay*. New York, 1938.

Homenaje del Partido Nacional al Autor de la Primera Legislación Obrera en el Uruguay, 1861—Carlos Roxlo—1927. Montevideo [1930?].

Idiarte Borda, C., and M. E. Idiarte Borda, *Juan Idiarte Borda. Su Vida. Su Obra*. Buenos Aires, 1939.

Ipuche, Pedro Leandro, *El Gran Solitario de Piedras Blancas*. Montevideo, 1915.

Jalabert, Ricardo M., and Rodolfo Cabal, *Album Biográfico Ilustrado y Descripción Histórico Geográfico de la República Oriental del Uruguay*. Montevideo, 1903.

Jiménez de Aréchaga, Justino E., *Evolución de la Propiedad Territorial*. Montevideo, 1908.

Johnson, John J., *Political Change in Latin America: The Emergence of the Middle Sectors*. Stanford, Calif., 1958.

Lloyd, Reginald, and others, editors, *Impresiones de la República del Uruguay en el Siglo Veinte*. London, 1911.

Maeso, Carlos M., *Tierra de Promisión*. Montevideo, 1904.

Manacorda, Telmo, *Itinerario y Espíritu de Jacobo Varela*. Montevideo, 1950.

Márquez, Alberto A., *Bosquejo de Nuestra Propiedad Territorial*. Montevideo, 1893.

Martin, Percy Alvin, "The Career of José Batlle y Ordóñez," *Hispanic American Historical Review*, X (November 1930), 413–428.
Martínez, José Luciano, *Cuestas y su Administración*. Montevideo, 1904.
Martínez, Martín C., *La Renta Territorial*. Montevideo, 1918.
Melián Lafinur, Luis, *La Acción Funesta de los Partidos Tradicionales en la Reforma Constitucional*. Montevideo, 1918.
Monegal, José, *Vida de Aparicio Saravia*. Montevideo, 1942.
Mongrell, Hugo, *Luis Mongrell (1858–1937) Político, Revolucionario y Periodista, Cabañero y Ruralista*. Vigo, 1958.
Mora Guarnido, José, *Batlle y Ordóñez: Figura y Transfigura*. Montevideo, 1931.
Morató, Octavio, *Economía y Finanzas; Notas y Apuntes*. Montevideo, 1906.
–––––– *Surgimientos y Depresiones Económicos en el Uruguay a Través de la Historia*. Montevideo, 1938.
Northrop, F. S. C., *Philosophical Anthropology and Practical Politics*. New York, 1960.
Oddone, Juan Antonio, *El Principismo del Setenta: Una Experiencia Liberal en el Uruguay*. Montevideo, 1956.
Palomeque, Alberto, *Eduardo Acevedo Díaz (Del Natural)*. Montevideo, 1901. Reprinted from *Vida Moderna*, vol. III, no. 7.
Pintos, Francisco R., *Batlle y el Proceso Histórico del Uruguay*. Montevideo, 1938.
–––––– *Historia del Uruguay (1851–1938): Ensayo de Interpretación Materialista*. Montevideo, 1946.
Pintos, Diago, C., *Anécdotas de Saravia*. Montevideo, 1928.
Pivel Devoto, Juan E., *Los Partidos Políticos en el Uruguay 1811–1897*. 2 vols., Montevideo, 1942.
–––––– *Uruguay Independiente*. Barcelona, 1949. vol. XXI of *Historia de América y de los Pueblos Americanos*, edited by Antonio Ballesteros y Berreta.
–––––– and Alicia Ranieri de Pivel Devoto, *Historia de la República Oriental del Uruguay*. Montevideo, 1945.
Ponce de León, Luis R., *Aparicio Saravia: Héroe de la Libertad Electoral*. Montevideo, 1956.
Pontac, M. Ferdinand (Luis Bonavita), "En Torno a la Figura de Don José Batlle y Ordóñez," *El Día—Suplemento*, April 9, 1961.
Quinteros Delgado, Juan Carlos, *Historia, Legislación y Jurisprudencia de Aduanas*. 2 vols., Montevideo, 1939.
–––––– *La Industria y el Estado en el Uruguay*. Montevideo, 1919.
Ramos Montero, Dionisio, *Los Progresos de un País Sud-Americano, la República Oriental del Uruguay*. Santiago de Chile, 1905.
Rippy, J. Fred, *British Investments in Latin America, 1822–1949: A Case Study in the Operations of Private Enterprise in Retarded Regions*. Minneapolis, 1959.
Robido, Cándido, *Colección de Artículos Sobre Asuntos Militares*. Montevideo, 1905.
Rodríguez Fabregat, Enrique, *Batlle y Ordóñez, el Reformador*. Buenos Aires, 1942.
Ruano Fournier, Agustín, *Estudio Económico de la Producción de Carnes del Río de la Plata*. Montevideo, 1936.
Sangre de Hermanos: Crónica Completa de los Sucesos Militares y Políticos

Durante la Revolución de 1904, vol. I. Montevideo, 1905. (Only one volume published.)

Seoane, Pedro, *La Industria de las Carnes en el Uruguay.* Montevideo, 1928.

Trías, Walter, *Batlle Periodista.* Montevideo, 1958.

Vidart, Daniel D., *Tomás Berreta. Apología de la Acción.* Montevideo, 1946.

Villegas Suárez, Ernesto, *La Contribución Inmobiliaria; Bosquejo Histórico —Legislación—Disposiciones.* Montevideo, 1941.

Visca, Carlos, "Aspectos Económicos de la Época de Reus," *Revista Histórica de la Universidad.* [Montevideo] Segunda Época 1 (February 1959), 39–55.

Welker, Juan Carlos, *José Serrato: Un Ejemplo.* Montevideo, 1944.

Williman, J. C. *El Dr. Claudio Williman: Su Vida Pública.* Montevideo, 1957.

Zavala Muniz, Justino, *Batlle, Héroe Civil.* México, 1945. Colección Tierra Firme, no. 16.

—— *Crónica de Muniz.* Montevideo, 1921.

Zum Felde, Alberto, *Proceso Histórico del Uruguay: Esquema de una Sociología Nacional.* Montevideo, 1919.

—— (Aurelio del Hebrón, pseud.), *El Uruguay Ante el Concepto Sociológico.* Montevideo, 1911.

Notes

I. Uruguay—1902

1. "Realidades," *El Siglo*, January 17, 1902.
2. Dirección General de Estadística, *Anuario Estadístico de la República Oriental del Uruguay, 1902–1903* (2 vols., Montevideo, 1903), I, 3–5 (hereinafter cited as *Anuario Estadístico*).
3. Juan Carlos Blanco, *El Puerto de Montevideo* (Montevideo, 1912), 26–27; *Diario de Sesiones de la H. Asamblea General*, X, 113–114 (hereinafter cited as *Asamblea General*).
4. Federico Rahola, *Sangre Nueva. Impresiones de un Viaje a la América del Sud* (Barcelona, 1905), 238; Lincoln Hutchinson, *Report on Trade Conditions in Argentina, Paraguay, and Uruguay* (Washington, 1906), 20–21.
5. J. Fred Rippy, *British Investments in Latin America, 1822–1949. A Case Study in the Operations of Private Enterprise in Retarded Regions* (Minneapolis, 1959), 142. Rippy's figures are for 1900. W. Herbert Coates, "Situación Comercial," in Reginald Loyd and others, editors, *Impresiones de la República del Uruguay en el Siglo Veinte* (London, 1912), 83.
6. Juan Carlos Quinteros Delgado, *Historia, Legislación y Jurisprudencia de Aduanas* (2 vols., Montevideo, 1933), I, 271.
7. *Anuario Estadístico, 1902–1903*, II, 259.
8. "Las Huelgas," *La Nación*, January 21, 1902.
9. Juan José Castro, *Estudio sobre los Ferrocarriles Sud-Americanos y las Grandes Líneas Internacionales* (Montevideo, 1893), 14–17.
10. Juan Ángel Álvarez Vignoli, *Evolución Histórica de la Ganadería en el Uruguay. Tésis presentada para optar al título de Ingeniero Agronómico* (Montevideo, 1917), 101–116; Honorio Camps Fajardo, "Ganadería," *Diario del Plata 1930* (Montevideo,1930), 195–208; Simon G. Hanson, *Utopia in Uruguay. Chapters in the Economic History of Uruguay* (New York, 1938), 215–216.
11. *Diario de Sesiones de la H. Cámara de Representantes*, CLXVII, 164–165, 691 (Hereinafter cited as *Cámara*); *Anuario Estadístico, 1902–1903*, II, 52; José Serrato, "Economía Rural," *El Siglo*, June 8, 1902.
12. *Anuario Estadístico, 1915*, 441; *Anuario Estadístico, 1902–1903*, II, 52.
13. *Ibid.*
14. Alberto A. Márquez, *Bosquejo de Nuestra Propiedad Territorial. Tésis presentada para optar el grado de doctor en Jurisprudencia* (Montevideo, 1893). Márquez estimated in 1893 that at least 1,000 of the 7,000 leagues of land in Uruguay were *tierras fiscales, ibid.*, 378. Martín C. Martínez, *La Renta Territorial* (Montevideo, 1918), 228–236.
15. "Asociación Rural del Uruguay," *El Nacional*, July 26, 1902.
16. *Anuario Estadístico, 1902–1903*, I, 110–112.
17. Adolfo H. Pérez Olave, *El Problema de la Instrucción Pública* (Montevideo, 1904), 51–52.
18. *Anuario Estadístico, 1902–1903*, I, 116, 387.
19. *Ibid.*, I, 172.

20. *Ibid.*, I, 7; *Anuario Estadístico, 1901, 850.*

21. "Un Proyecto Innocuo," *La Nación,* April 15, 1902; *Cámara,* CLXVII, 343–351.

22. Carlos Visca, "Aspectos Económicos de la Época de Reus," *Revista Histórica de la Universidad* [Montevideo], Segunda Época 1 (February 1959), 39–55.

23. Octavio Morató, *Surgimientos y Depresiones Económicos del Uruguay a Través de la Historia* (Montevideo, 1938), 15–40. Eduardo Acevedo, *Anales Históricos del Uruguay* (Montevideo, 1934), V, 172.

24. *Anuario Estadístico, 1916, 472.*

25. *Anuario Estadístico, 1902–1903,* I, 416; *Anuario Estadístico, 1915,* 98–100; Antonio N. Grompone, "Comercio," *Diario del Plata, 1930,* 189.

26. *Anuario Estadístico, 1915,* 467–468; José Serrato, "Problemas Económicos," *El Siglo,* June 4, 1902.

27. *Anuario Estadístico, 1902–1903,* II, 487. The difference between government income and the lesser amount of the budget resulted from the practice of not including nonrecurring items of government income, like the port construction revenues, in the budget.

28. *Anuario Estadístico, 1915,* 333; *Asamblea General,* X, 117.

29. Eduardo Acevedo, *Notas y Apuntes. Contribución al Estudio de la Historia Económica y Financiera de la República Oriental del Uruguay* (Montevideo, 1903), I, 5–7.

30. Juan Antonio Oddone, *El Principismo del Setenta. Una Experiencia Liberal en el Uruguay* (Montevideo, 1956) presents a more sympathetic appraisal.

31. Among the standard works on Uruguayan history are: Juan E. Pivel Devoto, *Los Partidos Políticos en el Uruguay, 1811–1897* (2 vols., Montevideo, 1942) and *Uruguay Independiente* (Barcelona, 1949); Alberto Zum Felde, *Proceso Histórico del Uruguay* (3rd edition, Montevideo, 1945); Eduardo Acevedo, *Manual de Historia Uruguaya* (2 vols., 3rd edition, Montevideo, 1943), and *Anales Históricos del Uruguay* (6 vols., Montevideo, 1933–1936). Francisco Pintos presents a Marxist view in *Historia del Uruguay (1851–1938). Ensayo de Interpretación Materialista* (Montevideo, 1946).

32. Saravia's papers have recently been published, interspersed with the comments of his son Nepomuceno, by Saravia's grandson and Nepomuceno's son, Nepomuceno Saravia García, *Memorias de Aparicio Saravia* (Montevideo, 1956), hereinafter cited as *Memorias de Saravia.* The son of Saravia's secretary used his father's archive in preparing *Aparicio Saravia. Héroe de la Libertad Electoral* by Luis R. Ponce de León (Montevideo, 1956), hereinafter cited as *Ponce de León—Saravia.* There are as well a number of pro-Saravia biographies. The best is José Monegal, *Vida de Aparicio Saravia* (Montevideo, 1942).

33. Cuestas, who did some writing, describes the scene in Juan Lindolfo Cuestas, *Páginas Sueltas* (3 vols., Montevideo, 1897–1901), III, 351–352. Borda's daughters defend his memory in C. Idiarte Borda and M. E. Idiarte Borda, *Juan Idiarte Borda, Su Vida, Su Obra* (Buenos Aires, 1939).

34. José Luciano Martínez, *Cuestas y su Administración* (Montevideo, 1904), the only full-length treatment, written by a hostile Colorado, includes all the vexations.

35. *Memorias de Saravia,* 300.

II. Campaigners

1. In 1897, after the revolution, Saravia supposedly told friends, "I expect to triumph through the ballot. If the Pact of La Cruz [which ended the war] is respected, the National Party will win by the time three legislative elections have passed, and only if they don't want to turn over to us the positions we have legitimately gained will I have to turn to arms." César Pintos Diago, *Anécdotas de*

Saravia (Montevideo, 1928), 155. By the time the 1901 electoral acuerdo was being negotiated, Saravia's confidence had shifted. He told Acevedo Díaz, "I believe that without the use of force the party will not achieve power." Eduardo Acevedo Díaz (h), *La Vida de Batalla de Eduardo Acevedo Díaz* (Buenos Aires, 1941), 143.

2. J. Muñoz Miranda, *Milicias Nacionales, Escalafón Militar del Partido Nacional* (Montevideo, 1902), 8–102.

3. *Memorias de Saravia,* 314.

4. Parts of a memoir Cuestas prepared, probably for posthumous publication, have been published by Federico Grunwaldt Ramasso, "Apuntes de Don Juan L. Cuestas. La Elección del 1 o. de Marzo de 1903," *El Día—Suplemento,* February 28, 1954 (hereinafter cited as *Apuntes—Cuestas*); Federico Grunwaldt Ramasso, *Páginas Sueltas Sobre la Personalidad y Obra de Don Juan Lindolfo Cuestas al Celebrarse el Cincuentenario del Puerto de Montevideo* (Montevideo, 1951), 28.

5. Ponce de León—*Saravia,* 58–59.

6. Batlle himself did not accent the second "o" in Ordoñez when signing his name, even though the accent appears in official documents. The practice here will be not to use the accent.

The book-length biographies of Batlle y Ordoñez are all written by political supporters. In 1928, during Batlle's lifetime, Roberto B. Giúdici and Efraín González Conzi published the thousand-page *Batlle y el Batllismo,* culled principally from *El Día* articles. Although basically a campaign biography, it contains long excerpts from Batlle's articles and projects. Batlle himself made marginal notes on his copy of the book, notes almost certainly designed for publication. The book, with the marginal notations, has recently been reprinted. The other large work, more novelistic in format, is Enrique Rodríguez Fabregat, *Batlle y Ordóñez, el Reformador* (Buenos Aires, 1942). Justino Zavala Muniz, who was close to Batlle in Batlle's later years, wrote *Batlle, Héroe Civil* (Mexico, 1945). José Mora Guarnido, an *El Día* newspaperman from Spain, wrote *Batlle y Ordóñez—Figura y Transfigura* (Montevideo, 1931).

A number of pamphlets deal with various phases of Batlle's career. Antonio Grompone's introductory essay to *La Ideología de Batlle, Sus Artículos* (Montevideo, 1943) stands out. Francisco Pintos, though a Communist, is sympathetic to Batlle in *Batlle y el Proceso Histórico del Uruguay* (Montevideo, 1938).

In 1956, the newspaper *Acción* published a series of articles by distinguished contributors. The articles, commemorating the centennial of Batlle's birth, have been published in book form as *Batlle, Su Vida, Su Obra* (Montevideo, 1956).

The most intimate picture of Batlle was painted by his lifelong collaborator Domingo Arena, in scattered articles and speeches. They are collected in Domingo Arena, *Batlle y los Problemas Sociales* (Montevideo, 1939) and "Escritos y Discursos del Dr. Domingo Arena Sobre el Señor José Batlle y Ordoñez," Biblioteca "Batlle," I (Montevideo, 1942), hereinafter cited as *Biblioteca "Batlle."*

7. Rodríguez Fabregat, *Batlle y Ordóñez, el Reformador,* 13–57.

8. Arturo Ardao, *Espiritualismo y Positivismo en el Uruguay* (Mexico, 1950) has detailed the intellectual history of the period when the attitudes of a generation were formed.

9. *Anales del Ateneo* (9 vols., Montevideo, 1881–1886) and *Revista de la Sociedad Universitaria* (3 vols., Montevideo, 1884–1885) contain the speeches and essays of the participants. Ardao has published the minutes of "La Sección de Filosofía del Ateneo (1879–1881)," *Revista de la Facultad de Humanidades y Ciencias* [Montevideo] año IV, no. 5 (June 1950), 129–144, in which Batlle took part.

10. Vázquez y Vega wrote Batlle: "I subordinate *everything* to the moral question." F. Fernández Prando, *Escritos y Discursos de Prudencio Vázquez y Vega, 1875–1882* (Montevideo, 1958), 16.

11. E. Ahrens, *Curso de Derecho Natural ó de Filosofía del Derecho* (6th edition, Paris and Mexico, 1880). First printing of 6th edition, 1868, translated by Pedro Rodríguez Hortelano and Mariano Ricardo de Asensi.

12. Arturo Ardao, *Batlle y Ordóñez y el Positivismo Filosófico* (Montevideo, 1951), 166. Ardao's research marks an encouraging development in studies on Batlle, shifting the polemic from partisan politics to questions of historical interpretation. Those who still hold, after Ardao's publications, that Batlle was a Positivist are hard pressed in their proofs. Ardao's research has been presented to American readers by F. S. C. Northrop—with startling misconceptions—in the chapter "The Nation of Uruguay's Batlle y Ordóñez" of his *Philosophical Anthropology and Practical Politics* (New York, 1960), 123–142.

13. Lorenzo Batlle to Luis Batlle y Ordoñez, October 10, 1883, Batlle Archive.

14. José Batlle y Ordoñez, Paris, to Lorenzo Batlle, March 7, 1880, Batlle Archive. Caro and Janet were Idealists, Laffitte a Comtian Positivist. The belief that Batlle was a Positivist stemmed from knowledge that he had attended Laffitte's classes in Paris. The fact that he also attended other classes is an important piece of evidence in the polemic over Batlle's early philosophical position.

15. Lorenzo Batlle to Luis Batlle y Ordoñez, February 14, 1883, Batlle Archive.

16. Pages from diary for January 1883, Batlle Archive.

17. Pedro Leandro Ipuche, *El Gran Solitario de Piedras Blancas* (Montevideo, 1915), 7.

18. Walter Trías, *Batlle Periodista* (Montevideo, 1958), 53–55; Benjamín Fernández y Medina, *La Imprenta y La Prensa en el Uruguay* (Montevideo, 1910), 54–55; Francisco Guevara Rosell, "Los 75 Años de 'El Día,'" *El Día. 1886—Junio —1961* (Montevideo, 1961).

19. C. Idiarte Borda and M. E. Idiarte Borda, *Juan Idiarte Borda, Su Vida, Su Obra* (Buenos Aires, 1939), 459–460.

20. Pedro Figari, *El Momento Político, 1910–1911* (Montevideo, 1911), 54–55; Arena, "La Primera Presidencia de Batlle," *Biblioteca "Batlle,"* I, 183–185.

21. Partido Nacional Archivo, Actas del Directorio, Series I, VI, 46–50; *Diario de Sesiones de la H. Cámara de Senadores,* LXXVI, 624–626 (hereinafter cited as *Senadores*).

22. The speech was reprinted in the third person in "El Error de la Razón," *El Día,* February 16, 1902.

23. Undated draft of letter (approximately September 1900), Batlle to Raimundo Pencifort, Fray Bentos, Río Negro, Batlle Archive.

24. Arena, "La Primera Presidencia de Batlle," *Biblioteca "Batlle,"* I, 186.

25. Interview, José Serrato, September 21 and 24, 1952.

26. Recollection of Rafael Batlle Pacheco.

27. *Apuntes—Cuestas.*

28. Eduardo Acevedo Díaz (h), *La Vida de Batalla de Eduardo Acevedo Díaz* (Buenos Aires, 1941), is the filial biography. Alberto Palomeque, *Eduardo Acevedo Díaz (Del Natural)* (Montevideo, 1901), is unsympathetic.

29. José M. Fernández Saldaña, *Diccionario Uruguayo de Biografías, 1810–1940* (Montevideo, 1945), 207–210.

III. The Presidential Campaign Begins

1. Domingo Arena, "La Primera Presidencia de Batlle," *Biblioteca "Batlle,"* I, 193.

2. José Batlle y Ordoñez, "Nuevos Rumbos," *El Día,* January 13, 1902.

3. José Batlle y Ordoñez, "Las Luchas de los Partidos," *El Día,* January 18, 1902.

4. José Batlle y Ordoñez, "Nuevos Rumbos," *El Día,* January 13, 1902. Batlle did not sign many articles, although he sometimes used well-known pseudonyms. Most of his articles must be identified stylistically.

5. Eduardo Acevedo Díaz, "Separación de 'El Nacional.' A Mis Correligionarios y Amigos," *El Nacional,* April 8, 1902.

6. Partido Nacional Archivo, *Actas del Directorio,* Series I, IV, 434–435; *Memorias de Saravia,* 306–307.

7. "Informaciones Políticas," *El Día*, April 26, 1902.

8. "Entrevista Cuestas-Batlle," *El Siglo*, April 28, 1902.

9. "La Elección Presidencial," *La Prensa*, May 15, 1902; "La Actualidad," *ibid.*, June 1, 1902.

10. In later years, Batlle insisted on the incompatibility of a legislator's taking an executive position. His speech on Cuestas' project appears in *Senadores*, LXXIX, 404-406. The debates are in *ibid.*, 283-284, 392-407, 461-462.

11. *Ibid.*, 469-503, 506-547, 584-594. José Batlle y Ordoñez, "La Senatoría de la Colonia," *El Día*, June 13, 1902, and June 27, 1902.

12. *Asamblea General*, X, 9-39; *Senadores*, LXXX, 101-104; *Diario de Sesiones de la H. Comisión Permanente*, XI, 328 (hereinafter cited as *Comisión Permanente*); "El Complot Contra la Vida del Señor Presidente Cuestas," *La Nación*, July 8, 1902; Partido Nacional Archivo, *Actas del Directorio*, Series I, V, 6-7.

13. "Una Carta del Dr. Rodríguez Larreta," *La Prensa*, July 20, 1902; "El Problema en Su Aspecto Nacional," *ibid.*, July 27, 1902.

14. The letter from Ramírez, dated August 13, 1902, was published in "Contra el Doctor Ramírez," *El Día*, September 21, 1906. Ramírez, Blanco, and Rodríguez Larreta had served in and resigned together from Santos' famous post-Quebracho "Ministry of Conciliation" in 1886.

15. Archivo del Partido Nacional, *Notas Recibidas por el H. Directorio*, II, II, 49-56.

16. The lead editorials of *El Nacional*, variously titled, for July 2, 5, 26, 27, and August 1, 2, 3, 5, 8, 10, 1902, elaborate Acevedo Díaz' position. The Directorio newspaper rejected it in "Las Generalidades del Problema Presidencial," *La Prensa*, August 12, 1902, but *El Nacional* reaffirmed this position on August 14, 1902, in "Planes de Política Práctica y Partidarismo a la Violeta."

17. "La Futura Presidencia," *El Siglo*, August 6, 1906; José Espalter, "El Problema Presidencial," *El Día*, August 20, 1906.

18. Arena, "La Primera Presidencia de Batlle," *Biblioteca "Batlle,"* I, 187.

19. *Ibid.*, 188-191; "Política de Verano," *El Siglo*, October 22, 1902.

20. "Manifestación de Propósitos de los Senadores y Representantes Afiliados al Partido Nacional," *La Prensa*, November 5, 1902.

21. Eduardo Acevedo Díaz (h), *La Vida de Batalla de Eduardo Acevedo Díaz* (Buenos Aires, 1941), 152-153; *Memorias de Saravia*, 357-359.

22. "Día Político," *El Nacional*, November 4, 1902.

23. "La Entrevista del Dr. Imas," *La Prensa*, November 12, 1902; "La Conferencia del Señor Imas con el Presidente de la República," *La Nación*, November 12, 1902. In his later memoir, Cuestas wrote that although ostensibly for Juan Carlos Blanco, the Nationalists "were playing with a marked deck, because through friends of the Directorio they were offering their support in the presidential election to Sr. Eduardo Mac-Eachen." *Apuntes—Cuestas*.

24. Partido Nacional Archivo, *Actas del Directorio*, I, V, 33-34, 40-42.

25. "Nuestra Proclamación," *La Nación*, November 21, 1902.

26. Alfredo Vidal y Fuentes, *Verdades* (Montevideo, 1903), 9. Vidal y Fuentes, Blanco's supporter in the Directorio, wrote this exposé in mid-1903. It is one of the few inside accounts of the presidential campaign.

27. "La Reunión Colorada de Ayer," *El Día*, November 22, 1902.

28. "Información Política," *El Día*, November 25, 1902.

29. "Plebiscito Nacional," *La Prensa*, November 4, 1902.

30. Vidal y Fuentes, *Verdades*, 12.

31. "Las Elecciones," *El Siglo*, December 1, 1902.

32. Vidal y Fuentes, *Verdades*, 16.

33. *Ponce de León—Saravia*, 64.

34. "La Nueva Presidencia en el Campo Nacionalista," *La Prensa*, December 2, 1902.

35. "Los Legisladores Colorados," *La Prensa*, December 6, 1902; "La Cuestión Presidencial," *El Siglo*, December 6, 1902.

36. "Conferencia Política," *El Siglo*, December 10, 1902.
37. "Los Peligros de la División," *La Nación*, December 19, 1902.
38. "Información Política," *El Día*, December 20, 1902; "La Reunión de Ayer," *El Siglo*, December 20, 1902.
39. "Alrededor de una Noticia," *La Nación*, December 23, 1902.
40. "Entrevista Cuestas-Batlle," *El Siglo*, December 27, 1902; "Cuestión Presidencial," *El Siglo*, December 27, 1902.
41. "Información Política," *El Día*, December 28, 1902; "El Teniente General Tajes," *El Siglo*, December 24, 1902.
42. "Cosas Muy Serias Imprudentemente Encaminadas," *El Nacional*, December 27, 1902; "Día Político," *El Nacional*, December 31, 1902; "Aclaración Necesaria," *El Siglo*, December 31, 1902; "Alrededor de una Entrevista," *La Prensa*, December 31, 1902.
43. *Memorias de Saravia*, 329-330.
44. "El Candidato de Saravia," *El Siglo*, December 30, 1902.

IV. Election

1. Confirmación Plena de un Nuevo Desacierto," *El Nacional*, January 1, 1903.
2. D. Mendilaharsu, "Contestando," *El Nacional*, January 23, 1903; D. Mendilaharsu, "Ampliando Informaciones," *El Nacional*, January 24, 1903.
3. [Batlle] "Sobre Aspiraciones," *El Día de la Tarde*, October 7, 1926. This account which Batlle published in the heat of a later political campaign was designed to show his disinterest, not his subtlety.
4. Partido Nacional Archivo, *Actas del Directorio*, Series I, V, 73-74.
5. "Día Político," *El Nacional*, January 9, 1903, January 20, 1903.
6. "Día Político," *El Nacional*, January 20, 1903; "Actualidad," *El Siglo*, January 18, 1903.
7. "Informaciones Políticas," *El Día*, January 23, 1903.
8. "Cuestión Presidencial," *El Siglo*, January 25, 1903.
9. "Quienes Faltaron al 'Compromiso,'" *El Nacional*, January 21, 1903; "Candidatos Imposibles," *La Prensa*, January 21, 1903.
10. *Memorias de Saravia*, 351-352.
11. *Memorias de Saravia*, 351.
12. "Declaraciones Políticas del Señor Batlle y Ordóñez," *El Día*, January 24, 1903.
13. "La Elección Presidencial," *La Prensa*, January 30, 1903.
14. Partido Nacional Archivo, *Notas del Directorio*, Series III, V, 229.
15. "Los Legisladores Nacionalistas," *La Prensa*, January 31, 1903.
16. Ramón P. González, *Aparicio Saravia en la Revolución de 1903* (Montevideo, 1949), 37.
17. "Día Político," *El Nacional*, February 1, 1903.
18. *La Prensa*, February 3, 1903.
19. *Memorias de Saravia*, 360-361; Monegal, *Vida de Aparicio Saravia*, 471-472.
20. *Apuntes—Cuestas*.
21. "La Candidatura Oficial," *La Prensa*, February 5, 1903; "Cuestión Presidencial," *El Siglo*, February 5, 1903.
22. "Información Política," *El Día*, February 6, 1903.
23. Arena, "La Primera Presidencia de Batlle," *Biblioteca* "*Batlle*," I, 192.
24. This is the version Acevedo Díaz gave when he published his defense of his actions in the presidential campaign as "Carta Política," *El Nacional*, September 16, 1903; reprinted as a pamphlet, *Carta Política* (Montevideo, 1903). The Directorio minutes merely note that the delegation reported, not *what* they reported. Partido Nacional Archivo, *Actas del Directorio*, Series I, V, 83-84.
25. "Información Nacionalista," *La Prensa*, February 5, 1903.
26. Acevedo Díaz, *Carta Política*.

27. *Memorias de Saravia*, 355; "Por la Unificación," *La Prensa*, February 17, 1903.

28. "Reflexiones Oportunas," *La Prensa*, February 8, 1903.

29. "La Reunión Nacionalista," *La Prensa*, February 10, 1903; Partido Nacional Archivo, *Actas del Directorio*, Series I, V, 89–90.

30. Vidal y Fuentes, *Verdades*, 21–22; "Cuestión Presidencial," *El Siglo*, February 10, 1903.

31. Vidal y Fuentes, *Verdades*, 23–33; "Legisladores Nacionalistas," *La Prensa*, February 11, 1903.

32. *Memorias de Saravia*, 362.

33. Joaquín Fajardo to Batlle, October 26, 1903, Batlle Archive.

34. "Informaciones Políticas," *El Día*, February 12, 1903.

35. Domingo Arena, "La Primera Presidencia de Batlle," *Biblioteca "Batlle,"* I, 195.

36. "Informaciones Políticas," *El Día*, February 12, 1903.

37. "Cuestión Presidencial," *El Siglo*, February 12, 1903.

38. Vidal y Fuentes, *Verdades*, 36–49; Partido Nacional Archivo, *Actas del Directorio*, Series I, V, 92–94. Vidal y Fuentes says that Batlle told him he would not give another *Jefatura*, but evidence suggests otherwise.

39. "Informaciones Políticas," *El Día*, February 15, 1903; Vidal y Fuentes, *Verdades*, 46.

40. Partido Nacional Archivo, *Actas del Directorio*, Series I, V, 90–91. Cuestas in his memoirs may have intentionally confused this later Nationalist move with the scheme he accused them of planning earlier. In this way he could picture himself as Batlle's supporter before February 11.

41. "La Presidencia del Senado," *El Día*, February 15, 1903; Acevedo Díaz, *Carta Política; Senadores*, LXXX, 464–467.

42. *Apuntes—Cuestas*.

43. Juan L. Cuestas to Batlle, February 14, 1903, Batlle Archive.

44. The exchange was first made public by Acevedo Díaz in his *Carta Política* of September, 1903. Draft copies of Batlle's promises, carefully corrected by Batlle, are in his archive.

45. Lauro V. Rodríguez to Batlle, February 5, 1905, Batlle Archive.

46. "Información Política," *El Día*, February 19, 1903.

47. *Ponce de León—Saravia*, 68–69.

48. "Propaganda de Paz y Legalidad," *La Prensa*, February 22, 1903.

49. Archivo del Partido Nacional, *Notas Recibidas por el H. Directorio*, Series II, II, 81.

50. Giúdici and González Conzi's massive *Batlle y el Batllismo*, published in 1928, gave currency to the legend. Even Batlle, as the next footnote indicates, felt obliged to correct the authors on some points. American academic readers were introduced to Batlle in 1930 by Percy Alvin Martin, "The Career of José Batlle y Ordóñez," *Hispanic American Historical Review*, X (November 1930), 413–428, which gives evidence of following Giúdici and González Conzi. I suspect that American textbook writers have taken their lead from Martin and from Simon Hanson, *Utopia in Uruguay: Chapters in the Economic History of Uruguay* (New York, 1938). Hanson, whose impressive treatment of the operations of the Uruguayan state-owned enterprises has perhaps given excessive authority to his incidental treatment of political matters, introduces Batlle on taking office in 1903 as follows: "Batlle's prestige was greater than that of his party. He was the son of a former president, had led the fight for honest government for a quarter of a century, and had demonstrated ability as the head of a department and in the legislature. He was the most influential journalist in the country. He had resurrected his party and given it his ideals, chief of which was that Uruguay should become a true democracy" (19). Russell H. Fitzgibbon's chapter "The Lengthened Shadow of a Man" in his *Uruguay: Portrait of a Democracy* (New Brunswick, N.J., 1954) follows in the tradition of Martin and Hanson.

51. Batlle's corrections to the Giúdici and González Conzi biography, p. 265, Batlle Archive. Batlle makes Cuestas more pro-Batlle than he actually was by neglecting to explain that he lost the Nationalist votes and Cuestas' support because he broke with Cuestas' policy of conciliation toward the Nationalists.

52. Domingo Arena, "La Primera Presidencia de Batlle," *Biblioteca "Batlle,"* I, 183, 194, 197.

V. Dangerous Inauguration

1. "Información Política," *El Día*, February 28, 1903.

2. Batlle had not wanted the traditional presidential expense account because he would have felt obliged to keep detailed records. Instead, the Assembly voted him a salary equal to the previous presidential salary plus an expense account. Domingo Arena, "Anécdotas de Excepcional Valor Documentario," *Biblioteca "Batlle,"* I, 165.

3. *Asamblea General*, X, 325–335.

4. "La Elección Presidencial," *El Siglo*, March 2, 1903.

5. *Ibid.*

6. *Ibid.;* Federico Grunwaldt Ramasso, *Páginas Sueltas Sobre la Personalidad y Obra de Don Juan Lindolfo Cuestas al Celebrarse el Cincuentenario del Puerto de Montevideo* (Montevideo, 1951), 29.

7. "La Elección Presidencial," *El Día*, March 2, 1903.

8. Domingo Arena, "Batlle, Director de El Día," *Bliblioteca "Batlle,"* I, 133.

9. Dr. Francisco Soca, who had been the formal leader of the MacEachenites at the end of the campaign, felt Batlle owed him the Senate presidency. Batlle was reluctant to antagonize Castro—early in the campaign Don Pepe had encouraged Castro's hopes that he, not Batlle, might be elected President of the Republic by telling him that whoever got the most votes among the Colorado legislators would be the party's candidate—and insisted to Soca that his own political position was not secure enough to permit him to influence the election of the Senate President. There are several undated letters from Soca to Batlle on this matter in the Batlle Archive. Batlle's conversation with Castro and the Castro-Soca rivalry are mentioned by César Batlle Pacheco, in a somewhat different context, in an interview with M. Ferdinand Pontac [Luis Bonavita], "En Torno a la Figura de Don José Batlle y Ordoñez," *El Día–Suplemento*, April 9, 1961. Arena described Don Pepe's tactic of holding his group together by telling its members that he would step aside should another member of the group secure more votes. The vague presidential hopes of various members of the group were thus channeled toward getting more votes for the group—and Batlle. Domingo Arena, "La Primera Presidencia de Batlle," *Biblioteca "Batlle,"* I, 188–189.

Senadores, LXXXI, 26–27; "Manifiesto del Directorio del Partido Nacional al País," *La Prensa*, March 4, 1903.

10. Partido Nacional Archivo, *Actas del Directorio*, Series I, V, 120–121.

11. Vidal y Fuentes, *Verdades*, 71–72.

12. *Memorias de Saravia*, 370.

13. "Asuntos Militares," *El Día*, March 12, 1903; "El Acuerdo de Ministros," *La Prensa*, March 12, 1903.

14. [Batlle] "Las Empresas Tranviarias y el Partido Oribista," *El Día de la Tarde*, January 23, 1927; *Asamblea General*, X, 345–349.

15. Partido Nacional Archivo, *Actas del Directorio*, Series I, V, 124–129; "Información Nacionalista," *La Prensa*, March 14, 1903; "Asuntos Nacionalistas," *El Siglo*, March 14, 1903.

16. "Información Nacionalista," *La Prensa*, March 15, 1903; "Del Doctor Quintela," *La Prensa*, March 17, 1903; "Informaciones Políticas," *El Día*, March 15, 1903.

17. *Memorias de Saravia*, 371–373.

18. Interview, Alfonso Lamas, September 25, 1952.
19. *Memorias de Saravia*, 374.
20. Francisco Susviela Guarch, Rio de Janeiro, to Batlle, March 19, 1903, Batlle Archive.
21. Daniel Muñoz, Buenos Aires, to Batlle, March 19, 20, 21, 22, 1903, Batlle Archive.
22. *Memorias de Saravia*, 374, 375.
23. Pedro Cosio, *Crónica de los Sucesos de Rivera* (Montevideo, 1903), 91. The famous playwright Florencio Sánchez spent some time with João Francisco, and wrote a frightening pamphlet on his experience in *El Caudillaje Criminal en Sud América* (Montevideo, 1913).
24. "La Insurrección," *El Día*, March 22, 1903.
25. Francisco Susviela Guarch, Rio de Janeiro, to Batlle, March 19, 1903, Batlle Archive.
26. Daniel Muñoz, Buenos Aires, to Batlle, March 25, 1903, Batlle Archive.
27. "La Insurrección," *El Día*, March 19, 1903.
28. "La Insurrección," *El Día*, March 21, 1903; "La Insurrección," *El Siglo*, March 21, 1903.
29. Ramírez and Lamas, Melo, telegram to Batlle, Batlle Archive.
30. [Batlle] "Una Mala Causa," *El Día*, March 26, 1913 [*sic*].
31. *El Día* published the conversation in "La Paz" on March 24, 1903. The originals are in the Batlle Archive.
32. "Hora Sombría," *El Siglo*, March 21, 1903.
33. "La Insurrección," *El Día*, March 22, 1903.
34. "La Insurrección," *El Día*, March 23, 1903.
35. "La Paz," *El Día*, March 24, 1903.
36. Lamas, Nico Pérez, telegram to Batlle, Batlle Archive.
37. "La Paz," *El Día*, March 28, 1903.
38. Nobody counted and Nationalist estimates have varied from 14,000 to 20,000, but there is no doubt that a large mounted army had assembled at Nico Pérez. "La Paz," *La Prensa*, March 29, 1903; *Memorias de Saravia*, 389–390; Monegal, *Vida de Aparicio Saravia*, 331.
39. Saravia's secretary wrote his fiancé from Nico Pérez: "Acevedo Díaz and his group, the only ones who caused the conflict." *Ponce de León—Saravia*, 71.
40. Ramón P. González, *Aparicio Saravia en la Revolución de 1904* (Montevideo, 1949), 46.
41. "La Paz," *El Día*, March 28, 1903.
42. "La Paz," *El Siglo*, March 29, 1903.
43. "En Celebración de la Paz," *El Día*, March 31, 1903.
44. "Proclama del General Saravia," *La Prensa*, March 31, 1903.
45. "El Manifiesto del General Saravia," *La Prensa*, March 24, 1903.

VI. Uneasy Year

1. *Cámara*, CLXXI, 163–184; *Senadores*, LXXXI, 69–72.
2. *Memorias de Saravia*, 387–388; Archivo del Partido Nacional, *Notas Recibidas por el H. Directorio*, Series II, XI, 138–156; Partido Nacional Archivo, *Actas del Directorio*, Series I, V, 133–143; "Conferencia Batlle-Campisteguy-Imas," *El Siglo*, April 10, 1903; "Jefaturas Nacionalistas," *El Siglo*, April 12, 1903.
3. "Cambio de Ministros," *La Prensa*, April 3, 1903.
4. "El Telegrama del Doctor Imas," *La Prensa*, April 3, 1903; "Información Política," *El Día*, April 4, 1903; "La Paz," *El Día*, April 6, 1903.
5. "La Fiesta de Anoche," *El Día*, April 19, 1903; "El Gran Banquete," *El Siglo*, April 19, 1903.
6. *Cámara*, CLXXII, 322–325.
7. Carlos Burmeister to Batlle, April 30, 1903, Batlle Archive.

8. "Derecho de los Militares," *El Día*, April 23, 1903; "Informaciones Políticas," *El Día*, April 23, 1903.

9. *Memorias de Saravia*, 400; Partido Nacional Archivo, *Actas del Congreso Elector de Directorio*, Series VII, I, 93–95.

10. "El Nuevo Directorio," *La Prensa*, May 7, 1903.

11. Saravia to Lamas, May 11, 1903, Archivo del Partido Nacional, *Notas Recibidas por el Directorio del Partido Nacional*, Series II, XIII, 11.

12. *Memorias de Saravia*, 400.

13. Eusebio Pedragosa, Rivera, May 1, 1903, Batlle Archive.

14. The Executive sent bills, together with a covering message, directly to the legislature. *Cámara*, CLXXI, 295–309, 350–355; *Senadores*, LXXXI, 195–200.

15. *Memoria de la Jefatura Política y de Policía de la Capital. Administración: Coronel Juan Bernassa y Jerez, 1903 a 1906* (Montevideo, 1907), 57–62; "El 1o. de Mayo," *El Día*, May 2, 1903.

16. [Batlle] "Por Nuestras Industrias," *El Día*, June 10, 1903.

17. In later years, Batlle tried to turn aside Aguirre's priority in proposing a plural executive, the spinal column of the Batllista program. [Batlle] "Inconsecuencia que no Existe," *El Día*, September 8, 1916.

18. "La Reforma Constitucional," *El Día*, May 9, 10, 19, June 10, 1903; "En el Ateneo," *El Siglo*, June 16, 1903.

19. During 1903, Batlle changed the commanders of most army units. Florencio César González, *Ejército del Uruguay* (Montevideo, 1903), 18–118.

20. "Informaciones Políticas," *El Día*, May 19, 1903.

21. "De Mal en Peor," *El Siglo*, May 10, 1903; "El Meeting del 31," *El Día*, May 13, 1903.

22. *Memorias de Saravia*, 403–405.

23. Campisteguy to Batlle, May 25, 1903, Batlle Archive.

24. Partido Nacional Archivo, *Actas del Directorio*, Series I, V, 201–205.

25. According to its sponsors, some 5,000 demonstrators, who cheered when they passed *El Día*, took part. "El Meeting de Ayer," *El Día*, June 1, 1903. The pros and cons of the demonstration are presented in: Biblioteca del Club Vida Nueva, *Protesta Contra el Crimen* (Montevideo, 1903), and Comité Defensa Nacionalista, *Contra la Calumnia. Gestiones de Protesta por las Invectivas del Club "Vida Nueva"* (Montevideo, 1903).

26. *Memorias de Saravia*, 405–407.

27. "Con 'La Prensa,'" *El Día*, June 16, 1903.

28. *Cámara*, CLXXII, 322–406.

29. "El Presidente Batlle y el Partido Nacional," *La Prensa*, July 15, 1903; *Cámara*, CLXXII, 407; *Senadores*, LXXXII, 37–41.

30. Biblioteca del Club Colorado "Defensa de Montevideo," *Proceso de la Gran Asamblea de Villa Colón Julio 19 de 1903* (Montevideo, 1905), 2–116; "La Reunión Colorada de Ayer," *El Día*, July 20, 1903.

31. "Las Alarmas del País," *El Día*, July 22, 1903.

32. Partido Nacional Archivo, *Actas del Directorio*, Series I, V, 289–290; "Informaciones Políticas," *El Día*, July 28, 1903; "La Entrevista de Ayer," *La Prensa*, July 28, 1903.

33. "El Directorio del Partido Nacional AL PAÍS y a los Correligionarios," *La Prensa*, July 28, 1903; "La Tranquilidad," *El Día*, July 30, 1903.

34. Domingo Arena, "Anécdotas de Excepcional Valor Documentario," *Biblioteca "Batlle,"* I, 167–168; José Serrato interview, September 21 and 24, 1952; "El Presidente de la República," *El Día*, August 28, 1903. Batlle wanted posterity to know of his government's honesty. On the margin of a letter from Strauch & Co., September 18, 1903, which protested that the Ministry of War had accepted a bid from a competitor after bids were closed, Batlle noted "Nothing at all of what Strauch & Co. describe took place. JBO." Batlle Archive.

35. Telegram to Cardinal Rampella, Rome, July 9, 1903, Batlle Archive.

36. On September 5, 1903 *Diario Nuevo* supported the labor proposals of the Argentine Socialists; on September 6 it proposed taxes on dividends going abroad; on September 7 it proposed taxes on bank deposits and mortgages to force capital into circulation; on September 12 it proposed the expropriation of the foreign-owned Montevideo waterworks.

37. "La Visita a Saravia," *El Día*, August 10, 1903.

38. "La Legación en Norte América," *El Día*, August 19, 1903; *Comisión Permanente*, XI, 425; *Senadores*, LXXXII, 109–112; Partido Nacional Archivo, *Actas del Directorio*, Series I, V, 305–306, 324–325.

39. *Memorias de Saravia*, 411–412.

40. "La Reorganización Colorada," *El Día*, August 10, 1903.

41. "El Remedio del Mal," *El Día*, August 26, 1903.

42. The documents on these negotiations were later published as *Bases de Unificación del Partido Colorado* (Montevideo, 1903).

43. Domingo Arena, "El Humanitarismo de Batlle," *Biblioteca "Batlle*," I, 138.

44. Vázquez Acevedo insisted that the Constitution required the President of the Republic to delegate the executive power on leaving the capital. The motion was defeated in a party vote. *Senadores*, LXXXII, 130–137; Partido Nacional Archivo, *Actas del Directorio*, Series I, V, 345–348.

45. "Reportaje al Señor Batlle y Ordoñez," *El Día*, September 28, 1903.

46. Batlle may have been responding to the novelist-rancher Carlos Reyles, who had just proposed a producers' league as a new force in Uruguayan politics. Carlos Reyles, "El Ideal Nuevo," *El Siglo*, August 16, 1903.

47. "La Gira Presidencial," *El Día*, September 28, 1903.

48. "El Discurso Presidencial," *La Prensa*, September 30, 1903.

49. "La Gira Presidencial," *El Día*, September 29, 1903.

50. "La Gira Presidencial," *El Día*, September 30, 1903.

51. Román Freire to Luis P. García, October 7, 1903. Batlle Archive.

52. "Organización Colorada," *El Día*, October 25, 1903.

53. *Cámara*, CLXXIII, 217–221; *Senadores*, LXXXII, 209–213.

VII. The Regiments in Rivera

1. Cabrera published a long press account in 1936, reprinted in *Memorias de Saravia*, 418–421. The Uruguayan Consul in Santa Ana do Livramento, Gabriel Vázquez, sent Batlle a detailed description on November 2, 1903, Batlle Archive.

2. "1904! Colección Completa de Documentos Oficiales Relacionados con la Guerra Civil," *El Día*, August 26, 1919.

3. Vice Consul Brasilero, Rivera, telegram to Consul Gral. del Brasil, Montevideo, November 1, 1903, and Gómes Freitas, Rivera, telegram to Ministro Brasilero, Montevideo, November 1, 1903, Batlle Archive.

4. Jefe Político, Rivera, telegram to Presidente de la República, November 1, 1903, Batlle Archive.

5. "1904!," *El Día*, August 26, 1919.

6. González, *Aparicio Saravia en la Revolución de 1904*, 56.

7. Gabriel Vázquez, Consul, Rivera, telegram to Presidente de la República, November 2, 1903, Batlle Archive.

8. C. L. Cabrera, Rivera, telegram to Presidente de la República, November 2, 1903, Batlle Archive.

9. "1904!," *El Día*, August 26, 1919.

10. "Los Sucesos de Rivera," *El Día*, November 2, 1903.

11. Partido Nacional Archivo, *Actas del Directorio*, Series I, V, 407–410.

12. "Los Sucessos de Rivera," *El Día*, November 3, 1903.

13. *Comisión Permanente*, XI, 450–451.

14. The Martín C. Martínez interview was published in *El Día*, February 7, 1904.

It was reprinted in *Sangre de Hermanos. Crónica Completa de los Sucesos Militares y Políticos de 1904* (Vol. I, only volume published, Montevideo, 1905), 227–228 (hereinafter cited as *Sangre de Hermanos*).

15. The José Pedro Ramírez interview appeared in *El Tiempo*, February 6, 1904, and *Sangre de Hermanos*, 218–219.

16. The Batlle interview appeared in *El Día*, February 7, 1904, and *Sangre de Hermanos*, 225–226.

17. "Del Dr. Alfonso Lamas," *El Día*, February 18, 1905.

18. The second José Pedro Ramírez interview, *El Siglo*, February 9, 1904, and *Sangre de Hermanos*, 228–230.

19. [Batlle] "En 1904," *El Día*, September 18, 1923; [Batlle] "1904," *El Día*, August 29, 1919; Colonel Cándido Viera, Tranqueras, to Batlle, November 19, 1903, Batlle Archive.

20. Batlle's annotation on the Giúdici biography, 327–329, Batlle Archive.

21. The Juan Andrés Ramírez interview, *El Siglo*, February 9, 1904, and *Sangre de Hermanos*, 230–231.

22. Saravia to Lamas, May 11, 1903, Partido Nacional Archivo, *Notas Recibidas por el Directorio*, Series II, XIII, 9–11.

23. "Cual es el Pacto," *Diario Nuevo*, November 12, 1903.

24. "Más Exigencias," *Diario Nuevo*, November 27, 1903.

25. "El Restablecimiento Constitucional," *El Día*, November 14, 1903.

26. "Saravia y la Paz," *El Siglo*, November 12, 1903.

27. *Memorias de Saravia*, 428–430.

28. "Año de Lucha," *La Prensa*, November 28, 1903.

29. "Día Político," *El Tiempo*, November 5, 1903; "Asuntos Políticos," *Diario Nuevo*, November 6, 1903; "Política Colorada," *El Siglo*, November 11, 1903; "Organización Colorada," *El Día*, November 14, 1903.

30. "La Acción Partidaria en los Departamentos," *Diario Nuevo*, December 6, 1903; "Organización Colorada," *El Día*, November 20, 1903; J. A. Abellá y Escobar, Rivera, to Julio Abellá y Escobar, November 25, 1903, Batlle Archive.

31. M., "Actividad Colorada," *El Día*, December 10, 1903, and N. [Batlle?], "Actividad," *El Día*, December 11, 1903.

32. Julio María Sosa, *Deberes Partidarios* (Montevideo, 1903), 20–21; Adolfo H. Pérez Olave, *Conferencia Política Dada en el Instituto Verdi el 12 de Noviembre de 1903 Bajo los Auspicios del Club "Vida Nueva"* (Montevideo, 1903), 27.

33. "La Gira Presidencial," *El Día*, October 5, 1903.

34. *Cámara*, CLXXIV, 85.

35. *Ibid.*, 143–160.

36. *Ibid.*, 156, 180, 204–271.

37. *Cámara*, CLXXIII, 419, 432; *Cámara*, CLXXIV, 13; "Las Compañías de Seguros," *El Siglo*, October 31, 1903.

38. The Montevideo municipality was the legal owner of the power plant, but the national government operated it. The ownership complications were an inheritance from the collapse of the Banco Nacional.

39. Federico Paullier to Batlle, December 17, 1903, Batlle Archive; "Por fin," *El Siglo*, December 18, 1903.

40. "El Derecho a la Huelga," *El Día*, November 27, 1903.

41. "Las Dos Tendencias," *La Prensa*, December 1, 1903.

42. *Memorias de Saravia*, 433–434.

43. "La Entrevista con el General Saravia," *La Prensa*, December 17, 1903.

44. There are no verbatim accounts of what transpired. My sources are *Memorias de Saravia*, 421–439; *Sangre de Hermanos*, 265–271; Partido Nacional, *Exposición. El Directorio Saliente á la Nueva Corporación, Abril, 1905* (Montevideo, 1905), 16–17; interview with Alfonso Lamas, September 25, 1952.

45. "Cuestas 'El Insufrible' y Batlle 'El Bueno,'" *La Prensa*, December 17, 1903.

46. Batlle annotation on Giúdici biography, 139, Batlle Archive. Batlle put

much thought and effort into blackening José Pedro Ramírez' reputation in later years, even to the point of denying him a state funeral.

47. There is such a plan in the Batlle Archive. The Nationalists also were aware of it. Partido Nacional, *Exposición* . . . *1905*, 16,

48. Undated, Batlle Archive.

49. Partido Nacional Archivo, *Notas Recibidas por el H. Directorio*, Series II, XII, 36–40.

50. *Memorias de Saravia*, 441; Juan José Muñoz, *Apuntes Históricos* (Montevideo, 1952), 35, 63.

51. *Memorias de Saravia*, 421–423.

52. "Los Sucesos," *El Día*, January 2, 1904.

53. Partido Nacional Archivo, *Actas del Congreso Elector del Directorio*, Series VII, I, 130–143; Partido Nacional Archivo, *Actas del Directorio*, Series I, V, 454.

54. Gonzalo Ramírez interview, *El Día*, February 5, 1904, and *Sangre de Hermanos*, 224–225.

55. [Batlle] "Otras Verdades," *El Día*, January 9, 1904; Pedro Manini y Ríos, *La Culpa de la Guerra* (Montevideo, 1905), 103.

56. *Memorias de Saravia*, 443

57. *Ibid.*, 444.

58. "Los Sucesos," *El Día*, January 2, 1904; Pedro Erasmo Callorda, *Evocando el Pasado. Batlle* (Habana, 1920), 38.

59. *Memorias de Saravia*, 445.

60. "1904," *El Día*, August 31, 1919. In 1919, Batlle published the war telegrams under the title "1904" as a daily feature of the new afternoon edition of *El Día*.

61. *Memorias de Saravia*, 452.

62. [Batlle] "Otras Verdades," *El Día*, January 9, 1904; Manini y Ríos, *La Culpa de la Guerra*, 108.

63. [Batlle] "La Guerra," *El Día*, January 10, 1904.

64. Partido Nacional Archivo, *Actas del Directorio*, Series I, V, 454–455.

65. *Memorias de Saravia*, 453.

66. Partido Nacional, *Exposición* . . . *1905*, 31; Manini y Ríos, *La Culpa de la Guerra*, 110.

67. *Memorias de Saravia*, 450.

68. "1904," *El Día*, September 1, 1919.

69. Juan José Muñoz, *Apuntes Históricos*, 36.

70. Telegrams of January 4 and 5, 1904, "1904," *El Día*, September 2, 3, 4, 5, 1919.

71. *Comisión Permanente*, XI, 455–456.

72. "1904," *El Día*, September 16, 18, 1919.

73. *Memorias de Saravia*, 450–451, reprints an article by Rómulo Muñoz Zeballos which first appeared in *El País*, August 20, 1955. Rodríguez Larreta told the story to Muñoz Zeballos.

74. Batlle defended his 1903–1904 actions in his annual message to the legislature in February 1905. *Asamblea General*, X, 492–497. The Directorio answered with *Exposición* . . . *1905*, which provoked Manini y Ríos' *La Culpa de la Guerra*. These three statements are the most solid bases for later polemics.

75. Domingo Arena, "Los Últimos Días de Batlle," *Biblioteca "Batlle,"* I, 209.

VIII. The War of 1904

1. José Serrato, "Don José Batlle y Ordoñez," [*Acción*], *Batlle, Su Vida, Su Obra* (Montevideo, 1956), 5.

2. Justino Zavala Muniz, *Crónica de Muniz* (Montevideo, 1921), 260–288.

3. "1904," *El Día*, *Edición de la Tarde* (hereinafter cited as *El Día—Tarde*), September 21, 1919. Batlle, especially at the beginning, supplied editorial comment to the telegrams he was publishing.

4. Nationalist sources are reluctant to criticize Saravia as a strategist. Inferential

criticisms do emerge when writers and editors try to clear the reputations of Saravia's subordinates, especially when sons write of their fathers.

Juan José Muñoz, *Apuntes Históricos*, 37-68; *Memorias de Saravia*, 460-461; Arturo Ardao and Julio Castro, *Vida de Basilio Muñoz* (Montevideo, 1938), 113-115. The novelist Javier de Viana wrote a propaganda account during the war, *Con Divisa Blanca* (2nd edition, Buenos Aires, 1921), 22-24.

5. "1904," *El Día—Tarde*, September 21, 22, 1919.

6. "Trabajos por la Paz," *El Siglo*, January 12, 1904; "Gestiones de Paz," *El Día*, January 12, 1904.

7. Daniel Muñoz, Buenos Aires, to Batlle, January 13, 1904, Batlle Archive.

8. "Las Gestiones de Paz," *El Día*, January 13, 14, 15, 1904.

9. *Ponce de León—Saravia*, 87; *Sangre de Hermanos*, 49-50; Juan José Muñoz, *Apuntes Históricos*, 37.

10. "1904," *El Día—Tarde*, October 13, 1919.

11. "1904," *El Día—Tarde*, October 10, 1919.

12. "La Insurrección," *El Día*, January 29, 1904.

13. *Memorias de Saravia*, 467-487; the account is by son Nepomuceno; Viana, *Con Divisa Blanca*, 60-67; *Sangre de Hermanos*, 79-83; interview with Alfonso Lamas, September 25, 1952.

14. The fact that Batlle ordered Vázquez to walk his horses makes this interpretation more reasonable than Batlle's later claim (in the editorial notes for October 25, 1919) that he was sending Vázquez to take over Muñoz' command. "1904," *El Día—Tarde*, October 22, 23, 24, 27, 1919.

15. *Sangre de Hermanos*, 115-134.

16. "1904," *El Día—Tarde*, October 28, 1919.

17. *Sangre de Hermanos*, 115-134; *Ponce de León—Saravia*, 91; Daniel Vidart, *Tomás Berreta. Apología de la Acción* (Montevideo, 1946), 239-262; Monegal, *Vida de Aparicio Saravia*, 346-358.

18. [Batlle] "1904," *El Día—Tarde*, October 30, 1919.

19. *Sangre de Hermanos*, 135-148.

20. "1904," *El Día—Tarde*, November 1, 2, 1919.

21. Ejército Nacionalista, *Campaña de 1904. Colección Completa de Órdenes Generales Dictadas por el Estado Mayor General del Ejército* (Montevideo, 1905), 5; *Memorias de Saravia*, 479-480.

22. Viana, *Con Divisa Blanca*, 114.

23. "Uruguay," *La Nación* (Buenos Aires), February 6, 7, 1904; *Sangre de Hermanos*, 240-249; "Por los Fueros Nacionales," *Diario Nuevo*, February 5, 1904.

24. "Los Sucesos Uruguayos," *La Nación* (Buenos Aires), February 2, 1904.

25. *Cámara*, CLXXV, 29; *Senadores*, LXXXIII, 25; the text of the law was published in *Sangre de Hermanos*, 268-276; [Batlle] "1904," *El Día—Tarde*, November 6, 1919; "Para Contener la Ruina," *El Día*, February 29, 1904.

26. *Senadores*, LXXXII, 15-17; *Sangre de Hermanos*, 237-239.

27. Angel Floro Costa, Buenos Aires, to Batlle, February 2, 1904, Batlle Archive.

28. "1904," *El Día—Tarde*, November 8, 12, 1919.

29. *Memorias de Saravia*, 497-498.

30. Fernando Gutiérrez, *Paso del Parque* (Montevideo, 1921), 38-55.

31. *Ibid.*, 71-103; *Memorias de Saravia*, 506; Juan José Muñoz, *Apuntes Históricos*, 40-42; Ardao and Castro, *Vida de Basilio Muñoz*, 118-122; Monegal, *Vida de Aparicio Saravia*, 358-372.

32. "1904," *El Día—Tarde*, December 19, 1919.

33. Benjamín Victorica, Buenos Aires, to Batlle, February 27, 1904; Batlle to Victorica, February 28, 1904, Batlle Archive.

34. "Los Delegados de la Paz," *El Día*, March 17, 1904.

35. Batlle to Bernardo Irigoyen and Benjamín Victorica, Buenos Aires, March 18, 1904, Batlle Archive; Irigoyen and Victorica to Batlle, March 15, 1904, Batlle Archive; "Los Delegados de la Paz," *El Día*, March 17, 1904.

36. On March 15, before the peace mission arrived, the American Consul in Montevideo, John E. Hopely, reported to Washington: "Much of the business done here is done by foreigners. All these complain of the serious effect of the war on business and are anxious for any termination of the struggle, and anxious for a peaceful government of this country, whether by either of the local parties or by any foreign power. The native population are equally anxious for a speedy termination of the trouble, and rather than have the existing condition of affairs continue would probably not object to Argentina or Brazil insisting on some permanent settlement." *Foreign Relations of the United States, 1904* (Washington, 1905), 850–851.

37. "Porqué No Se Pide La Paz," *El Día*, March 24, 1904; "Los Sucesos," *El Siglo*, March 29, 1904.

IX. No Peace

1. "1904," *El Día—Tarde*, January 3, 19, 26, 27, 31, 1920.
2. *Memorias de Saravia*, 507–518; Ardao and Castro, *Vida de Basilio Muñoz*, 125; Ponce de León—*Saravia*, 97.
3. "La Insurrección," *El Día*, March 26, 1904.
4. "El Asilo del Coronel Pampillon," *La Nación* (Buenos Aires), April 9, 1904; [Batlle] "Sucesos Internacionales de 1904," *El Día*, October 11, 1929.
5. Daniel Muñoz, Buenos Aires, to Batlle, March 28, 1904, Batlle Archive.
6. Interview, José Claudio Williman, September 1, 1952.
7. "Los Sucesos," *El Siglo*, March 30, April 1, 3, 1904.
8. "Uruguay," *La Nación* (Buenos Aires), April 12, 14, 1904; "Los Hacendados y la Insurrección," *El Día*, April 15, 1904.
9. Daniel Muñoz, Buenos Aires, to Batlle, April 17, 1904, Batlle Archive.
10. "La Defensa del Crimen," *El Día*, April 18, 1904.
11. "1904," *El Día—Tarde*, March 28, 1920.
12. "Sucesos Uruguayos," *La Nación* (Buenos Aires), May 9, 1904; Ejército Nacionalista, *Campaña de 1904*, 25.
13. Muñoz explained his actions in a letter to Foreign Minister Romeu, read in *Cámara*, CLXXVI, 27–33.
14. *Memorias de Saravia*, 529.
15. This is taken from an undated, unsigned document in the Batlle Archive titled (in Spanish): "Preliminary Bases indicated to the Military Chief of the Revolutionary Movement by the Executive Committee of the Ranchers Congress, which accepted by him, were expounded in the 'Memorandums' of last May 11, to his Excellency the President of the Republic and to General Aparicio Saravia. The President also found these bases acceptable, but the same was not the case with the Nationalist Directorio in Buenos Aires which in spite of the repeated representations of the Ranchers Congress evaded analyzing them or substituting others for them."
The peace efforts of the Ranchers' Committee during 1904 deserve further study.
16. Alberto Nin and João Baptista da França Mascarenhas to Batlle, May 11, 1904, Batlle Archive.
17. A. Rodríguez Larreta, Buenos Aires, to Alberto Nin, May 16, 1904, Batlle Archive.
18. "Sucesos Uruguayos," *La Nación* (Buenos Aires), May 16, 1904.
19. "Algunas Ampliaciones," *El Día*, May 17, 1904.
20. *Memorias de Saravia*, 529, 531–532.
21. "1904," *El Día—Tarde*, April 13, 1920.
22. Batlle's editorial comments to "1904," *El Día—Tarde*, February 14, 1920.
23. Daniel Muñoz, Buenos Aires, to Batlle, May 4, 1904, Batlle Archive. Muñoz

had warned of plots against Batlle's life in previous letters on March 10 and April 25, 1904.

24. Ardao and Castro, *Vida de Basilio Muñoz*, 129–131; *Memorias de Saravia*, 532–536; *Ponce de León—Saravia*, 99–100.

25. "1904," *El Día—Tarde*, April 13, 27, May 6, 23, 27, 1920; José Urrutia [Muniz' secretary] for Justino Muniz, Tarariras, to Batlle, May 27, 1904.

26. Juan José Muñoz, *Apuntes Históricos*, 40; *Ponce de León—Saravia*, 100–103.

27. *Memorias de Saravia*, 601; González, *Aparicio Saravia en la Revolución de 1904*, 104; Colonel Carlos Gaudencio, Salto, to Batlle, June 1, 1904, Batlle Archive.

28. "1904," *El Día—Tarde*, June 6, 8, 9, 1920.

29. "1904," *El Día—Tarde*, June 20, 1920.

30. "1904," *El Día—Tarde*, June 30, July 11, 13, 1920; Vicente Guillermo Etcheverry, *Guerras Civiles de 1897 y 1904. Campañas del General Benavente; Páginas de Mi Diario* (2nd edition, Montevideo, 1935), 156–157.

31. *Cámara*, CLXXVI, 100; "La Única Solución," *El Día*, June 2, 1904. Senator José Espalter proposed peace based on Constitutional reform, *Senadores*, LXXXIII, 203–237; revised and reprinted as José Espalter, *El Problema de la Actualidad* (Montevideo, 1904), 5–74.

32. Daniel Muñoz, Buenos Aires, to Batlle, June 8, 1904, Batlle Archive.

33. The proposals Mascarenhas reportedly was carrying with him were outlined in "Uruguay," *La Nación* (Buenos Aires), June 6, 1904.

34. Francisco Susviela Guarch, Rio Grande do Sul, to Batlle, June 5, 1904; Susviela Guarch, Petropolis, to Batlle, June 27, 1904, Batlle Archive.

35. "La Paz Uruguaya," *La Nación* (Buenos Aires), June 5, 1904; "Sucesos Uruguayos," *La Nación* (Buenos Aires), June 11, 1904.

36. *Cámara*, CLXXVI, 157–179.

37. *Ibid.*, CLXXVI, 206–207.

38. *Ibid.*, CLXXVI, 189–309 *passim.*

39. *Ibid.*, CLXXVII, 173–182. The million pesos voted in 1903 to pay the costs of the March revolution were used in 1904 and kept the deficit down. Several million pesos in war claims, to be adjudicated later, were not included in the modest deficit.

X. From Tupambaé to Masoller

1. "1904," *El Día—Tarde*, August 13, 1920. Batlle could not identify Mascarenhas, the peacemaker; to do so might make Benavente think Batlle's war spirit was flagging.

2. "El Delegado del Congreso Ganadero," *La Nación* (Buenos Aires), June 16, 1904.

3. "El Viaje de João Francisco," *La Nación* (Buenos Aires), June 22, 1904; Daniel Muñoz, Buenos Aires, to Batlle, June 10, 17, 1904, Batlle Archive; "Rumores Infundados," *La Nación* (Buenos Aires), June 23, 1904; "¿Intervenidos?," *El Siglo*, June 23, 1904; "Los Sucesos," *Diario Nuevo*, June 24, 1904.

4. Daniel Muñoz, Buenos Aires, to Batlle, June 8, 10, 17, 19, 1904, Batlle Archive.

5. Pablo Galarza, Campamento Santa Clara, to Eduardo Vásquez [sic], June 26, 1904, Batlle Archive.

6. "1904," *El Día—Tarde*, June 18, 1920.

7. "1904," *El Día—Tarde*, August 11, 1920.

8. "1904," *El Día—Tarde*, September 13, 15, 18, 26, 1920.

9. *Memorias de Saravia*, 542–544; *Ponce de León—Saravia*, 104.

10. The action at Tupambaé has been judged with violently different viewpoints. Galarza sent a long account of the battle to Batlle on June 25, 1904, Batlle Archive. Nepomuceno Saravia gives his version in *Memorias de Saravia*, 544–549; *Jornadas de Civismo* (Montevideo, 1905), 12–59; Fernando Gutiérrez, *Tupambaé* (3 Vols.,

Montevideo, 1915–1918); Juan José Muñoz, *Apuntes Históricos*, 47–50; González, *Aparicio Saravia en la Revolución de 1904*, 108–127.

11. "1904," *El Día—Tarde*, September 26, 1920.

12. *Memorias de Saravia*, 549–551.

13. Alberto Eirale, *Memorias de un Médico que Actuó en el Ejército del Sur Durante Toda la Guerra Civil de 1904* (Montevideo, 1951), 50–51; Luis Suárez, *De Tupambaé al Apa; Expedición de Auxilios a los Heridos de Tupambaé* (Montevideo, 1927?), 35–37.

14. *Memorias de Saravia*, 552.

15. "1904," *El Día—Tarde*, September 20, 1920.

16. "1904," *El Día—Tarde*, September 29, 1920.

17. Etcheverry, *Campañas del General Benavente* . . . , 184; Manuel Benavente to Batlle, July 18, 1904, Batlle Archive.

18. Federico Fleurquin to Batlle, June 29, 1904, Batlle Archive.

19. "1904," *El Día—Tarde*, October 15, 26, 1920.

20. "1904," *El Día—Tarde*, October 15, 1920.

21. *El Siglo* reprinted the *El Día* editorial. "La Paz," *El Siglo*, June 25, 1904.

22. *Senadores*, LXXXIII, 264–280, 302–351.

23 *Cámara*, CLXXVI, 405.

24. *Ibid.*, 408.

25. The notes exchanged during these negotiations were reprinted as *Documentos Relativos a las Gestiones del Comité del Comercio en Favor de la Paz* (Montevideo, 1904), 5–39.

26. Joaquín C. Márquez, President of the Comisión de Comercio Pro-Paz, to Batlle, July 10, 1904, Batlle Archive.

27. "Uruguay," *La Nación* (Buenos Aires), July 15, 1904; "Trabajos de Pacificación," *El Siglo*, July 15, 1904.

28. "Trabajos de Paz," *El Siglo*, July 19, 22, 1904.

29. "1904," *El Día—Tarde*, March 6, 1921.

30. "1904," *El Día—Tarde*, June 18, 1921; "La Revolución Uruguaya," *La Nación* (Buenos Aires), August 4, 1904.

31. Acevedo Díaz to John Hay, August 2, 1904, *Notes from Foreign Missions*, *Uruguay*, Vol. 2, National Archives. The original is in Spanish. I owe thanks to Mr. John P. Harrison, then Latin American Specialist, National Archives, who searched the records for me on the Uruguayan request for American assistance.

32. "Sucesos Internacionales de 1904," *El Día*, October 11, 1929. This article, written when Batlle was in the hospital where he died, links the request to the Pampillon asylum case, a more clearly Uruguayan-Argentine dispute than the Nationalist arms shipments. At the time, and since, Batlle was accused of offering the United States a coaling station in exchange for its intervention, or Uruguay's rights to the Island of Martín García in the Río de la Plata in exchange for three gunboats. Batlle categorically denied both accusations when they were made in "Sucesos Uruguayos," *La Nación* (Buenos Aires), September 4, 1904.

33. J. H. [John Hay] to Alvey Adee, undated, in response to communication from Adee dated August 24, 1904, *Diplomatic Dispatches*, *Uruguay*, Vol. 17, National Archives.

34. Finch to Department, August 4, 1904, *ibid.*

35. "Sucesos Uruguayos," *La Nación* (Buenos Aires), August 7, 1904.

36. "El Atentado de Ayer Contra el Presidente y su Familia," *El Día*, August 7, 1904; "Uruguay," *La Nación* (Buenos Aires), August 7, 1904. Both interviewed Batlle.

37. The draft, which Batlle revised before sending, is in the Batlle Archive; Domingo Arena, "Los Últimos Días de Batlle," *Biblioteca "Batlle,"* I, 210.

38. Juzgado de Instrucción del 1ᵉʳ Turno, August 1904. Sumario por Atentado Contra la Vida de S. E. el Señor Presidente de la República. Batlle Archive; Osvaldo Cervetti to Batlle, August 3, 7, 1904, Batlle Archive.

Batlle visited, and bore no hard feelings toward, the simple immigrant who had detonated the bomb. Arena points this out but does not point out that Batlle was implacable toward Cervetti, whom he wanted punished to the full extent of the law. Arena, "El Humanitarismo de Batlle," *Biblioteca "Batlle,"* I, 148; Cervetti to Batlle, August 12, 1904, Batlle Archive; "El Atentado," *El Día,* August 11, 12, 1904.

39. The police reports are in the Batlle Archive.

40. "1904," *El Día—Tarde,* July 16, 1921.

41. *Memorias de Saravia,* 566–571.

42. Finch to Department, August 23, 1904, *Diplomatic Dispatches, Uruguay,* Vol. 17, National Archives.

43. A.A.A. to Hay, August 24, 1904; J. H. [John Hay] to Adee, *ibid.*

44. "Uruguay," *La Nación* (Buenos Aires), August 20, 1904.

45. Luis Alberto de Herrera, Saravia's secretary after Ponce de León, wounded at Tupambaé, had been taken prisoner, revealed the offer in "Cotizando Jefaturas," *La Democracia,* December 25, 27, 1904. Batlle gave his version in "Las Jefaturas y la Insurrección," *El Día,* December 26, 1904. Mascarenhas supported Batlle's version in "Las Jefaturas y la Insurrección," *El Día,* December 28, 1904. It would be of considerable interest to have a copy of the terms Mascarenhas in fact outlined to Saravia.

46. "Uruguay," *La Nación* (Buenos Aires), September 3, 16, 1904.

47. *Memorias de Saravia,* 573–574.

48. "La Insurrección," *El Día,* September 2, 1904.

49. Vázquez, Sarandí del Mataojo, to Batlle, August 27, 1904, Batlle Archive.

50. "1904," *El Día—Tarde,* August 17, 1921.

51. Vázquez, Cuchilla del Mataojo, to Batlle, 8:00 A.M., August 30, 1904, sent by way of Tacuarembó, 8:40 P.M., August 31, 1904, Batlle Archive.

52. "1904," *El Día—Tarde,* August 24, 1921.

53. Vázquez, Gruta León, to Batlle, 7:00 A.M., August 31, 1904, sent by way of Laureles, August 31, 1904, Batlle Archive.

54. Marcelino Gómez Arias, *Revolución Uruguaya de 1904. Sus Operaciones en el Sud* (Buenos Aires, 1905), 23–35.

55. "Sucesos Uruguayos," *La Nación* (Buenos Aires), September 4, 1904; "Las Conspiraciones," *Diario Nuevo,* September 3, 1904.

56. Hugo Mongrell, *Luis Mongrell* (Vigo, 1958), 214–220. Mongrell, Batlle's agent, thought Pampillon expected the Colorado military to revolt and replace Batlle with Tajes, once Pampillon's "army" appeared before Montevideo.

57. Ardao and Castro, *Vida de Basilio Muñoz,* 139; Juan José Muñoz, *Apuntes Históricos,* 53; *Memorias de Saravia,* 577.

58. Vázquez to Batlle, September 8, 1904, Batlle Archive.

59. *Memorias de Saravia,* 580–582.

60. Only now are some of these dissensions being aired. They are summed up by Avelino C. Brena in his prologue to Ramón P. González, *Aparicio Saravia en la Revolución de 1904.*

61. *Memorias de Saravia,* 584.

62. "1904," *El Día—Tarde,* August 27, 1921.

63. Pedro Figari, *El Momento Político, 1910–1911* (Montevideo, 1911), 58–59.

64. Afterwards, each of the commanders claimed he wanted to continue but was betrayed by the others. *Memorias de Saravia,* 586–605; Juan José Muñoz, *Apuntes Históricos,* 54–73; González, *Aparicio Saravia en la Revolución de 1904,* 186–212; Ardao and Castro, *Vida de Basilio Muñoz,* 140–141; Gregorio Lamas to Sres. Comandantes en Jefes Interinos del Ejército Nacional, Coroneles Basilio Muñoz, José F. González and Juan José Muñoz, Archivo del Partido Nacional, *Revolución de 1904,* Series XII, V, 7–8.

65. "1904," *El Día—Tarde,* October 17, 1921.

66. "1904," *El Día—Tarde,* October 20, 1921.

67. "Aparicio Saravia," *La Nación* (Buenos Aires), September 14, 1904.

68. Batlle's telegraphed copy was forwarded by Casildo Carrión, Consul Bagé, September 22, 1904, Batlle Archive.

The bases, together with an extensive justification, were published in *El Programa de la Revolución, Las Verdaderas Bases de Paz* (Montevideo, 1904), 5–38.

69. Basilio Muñoz, Hijo, to Batlle, September 23, 1904, Batlle Archive.

70. "1904," *El Día—Tarde*, November 15, 20, 25, 26, 1921.

71. "La Paz," *El Día*, September 27, 1904.

72. "1904," *El Día—Tarde*, December 6, 1921.

73. "La Paz Uruguaya," *La Nación* (Buenos Aires), October 6, 1904.

74. *Las Jornadas del Civismo. Tupambaé y Masoller. El Caudillo y Sus Glorias* (Montevideo, 1905), 69–108.

75. Batlle comments on Giúdici biography, 339, Batlle Archive.

76. *El Siglo* reported this on June 20, 1904.

XI. Elections

1. Néstor [Batlle], "Se Aclaren las Cuentas," *El Día*, November 17, 1904.

2. Partido Nacional Archivo, *Actas del Directorio*, Series I, V, 461–468.

3. *Cámara*, CLXXVIII, 11–13.

4. Herrera y Obes had just written a series of newspaper articles claiming that a January election would be unconstitutional and, more to the point, would not give the dissident Colorados, who had refused to register since '97, enough time to prepare for the election. Herrera y Obes wanted elections postponed until November 1905. Julio Herrera y Obes, "Una Ley Revolucionaria," *Diario Nuevo*, October 21, 22, 1904, and "Proyecciones Políticas de una Ley," *Diario Nuevo*, October 26, 1904.

5. Partido Nacional Archivo, *Actas del Directorio*, Series I, V, 60.

6. *Cámara*, CLXXVII, 170–171.

7. *Cámara*, CLXXVII, 49, 79–81; *Senadores*, LXXXIV, 135.

8. *Cámara*, CLXXVII, 175, 314, 434; *Cámara*, CLXXVIII, 79–81.

9. *Cámara*, CLXXVII, 419.

10. One Senator and four alternates were elected by each department. In case of the Senator's illness, leave of absence, or death, the first alternate took over.

11. [Batlle] "Cosas de 'El Tiempo,'" *El Día*, November 18, 1904.

12. The departments were not divided into electoral districts.

13. *Cámara*, CLXXVIII, 222–224.

14. "Ley del Mal Tercio," *La Democracia*, November 12, 1904.

15. Martín C. Martínez' three articles, "La Reforma de la Ley Electoral," "En el Terreno de los Principios," and "Cuentas Claras," appeared in *El Siglo*, November 12, 15, 17, 1904; Néstor [Batlle], "Lecciones de la Experiencia," "Palabras que no Corresponden a Ideas," and "Se Aclaren las Cuentas," *El Día*, November 14, 16, 17, 1904.

16. Néstor [Batlle], *El Día*, November 16, 1904.

17. Martínez, *El Siglo*, November 12, 1904.

18. Néstor [Batlle], *El Día*, November 17, 1904.

19. Martínez, *El Siglo*, November 15, 1904.

20. Néstor [Batlle], *El Día*, November 14, 1904.

21. Néstor [Batlle], *El Día*, November 17, 1904.

22. Néstor [Batlle], *El Día*, November 14, 1904.

23. [Batlle] "Sobre Representación Proporcional," *El Día*, August 7, 1911.

24. *Cámara*, CLXXVIII, 222–224.

25. There was supposed to be a club in each of the twenty-one judicial sections of Montevideo. First-line politicians, not neighborhood leaders, were appointed as club presidents.

26. "Herrera, Tajes, Estevan, etc.," *El Día,* November 9, 1904.
27. Lauro V. Rodríguez to Batlle, February 5, 1905, Batlle Archive.
28. [Batlle] "Las Elecciones y Los Agentes Policiales," *El Día,* November 21, 1904.
29. [Batlle] "Revista de la Prensa," *El Día—Tarde,* February 25, 1920.
30. Pablo Galarza, Durazno, to Batlle, November 11, 1904, Batlle Archive.
31. Miguel H. Lezama, Rocha, to Batlle, November 24, 1904, Batlle Archive.
32. *Cámara,* CLXXIX, 46–47.
33. "La Reforma," *La Democracia,* November 30, 1904.
34. Minor Senate amendments were accepted. *Senadores,* 171–199; *Cámara,* CLXXIX, 28; *Asamblea General,* X, 477–481.
35. José Serrato, "Don José Batlle y Ordóñez," [*Acción*] *Batlle, Su Vida, Su Obra,* 5.
36. Arturo Brizuela, head of the special police, was alerted by his Buenos Aires agent on December 17, 1904; about that time, Jefe Político Maurente of Maldonado reported to Batlle that he was concerned about a revolutionary outbreak. Batlle Archive.
37. Domingo Arena, "Artículo publicado por el Dr. Domingo Arena en el suplemento de 'El Día' el 20 de Octobre de 1933," *Biblioteca "Batlle,"* I, 159.
38. "La Reforma de la Constitución," *El Siglo,* January 1, 1905.
39. Nemo [Batlle], "Palo Porque Remas y Porque No Remas, Palo," *El Dia,* January 4, 1905.
40. "El Compromiso Colorado," *El Día,* February 3, 1905.
41. Amaro F. Ramos, San Eugenio, to Batlle, January 13, 1905, Batlle Archive.
42. Jefe Político, San Eugenio, telegram to Batlle, January 18, 1905, Batlle Archive.
43. Dámaso Vaeza, Melo, to Román Freire, Presidential Secretary, January 18, 1905, Batlle Archive. There is extensive correspondence on the situation in Cerro Largo in the Batlle Archive.
44. "Electorales," *El Día,* January 8, 1905.
45. "Dentro de Filas y Fuera de Filas," *El Día,* January 10, 1905.
46. "Electorales," *El Día,* January 14, 18, 1905; "Las Listas de Diputados," *El Día,* January 18, 1905; "Proceso Electoral," *Diario Nuevo,* January 17, 1905.
47. Eduardo Acevedo, *Anales Históricos del Uruguay* (6 Vols., Montevideo, 1933–1936), V, 292.
48. Partido Nacional Archivo, *Actas del Directorio,* Series I, VI, 7–8.
49. Batlle, fearful that the negotiations were a prelude to revolution, had the police watch Herrera y Obes and Tajes. The police reports are in the Batlle Archive.
50. The negotiations are carried in great detail in Partido Nacional Archivo, *Actas del Directorio,* Series I, VI, 54–78.
51. Partido Nacional Archivo, *Actas del Directorio,* Series I, VI, 59–60.
52. Archivo del Partido Nacional, *Notas Recibidas por el H. Directorio,* Series II, XIV, 99–104.
53. Eugenio Martínez Thedy, *Conferencia Política . . .* (Montevideo, 1905), 20; Daniel D. Vidart, *Tomás Berreta. Apología de la Acción* (Montevideo, 1946), 314; Florencio Aragón y Etchert and Julio María Sosa, *Conferencia Política . . .* (Montevideo, 1904), 17; "La Coalición," *El Día,* January 21, 1905.
54. "Hacia la Luz," *El Siglo,* January 23, 1905; "Las Elecciones," *La Democracia,* January 24, 1905.
55. The debates in the Chamber on disputed elections are a mine of information on the techniques of electoral manipulation. *Cámara,* CLXXX, 312–454 *passim.*
56. The official returns were never published, indicative of the absence of any felt need for complicated vote analysis. Even the all-encompassing Eduardo Acevedo had to content himself with publishing an estimate in *Anales Históricos del Uruguay,* V, 291–292.

On November 27, 1907, *El Día* did publish a department-by-department break-down in "La Derrota Nacionalista" (an error in the figures for Maldonado was rectified the next day):

Department	Colorado	Nationalist
Montevideo	8,869	5,452
Canelones	2,157	1,117
Tacuarembó	1,235	347
Flores	394	504
Durazno	937	554
Maldonado	1,365	999
San José	804	965
Paysandú	1,058	398
Treinta y Tres	574	540
Soriano	916	528
Rivera	457	0
Colonia	1,209	774
Florida	1,374	1,030
Rocha	1,587	1,653
Minas	1,132	747
Cerro Largo	482	536
Río Negro	537	366
Salto (two lists)	781 \ 142 }	366
Artigas	695	8
Total	26,705	16,871

57. Partido Nacional Archivo, *Actas del Directorio*, Series I, VI, 88–89.

58. According to the Constitution, male citizens aged twenty and over, native and naturalized, who were literate and were not day laborers could vote. The two restrictions were not enforced: electoral literacy meant the ability to sign one's name; no one was classed as a day laborer, since the electoral definition of that term was a man hired by written contract, and written contracts were not used for day laborers.

The 1908 census listed 171,898 men eligible to vote. The figure 150,000 is probably low for 1905. *Anuario Estadístico 1907–1908*, Vol. II, Part III, xliii.

XII. New Situation

1. *Asamblea General*, X, 548, 492–562.

2. *Anuario Estadístico, 1915*, 333, 20, 72; *Anuario Estadístico, 1904–1906*, II, 264; Criadores del Uruguay, *Cincuentenario de la Fundación de los Registros Genealógicos de la Asociación Rural del Uruguay* (Montevideo, 1937), 428–429.

3. *Banco de la República Oriental del Uruguay, 1896—24 de Agosto—1917* (Montevideo, 1918), 85.

4. "La Tracción Eléctrica," *El Día*, December 3, 1904.

5. Domingo Arena, "Anécdotas de Excepcional Valor Documentario," *Biblioteca "Batlle*," I, 175; "El Presidente de la República," *Diario Nuevo*, February 16, 1905.

6. *Asamblea General*, X, 492.

7. "Renuncia del Directorio," *La Democracia*, March 4, 1905; Partido Nacional Archivo, *Actas del Directorio*, Series I, VI, 109–115. The message, the official Nationalist position on the causes of the War of 1904, was published in November 1905, as Partido Nacional, *Exposición. El Directorio Saliente a la Nueva Corporación. Abril [sic], 1905*.

8. "El Gobierno y el Adversario," *Diario Nuevo*, March 21, 1905; "Con el

Señor Basilio Muñoz (Hijo)," *El Siglo*, April 13, 1905; Ardao and Castro, *Vida de Basilio Muñoz*, 153-154.

9. Basilio Muñoz (Hijo) to Batlle, March 24, 1905, Batlle Archive.

10. Partido Nacional Archivo, *Actas del Congreso Elector de Directorio*, Series VII, I, 23-29.

11. "Aceptamos y Retribuimos," *La Democracia*, April 15, 1905. The Directorio objected to the newspaper's free swinging style and no longer called it the official Directorio newspaper.

12. Partido Nacional Archivo, *Actas del Directorio*, Series I, VI, 148.

13. "El Directorio del Partido Nacional á las Comisiones Departamentales," *La Democracia*, April 18, 1905.

14. "Actualidad," *El Siglo*, May 6, 1905.

15. "Reorganización Colorada," *El Día*, April 14, 1905; "Reorganización Partidaria," *Diario Nuevo*, April 14, 1905.

16. "En Santa Lucía," *El Día*, April 10, 1905. After the war, Serrato retained the Finance ministry and relinquished the Fomento portfolio. Batlle named an engineer, Juan A. Capurro, as new Minister of Fomento.

17. X, "El Mal del País," *Diario Nuevo*, April 5, 1905, and *El Día*, April 6, 1905.

18. "Sobre la Senda . . . ," *El Diario*, July 26, 1905. *Diario Nuevo* had changed its name to *El Diario*.

19. *Senadores*, LXXXIV, 504.

20. *Cámara*, CLXXXI, 493.

21. "Recibos de Legisladores," *El Día*, May 8, 1905.

22. "Los Recibos Presidenciales," *El Día*, May 11, 1905.

23. "En la Casa del Presidente," *El Día*, May 27, 1905.

24. *Cámara*, CLXXXI, 226-422 *passim; Cámara*, CLXXXII, 177-201; *Senadores*, LXXXV, 347-348, 405-434; "El Tranvía Oriental," *El Día*, May 20, 1905; "Los Trenvías [*sic*] Sub-Urbanos," *El Día*, July 23, 1905; José L. Buzzetti, *La Magnífica Gestión de Batlle en Obras Públicas* (Montevideo, 1946), 360.

25. The network would be patterned after the French road system. The influence of France on Uruguay was very great and ought to be seriously investigated. Much legislation followed French models; French authorities were cited on all questions, with Paul Leroy Beaulieu a particular favorite of conservatives.

26. Luis Mongrell, Fray Bentos, to Batlle, December 6, 1904, Batlle Archive.

27. *Cámara*, CLXXXI, 340-347, 382-517; *Cámara*, CLXXXII, 12-75; Federico E. Capurro, *Una Memoria Más, 1898-1948* (Montevideo, 1950), 38.

28. *Cámara*, CLXXXII, 493-495; *Senadores*, LXXXV, 476-478.

29. Antonio Bachini, Buenos Aires, to Jacobo Varela Acevedo, July 11, 22, 31, 1905, Batlle Archive. Varela Acevedo had replaced Freire, now a deputy, as Batlle's secretary. Bachini to Batlle, August 12, 1905, and Daniel Muñoz, Buenos Aires, to Batlle, July 24, 1905, Batlle Archive. Police reports on Nationalist meetings in Montevideo, August 2, 3, 4, 1905, Batlle Archive.

30. *Comisión Permanente*, XI, 612-614; "Aclaraciones," *El Día*, August 30, 1905; Urrutia for Justino Muniz, Melo, to Batlle, August 17, 1905, Batlle Archive; Daniel Muñoz, Buenos Aires, to Batlle, August 10, 1905, Batlle Archive.

31. "La Religión en el Hospital," *El Día*, August 30, 1905; "La Comisión N. de Caridad," *El Día*, July 20, 22, 25, August 4, 17, 1905.

32. Domingo Arena, "El Humanitarismo de Batlle," *Biblioteca "Batlle,"* I, 146.

33. *Cámara*, CLXXXIII, 134-562 *passim*.

34. *Cámara*, CLXXXII, 122-127.

35. *Anuario Estadístico, 1915*, 365-366.

36. *Cámara*, CLXXXII, 233.

37. *Ibid.*, 122-254 *passim; Senadores*, LXXXVI, 422-467.

XIII. Reform

1. Rippy, *British Investments in Latin America, 1822–1949*, 148; Hanson, *Utopia in Uruguay*, 199–200, 219; Acevedo, *Notas y Apuntes*, II, 22–23.
2. *Cámara*, CLXXX, 273-274, 175-506 *passim; Cámara*, CLXXXI, 133-199.
3. "Nuestras Huelgas," *El Día*, January 11, 12, 13, 14, 1905; "La Huelga Ferroviaria," *El Siglo*, January 11, 12, 13, 14, 17, 1905; Emilio Frugoni, "La Huelga de los Ferrocarrileros," *El Día*, January 6, 1905; *Memoria de la Jefatura Política y de Policía de la Capital, 1903-1906*, 65–66.
4. "Obras Son Amores," *Diario Nuevo*, May 6, 1905; "Hechos que Enseñan," *El Día*, May 19, 1905; [Batlle] "¡Palabras! . . . ," *El Día*, June 17, 1905.
5. Strike news was carried daily by *El Día* under the title "Nuestras Huelgas," and by *El Siglo* as "La Huelga," from May 24, 1905, to July 12, 1905.
6. "La Huelga," *El Día*, May 29, 1905; "Las Iras de Arriba," *La Democracia*, June 18, 1905.
7. Herrera's purpose was to anticipate the Colorados and claim Nationalist priority of concern for labor. In this he was successful, for the project is still exhumed to show early Nationalist labor sympathies. *Cámara*, CLXXX, 81–85.
8. *Cámara*, CLXXXII, 86–95; "En la Industrial Uruguaya," *Diario Nuevo*, May 13, 1905.
9. They appear in Domingo Arena, *Batlle y los Problemas Sociales en el Uruguay* (Montevideo, 1939), 59–90.
10. [Arena] "La Razón de las Huelgas," *El Día*, June 16, 1905.
11. *Ibid.*
12. [Arena] "Los Agitadores," *El Día*, June 19, 1905.
13. "¡No nos Animamos! . . . ," *El Día*, July 2, 1905.
14. *Cámara*, CLXXXII, 265–286; *Senadores*, LXXXVI, 515, 519–521.
15. *Cámara*, CLXXXIII, 396; *Cámara*, CLXXXIV, 46–501 *passim*.
16. "Legislación del Trabajo," *El Día*, September 8, 1905.

XIV. Preparing the Way

1. "El Comité Ejecutivo Nacional Provisorio y Los Legisladores Colorados a sus Correligionarios," *El Día*, September 23, 1905.
2. "Las Autoridades Coloradas," *El Día*, September 25, 1905.
3. "La Voluntad Nacional," *El Siglo*, October 15, 1905.
4. "La Futura Presidencia," *El Uruguay*, October 25, 1905; "Los Legisladores Colorados," *El Día*, October 20, 1905. *El Uruguay* was a newspaper Batlle published for a short time, perhaps with the intention of using it to propagandize Williman's candidacy, if needed.
5. "Cuestión Presidencial," *El Día*, October 31, 1905.
6. [Batlle] "Invenciones a Granel," *El Día*, November 19, 1905.
7. [Batlle] "Cosas de 'El Siglo,'" *El Día*, June 23, 1906.
8. Interview with José Claudio Williman, September 1, 1952. José Claudio Williman has compiled a biography of his father, publishing only selections from his father's public papers, in *El Dr. Claudio Williman. Su Vida Pública* (Montevideo, 1957).
9. José Espalter, "La Oportunidad de la Proclamación," *El Día*, October 30, 31, 1905, and José Espalter, "La Candidatura," *El Día*, November 6, 1905.
10. "Cuestión Presidencial," *El Día*, October 29, 1906; "En el Aniversario," *El Día*, October 29, 1906; José T. Abad, *La Candidatura Williman* (Montevideo, 1905), 7–16; Avelino G. Buela, *Conferencia Política Sobre la Candidatura del Doctor Claudio Williman* (Montevideo, 1908), 3–15; Víctor Albístur, *El Problema Presidencial de 1907 y el Manifiesto Nacionalista* (Montevideo, 1907), 9–45; J. C. Williman, *El Dr. Claudio Williman. Su Vida Pública*, 11–167.

11. "Cuestión Presidencial," *El Día*, November 30, 1905.
12. [Batlle] "Los Restos de Cuestas," *El Día*, November 11, 1905.
13. "Moral de lo que no es Cuento," *La Democracia*, October 26, 1905; "Votos Inoportunos," *La Democracia*, November 1, 1905.
14. S. Retamoso, Santa Rosa, to Colonel Juan A. Pintos, October 25, 1905, Batlle Archive.
15. Daniel Muñoz, Buenos Aires, to Batlle, October 28, 1905, Batlle Archive; José Romeu to Batlle, November 20, 1905, Batlle Archive; Claudio Williman to Batlle, November 24, 1905, Batlle Archive.
16. Carlos Blixen, Santa Rosa, to Batlle, November 27, 1905, Batlle Archive.
17. Arturo Brizuela, head of police investigations section, December 2, 3, 5, 1905, Batlle Archive.
18. Partido Nacional Archivo, *Actas del Directorio*, Series I, VI, 247; "Disipando Alarmas," *La Democracia*, December 8, 1905.
19. José Romeu to Batlle, December 11, 1905, Batlle Archive.
20. *Cámara*, CLXXXIV, 195.
21. "Sépanlo Así Todos los Hacendados del País, Tanto Nacionalistas Como Colorados," *La Democracia*, December 28, 1905.
22. *Cámara*, CLXXXIV, 163–435, *passim*.
23. *Asamblea General*, XI, 49–50.
24. *Cámara*, CLXXXIV, 353.
25. The Uruguayan government had guaranteed the bank that a minimum of 6,000,078 pesos of new bonds would be issued to redeem old bonds. If all old bondholders wanted to redeem, the bank would be able to sell 13,670,050 pesos in new bonds.
The 19 million pesos of unissued bonds would not be sold directly to the public. They would be issued to creditors of the Uruguayan government, and would then be listed on the Paris exchange. The Bank charged a 2.5-percent commission for this service, but charged no commission on bonds given to convert present bonds.
26. *Cámara*, CLXXXIV, 282–418 *passim; Senadores*, LXXXVII, 31–242, *passim*.
27. *Asamblea General*, XI, 319.
28. *Cámara*, CLXXXIV, 592–598; *Senadores*, LXXXVII, 314, 320–335.
29. Batlle called in legislators to urge them to approve the contracting of foreign professors for the medical school. *Cámara*, CLXXXV, 62.

XV. The Nationalists Humbled

1. "Candidatura Williman," *El Siglo*, December 28, 1905.
2. [Batlle] "Conciliaciones y Acercamientos," *El Día*, January 12, 1906.
3. "La Utopía de la Coparticipación," *El Día*, January 15, 1906.
4. "Sobre el Tema Anterior," *El Día*, January 16, 1906.
5. [Batlle] 'Más Sobre la Utopía," *El Día*, January 19, 1906.
6. Batlle always referred to the National Party as the Nationalist Party; to call it the National Party was to suggest that it was the party of the entire nation. Now he began to call the Nationalists "Saravistas," to implant the idea that they were primarily a group of professional revolutionaries.
7. [Batlle] "El Gobierno de Partido no es Gobierno Exclusivista," *El Día*, January 25, 1906.
8. Gabriel Cabrea, Concordia, unaddressed, January 24, 1906, Batlle Archive.
9. J. C. Williman, *El Dr. Claudio Williman. Su Vida Pública*, 220–221; "Un Compromiso Deprimente," *La Democracia*, January 27, 1906.
10. Eduardo Iglesias, Paris, to Batlle, June 15, 1906, Batlle Archive.
11. Batlle to Colonel Américo Pedragosa, Melo, January 20, 1906, Batlle Archive.
12. [Batlle] "Reforma Radical," *El Día*, March 29, 1913.
13. "Del Doctor Castro," *La Democracia*, February 16, 1906.

14. "Interesante Entrevista," *El Día*, February 14, 1906.
15. *Senadores*, LXXXVII, 281–282.
16. *Asamblea General*, XI, 132–134.
17. Julio Abellá y Escobar, Rivera, to Batlle, February 24, 1906, Batlle Archive.
18. "Los Sucesos Políticos," *El Día*, March 7, 1906.
19. Ardao and Castro, *Vida de Basilio Muñoz*, 155–156.
20. "Partido Nacional," *El Siglo*, March 3, 1906.
21. *Asamblea General*, XI, 119.
22. General Eduardo Vázquez to Colonel Cándido Viera and Julio Abellá y Escobar, Rivera, March 3, 1906, Batlle Archive.
On March 3 and March 9, João Francisco offered to sell horses to the Uruguayan government. Pablo Minelli to Batlle, March 10, 1906, Batlle Archive.
23. "Los Sucesos Políticos," *El Día*, March 7, 1906.
24. *Asamblea General*, XI, 87, 63–181.
25. "Ayer y Hoy," *El Día*, March 23, 1906.
26. Partido Nacional Archivo, *Actas del Directorio*, Series I, VI, 260–262.

X V I. Onward

1. "Nuestro Directorio," *La Democracia*, March 29, 30, 1906; Partido Nacional Archivo, *Actas del Directorio*, Series I, VI, 265–266; "En Jira Política," *La Democracia*, April 8, 1906;
2. "La Coalición Argentina y La Coalición Oriental," *El Siglo*, March 27, 1906; "Las Ideas Buenas," *La Democracia*, April 3, 1906.
3. "El Partido Nacional y la Actualidad Política," *La Democracia*, April 8, 1906.
4. José Romeu to Batlle, April 10, 1906, Batlle Archive; Antonio Bachini, Buenos Aires, to Romeu, April 18, 1906, Batlle Archive.
5. [Batlle] "Soñando con los Cañones," *El Día*, April 17, 1906.
6. During the Nationalist meeting in Buenos Aires, the Police Chief of Montevideo kept Batlle advised of where he was going to dinner, in case Batlle needed to reach him. Juan Bernassa y Jerez to Batlle, April 6, 1906, Batlle Archive.
7. The article was published in *La Democracia* on April 22, 1906, and reprinted on April 24, 1906.
8. [Batlle] "¿Quién Dijo Miedo?," *El Día*, April 22, 1906.
9. "Incidente Personal," *La Democracia*, April 24, 1906; "Un Incidente," *El Día*, April 24, 1906.
10. Nemo [Batlle], "La Cuestión del Miedo," *El Día*, April 24, 1906.
Batlle, the moralist, could not approve of dueling, but he dueled, and twenty years later killed Washington Beltrán in a duel. He now explained: "That dueling proves nothing? Agreed. In our view it proves only a certain class of valor or a certain class of preoccupations.
"But, has the President challenged anyone to a duel? No. He has limited himself to saying that certain words were said by him, not by another; that he is not disposed to change them and that he accepts all their consequences. Nothing more. Why should the President be denied the right to say what he considers just in any given moment and the right to announce that he has said it? Does he not submit himself to all the laws, including those of knight-errantry?" Néstor [Batlle], "La Cuestión del Miedo," *El Día*, April 21, 1906.
11. Capurro, *Una Memoria Más, 1898–1948*, 38–40.
12. "Obras Públicas," *El Día*, May 8, 1906.
13. *Cámara*, CLXXXV, 331–396 *passim*.
14. *Ibid.*, 338–343; *Cámara*, CLXXXVI, 188–195.
15. "Impuestos," *La Prensa*, April 29, 1906.
16. *Cámara*, CLXXXVI, 22–33.
17. The program, written by the young Nationalists Herrera, Roxlo, and Quintana, was more explicit than the Colorado one written by Manini. Among other

proposals, it called for the eight-hour day. Neither the National Party nor the program's authors took the program seriously. "El Partido Nacional," *La Democracia,* June 16, 1906.

18. Partido Nacional Archivo, *Actas del Congreso Elector de Directorio,* Series VIII, I, 40–58; Partido Nacional Archivo, *Actas del Directorio,* Series I, VI, 272–274, 294.

19. Antonio Bachini, Buenos Aires, to Batlle, June 5, 1906, Batlle Archive. Daniel Muñoz had been appointed Minister to England, to make room for Acevedo Díaz.

20. "Del General Galarza," *El Día,* May 7, 1906.

21. "Nuestra Actualidad Política," *El Día,* June 3, 1906.

22. *Ibid.*

23. "Las Próximas Senaturías," *El Día,* May 31, 1906; "Notas Diversas," *El Siglo,* May 15, 1906.

24. *Cámara,* CLXXXVII, 71.

25. *Cámara,* CLXXXVII, 398; *Cámara,* CLXXXVI, 26–31, 666–673; *Cámara,* CLXXXVII, 27–34, 213–399 *passim; Senadores,* LXXXVIII, 334–337.

26. *Cámara,* CLXXXVII, 387.

27. *Cámara,* CLXXXVII, 515, 518, 387–523 *passim; Senadores,* LXXXVIII, 518–527.

28. N. [Batlle], "Sobre Liebig," *El Día,* July 24, 1906. Batlle did not convince *El Siglo,* which the next day in "Puerto, Alcohol, y Oro," answered: "Gold does not need citizenship papers."

The Senate committee had anticipated Batlle's objections by explaining that Liebig's, rather than extracting capital from Uruguay, sent capital to Uruguay to pay ranchers for their cattle; Liebig's 20-percent profits came from European consumers, not from Uruguayan operations. The committee did not raise the question of whether such a profitable company needed tax relief. *Senadores,* LXXXVIII, 348.

29. Arena, who liked to picture Don Pepe as unwilling to compromise the right, insists that Batlle would have resigned as President before authorizing an execution. Domingo Arena, "Los Últimos Días de Batlle," *Biblioteca "Batlle,"* I, 220.

30. *Cámara,* CLXXXVII, 6–7.

31. *Ibid.,* 89–91.

32. *Ibid.,* 111.

33. *Ibid.,* 91–146; Domingo Arena, "El Humanitarismo de Batlle," *Biblioteca "Batlle,"* I, 143–144.

34. Judas [Batlle], "La Resurrección," *El Día,* April 17, 1906.

35. José Enrique Rodó, *Liberalismo y Jacobinismo* (Valencia, n.d.), 103–195. Rodó published the original as a letter to *La Razón* (owned by *El Siglo*) on July 5, 1906. It was reprinted as a pamphlet in Montevideo in 1906.

36. Rodó, *Liberalismo y Jacobinismo,* 113.

37. "Resabios Godos," *El Siglo,* July 8, 1906; "Liberalismo Real," *El Siglo,* July 10, 1906; "El Cristo de los Hospitales," *La Democracia,* July 15, 1906; "Los Dos Liberalismos," *La Democracia,* August 21, 1906.

38. [Batlle] "Cosas de 'El Siglo,'" *El Día,* July 11, 1906.

39. "La Ira Arzobispal," *El Día,* August 8, 1906.

40. "Conspiración Prelática," *El Día,* August 8, 9, 1906; "La Nota del Día," *El Siglo,* August 9, 1906.

XVII. Tidying Up

1. Police reports in the Batlle Archive.

2. Manuel Amare, Rivera, to General Eduardo Vázquez, September 9, 12, 1906, Batlle Archive; Jaime Gómez, Santa Ana, to Pedro Espartero, September 12, 1906, Batlle Archive.

3. *Cámara,* CLXXXVIII, 208–329.

4. "El Periodista Micelli Visitando al Presidente," *El Día,* October 24, 1906.

5. *Cámara*, CLXXXIX, 289–298, 365–370.

6. *Ibid*, 21–145 *passim*.

7. "El Documento Parlamentario," *La Prensa*, October 28, 1906; "En el Aniversario," *El Día*, October 29, 1906.

8. Partido Nacional Archivo, *Actas del Directorio*, Series I, VI, 354–355, 364–365; Archivo del Partido Nacional, *Notas Recibidas por el H. Directorio*, Series II, XV, 416–473.

9. "Las Senaturías," *El Día*, November 14, 1906.

10. "¡Una Trampa!," *El Día*, November 21, 1906; Martín Suárez, Rocha, to Batlle November 20, 1906, Batlle Archive.

11. "Lealtad Electoral," *El Día*, November 23, 1906; "Las Senaturías," *El Día*, November 24, 1906.

12. Colonel Juan Pintos, Melo, to General Eduardo Vázquez, November 3, 1906, Batlle Archive.

13. "Las Elecciones," *El Día*, November 27, 1906.

14. Capurro died shortly after the election and was replaced as Senator by Magariños Veira.

15. Receipt of the project was acknowledged on December 29, 1906, in *Cámara*, CLXXXIX, 454. The project itself was not published officially until 1913 in *Cámara*, CCXXIII, 147–152.

16. "El Gobierno de un Periodista," *El Día*, December 24, 1906.

17. *Cámara*, CCXXIII, 147–149.

18. *Ibid.*, 150, 149–152.

19. "Legislación Obrera," *El Siglo*, December 27, 1906; "All exaggeration is bad and a legal workday of eight hours, given the conditions of our country, is a veritable exaggeration." "Horas de Labor," *La Democracia*, December 29, 1906.

20. *Cámara*, CLXXXIX, 424–521 *passim*.

21. "El impuesto Sobre las Herencias," *El Día*, January 3, 1907.

22. *Cámara*, CLXXXIX, 550–551.

23. *Ibid.*, 550–559.

24. [Batlle] "La Ley de Divorcio," *El Día*, March 6, 1922.

25. *Cámara*, CLXXXIX, 602, 572–606.

26. *Cámara*, CXC, 16–52.

XVIII. Departure

1. Partido Nacional Archivo, *Actas del Congreso Elector de Directorio*, Series VII, III, 9–11; "El Nuevo Directorio," *La Democracia*, January 9, 1907.

2. "Circular del Directorio," *La Democracia*, January 19, 1907.

3. Batlle opposed as unnecessary the adding of Nationalist votes to Williman's total; [Batlle] "La Ley de Interdicciones y la Cuestión Presidencial," *El Día*, January 5, 1907. *El Día* grew increasingly violent on the issue, proclaiming, "the politics of give and take, with popular influences left out, is more than immoral, it is villainy, it is a social crime"; "Lo Que Quiere 'El Día,'" *El Día*, January 31, 1907.

4. Partido Nacional Archivo, *Actas del Directorio*, Series I, VI, 418–419, 428–432, 444–445; "Reunión de Legisladores Nacionalistas," *La Democracia*, January 22, 1907; "Actitudes Claras," *La Democracia*, January 23, 1907.

5. *Senadores*, LXXXIX, 276–278; "La Presidencia del Senado," *El Siglo*, February 8, 10, 14 1907.

6. *Senadores*, LXXXIX, 149–290 *passim*.

7. *Asamblea General*, XI, 272, 271–333.

8. "Exit Batlle," *The Montevideo Times*, March 1, 1907.

9. "El Futuro Presidente," *El Día*, February 19, 1907. Williman, in later years, always bridled when it was suggested that he had agreed to act as Batlle's stand-in. In 1919, he bitterly criticized Vázquez Acevedo for claiming this; "Del Dr. Williman," *El Día*, January 16, 1919. In 1925, he corrected an

Argentine historian: "Neither by temperament, by education, nor by the principles I have always maintained would I have agreed to a merely inert and purely decorative retention of the government. And if I am not a man capable of accepting such a situation, neither was my predecessor a man capable of making such a demand, be it said in his honor." Mario Falcao Espalter, "La Presidencia Williman," *Revista Nacional*, XIII (February 1941), 205.

10. "La Convención N. Colorada," *El Día*, February 24, 25, 1907; "Movimiento Político," *El Siglo*, February 22, 1907.

11. [Batlle] "Sobre Representación Proporcional," *El Día*, July 3, 1911.

12. "En la Convención," *El Día*, February 27, 1907.

13. Partido Nacional Archivo, *Actas del Directorio*, Series I, VI, 456–457; "Legisladores y Directorio," *La Democracia*, February 26, 1907; "Manifiesto Político," *La Democracia*, February 27, 1907.

14. "La Cuestión Presidencial," *La Democracia*, February 28, 1907; "Punto Final," *La Democracia*, March 1, 1907.

15. *Asamblea General*, XI, 336–345.

16. *Ibid.*, 345–349.

17. Batlle's comments on Giúdici biography, p. 368, Batlle Archive.

18. "El Gran Acto de Ayer," *El Día*, March 2, 1907.

19. Constancio C. Vigil, "José Batlle y Ordoñez," *El Día*, February 28, 1907.

20. "En Honor de Williman y Batlle," *El Día*, March 3, 1907.

21. "El Gran Mitín de Ayer," *El Día*, March 4, 1907.

22. *Asamblea General*, XI, 358.

23. *Cámara*, CXC, 76; *Senadores*, LXXXIX, 325–331; "El Pueblo de Nico Pérez y el Presidente de la República," *El Día*, July 25, 1906.

24. "El Homenaje a Batlle y Ordoñez," *El Día*, March 24, 1907.

Index